THREAT
OF
DISSENT

THREAT

OF

DISSENT

A History of Ideological Exclusion
and Deportation in the United States

Julia Rose Kraut

Harvard University Press

Cambridge, Massachusetts, and London, England

First Harvard University Press paperback edition, 2023
First printing

Publication of this book has been supported through the generous
provisions of the S. M. Bessie Fund.

Library of Congress Cataloging-in-Publication Data

Names: Kraut, Julia Rose, 1981– author.
Title: Threat of dissent : a history of ideological exclusion and
    deportation in the United States / Julia Rose Kraut.
Description: Cambridge, Massachusetts : Harvard University Press, 2020. |
    Includes index.
Identifiers: LCCN 2019047965 | ISBN 9780674976061 (cloth) |
    ISBN 9780674292352 (pbk.)
Subjects: LCSH: Emigration and immigration law—United States—History. |
    Deportation—United States—History. | United States—Emigration and
    immigration—Political aspects.
Classification: LCC KF4819 .K73 2020 | DDC 342.7308/2—dc23
LC record available at https://lccn.loc.gov/2019047965

For my parents,
Alan M. Kraut and Deborah A. Kraut,
with love, gratitude, and appreciation

Contents

Introduction

ON APRIL 10, 2019, a prominent Palestinian activist named Omar Barghouti arrived at Ben Gurion International Airport in Israel and learned that he could not board his flight to the United States because he was barred from entry. The Arab American Institute in Washington, DC, had invited Barghouti to come to the United States to participate in a series of lectures, debates, conversations, and interviews on Israel and human rights. Barghouti had scheduled speaking engagements at New York University and Harvard University, and he had planned to attend his daughter's wedding in Texas. Barghouti had previously visited the United States, accepting the Gandhi Peace Award at Yale University in 2017, and possessed Israeli travel documents and a valid US visa, yet, US Citizenship and Immigration Services (USCIS) instructed the US consulate to exclude him. According to Barghouti, USCIS did not provide a reason, stating at the time, it was an "immigration matter." He believed it was an "ideologically and politically motivated measure" taken by the US government based on his associations and expressions.[1]

Barghouti was born in Qatar in 1964, the son of a founding member of the Palestine Liberation Organization (PLO). He grew up in Egypt, earned a master's degree in electrical engineering from Columbia University, and, in 1993, settled in Israel. In 2005, Barghouti co-founded the Boycott, Divestment, and Sanctions movement (BDS), which seeks to pressure Israel to change its policies toward and treatment of Palestinians by ending international support for Israel through a global campaign of boycotts, economic sanctions, and public criticism.[2]

BDS has gained international attention and growing popularity on college and university campuses, where it has drawn comparisons to the anti-apartheid student movement. Yet, BDS remains controversial within in the United States, described by some as an anti-Semitic movement that threatens Israel's existence and jeopardizes US foreign relations with Israel.[3] The Israeli government has condemned BDS and, in 2017, passed an entry law excluding foreign nationals who "have issued a public call to boycott the State of Israel or pledged to participate in the said boycott."[4] Some American universities and colleges have sought to restrict or prevent BDS activism on their campuses, and the US Senate and various states have passed legislation to prohibit and penalize associations with BDS. Yet, these efforts have met public criticism and legal challenges as violations of the First Amendment's constitutional protections of freedom of speech and association, which, according to the US Supreme Court, include participation in economic boycotts.[5]

After being prevented from entering the United States, Barghouti remarked, "I am hurt, but I am not deterred."[6] While he arranged to give interviews and participate in events and discussions via live-streamed video conference calls, his exclusion drew more public and media attention to his criticism of Israel and his BDS activism. Barring Barghouti also raised questions about the right of a sovereign nation to exclude or deport, the right of those who invited him to come to the United States to engage with him and his ideas, and whether his exclusion was a suppression of dissent that undermined the nation's values and identity as a liberal democracy. Barghouti described his exclusion as part of Israel's repression of BDS—"outsourcing its anti-democratic tactics to the US."[7] Yet, others viewed it as an authentically American tool.

"This looks like an ideological exclusion, which is a long-discredited form of government censorship that prevents Americans from meeting with and hearing from a speaker whose views the government dislikes," remarked Hina Shamsi, director of the American Civil Liberties Union's National Security Project, when asked to comment on the decision to bar Barghouti from the United States. "Ideological exclusion was used in the past to revoke or deny visas to some of the world's leading writers, artists, and thinkers. If the Trump administration is using this political censorship tool again, it's a disgrace and a violation of Americans' First Amendment rights."[8]

If Shamsi is correct, Barghouti's name will be added to the list of foreign-born visitors or immigrants barred or expelled because of their political beliefs, expressions, and associations. The United States has a very long history of such ideological exclusions and deportations. *Threat of Dissent* traces that history from the late eighteenth century to the War on Terror.

————

Beginning with the Alien Friends Act of 1798, Congress has passed or revised ideological exclusion and deportation laws in the name of national security during wartime or when on the brink of war, in the aftermath of a dangerous attack or act of violence, in an economic depression, and amid labor strikes or international tensions. These laws reveal an underlying, perpetual fear of internal and external subversion in the United States, as well as the perception of foreigners as the source of subversion, responsible for instigating dissent and importing radical ideologies. Conflating foreigners and subversion in the United States, the passage and enforcement of ideological exclusion and deportation laws both reflected and manipulated the nation's anxieties and fears.

American political theorist Corey Robin describes political repression as one of the consequences of "political fear." He defines this fear as "a people's felt apprehension of some harm to their collective well-being" and a response to "the intimidation wielded over men and women by governments or groups." Thus, political repression includes policies and restrictions suppressing free expression, belief, and association, as well as intimidation and fear. Public officials choose, identify, define, interpret, and respond to "objects of fear" in ways that are "influenced by their ideological assumptions and strategic goals." According to Robin, liberal democracy and "constituent elements in the American polity can be both instruments of freedom and weapons of fear." The rule of law and the political system can provide protection from political repression, but can also serve to uphold and legitimate it.[9]

I argue that ideological exclusions and deportations are a consequence of the political fear of subversion. They are enduring tools of political repression used to suppress the threat of dissent. This threat includes criticism of the United States and its politicians, laws, and foreign and domestic policies; challenges to the status quo and capitalism; calls for reform or revolution; as well as associations with anarchist, Communist, or terrorist organizations perceived to subvert the United States and its government and / or commit, support, or encourage acts of violence. Rooted in earlier laws, ideological exclusions and deportations have continuously served to suppress the threat of dissent throughout the twentieth century and into the twenty-first.

When public officials identify foreigners as objects of fear and deem dissent subversive and "un-American," they are expressing "anti-radical nativism," which historian John Higham defined as arising when the nation loses its "confidence" in the "stability of American institutions" and "nationalistic fears of revolution" reemerge.[10] I contend that the fear of foreigners and subversion is constant. Ideological exclusions and deportations do not necessarily reflect a loss of confidence; rather, they employ suppression as a way to alleviate or increase this fear, extinguish the threat of dissent, promote political interests, or reflect national identity.

Ideological deportation laws, as well as denaturalization and restrictions on obtaining citizenship that facilitate deportation efforts, attempt to eliminate a perceived internal threat of subversion by exploiting the vulnerability of foreign residents to expulsion. Conversely, ideological exclusion laws have prohibited foreign visitors and immigrants from entering the United States to prevent an external threat of subversion from becoming an internal one.

There are two types of ideological exclusion and deportation laws, which I refer to as "explicit" and "implicit." Explicit restrictions are those that bar or eject noncitizens based on specific beliefs, expressions, or associations listed and defined within the text of a federal statute, typically an immigration law (such as barring anarchists, members of Communist organizations, or those who espouse, endorse, or materially support terrorism). Challenges to exclusion or deportation of individuals under explicit restrictions focus on the interpretation and meaning of the specific language, syntax, and grammar used in the text of the statute, as well as the breadth or narrowness of the categories of beliefs, associations, and expressions listed in the statute.

Implicit restrictions are those that bar or eject noncitizens at the discretion of a public official (such as the president, attorney general, or secretary of state), who determines that a foreign noncitizen would be prejudicial to the public interest or endanger the welfare, safety, or security of the United States if he or she were to enter or remain. Challenges to exclusion or deportation under implicit restrictions focus on the reasons behind an official's decision to exclude or deport, the use or abuse of the official's discretion and authority, and demonstrating the foreign noncitizen does not pose an actual threat to national security or to US foreign policy.

Selective ideological exclusions and deportations are a form of retaliation by the government to punish or suppress a specific foreign noncitizen because of his or her beliefs, expressions, or associations, including criticisms of the US government and its policies and participation in or association with organizations advocating reform or radical change. Public officials exclude or deport these individuals under implicit and explicit ideological laws, as well as nonideological restrictions, such as barring or expelling individuals for illegal entry or for violating visa requirements. They may also advance a deferred deportation or revoke a visa as a form of retaliation for dissent. The statutory basis is often a pretext used to selectively target individuals and to conceal the motivation to punish and suppress dissent. Challenges to selective exclusions or deportations focus on exposing the government's motivation behind excluding or deporting this individual and the government's abuse of authority and discretion under the law.

The legislative and executive branches of government have continuously struggled over the passage and revision of exclusion and deportation laws. Tensions have also arisen within and between these branches regarding the implementation and enforcement of these laws and specific instances of ideological exclusions and deportations under them. Some of these tensions concerned discretionary authority held by public officials charged with enforcing restrictions.

Legal scholar Daniel Kanstroom has distinguished three main categories of discretion. "Prosecutorial discretion" is the exercise of authority to choose *not* to exclude or deport despite an explicit restriction or to defer or delay taking action to deport. "Ultimate discretion" is the exercise of absolute authority to admit, deport, or exclude, with the final decision often left in the hands of a particular individual, such as the attorney general or the president. "Interpretive discretion" is the exercise of authority by public officials to interpret the meaning of the explicit or implicit restrictions within the text of the statute to determine whether to exclude or deport.[11]

Immigration restrictionists have sought to prevent use of prosecutorial discretion, while advocates for more liberal immigration policies and opponents of ideological exclusion and deportation have supported it and ultimate discretion to admit, while pushing for reforms to immigration restrictions. They have also sought to prevent public officials' abuse of ultimate or interpretive discretion when enforcing implicit and explicit restrictions and argued for judicial review. Immigration restrictionists and advocates for liberal immigration policies have both engaged in congressional oversight of public officials' use of discretion to exclude or deport.

Ideological exclusions and deportations present a unique intersection of immigration and First Amendment legal doctrine and precedent. While the Supreme Court has placed limits on public officials' ultimate discretion to exclude or deport, the court has looked to immigration legal doctrine and precedent to guide its interpretation and evaluation of ideological restrictions and their constitutionality. Despite acknowledgment of the First Amendment implications of these restrictions, the majority of the court has consistently interpreted cases of ideological exclusion or deportation as an immigration issue, rather than as a First Amendment issue.

The court's application of immigration legal doctrine and judicial deference under it has served to insulate ideological exclusions and deportations from substantive judicial review under current First Amendment standards, including strict scrutiny, requiring restrictions to be narrowly tailored to serve a compelling governmental interest. It has also insulated ideological deportation from constitutional protections under the Fifth Amendment, guaranteeing that no "person" in a criminal case be "compelled" to self-incriminate, "nor be deprived of life, liberty, or property without due process of law," including a fair, impartial hearing and constitutional rights and protections. Deportation is considered a civil, not criminal, proceeding, and thus, is not subject to the same protections under the Fifth Amendment. I argue that by making this distinction and choosing to apply immigration legal doctrine and legal precedent, the majority of the court has helped to maintain and perpetuate the use of ideological exclusions and deportations as tools to suppress dissent and restrict free expression, association, and belief of citizens and noncitizens within the United States.

Taking the opposite approach of the majority of the Supreme Court, civil liberties and immigration advocates, members of the press and the public, and those excluded or deported have interpreted ideological restrictions not as an immigration issue, but rather as a violation of First Amendment rights. They have described ideological exclusions and deportations as effectively transforming public officials into censors and have argued that barring foreigners from entry and expelling foreigners from the United States restrict Americans' free speech and exchange, including the right to hear and receive information protected by the First Amendment.

Those critical of ideological restrictions have also noted that whereas the First Amendment makes no distinction between native or foreign-born citizens or between citizens and noncitizens, ideological deportation and denaturalization punish foreigners in the United States for their beliefs, associations, and expressions through expulsion or the threat of expulsion. The result is thus another violation of the First Amendment, referred to as the "chilling effect," that leads to self-censorship, inhibiting and restricting expression, suppressing and concealing belief, and limiting and precluding association due to intimidation and fear.

Foreign-born residents share the fear of repression and prosecution under laws suppressing free expression, belief, and association felt by American-born citizens, but they also experience the fear of potential denaturalization, deportation, and detention. Even if these foreign-born residents are never arrested and expelled or lose their citizenship, the intimidation and fear may prove equally or more potent as a form of repression. In the past, public officials exploited the fears and vulnerabilities of foreign residents through deportation drives and mass arrests, public announcements of the intention to deport thousands of foreigners, lengthy detentions and excessive bail, and burdensome supervisory parole requirements. This intimidation caused foreigners to fear deportation and some to preemptively leave the United States. Foreign visitors and immigrants worried about being excluded were also intimidated by long delays to obtain visas, intrusive interrogations and investigations, and the embarrassment of being barred if their visas were denied. Some simply decided not to come to the United States.

When Americans challenged the constitutionality of state and federal laws that suppressed free expression, belief, and association, state and federal courts often upheld these laws and legitimized prosecutions under them. Yet, when the Supreme Court struck them down and created speech-protective standards to evaluate the constitutionality of restrictions under the First Amendment, many jurists chose not to apply these new standards to cases involving foreigners facing ideological exclusion or deportation. For foreigners, the rule of law has served to reinforce political repression, rather than remove it. While for some the response to ideological restrictions has been fear, for others it has been defiance. In those cases, suppression tactics have often backfired, drawing more attention to First Amendment values and their violation and creating more support for radical movements and defense of free speech.

Critics of ideological exclusion and deportation laws have argued that these policies portray the United States as fearful and repressive and as turning its back on its core values and its identity as a nation of immigrants. They have claimed that such restrictions damage America's reputation abroad by undermining its image as a liberal democracy, which preserves and protects the free expression and exchange that are essential to self-government. Some have also criticized the application of immigration legal doctrine as threatening the founding constitutional principles of separation of powers and checks and balances by placing so much unchecked power in the legislative and executive branches to decide whom to bar or expel from the United States. To these critics, ideological exclusions and deportations do not reflect a country that is a strong, fearless nation, upholding its democratic ideals and values, and welcoming of foreigners as a beacon of freedom; instead, exclusions and deportations reflect an insecure, repressive nation that fears and punishes dissent and banishes and bars foreigners.

Political scientist Aristide Zolberg characterized the United States as a "nation by design," one that creates a national identity by controlling who can enter and reside within its borders.[12] Thus, the nation's identity is defined not only by whom it chooses to include, accept, and protect, but also by whom it chooses to exclude, deport, and suppress. Daniel Kanstroom and historian Deirdre Moloney have described immigration restrictions as filters or a form of social control used to shape America's population and as reflections of societal values and prejudices.[13] The same can be said of restrictions on free expression, belief, and association. The history of ideological exclusion and deportation in the United States reveals a national identity that has been shaped by fear of the threat of dissent and by the political repression of dissent.

The subject of ideological exclusion and deportation straddles immigration and free expression law and history and appears across works by historians and legal scholars. Some describe ideological exclusion or deportation within a limited time period, such as historian William Preston Jr.'s examination of the suppression of radicals during and after World War I in *Aliens and Dissenters*, or historian David Caute's discussion of Cold War anti-Communism during the 1940s and 1950s in *The Great Fear*.[14] Immigration scholars have included examples of particular ideological restrictions in larger works on citizenship, deportation, exclusion, or refugee policy based on racial, economic, or religious discrimination.[15] Civil liberties scholars have incorporated ideological exclusion and deportation in broader histories of American political repression or First Amendment jurisprudence, such as legal scholar Geoffrey Stone's examination of restrictions on freedom of speech during wartime in *Perilous Times*.[16]

Threat of Dissent is the first book to focus exclusively on ideological exclusion and deportation in the United States and to trace the legal, political, and social history of these restrictions over an extensive time period. This focus provides a fresh perspective on immigration and First Amendment law and history, while exploring their intersection.

This long, narrative examination reveals the dynamics and motivations behind the passage and use of ideological exclusion and deportation laws. It includes the vast network of legal and nonlegal actors who shaped, enforced, interpreted, and challenged these laws, as well as the foreign-born immigrants and visitors who have faced ideological exclusion or deportation under them. This history also serves as a window to understandings of national identity, security, sovereignty, and foreign policy, the role of fear, dissent, and censorship in society, xenophobia and nativism within legislation, and challenges to immigration and free speech restrictions and their constitutionality.

Threat of Dissent highlights the changes as well as the striking continuities within the history of ideological exclusion and deportation in the United States. Many of the figures described in the book include Supreme Court justices; legal advocates; deported or excluded foreign radicals; scholars, artists, and writers; and public officials. Some are familiar names, such as Justices Thurgood Marshall and Robert Jackson, Clarence Darrow, Emma Goldman, John Lennon, Charlie Chaplin, Carlos Fuentes, Frances Perkins, and J. Edgar Hoover. Others may be less familiar, such as Justice Frank Murphy, Carol King, Harry Bridges, Louis F. Post, Ernest Mandel, Senator Patrick McCarran, and Leonard Boudin. Some of these figures appear in more than one chapter. Like the narrative itself, they examine the meanings and effects of ideological exclusion and deportation within the United States. They also compare current restrictions with those in previous periods, placing them in historical context, as well as in light of American values, ideals, and legal precedent.

While this book covers such a long time period, it does not intend to serve as a general, all-encompassing history of immigration restriction and civil liberties, and leaves discussions of discrimination and restriction based on race, ethnicity, gender, nationality, sexual orientation, religion, and socioeconomic status to past and future scholarship. Other countries have barred or expelled foreigners from their borders, but this book is limited to analyzing ideological exclusion and deportation laws and challenges to them within the United States. Its goal is to explore the constitutionality of ideological restrictions as interpreted by American courts, as well as to examine this specific intersection of American immigration and First Amendment law and history. The book demonstrates how ideological restrictions fit within American jurisprudence and history, as well as their role in civil liberties and immigration advocacy, including the legal challenges and public responses to exclusion and deportation in the United States.

Threat of Dissent begins with the Alien Friends Act of 1798—the first implicit ideological restriction—and continues through the nineteenth century with a discussion of sovereignty, self-preservation, and the establishment of federal immigration restriction and the plenary power doctrine. It enters the twentieth century during the War on Anarchy after the assassination of President William McKinley in 1901, when Congress passed the first explicit ideological restriction in the United States, and the Supreme Court upheld its constitutionality. The narrative then traces this explicit restriction's revisions and expansions—and deportations under them. It also examines questions of interpretation and enforcement and the shift from the threat of anarchism to that of Communism, from World War I to the Great Depression.

The book continues to explore these questions in the second half of the twentieth century, when foreigners faced deportation drives and visa denials during the Cold War. It then describes the response to the Nixon and Reagan administrations' suppression of dissent and critics of their foreign policies under the McCarran-Walter Act of 1952, and the subsequent legal challenges. The book examines efforts in Congress to repeal ideological restrictions as the Cold War came to a close and how it introduced new restrictions as the threat of Communism shifted to that of terrorism. *Threat of Dissent* concludes with a discussion of ideological restrictions in the twenty-first century during the War on Terror, including the use of social media and guilt by association to chill speech, and the extreme vetting measures pursued by the Trump administration.

1

Sovereignty and Self-Preservation

IN HIS 1796 FAREWELL ADDRESS, President George Washington spoke to the American people as their "fellow-citizen" and an "old and affectionate friend." Washington warned about the dangers of foreign influence, as well as political factions and divisions within the nation, for they "are likely, in the course of time and things, to become potent engines, by which cunning, ambitious, and unprincipled men will be enabled to subvert the power of the people and to usurp for themselves the reins of government."

Turning to foreign affairs, the departing president advised the young country not to have "excessive partiality for one foreign nation and excessive dislike of another," which he argued "gives to ambitious, corrupted, or deluded citizens (who devote themselves to the favorite nation), facility to betray or sacrifice the interests of their own country, without odium, sometimes even with popularity." Washington spoke of "the insidious wiles of foreign influence," and that "a free people ought to be constantly awake, since history and experience prove that foreign influence is one of the most baneful foes of republican government."

Washington cautioned against one political faction dominating and controlling the government, claiming this could lead to a "more formal and permanent despotism" and would result in a gradual inclination by men to seek revenge and security through absolute power. He emphasized the importance of the separation of powers within the federal government and the need to guard against the "spirit of encroachment" and too much power held by one department without a check by others. Washington called for unity and for a focus on a shared story of fighting for liberty and forging a new nation together.[1]

The nation that Washington addressed was a deeply divided one. The arguments over the ratification of the Constitution in 1787 had extended into the 1790s, reflecting a fundamental, perpetual disagreement over the role of the federal government and of the states in the new democratic republic. The Federalists, led by Washington, John Adams, and Alexander Hamilton, favored a strong central government, which encouraged business and trade. The Democratic-Republicans, led by Thomas Jefferson and James Madison, opposed a strong central government, favored independent farmers, and were concerned that the new Constitution had given too much power to the federal government, which could infringe upon the states' autonomy and power.[2]

Washington's warning about factions reflected his apprehension regarding the rise of Democratic-Republican societies, where people gathered to discuss politics and their opposition to his administration. These societies viewed themselves as preserving the "legacy of the Revolution," which they argued Washington's administration undermined with its financial policies and foreign relations with Great Britain. They considered open challenges to Washington's decision-making as a patriotic check on federal power, and they believed sovereignty was held by the people and the individual states, and not by the federal government. The Federalists viewed these Democratic-Republican societies as subversive, undermining the interests of the people and the government by expressing dissent and criticism in their own circles, and not through the electoral process and political petitions to Congress.[3]

The United States faced crisis not only at home, but also abroad. Internationally, the United States was caught in the middle of tensions between Great Britain and France following the French Revolution. In the 1790s, the Federalists were pro-British, while the Democratic-Republicans were sympathetic to France.[4] When France declared war on Great Britain in 1793, Washington issued a Proclamation of Neutrality, but in 1795, Washington signed the Jay Treaty with Great Britain. The treaty granted the United States "most favored nation status" and sent compensation for prerevolutionary debts and British seizure of American ships into arbitration.[5] It exacerbated tensions with France, which considered the Jay Treaty a step away from neutrality and a step toward the United States' open alliance with Great Britain.[6] Because of this perceived partiality toward Great Britain and a step away from France, the Jay Treaty was also incredibly unpopular with Democratic-Republicans and was denounced by Jefferson.[7]

Both the Federalists and the Democratic-Republicans shared Washington's concerns about foreign influence, but this consensus also served to contribute to the political chasm and increasing enmity within the United

States. Desperate to distinguish the United States from Europe and to increase partisan political gains, the Federalists and the Democratic-Republicans accused each other of changing the nature of the United States through its alliances and partiality. The Democratic-Republicans charged the Federalists with bringing elements of British aristocracy to the United States, thus corrupting the new nation's experiment in democracy. The Federalists charged the Democratic-Republicans with bringing terror and chaos to the United States with their support of the French Revolution and referred to Democratic-Republicans as American "Jacobins."[8]

By 1798, the Federalists controlled Congress and, with the election of John Adams, the presidency as well. The nation's division had grown even sharper and more contentious, and the United States was in a quasi-war with France. The infamous "XYZ Affair" was primarily responsible for Adams's decision that the nation would enter this "virtual state of undeclared war."[9] This diplomatic scandal involved three French agents (referred to as "X, Y, Z") who demanded enormous concessions as a condition for continuing bilateral peace negotiations, including a $10 million loan and a $250,000 personal bribe to French foreign minister Charles Maurice de Talleyrand. The American delegates sent to France rejected these demands, replying "No. Not a sixpence."[10] When this news broke, the Federalists urged war with France, while the Democratic-Republicans supported maintaining neutrality and openly denounced Adams.[11]

On the brink of open war with France, the Federalists passed legislation that conflated foreigners with dissent and subversion, and they abused their political power in the executive and legislative branches to exploit the vulnerability of foreign noncitizens. In addition to changing naturalization requirements and criminalizing criticism of Adams, Congress, and the quasi-war, the Federalists also passed the Alien Friends Act in 1798, the first implicit ideological deportation law. This act gave the president absolute power and discretion to deport any foreigner he deemed "dangerous to the peace and safety of the United States." One of the legal justifications for the Alien Friends Act's passage—Congress's power to regulate commerce with foreign nations—was later used to support and strengthen federal power and regulation throughout the nineteenth century. Other justifications, including national sovereignty and the inherent right of self-preservation, served as the basis for Congress's plenary (absolute) power and the plenary power doctrine to uphold the constitutionality of federal immigration restriction.

The Four Acts Passed in 1798

Before the American Revolution, individual colonies restricted their borders and expelled undesirable foreign newcomers.[12] After the Revolution, these colonies-turned-states continued their practice of exclusion and ejection. Thus, individual states, and not the federal government, were responsible for the restrictions on foreigners coming to and residing in the United States.

By the late 1790s, the United States had become a haven for various refugees, including French radicals and aristocrats, French planters escaping the Haitian Revolution, and persecuted Irish fleeing British rule.[13] Approximately, 80,000 had emigrated from Great Britain, 60,000 had arrived from Ireland, and 30,000 French immigrants were living in the United States, many of them residing in Philadelphia.[14]

The Democratic-Republicans worried that the Haitian planters would bring their sympathies for monarchy and fear of revolution to the United States and support the Federalists. They were also concerned that the free black Haitian émigrés would import radicalism and insurrection to the slave-holding states.[15] Meanwhile, the Federalists focused on the anti-British, anti-monarchical Irish, who they feared would become Democratic-Republicans.[16] Irish immigrants who had been members of the United Irishmen, a secret organization fighting against British rule and for Irish independence, established similar societies in the United States and voted Democratic-Republican.[17] The Federalists worried the Irish and French immigrants would unite and work together to bring rebellion against the United States and its government.[18]

The Federalists in Congress and members of the Adams administration had also become increasingly angered by the verbal and published attacks hurled at them by the Democratic-Republicans.[19] In the 1790s, newspapers and their circulation increased, as did their partisanship and use by Hamilton and Jefferson as organs of the Federalists and the Democratic-Republicans, respectively.[20] Encouraged by Jefferson, Benjamin Franklin Bache (Benjamin Franklin's grandson), the editor of the *Aurora*, the leading Democratic-Republican newspaper published in Philadelphia, explicitly and forcefully opposed the Jay Treaty. Bache turned the paper into an organizing vehicle for the Democratic-Republicans and their support for Jefferson.[21] He denounced the Federalists and described the president as "old, querulous, Bald, blind, crippled, Toothless Adams."[22]

As war with France loomed, the Federalists seized the opportunity to curb the Democratic-Republicans' vitriol by turning them into the enemy. They characterized the Democratic-Republicans as "foreign" and attacked their patriotism by casting them as disloyal and subversive. Jefferson was the Federalists' main target. The *Porcupine's Gazette*, Philadelphia's Federalist newspaper and rival to Bache's *Aurora*, described Jefferson, as "the head of the democratic frenchified faction in this country." At a Federalist rally to celebrate the Fourth of July, all raised their glasses to Adams: "May he, like Samson, slay thousands of Frenchmen with the jawbone of Jefferson."[23] The Federalists declared that an American who opposed the Adams administration was a "traitor." Another Federalist newspaper, the *Gazette of the United States*, coined the political slogan: "He that is not for us, is against us."[24]

The Federalists' turn toward federal legislation as a tool to suppress the threat of dissent began with naturalization. Under Article I of the Constitution, Congress held the power to "establish an uniform rule of Nationalization," and in 1790, it passed the first Naturalization Act. Attempting to encourage immigration to the new nation and increase citizenry, the act granted citizenship to "free white persons" of "good moral character" who had resided for two years in the United States.[25] Fears of foreign influence and foreigners' political participation and support for the Democratic-Republicans led Congress, which was then controlled by the Federalists, to revise the Naturalization Act in 1795, lengthening the time to become a US citizen by increasing the US residency requirement to five years.[26]

Now, on the brink of war, Federalists sought to more than double the residency requirement. On June 18, 1798, Congress passed a new Naturalization Act, which increased the residency requirement to fourteen years. The act also included a requirement for all foreigners over the age of twenty-one to register with a clerk at the nearest US district court to entry or residence and provide identification information, including gender, place of birth, age, nation of origin and citizenship, occupation or status, and residence in the United States.[27]

One week later, on June 25, Congress passed an "An Act concerning Aliens" also known as the "Alien Friends Act." It authorized the president "at any time during the continuance of this act, to order all such aliens as he shall judge dangerous to the peace and safety of the United States, or shall have reasonable grounds to suspect are concerned in any treasonable or secret machinations against the government thereof, to depart out of the territory of the United States, within such time as shall be expressed in such order."[28]

Under the act, foreigners ordered deported could obtain a license from the president to remain if they could prove their presence posed "no injury or danger to the United States." If a foreigner ordered deported did not obtain a license and attempted to evade deportation, he or she could be imprisoned for up to three years, and the president could deport the foreigner at any time "if public safety requires a speedy removal." If a foreigner who was deported returns without permission from the president, the foreigner could be imprisoned at the president's discretion and for as long as the president is of the opinion that the public safety requires it. The act was passed as a temporary measure and set to expire two years from its passage.[29]

Anticipating war with France, the Federalists in Congress also pushed for a law to control, contain, and deport French residents during wartime. The following week, on July 6, 1798, Congress passed "An Act Respecting Alien Enemies," which stated that during "a declared war between the United States and any foreign nation or government, or any invasion or predatory incursion . . . all natives, citizens, denizens or subjects of the hostile nation or government, being males of the age of fourteen years and upwards, who shall be within the United States, and not actually naturalized, shall be liable to be apprehended, restrained, secured and removed, as alien enemies."[30]

The Federalists next turned their attention to the Democratic-Republicans' criticisms, passing "An act for the punishment of certain crimes against the United States," referred to as the "Sedition Act," on July 14, 1798. It punished anyone who "shall write, print, utter or publish" any "false, scandalous and malicious writing or writings against the government of the United States, or either house of the Congress of the United States, or the President of the United States, with intent to defame the said government, or either house of the said Congress, or the said President, or to bring them, or either of them, into contempt or disrepute; or to excite against them, or either or any of them, the hatred of the good people of the United States, or to stir up sedition within the United States."[31] While proving the "truth" of the expression was a defense under the Sedition Act, Democratic-Republicans argued this was near impossible to do with statements of political opinion.[32] Those convicted under the Sedition Act faced a $2,000 fine and two years in prison. Like the Alien Friends Act, the Sedition Act was also a temporary measure, set to expire on March 3, 1801.

Over the course of four weeks in 1798, Congress had passed what would become considered the most despotic legislation in American history. The Democratic-Republicans denounced the passage of this restrictive legislation as unconstitutional and undermining American values in democracy, including the separation of powers and sovereignty held by the people and the states, as well as freedom of speech and press. Jefferson wrote to Madison that the Sedition Act and the Alien Friends Act were both "so palpably in the teeth of the Constitution as to shew they mean to pay no respect to it."[33]

The Alien Friends Act

Crafted by a Federalist committee and passed quickly in the Senate, the Alien Friends Act faced two days of debate in the House of Representatives before its passage.[34] The Democratic-Republicans in the House voiced their opposition, raising a number of arguments challenging its constitutionality and the power of the federal government to deport. The Democratic-Republicans first dismissed the Alien Friends Act as alarmist and unnecessary. They argued that the Federalists had failed to prove any threat or danger posed by foreigners in the United States and that the Alien Friends Act was too broad.[35] Not only was it unnecessary and excessive, but also existing state laws were sufficient to punish those who presented an actual threat.[36]

The Federalists declared that the United States had the right to expel whomever it wished. Furthermore, as a sovereign nation, the United States possessed the inherent right to self-preservation and could pass laws "necessary and proper" to expel those foreigners who threatened that preservation and who sought to overthrow the government. The Federalists pointed to the preamble of the Constitution, "We, the people of the United States," which established sovereignty and the right of the government to pass laws to maintain "domestic tranquility," "provide for the common defence," and "promote the general Welfare."[37] The Democratic-Republicans responded by arguing that the sovereign power was held not by the federal government, but rather by the people and the states.[38]

While the Democratic-Republicans did not dispute that every nation held an inherent right to self-preservation to exclude foreigners from its borders, they insisted that the Constitution did not delegate that power to the federal government. Instead, the individual states held the exclusive power over the admission and expulsion of foreigners. The Democratic-Republicans cited the Tenth Amendment: "Powers not delegated to the United States by the Constitution, nor prohibited by it to the States, are reserved to the States respectively, or to the people."[39] The Federalists sarcastically dismissed this argument as suicidal at a time when the nation was on the brink of open war with France and there was an enemy within: "Though we see the knife of the traitor held to our throats, we are to wait until the State Governments come in and snatch it away."[40]

17

In an attempt to find more constitutional support for passage of the Alien Friends Act, the Federalists argued that because Congress held the power to regulate commerce with foreign nations, and foreigners generally came to the United States for commercial purposes, the Alien Friends Act was constitutional as a permissible regulation of commerce.[41] The Democratic-Republicans assailed that argument as ridiculous, insisting that immigrants were not articles of commerce; the Alien Friends Act was a political measure, not a commercial one.[42]

The Democratic-Republicans then contended that even if the Federalists were correct and Congress did hold the power to regulate foreigners, it could not exercise that power now. The Migration Clause in Article I, Section 9 of the Constitution prevented Congress from prohibiting the "migration" or "importation" of those "the States now existing shall think proper to admit" until 1808.[43] The Federalists interpreted the clause differently. They first argued that the prohibition applied only to the importation of slaves, not to immigration or expulsion of free, European, white foreigners.[44] The Federalists then insisted that even if the clause did apply to foreigners, importation and migration could be considered "admission," and not expulsion. While the states controlled the admission of foreigners and the Migration Clause barred Congress from regulating such admission, it did not address or prohibit deportation. Thus, the Migration Clause did not bar Congress from passing an act authorizing the president to deport.[45]

In their final attempt to defeat the Alien Friends Act, the Democratic-Republicans, led by New York Congressman Robert Livingston, argued that the act violated the separation of powers, the underlying principle of the nation's democratic, republican government, which had distinguished it from Europe's monarchies. By placing absolute power and discretion to deport solely in the hands of the president, without a judicial check, and without due process protections under the Fifth Amendment, or legislative balance, the Alien Friends Act would create the potential for despotism. Enforcement of the act would be completely discretionary, and foreign residents could simply be deported at the whim of the president. Livingston predicted the Alien Friends Act would also cause foreigners to flee the United States in fear:

A careless word, perhaps misrepresented, or never spoken, may be sufficient evidence; a look may destroy, an idle gesture may insure punishment; no innocence can protect, no circumspection can avoid the jealousy of suspicion; surrounded by spies, informers, and all that infamous herd which fatten under laws like this, the unfortunate stranger will never know either of the law, or of the accusation, or of the judgment, until the moment it is put in execution; he will detest your tyranny, and fly from a land of desolators, inquisitions, and spies.[46]

Despite their efforts, Democratic-Republicans were unable to prevent the Alien Friends Act from becoming law; it passed in a partisan vote in the House of Representatives before Adams signed it. By this time, Livingston's fears of fleeing foreigners had already come true, and his concerns regarding the Act's arbitrary and capricious enforcement would prove prescient.

Even before passage of the Alien Friends Act, Jefferson observed that many who were frightened had begun to flee the United States.[47] In July and August, over a dozen ships filled with "anxious Frenchmen" transported them back to France or to Santo Domingo in Haiti. The Federalists celebrated their departure. "When the state is in danger and strong remedies are necessary . . . none but an ENEMY can resist their use," proclaimed the *Albany Centinel*. "Such remedies have been provided by the late Session of Congress; and however long the partisans of France may declaim against them, every good citizen rejoices in the provision, and will aid in giving it efficacy."[48]

Secretary of State Timothy Pickering was a zealous, pro-British Federalist who had opposed neutrality and any attempt to negotiate with France and had actively encouraged Adams to go to war. He was the chief enforcement officer for the Alien Friends Act, as well as the Sedition Act.[49] While Adams did not deport a single foreigner under the Alien Friends Act, he did nevertheless sign it into law, and he and Pickering did seek to deport foreigners under it. Ultimately, it is their use of the law, their attempts or refusal to deport, and the unchecked, absolute power and discretion Adams held under the Alien Friends Act that is most significant.

Pickering proposed that Adams should sign a few blank deportation warrants that Pickering and the cabinet would fill in later, and that Adams should find a person to assist with licenses for deportees if Adams saw fit to issue one to permit the deportee to stay.[50] While Adams preferred to make the decision to deport himself, he signed three blank warrants.[51]

Georges-Henri-Victor Collot was one of the top names on Adams' list to deport. Collot led an expedition of the western border, funded by the French government to learn more about the western and southern states and their attitude toward France and the United States. The purpose was to encourage states to "secede from the Union, and form a separate connection with a foreign power." Believed to be a spy for France, it was assumed that Collot was one of the intended targets of the Alien Friends Act and would be one of the

Act Concerning Aliens. June 25, 1798, blank warrant, signed by John Adams.
Timothy Pickering Papers
Collection of the Massachusetts Historical Society.

first deported. It was understood between Adams and Pickering that one of the blank warrants was for Collot.[52]

Yet, Collot was never deported. Pickering was busy enforcing the Sedition Act and expressed his reservations about enforcing the Alien Friends Act when there was no mechanism within the act to detain foreigners once they received a deportation order. He believed deportees could simply flee or go into hiding. While Adams was eager to use the act to deport Collot, Pickering was more concerned about Collot returning to France and helping to plot an attack on the United States. Pickering arranged to withhold Collot's passport to prevent him from returning to France. Collot found another way to travel to France and left the United States in 1800.[53]

Médéric-Louis-Elie Moreau de St. Méry was a French scholar and a former member of the French Assembly. Moreau had fled the Reign of Terror and settled in the United States; he opened a bookstore in Philadelphia in 1794. Members of Washington's administration patronized the store, and Adams was a customer. It was not until 1798 that Moreau fell under the Federalists' suspicions. Moreau ended up on Adams's list of Frenchmen to be deported under the Alien Friends Act. When questioned why Moreau was on the list, Adams replied, "Nothing in particular, but he's too French." Moreau and his family resolved to voluntarily depart rather than face deportation under the Alien Friends Act. Pickering did not remove Moreau from the list, but he did help to provide Moreau with a "letters of safe conveyance" in order to hasten his voyage back to France. Moreau and his family left the United States in August 1798.[54]

Adams did not just use his authority and discretion to deport, but also to exclude foreigners from the United States. In July 1798, Rufus King, the American minister to England, informed Adams that French philosopher Pierre DuPont de Nemours and a delegation of French colleagues wished to obtain permission to come to the United States on a mission to improve and extend the sciences. Adams explained he was not willing to grant permission to DuPont or his delegation at present. "We have had too many French philosophers already," Adams wrote, "and I really begin to think, or rather to suspect, that learned academies, not under the immediate inspection and control of government, have disorganized the world, and are incompatible with social order."[55]

Adams and Pickering also sought to use the Alien Friends Act and Sedition Act to supplement each other to suppress dissent and Democratic-Republican criticisms. Irish immigrant John D. Burk headed the New York local lodge of the United Irishmen and co-edited the Democratic-Republican journal, *New York Time Piece*. Pickering believed prosecuting Burk under the Sedition Act would prove more expedient in silencing him, but also intended to deport him under the Alien Friends Act after his prosecution and punishment for sedition. Burk attempted to strike a deal with the Adams administration. If Adams agreed to authorize the dismissal of his case and release him on bail, Burk promised to voluntarily depart the United States. Adams agreed. While Burk led Pickering to believe he would honor their agreement, he subsequently went into hiding in Virginia and waited until the Alien Friends Act expired.[56]

The Federalists were adamant in their desire to suppress Benjamin Franklin Bache and his Democratic-Republican newspaper *Aurora*, and they could not wait for Congress. Three weeks before Adams signed the Sedition Act into law, the Federalist-dominated government arrested Bache and charged him with violating common law seditious libel.[57] Before he could be brought to trial, Bache died of yellow fever.

The Federalists then shifted their efforts to silence Bache's successor, William Duane. Pickering directed William Rawle, a federal district attorney, to bring a sedition prosecution against Duane. He also urged Adams to deport Duane under the Alien Friends Act. Pickering argued that while Duane "pretends to be an American citizen, saying that he was born in Vermont," he was born in America "before our revolution" and remained a British subject when he was raised in Ireland as a child. "He is doubtless a United Irishman, and the company is probably formed, to oppose the authority of the Government; and in case of war and invasion by the French, to join them."[58] Adams agreed to authorize Duane's deportation. Pickering proceeded with the Sedition Act prosecution, and intended to subsequently deport Duane. The prosecution was unsuccessful and eventually dismissed, and Duane was never deported.[59]

While Adams intended to deport under the Alien Friends Act, he would not act as a rubberstamp, and he used his absolute authority and ultimate discretion to refuse to deport a former friend and supporter. Dr. Joseph Priestley was an eminent scientist and theologian whom Adams had met in England. Priestley settled in Pennsylvania in 1796 and published a series of his sermons, which he dedicated to Adams. When Adams became president, Priestley wrote to him, recommending Thomas Cooper for a political appointment. Adams did not answer him—it was his practice never to reply to solicitations.[60] Priestley then began to circulate articles Cooper had written that were critical of Adams and published in Democratic-Republican newspapers. When Cooper would later face prosecution under the Sedition Act,

Pickering recommended Priestley's deportation under the Alien Friends Act.[61] Perhaps seeking to justify his decision to let Priestley remain in the country despite his views and criticisms, Adams described Priestley as "weak as water, as unstable as Reuben or the wind. His influence is not an atom in the world."[62]

Separation of Powers

The Democratic-Republicans immediately and vehemently denounced the Alien Friends Act and Sedition Act. They condemned the acts in the press and organized drives to send petitions demanding that Congress repeal them.[63] The Virginia and Kentucky Resolutions, drafted by Madison and Jefferson, respectively, attacked the Alien Friends Act and Sedition Act as unconstitutional, exceeding the delegated power to the federal government.

In the Virginia Resolution, Madison declared that both acts would "transform the present republican system of the United States, into an absolute, or at best a mixed monarchy."[64] Madison argued that the Alien Friends Act "subverts the general principles of free government." Adams's unchecked, unlimited power and discretion to deport anyone he deemed "dangerous to the peace and safety of the United States" violated the constitutional principle of separation of powers "by uniting legislative and judicial powers to those of executive."[65]

Pennsylvania Congressman Albert Gallatin, a Democratic-Republican who was an emigrant from Switzerland, helped to lead the charge against passage of the Alien Friends Act. During the debates in the House of Representatives, Gallatin argued that the Alien Friends Act's authorization of deportation of foreigners violated the Fifth Amendment, which specified no "person" should be deprived of due process protections and thus applied to foreign noncitizens, as well as American citizens within the United States.[66] In 1799, Gallatin denounced the Alien Friends Act and called for its repeal. He contended the act was not a necessary measure to protect the United States, but rather one used to try to suppress political opinion and dissent. The act exploited the vulnerability of noncitizens to potential deportation and coerced their silence through fear. Gallatin described the justification of the Alien Friends Act as part of a fear of "subversion of religion, morality, law and government." Gallatin called these fears "pretended dangers" in America, "the visionary phantoms of a disordered imagination," used to establish Congress's power and its "substantial despotism on the ruins of our Constitution."[67]

Addressing the effect and dangers of the Alien Friends Act, Gallatin decried the absolute power it gave President Adams to deport foreigners, "holding the rod of terror over their heads, and leaving their fate at his sole disposal." He argued such power "renders them complete slaves of the President, and makes them proper instruments for the execution of every project which ambition may suggest, which faction may dictate." He asked, "Is that a government of laws which leaves us no security but in the confidence we have in the moderation and patriotism of one man?" Foreshadowing the dangers of laws placing unlimited power in the president, Gallatin urged his colleagues to think about that power left in the wrong hands. Congress might think such power was safe with the president when it passed the law, but one day that power could be left with another president in "whom they do not place the same confidence."[68]

The Democratic-Republican petitions and the Virginia and Kentucky Resolutions were unsuccessful in persuading members of Congress to repeal the Alien Friends Act and Sedition Act. Federalists arrested twenty-five Democratic-Republicans under the Sedition Act, with ten indicted, tried, and convicted, including leading critics of Adams and his administration: Matthew Lyon, Thomas Cooper, and James Callender.[69]

Yet, if the intention of these prosecutions was to suppress dissent, it backfired. Since passage of the Alien Friends Act and Sedition Act, the number of Democratic-Republican newspapers had tripled, and they continued to publish denunciations of both acts and of Adams.[70] A year after passage of the acts, tensions between France and the United States eased, Adams opened peace negotiations, and the quasi-war ended in 1799. Peace could not save Adams's presidency, however. The unpopularity of the Alien Friends Act and Sedition Act led to his losing reelection to Jefferson. As president, Jefferson did not repeal the Alien Friends Act and Sedition Act, but rather allowed them to expire. He did sign the Naturalization Act of 1802, which repealed the fourteen-year residency requirement in the 1798 Act. Even though the United States never went to war with France, the Alien Enemies Act remained in place and was later used in the War of 1812 and during World War I.

Since their expiration, the Alien Friends Act and Sedition Act of 1798 have been recalled in popular memory only as repressive laws, which undermined the Constitution and America's democratic values and protection of free press and speech. The Sedition Act, and the prosecutions under it, sought to suppress Democratic-Republicans' criticisms. Although there were no deportations under the Alien Friends Act, it was a politically motivated tool to suppress dissent and internal subversion. While the Alien Friends Act expired, the threat of deportation and use of fear and intimidation to force foreigners to choose removal or voluntary departure would persist, as would arguments about due process protections, the dangers of consolidated absolute power, and the Federalists' legal arguments supporting the Alien Friends Act's passage.

Developing the Plenary Power Doctrine

During the nineteenth century, the United States experienced various waves of immigration, which helped to forge its identity as a "nation of immigrants." Yet, immigration during this period was not open and unrestricted.[71] States continued to control their borders, and state legislatures passed restrictions under their "police power," an inherent power held by each sovereign state to regulate, protect, and promote the health, safety, morals, and general welfare.[72]

States expressed their sovereignty through restrictions, which reflected their focus on self-preservation and their fears of subversion through poverty, labor competition, race, and revolution. Tensions developed over the extent of state and federal power under the Constitution to restrict people from entering and moving within the United States. The Supreme Court began to strike down state laws as violating Congress's power to regulate commerce with foreign nations under the Constitution. Its decisions helped open the door to federal immigration restrictions in the late nineteenth century. The court upheld the constitutionality of these restrictions as a part of Congress's power to protect national security. It located this plenary (absolute) power to restrict immigration in a nation's sovereignty and its inherent right to self-preservation.

The nineteenth century saw an influx of Irish immigrants. Between 1820 and 1840, 700,000 Irish immigrants arrived in United States.[73] Between 1846 and 1855, as more left Ireland due to the potato blight and famine, 1.8 million immigrated to North America.[74] Pauperism among immigrants led to hostility toward newcomers and concern that they would become a burden on the state and its resources. States turned to the English poor laws for guidance. Under these laws, the poor were the responsibility of the local community where they were legally "settled." States such as Massachusetts passed legislation to prevent the poor or those likely to become a public charge from entering and becoming legally settled.[75] In response to an increase in immigration, New York began to create workhouses and almshouses in 1824, not for charitable purposes, but rather as a way to control the poor and save the state money.[76]

Massachusetts and New York both required bonds and / or a passenger or "head" tax to compensate the state for those likely to become a public charge. In 1820, Massachusetts began to demand security from vessels in the form of a bond to indemnify it for three years with respect to any passenger likely to become a public charge. In 1831, the state offered a choice to post security for each foreign passenger deemed likely to become a pauper or pay $5 per passenger to compensate the state. As more arrived, Massachusetts changed the requirements in anticipation of paupers settling within the state. In 1837, it required vessels to post bond for "high risk" foreign passengers likely to become a public charge and pay $2 per foreign passenger who was not a risk.[77] The New York Commissioners of Emigration helped enforce New York's exclusion laws, as well as facilitating the voluntary departure of foreign paupers back to Europe.[78]

With the discovery of gold in California in 1848, immigrants and native-born Americans all rushed to the West Coast to seek their fortune. Chinese, mostly men and traveling alone, arrived in California and worked alongside Irish immigrants in the mines and later on the railroads.[79] Many of the Chinese immigrants could not afford passage to the United States, and so they entered a contract labor system, similar to indentured servitude. Companies would arrange to bring Chinese immigrants to California, where the Chinese would work in the mines to pay off their debt. As competition grew, so did resentment and racial discrimination against the Chinese. Other miners argued they simply could not compete against contract laborers, who worked for small wages or none at all and lived cheaply without families to support.[80] They likened contract labor to slave labor and Chinese miners to African American slaves, while characterizing the Chinese as inferior, immoral heathens, who would never be able to assimilate into American society.[81] California legislators began to pass racially discriminatory laws, including a head tax, aimed at restricting the Chinese, and a "Foreign Miners' Tax."[82]

While state self-preservation focused on economics, race and nationality, and labor competition, it also included rebellion and the subversion of slavery within the United States and from those abroad. As slavery split the nation, it also led to both Northern and Southern states passing restrictions on the residence and migration of free African Americans. In the North, many of those who opposed slavery also opposed a racially integrated society. Some pushed for the exclusion of free African Americans from their states, fearing that their calls for abolition would lead to an influx.[83] The American Colonization Society (1816) advocated for gradual abolition and the deportation of freed African Americans out of the United States. The society worked with states that wanted to arrange to send African Americans out of the United States, and it sponsored colonies to establish settlements in Liberia in 1821 for this purpose.[84]

In the South, slave-holding states feared that free black individuals residing in their states would present a grave threat to slavery and would inspire and encourage slave escapes, conspiracies, and revolts. States began by excluding Haitians in fear that those who fled on their own, or were expelled, would infect American slaves with the dangerous idea of revolt.[85] With a growing abolitionist movement, slave-holding states barred entry of free black people who were not already residents, and imposed penalties on those bringing in free black people from other states. Some states required individuals to leave the state upon emancipation. Those permitted to remain within these states faced restrictions, including registration requirements and proof of their free status, without which they could face expulsion.[86]

In the wake of Denmark Vesey's slave revolt conspiracy in 1822, South Carolina passed a "Negro Seamen Act" to prevent the "moral contagion" of freedom from spreading and infecting its slaves. The act required "free negroes or persons of color" to remain on their vessels docked at local ports, and they were barred from entry. Other states including Florida, Alabama, Georgia, North Carolina, Louisiana, Texas, and Mississippi would pass similar acts to prevent this moral contagion of freedom from threatening slavery within their states.[87]

While states passed restrictions to control their borders and alleviate concerns and economic burdens presented by increased migration and immigration, this use of their police power also faced legal challenges under the Constitution. Federal courts struck down state restrictions under Article VI of the Constitution. Referred to as the "Supremacy Clause," this section of the Constitution prevents the states from exercising or interfering with a power held by Congress.[88] The federal courts that struck down these laws focused on conflicts with Congress's power to regulate commerce with foreign nations. This was one of the justifications the Federalists articulated to support passage of the Alien Friends Act and its constitutionality.

In *Elkison v. Deliesseline* (1823), a Jamaican sailor challenged his detention under South Carolina's Negro Seaman Act. The circuit court held the law was an unconstitutional restriction of commerce with foreign nations and treaties with foreign nations, which was a specific power delegated to Congress under the Constitution. The foreign vessels coming into the port and navigating the seas were part of foreign commerce, and the exclusion and detention of individuals on those vessels interfered with commerce and international relations.[89]

In *Gibbons v. Ogden* (1824), the Supreme Court issued a landmark decision striking down a New York law granting Robert R. Livingston and Robert Fulton exclusive rights to navigating New York waterways with steamboats. The court held that Congress's power to regulate interstate and foreign commerce under the Constitution extends to "navigation" and commercial intercourse through connected waterways. It described Congress's power over interstate and foreign commerce as "plenary" within its sovereignty as "a single government."[90]

In 1849, the Supreme Court struck down a head tax imposed in New York and Boston ports as an unconstitutional regulation of interstate and foreign commerce. In what were referred to as the *Passenger Cases*, the court held the requirement of vessels to pay the state per passenger interfered with the exercise of "commercial power," which was "vital" to the Union. Congress, and not the states, had exclusive jurisdiction to regulate it. The state's police power, including "safety, health, and morals of its citizens," was restricted by the Constitution. "The police power of the state cannot draw within its jurisdiction objects which lie beyond it. It meets the commercial power of the Union in dealing with subjects under the protection of that power, yet it can only be exerted under peculiar emergencies and to a limited extent." States circumvented this prohibition on head taxes, by requiring a bond for all passengers or voluntary payment.[91]

While the federal courts maintained that states still retained control over who resided within their borders under their police powers and state sovereignty, these decisions revealed a growing conflict between state regulation of immigration and powers held by Congress. They also foreshadowed the Supreme Court upholding federal regulation of immigration two decades later.

After the Civil War, the United States shifted from a union of states to one nation, and sought to reconstruct its national identity as it worked to incorporate newly freed slaves, and to provide citizenship and civil and political rights protections for African Americans.[92] During this period, Congress also began to pass laws to regulate immigration.

In 1868, the United States, seeking to improve relations and to increase trade and commerce with China, signed the Burlingame Treaty.[93] This agreement established an open immigration policy and permitted "free and voluntary" migration of Chinese to the United States and of Americans to China.[94] Both nations recognized "the inherent and inalienable right of man to change his home and allegiance, and also the mutual advantage of the free migration and emigration of their citizens and subjects respectively from the one country to the other for purposes of curiosity, of trade, or as permanent residents."[95] While the Burlingame Treaty stated that American and Chinese visitors or residents were entitled to the same privileges, immunities, and exemptions as its nation's citizens, the treaty also specified that this entitlement did not include citizenship.[96]

In 1870, Congress revised naturalization requirements intentionally seeking to prevent Chinese immigrants from becoming citizens.[97] Congress expanded naturalization to "aliens of African nativity and to persons of African descent," in addition to "free white persons" and those of "good moral character."[98] It implicitly excluded the Chinese, who were not considered "white."[99]

During the 1870s, the United States suffered an economic depression, which led not only to unemployment, but also to domestic concerns regarding increased poverty, prostitution, disease, and criminality. Foreigners became the scapegoats for these concerns, and their exclusion became the solution to the nation's problems. The main scapegoats were the Chinese, who were described as racially inferior and biologically incapable of assimilation. Some even likened the Chinese to an infectious disease that could contaminate American society and culture.[100] When labor unions, anti-Chinese advocates, and California legislators demanded protection and federal assistance against what they referred to as the "Yellow Peril," Congress took action.[101]

In 1875, Congress passed the Page Act.[102] It excluded foreign women "imported for the purposes of prostitution" (which was used to target Chinese women) and foreigners who were convicted of a felony (except for political crimes) or who agreed to emigrate instead of serving their sentence in their country.[103] The act's provisions also directly addressed the perceived threat of contract labor and, specifically, of Asian contract laborers. It punished any person involved in the contract labor system, including contractors and those transporting foreign contract laborers to the United States, as well as the transport of "any subject of China, Japan, or any Oriental country, without their free and voluntary consent, for the purpose of holding them to a term of service."[104]

A few months after Congress passed the Page Act, the Supreme Court declared state laws requiring bonds for immigrants in California, New York, and Louisiana unconstitutional because these restrictions interfered with Congress's power to regulate foreign commerce and relations.[105] In *Henderson et al. v. Mayor of City of New York* (1875), the Supreme Court held that the "passage of laws which concern the admission of citizens and subjects of foreign nations to our shores belongs to Congress, and not to the states. It has the power to regulate commerce with foreign nations; the responsibility for the character of those regulations and for the manner of their execution belongs solely to the national government." The court identified immigrants as part of commerce. "In addition to the wealth which some of them bring, they bring still more largely the labor which we need to till our soil, build our railroads, and develop the latent resources of the country in its minerals, its manufactures, and its agriculture."[106]

The court acknowledged that states held the police power to pass laws to protect their residents against "paupers and convicted criminals from abroad," but it was careful to note that such laws would be in the "absence of legislation by Congress." It also stated that these state laws should be "the subject of a uniform system or plan. The laws which govern the right to land passengers in the United States from other countries ought to be the same in New York, Boston, New Orleans, and San Francisco."[107] The court thus not only asserted the federal government's constitutional authority to regulate immigration, but also opened the door to Congress seizing that authority and passing more immigration restrictions.

By the late 1870s, Californian legislators continued to pressure Congress to exclude Chinese immigrants from the United States.[108] In 1880, Congress amended the Burlingame Treaty to allow the United States to "regulate, limit or suspend" the immigration of additional Chinese laborers, but permitted those who were already in the United States to "go and come of their own free will."[109] The amendment also authorized the United States to restrict entry or residence when it "affects or threatens to affect the interests of that country, or to endanger the good order of the United States or of any locality within the territory thereof." Under the treaty, however, the United States could not entirely prohibit immigration, and the power to suspend was limited to Chinese laborers.[110] These revisions to the Burlingame Treaty did not satisfy Chinese exclusion advocates, who pressed Congress for stricter restrictions.[111]

In 1882, Congress answered their calls with what was referred to as the "Chinese Exclusion Act." This act suspended immigration of Chinese "skilled and unskilled laborers and Chinese employed in mining" for ten years, and explicitly barred all Chinese from becoming United States citizens.[112] Two years later, Congress revised the Chinese Exclusion Act to require all Chinese in the United States to have a certificate stating their name, age, and occupation in order to remain, leave, and reenter the United States.[113] Anti-

Chinese advocates and anti-Chinese violence on the West Coast pushed Congress to amend the Chinese Exclusion Act in 1888.[114] This amendment prohibited all Chinese miners and skilled and unskilled laborers from entering the United States, and it invalidated the certificates, such that all Chinese who left the United States carrying certificates, were now excluded and denied reentry.[115]

Chinese residents ensnared by these restrictions and amendments, as well as those excluded from the United States, brought legal challenges against these federal immigration laws. Chae Chan Ping, a Chinese laborer who had left the United States with a certificate and was excluded under the 1888 amendment to the Chinese Exclusion Act, challenged the constitutionality of his exclusion and the act itself for violating the Burlingame Treaty.[116]

In *Chae Chan Ping v. United States* (1889), referred to as the "Chinese Exclusion Case," the Supreme Court unanimously upheld the constitutionality of the Chinese Exclusion Act and Ping's exclusion under it. The court held that Congress had the ability to pass legislation to amend, revise, or even revoke a treaty. Thus, it was the Chinese Exclusion Act, amended in 1888, and not the Burlingame Treaty, that applied to Ping and authorized his exclusion.[117] The court also held that Congress possessed the power to regulate immigration and exclude foreigners, and the judiciary should defer to Congress and not question this power or the motivations behind such regulation.[118]

Justice Stephen J. Field wrote the court's opinion. He was a former chief justice of California's supreme court and the justice who sat on the Ninth Circuit.[119] Field began his analysis by delivering a brief history of Chinese immigration to the United States and of the state and federal legislation restricting and excluding these newcomers. He described Chinese immigrants as "strangers in the land, residing apart by themselves, and adhering to the customs and usages of their own country."[120] He recounted California legislators' fears of being overrun by Chinese "in numbers approaching the character of Oriental invasion" and their concerns that Chinese laborers "had a baneful effect upon the material interests of the state and upon public morals" and were a "menace to our civilization."[121]

Defending Congress's passage of Chinese Exclusion in light of this perceived foreign threat to the United States and national security, Field wrote, "If, therefore, the government of the United States, through its legislative department, considers the presence of foreigners of a different race in this country, who will not assimilate with us, to be dangerous to its peace and security, their exclusion is not to be stayed because at the time there are no actual hostilities with the nation of which the foreigners are subjects."[122]

Field emphasized the importance of the United States as acting as "one people, one nation, one power" in foreign relations and regulating commerce with foreign nations.[123] Yet, he did not base Congress's constitutional authority to exclude immigrants on foreign commerce.[124] Instead, he rearticulated another one of the Federalists' justifications for the constitutionality of the Alien Friends Act of 1798 by locating the power held by Congress to regulate immigration within a nation's sovereignty, right to self-preservation, and "security against foreign aggression and encroachment."[125] Field explained that if an independent nation could not exclude foreigners from its shores, it would be subject to the control of another foreign power, and thus, an independent nation would cease to remain independent.[126]

A few months after passing the Chinese Exclusion Act, Congress began incorporating restrictions used by individual states into federal legislation. The Immigration Act of 1882 excluded "any convict, lunatic, idiot, or any person unable to take care of himself or herself without becoming a public charge."[127] This Act also levied a fifty-cent tax on every foreigner landing in the United States, collected by the United States Treasury Department and deposited into "an immigrant fund," which would be used to defray immigration regulation expenses, take care of immigrants, and enforce the Immigration Act.[128] The act left the inspection of foreigners and of enforcement of their exclusion to the state immigration commissions, boards, and officers, as well as state immigration charities, without compensation from the federal government.[129]

In 1891, Congress passed a comprehensive Immigration Act that excluded idiots, insane persons, paupers or persons likely to become a public charge; persons suffering from loathsome or a dangerous contagious disease; persons who have been convicted of a felony (except for political crimes) or other infamous crime or misdemeanor involving moral turpitude; polygamists; and contract laborers, or those whose passage was paid for by another.[130] It also established a Bureau of Immigration and a superintendent of immigration under the Treasury Department. Federal immigration officers appointed by the Treasury Department were responsible for enforcing immigration laws.[131]

This act marked the end of state-controlled immigration restrictions. In 1892, Ellis Island in New York harbor opened as a federal immigration depot, designed to enforce immigration laws and to sort, inspect, and detain immigrants pending entry to the United States or deportation to their country of origin. Ellis Island also featured a hospital where immigrants could receive medical treatment for curable diseases before their entry to the United States.

In 1892, a Japanese woman named Nishimura Ekiu challenged her exclusion under a provision in the Immigration Act of 1891, which barred those likely to become a public charge. In *Nishimura Ekiu v. United States*, the Supreme Court upheld Ekiu's exclusion under the 1891 act's provisions, reaffirmed the Chinese Exclusion Case, and articulated the plenary power doctrine,[132] establishing Congress's constitutional power to exclude foreigners:

> It is an accepted maxim of international law that every sovereign nation has the power, as inherent in sovereignty, and essential to self-preservation, to forbid entrance of foreigners within its dominions, or to admit them only in such cases and upon such conditions as it may see fit to prescribe.[133]

The court also upheld the constitutionality of the act's delegation of its enforcement to the Treasury Department and federal immigration officers.[134] These immigration officers were the sole judges of the facts leading to exclusion, and no other tribunal, unless expressly authorized by law, could question the decision or the sufficiency of the evidence on which these officials acted. The judiciary should defer to the decisions of Congress and of the immigration officers.[135]

In *Fong Yue Ting v. United States* (1893), a 6–3 decision, the Supreme Court reaffirmed the plenary power doctrine. Writing for the majority, Justice Horace Gray cited international law to support the doctrine, such as Swiss Political Philosopher Emmerich de Vattel's *Law of Nations*, which included the right to deport, as well as the right to exclude, those who could corrupt or disrupt, as what a sovereign nation "owes to itself, the care of its own safety." Gray then extended the plenary power doctrine to include Congress's power to deport foreigners residing in the United States, as well as to exclude. He eliminated any distinction between deportation and exclusion for due process purposes, and he dismissed the idea that deportation triggered more substantial procedural safeguards associated with punishment, including a fair hearing, access to counsel, and constitutional protections.[136]

Justice Field wrote a dissenting opinion. He described deportation as "banishment" and a "cruel and unusual" punishment without due process. Field argued that deportation should receive greater legal protection than exclusion, because, while constitutional protections did not apply to foreigners outside of the United States, such protections should apply to those residing within the nation's borders.[137] Field also distinguished this case from his holding in the Chinese Exclusion Case by emphasizing that the right to exclude was inherent in a nation's sovereignty, but the right to deport was not.

Field declared the people were sovereign.[138] Like Albert Gallatin, Field insisted that foreigners, as well as citizens, were entitled to due process protection under the Constitution. Field then likened the law to the Alien Friends Act, citing James Madison's condemnation of President Adams's ultimate power to deport foreigners he deemed dangerous and Madison's characterization of such deportation as "banishment" and a form of "punishment."[139]

In his farewell address, George Washington cautioned the American people against foreign influence, partiality for one nation and excessive dislike for another, and the ability of cunning, ambitious, and unprincipled men to subvert the power of the people and the values of the nation and to usurp the reins of government. He warned them of the despotism caused by men seeking revenge and security through absolute power and the danger of one branch of government holding too much power without a check by the others.

Examples of many of these dangers would appear at different points over the course of the next two centuries, beginning two years later in 1798, with passage of the Alien Friends Act and Sedition Act. Legislators and the American public would be haunted by this legislation that encapsulated Washington's warnings. Those who challenged subsequent immigration and speech restrictions looked to the Alien Friends Act and Sedition Act for a point of comparison.

The Alien Friends Act was the first implicit ideological restriction passed by Congress, and its passage and enforcement reveal the underlying conditions, suppression tactics, tensions, and contested interpretations that run through the history of ideological exclusion and deportation in the United States. Such explicit and implicit ideological restrictions place absolute power and ultimate discretion in the executive branch to admit, exclude, or deport, use restrictions of foreigners, including naturalization, as tools to suppress dissent, reflect a conflation of foreigners and radicals, and reveal a fear of foreigners as a source of subversion.

By the end of the nineteenth century, some of the Federalists' legal arguments to support passage of the Alien Friends Act would be used to strike down state laws regulating immigration, as well as to create the plenary power doctrine. National sovereignty and the authority to exclude and deport as being essential to self-preservation and national security had become the primary legal justifications for the federal power over foreigners and their entry to and residence in the United States. The Supreme Court had sanctioned this authority and insulated it from substantive judicial review. The Democratic-Republicans' insistence that deportation was subject to due process and constitutional protections would resurface in subsequent legal challenges.

In 1893, Congress established Boards of Special Inquiry, panels of three immigration inspectors who reviewed and decided exclusion and deportation cases, including those in which they had participated in collecting evidence to support exclusion or deportation. The hearings were closed to the public, and while detainees could have counsel at hearings, they were not provided with counsel during examination by the Board of Special Inquiry.[140] If the panel determined that a foreigner should be deported from the United States, it requested a warrant of deportation from the Secretary of the Treasury.

If ordered deported by the Secretary of the Treasury, foreigners, or their counsel, could file a writ of *habeas corpus* (a written demand "that you shall have the body" derived from the English common law) in a federal district court. It is a form of legal recourse for individuals who believe they are being unlawfully detained or imprisoned. They must be presented to a court to determine if their detention is lawful. Under the plenary power doctrine, the judicial branch defers to the legislative and executive branches to determine who should be excluded or deported, so substantive judicial review is limited in immigration cases. The federal district court judge could dismiss an exclusion or deportation only for a procedural error or a constitutional violation. An appeal of the federal district court judge's decision could eventually reach the Supreme Court.

In 1903, the Bureau of Immigration was transferred from the Treasury Department to the Commerce and Labor Department. In *Yamataya v. Fisher* (1903), referred to as the "Japanese Immigrant Case," the Supreme Court reaffirmed the plenary power doctrine. Decisions by immigration officers to exclude were final and conclusive; they were not reviewable by the judiciary, which should defer to their decisions. The court held that in deportation cases, notice and a hearing were sufficient due process. Deportation was not "punishment," and deportees were not constitutionally entitled to the same due process protections under the Fifth Amendment as those facing criminal prosecution.[141]

With the legal precedent establishing the plenary power doctrine, the stage was set for Congress to shift from explicit restrictions based on nationality, economic status, employment, and health to those based on belief, association, and expression. This shift began after "the shot that shocked the world": the assassination of the president of the United States in 1901.[142]

2

War on Anarchy

ON SEPTEMBER 6, 1901, President William McKinley greeted visitors at the Temple of Music at the Pan American Exposition in Buffalo, New York. A large crowd of people waited for hours to meet the president and to have a chance to shake his hand and exchange pleasantries.[1] Shortly after four o'clock in the afternoon, the last to meet McKinley was a twenty-eight-year-old man named Leon Czolgosz. Extending his hand, wrapped in a handkerchief, Czolgosz reached out to McKinley's. The handkerchief concealed a revolver, and just before the men's hands touched, Czolgosz fired twice into the president.[2] Secret Service agents immediately apprehended him. McKinley did not survive. He eventually succumbed to a gangrene infection from the bullet wounds and died a week later.[3]

The son of Polish immigrants, Czolgosz was born in Detroit, Michigan in 1873.[4] After losing his job as a steel wireworker in Cleveland in the Panic of 1893, he regained it under another name and identity, but had become depressed and disillusioned.[5] Czolgosz had turned to anarchism through friends who were anarchists. When asked what had motivated him to shoot McKinley, Czolgosz stated, "I never had much luck at anything and this preyed upon me. It made me morose and envious, but what started the craze to kill was a lecture I heard some time ago by Emma Goldman."[6] According to Czolgosz, Goldman's description of anarchist doctrine that "all rulers should be exterminated" had "set me on fire."[7] After the lecture, "I had made up my mind that I would have to do something heroic for the cause I loved."[8] Czolgosz was convicted of first-degree murder and sentenced to death, two months after the assassination. He made a final declaration prior to his electrocution: "I killed the President because he was the enemy of the good people—the good working people. I am not sorry for my crime."[9]

In the immediate aftermath of McKinley's assassination, an anti-anarchist fervor swept the nation. A day after Czolgosz shot McKinley, "a young man, well dressed, and apparently a student or professional man, created a sensation . . . making a series of speeches in which he urged volunteers to follow him over to Paterson [New Jersey] and exterminate the anarchists quartered there."[10] One observer wrote, "'I never in my life saw such an angry mob. There were men as well as boys in it and they seemed to have lost all control of themselves. If they had caught those anarchists . . . I believe they would have torn them to pieces.'"[11] After a few weeks, such incidents and calls for violence ceased and the fervor appeared to have subsided, but a fear of anarchist subversion and danger inside the United States remained.[12] Members of the public called on their government to protect them from this threat.[13]

In the years following McKinley's assassination, Congress, state legislatures, and law enforcement attempted to suppress anarchism in the United States by using current laws and passing new ones, including New York's Criminal Anarchy Law and the Alien Immigration Act of 1903, the first explicit ideological exclusion and deportation law in the twentieth century. Like the Alien Friends Act of 1798, these laws were passed in the name of national security and were used as tools of political repression. The response by legislators, the press, members of the public, and anarchists to this "War on Anarchy"[14] focused on free expression and articulating the importance of protecting this freedom against suppression. They also challenged the breadth of the test used to evaluate the legality of free speech restrictions, including restrictions on anarchist speech. While no one was deported under the Alien Friends Act of 1798, the federal government would use the Alien Immigration Act to exclude and deport. For the first time the Supreme Court would confront this intersection of First Amendment and immigration law and would have to decide how to interpret ideological restrictions and to evaluate their constitutionality.

Anarchists in America and Abroad

In 1798, the Federalists had attempted to demonize the Democratic-Republicans by characterizing them as "frenchified." In the wake of McKinley's assassination, some Americans dismissed anarchism as a "foreign" ideology, imported by immigrants. They rejected the idea that a "real" American could also be an anarchist and advocate for the abolition of all organized government.[15] In the nineteenth century, there were two strands of anarchism within the United States, individualist and communist, and both strands contained American homegrown roots as well as European origins. While some turned to anarchism after exposure to American and European writers and theorists, others became radicalized in response to governmental repression against anarchists and a growing labor movement in the United States.

Anarchism in the United States emerged partly from an antistatist undercurrent in its political history. Anarchists cited the American Revolution, a just rebellion against an oppressive government, as an example of their principles. They admired Thomas Jefferson's championing of individual rights and liberty and reprinted passages of the Declaration of Independence.[16] Anarchists also cited transcendentalist Henry David Thoreau and his argument for resistance to government and unjust, immoral laws: "government is best which governs not at all."[17]

Considered the father of American individualist anarchism, Josiah Warren, born in Massachusetts in 1798, believed in individual liberty and living in harmony without organized government and operating under a system of "mutualism," where private property existed but the price and the exchange of goods was based on the worth of the effort expended to produce it.[18] He founded an individualist utopian colony named "Modern Times" in New York in the 1850s. One of Warren's followers was an American named Benjamin Tucker, who identified as an individualist anarchist and "Jeffersonian." In the 1870s, Tucker traveled to France, where he met French philosopher Pierre-Joseph Proudhon, the father of individualist anarchism in Europe.

When Tucker returned to the United States, he translated and published Proudhon's 1840 text on anarchism, *What Is Property?*. In 1881, Tucker founded an American individualist anarchist newspaper, *Liberty: Not the Daughter but the Mother of Order*.[19] Tucker also continued to seek opportunities to introduce European anarchists to an American audience, translating and publishing works by Russian philosopher Prince Peter Kropotkin, the father of communist anarchism, and by Russian revolutionary Mikhail Bakunin. Influenced by Karl Marx, Kropotkin believed in publicly owned property, and he combined both communist and anarchist approaches to property and government to create communist anarchism.[20] Bakunin was an exponent of "propaganda by deed." Rather than focusing on writing and lectures as a method to influence the masses, propaganda by deed included resistance to and violence against the government as a demonstration of anarchist principles or solidarity.[21]

A young Bavarian socialist named Johann Most turned to Bakunin's anarchism. Most had been incarcerated for his radical activities and publications in Austria, Germany, and England, where he published a German anarchist newspaper called *Freiheit* (Freedom). Impressed with the labor organizing in the United States in the 1870s and eager to escape Europe, Most immigrated in 1882. In New York City, he led the International Working People's Association (IWPA) and resumed publication of *Freiheit*. A prolific publisher and charismatic orator, who delivered provocative speeches on anarchism, Most had become the leader of communist anarchism in the United States by the late 1880s.[22]

On May 4, 1886, the IWPA held a meeting of workers in Chicago's Haymarket Square to show solidarity with the McCormick Harvester factory strike and to protest police violence against the strikers.[23] Late in the evening, just as the protesters were beginning to leave, 180 policemen appeared and tried to disperse them. Someone threw a bomb at the police, and the police fired back into the crowd. Approximately seventy people were wounded by the bomb and gunfire, and seven policemen were killed. With the anarchist-led Chicago IWPA blamed for the attack, public outcries for cities to suppress anarchism swept the country.[24] Without any direct evidence, Chicago police arrested 150 people, and eventually eight anarchists in the IWPA were charged with conspiracy to commit murder. Of these eight, five were German immigrants.

Referred to as the "Haymarket Affair," the bombing, trial, conviction, and execution of several anarchists captured the public's attention abroad as well as in the United States. Anarchists followed the proceedings closely and held meetings to discuss and denounce them. The trial proved to be rife with judicial and prosecutorial misconduct and bias. Lacking any proof that these specific anarchist leaders had committed the crime, the prosecution played on the jury members' fears of violence and desire for revenge.[25] Addressing the jury, the prosecutor conflated anarchism and violence, directly linking the bombing to belief and ideology and treating the trial and conviction as a form of suppression of anarchism rather than prosecuting and punishing the actual bomb-thrower. "Law is on trial, anarchy is on trial. These men have been selected, picked out by the grand jury and indicted because they were leaders," he said. "Gentlemen of the jury; convict these men, make examples of them; hang them and you save our institutions, our society."[26] The jury convicted the anarchists, sentencing all but one to death. Four were hanged, one committed suicide, and two others had their death sentences commuted. In 1893, Illinois Governor John Peter Altgeld pardoned the remaining three anarchists, citing the trial's unfairness and prejudice against them.[27]

To some in the United States and abroad, the Haymarket Affair represented the connection between anarchism and violence and helped to inspire fear of the anarchist movement. To others, it provoked an interest in anarchism. It was not ideology, but rather the unjust trial and conviction of the "Haymarket martyrs" that pushed many toward anarchism. One person radicalized by the Haymarket Affair was a young woman named Emma Goldman.[28]

Goldman was born in 1869 to a Jewish family in Kovno, Lithuania, which was part of the Russian empire. She immigrated to the United States and settled with her family in Rochester, New York in 1885. She worked in a factory, and when she was eighteen, Goldman met and married an immigrant from Russia named Jacob Kersner. It was an unhappy marriage, and she divorced Kersner, only to remarry him when he threatened to commit suicide if they did not reunite.[29] Goldman was enthralled by the Haymarket Affair and marked the moment of her "social awakening" after listening to a speech about the Haymarket martyrs. Goldman became a devoted reader of Johann Most's *Freiheit*. In 1889, she left Rochester and Kersner, determined to move to New York City and to meet Most.[30]

When Goldman arrived in New York City, she joined anarchist circles and met Alexander Berkman, a Lithuanian-born Russian immigrant who had experienced his own social awakening in the United States; he had become an anarchist after the Haymarket Affair and observing America's poor treatment of immigrants and workers.[31] Berkman worked for *Freiheit* and introduced Goldman to Most.[32] Most encouraged Goldman's interest in anarchism, and she became his protégé. Over the next few years, Most taught Goldman how to deliver powerful, eloquent lectures to a public audience. Goldman would later replace him and become the leader of communist anarchism in America.

Beginning with the Haymarket Affair and through the 1890s, popular conceptions of anarchism identified it as not only a foreign ideology, but also a dangerous one. While the individualist and communist strands of anarchism remained, a much more prominent distinction had emerged, which divided anarchists into two categories: philosophical and violent. Philosophical anarchists advocated for the abolition of all organized government, attended meetings, read anarchist newspapers, and listened to anarchist lectures. Violent anarchists, however, not only advocated for an overthrow of government, but also took action to effect it.[33]

During the 1890s, some anarchists turned to Bakunin's propaganda by deed and committed acts of violence, including bombings and assassinations, referred to as *attentats* (a French term meaning "attacks" or "assassination attempts").[34] At this time, most anarchists in the United States were philosophical anarchists. While many of them might have celebrated the *attentats* in Europe, some considered them nothing more than murder, and others viewed such violence as damaging to the anarchist movement and inviting suppression.[35]

In 1892, Berkman attempted an *attentat*. During a steel strike in Homestead, Pennsylvania, Henry Clay Frick, chairman of the Carnegie Steel Company, had called in the Pinkerton detective agency to break up the strike. The Pinkertons were known for their rough methods; violence ensued, leaving seven workers and three Pinkertons dead. In the wake of the strike, Berkman sought revenge.[36] He shot and stabbed Frick, but did not succeed in killing him. Caught, convicted, and sentenced to twenty-two years in prison, Berkman later wrote that his attempt to kill Frick was "to express, by my deed, my sentiment toward the existing system of legal oppression and industrial despotism; to attack the institution of wage-slavery in the person of one of its most prominent representatives; to give it a blow—rather morally than physically—this was the real purpose and signification of my act."[37] Once a proponent of propaganda by deed, Most now condemned Berkman, insisting that such violence had no place in America. Most's repudiation caused a split among his followers. Outraged and heartbroken by his response, Goldman severed her relationship with Most.[38]

While Berkman's failed *attentat* captured the attention of the American public, the successful assassinations committed by foreign anarchists in Europe inspired more fear. Anarchists killed French President Marie François Sadi Carnot in 1894, Spain's Prime Minister Antonio Cánovas del Castillo in 1897, Austrian Empress Elisabeth in 1898, and King Umberto I of Italy in 1900. Most of the assassins were Italian anarchists, and like Berkman, they described their *attentats* as acts of revenge and retaliation in response to autocracy and repression.[39]

After each assassination, Germany, Russia, France, Italy, Spain, and Switzerland arrested anarchists and called for the suppression of anarchist newspapers; France and Spain expelled anarchists from their borders.[40] Raids and arrests of anarchists and expulsions ensued, as did reforms in laws to allow for extradition of anarchists and broad, sweeping provisions to deport anarchists at will.[41] In 1901, France issued an extradition order for Emma Goldman's deportation if she was found within its borders, declaring that her presence in the country would "compromise public security."[42] Such expulsions and extradition orders presented challenges and conflicts with other nations.

Many countries refused to admit those expelled as undesirable, and often anarchists sought refuge in England or the United States.[43]

American newspapers urged the United States to wage its own war against anarchists, warning that an influx of European immigrants would turn the nation into a "dumping-ground for all the vile brood of Anarchists and criminals."[44] Yet, Congress and state legislatures did not pass any restrictions. Nor did the United States participate in the first international Anti-Anarchist Conference held in Rome in 1898. For several weeks, delegates from every European nation discussed methods to defeat the anarchist threat, including forming an international police bureau to conduct investigations and track anarchist activities.[45] Each nation vowed to pass laws to suppress the anarchist press and prevent violence.[46]

After Czolgosz shot McKinley, nations were quick to offer support and sympathy and to disassociate themselves from the American-born assassin with a "foreign-sounding" name.[47] Russia and Germany, in a demonstration of solidarity, announced that both countries would completely suppress all anarchist newspapers.[48] Italian authorities renewed their anti-anarchist tactics through arrests and by suppressing anarchist meetings. France vowed to ban all anarchist literature, and Swiss authorities intended to pass more stringent anti-anarchist laws.[49] In Germany, Imperial Chancellor Count Bernhard von Bülow announced that he would place anarchists under constant surveillance, under the threat of arrest and deportation at any time.[50]

Anarchist violence abroad also helped to reinforce perceptions of anarchism as a violent, dangerous, foreign ideology. The New York Times reported that American law enforcement had considered anarchists a "foreign problem."[51] After McKinley's assassination, however, the United States could no longer think of itself as an exceptional nation in the War on Anarchy. This foreign problem had become an American one that demanded action.

The Suppression of Expression

A few months before McKinley's assassination, Emma Goldman had delivered a speech on "Modern Phases of Anarchy" in Cleveland, Ohio. Afterward, a young man approached her asking for suggestions on anarchist texts he should read. The man's name was Fred Nieman. He later followed Goldman to Chicago and accompanied Goldman to the railway station, where he met Abraham Isaak and some staff from Isaak's anarchist newspaper Free Society. Goldman recalled her encounter with Nieman as limited to a brief conversation about his desire to "get in touch with anarchists" while he was in

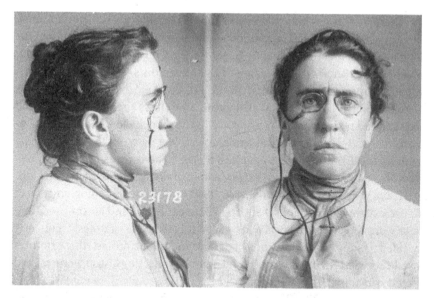

Emma Goldman's mug shot taken in 1901. Bain News Service,
George Grantham Bain Collection
Library of Congress, Prints & Photographs Division, LC-DIG-ggbain-00751.

Chicago before she boarded the train, and then they never saw each other again. But there was something about Nieman that concerned Isaak. He sent a warning to his readers. Nieman was an outsider, possibly a spy, who was not to be trusted.[52] Little did Isaak know that Nieman was an alias. The young man's real name was Leon Czolgosz.

After McKinley's assassination, initial demands for the governmental repression of anarchists focused on Goldman. Once Czolgosz explained how Goldman's speeches had "set me on fire," law enforcement raced to find and arrest her.[53] Goldman was charged with conspiracy to commit murder,[54] but there was no proof that she had anything to do with Czolgosz's plot to kill McKinley. After further questioning, Czolgosz insisted that Goldman knew nothing about his intentions.[55] Without evidence to support the charge, Goldman was set free, much to the dismay of those within the United States who blamed her and all anarchists for McKinley's assassination.[56] If the law could not hold Goldman, then perhaps new laws had to be passed in order to curb her activities and prevent her followers from becoming future assassins.[57]

There were no membership cards in the anarchist movement, but there were pockets of anarchist communities and activities in cities throughout the United States, most prominently in New York, Chicago, Cleveland, Detroit, St. Louis, and Paterson, New Jersey. In 1896, anarchists established an experimental community, the Mutual Home Colony Association, referred to as "Home Colony," in Tacoma, Washington. Anarchists attended meetings and lectures and read anarchist newspapers in German, Italian, Yiddish, and English. The newspapers were essential to create a network to communicate with each other and discuss anarchist ideas.[58] Thus, it was on the suppression of anarchist newspapers that law enforcement first focused its attention.

There were no specific anti-anarchy laws in effect, so law enforcement had to use existing laws in initial efforts. The most broad and accommodating laws were "breach of the peace" or "unlawful assembly" statutes. Frequently wielded to suppress expressions of dissent and public protest, these statutes would serve as the legal basis to raid anarchist meetings, stop lectures, and shut down anarchist newspapers.

On September 22, 1901, over two weeks after Czolgosz shot McKinley, New York City police arrested Johann Most.[59] The September 7 issue of *Freiheit* included excerpts from *Mord contra Mord* (Murder versus Murder), an essay written by German revolutionary Karl Heinzen in 1849. The passages included statements such as "despots are outlawed. . . . to spare them is a crime. . . . we say murder for murderers."[60] Most immediately pulled the issue when he heard about McKinley's assassination, but a few early editions had already been released.[61] Although there was no evidence linking any commission of a crime or violence to the *Freiheit* issue in New York, Most was convicted for "willfully and wrongfully" committing an act "which seriously endangers the public peace." Most was sentenced to one year in prison.[62]

Remarking on the power of speech, Judge John Hinsdale stated, "If we are to believe the murderer of our late President . . . the assassin declares that he was instigated and stimulated to consummate his foul deed by the teachings of Emma Goldman. He is now awaiting execution for the crime, while she is still at large in fancied security."[63] If the law could not punish the assassin's "teacher," than it should at least be used to punish Goldman's teacher. Hinsdale also insisted that anarchists did not deserve constitutional protection. "In the celebrated Somerset slave case 'No slave can breathe the free air of England.' It would be well if the laws of this country were such that it could be said truthfully, that no anarchist can breathe the free air of America."[64]

At this time, jurisprudential understandings of free speech derived from the English common law conceptions of free speech described in Sir William Blackstone's *Commentaries on the Laws of England* (1769). Blackstone considered the right of free speech as precluding prior restraints, but not restrictions on speech that had the *tendency* to harm the public welfare.[65] American courts relied on the bad tendency test to determine protected and unprotected speech, focusing on potential provocation to harm, rather than the actual results or likelihood of imminent unlawful action. Speech that possessed a "natural and probable tendency" to produce violence or immorality was not protected by the First Amendment or any state constitution's free speech protections. Judges evaluated the constitutionality of prosecution for violations of local laws under state constitutions, which provided free speech protections for those within the state.[66]

In 1902, the New York Court of Appeals upheld Most's conviction under the Blackstonian "bad tendency" test. The court of appeals concluded that Most's publication fell outside free speech protections within New York's state constitution, because *Freiheit* might have the tendency to harm the public.[67] "The public peace is in danger when a breach thereof is likely to occur in the ordinary course of events. The publication of the defendant manifestly tended toward this result, for he held forth murder as a duty and exhorted his readers to practice it upon their rulers. What would be more apt to alarm the people and disturb the peace of society? If the words used by him would not, what words could?"[68] This tendency was sufficiently amorphous to include expressions of dissent and radical speech that judges, legislators, or members of the public deemed threatening, and it opened the door for the legal suppression of expression.

Shortly after Most's arrest in New York City, the federal government attempted to shut down the anarchist newspaper *Discontent*, published in Home Colony. On September 24, 1901, three writers were arrested and charged with depositing "obscene, lewd or lascivious" literature in the mail under the federal "Act for the Suppression of Trade in, and Circulation of, Obscene Literature and Articles for Immoral Use" known as the "Comstock Act" of 1873. Because the act did not include a definition of "obscene literature," the federal statute could be used to ban any perceived objectionable material (often targeting sexual material or pamphlets on contraception) and to prosecute "sex radicals," men and women who wrote and published books and articles on birth control, sexual and social freedom, and reproductive health.[69] Deeming anarchism "obscene" as well as violent, law enforcement used the

Comstock Act and other postal regulations as another method to suppress anarchist publications when no anti-anarchy laws existed.[70]

While the Comstock Act and breach of the peace statutes would continue to be available to shut down anarchist newspapers and silence speakers, a few states began to pass anti-anarchy laws.[71] The first was New York. "We have no room for anarchists in this country.... Our laws just now do not meet the requirements," admitted Chairman George W. Dunn of the New York Republican State Committee. "But it will be no difficult matter to secure legislation which will induce the most rabid anarchists to believe that New York is not a very comfortable place."[72] On April 3, 1902, the New York legislature passed a Criminal Anarchy Law, which explicitly made anarchist expression illegal. Under this law, it was a felony to "advocate, advise, teach, print, publish, edit, circulate, sell, or publicly display" anything having to do with anarchism, which it defined as "the doctrine that organized government should be overthrown by force or violence, or by assassination of the executive head or of any of the executive officials of government, or by any unlawful means." If convicted, one faced ten years in prison or a $5,000 fine.[73]

Owners of lecture halls in New York refused to rent to Goldman for fear of prosecution.[74] When they did rent to Goldman, she found herself even more vulnerable to arrest than before. She began to arrive at her lectures carrying a book to read in case she was arrested and had to spend a night in jail.[75] The Comstock Act and the Criminal Anarchy Law became a rallying cry to gain support for a new free speech organization created to defend those facing prosecution.[76] Founded on May 1, 1902 by anarchists and sex radicals, the Free Speech League became the first organization that would fight to "maintain the right of free speech against all encroachments."[77]

The Alien Immigration Act of 1903

On December 3, 1901, Theodore Roosevelt delivered his first address to Congress as president of the United States. He declared, "Anarchy is a crime against the whole human race; and all mankind should band against the anarchist." Roosevelt urged Congress to take immediate action, including the exclusion and deportation of anarchists from the United States.[78] If the lack of anti-anarchy laws at the time of McKinley's assassination concerned fearful Americans, the absence of such laws was discomfiting to members of Congress, who recalled previous bills that excluded foreign anarchists and had subsequently died in debate in the past decade.[79]

After the Haymarket bombing, American newspapers called on Congress to pass protective legislation.[80] Anarchism was a foreign ideology, imported by immigrants, and spread like a contagious disease.[81] If the United States could constitutionally exclude paupers, convicts, and Chinese laborers, then it could constitutionally exclude anarchists.[82] Newspapers urged Congress to take action and bar anarchists from the country in the name of national security and self-preservation.[83]

Congress answered their calls and introduced bills that would include anarchists within the various categories of undesirable foreigners already excluded. Yet, these bills barring "anarchists," "nihilists," or anyone "who is personally hostile to the principles of the Constitution of the United States, or to the form of government of the United States" never made it out of committee.[84] Legislators struggled with how to define and identify anarchists, bar foreign anarchists who could change their political views once exposed to American democracy, rely on foreign governments who sought to expel dangerous anarchists from their borders by sending them to the United States, and effectively exclude anarchists during the inspection process at American ports.[85] Despite public pressure, Congress passed the Immigration Act of 1891 without including a provision to exclude or deport anarchists.

After an anarchist assassinated French President Carnot in 1894, members of Congress feared that dangerous foreign anarchists would seek refuge in the United States, bringing their desire to commit their *attentats* with them. Within two months, Senator David B. Hill (R-NY) had sponsored a bill that would exclude foreign anarchists from entry and provide for the deportation of foreign noncitizen anarchists currently residing in the United States.[86]

Many members in the House of Representatives supported the "Hill Bill" and the Senate pressed for its swift passage. "We are advised that a large number of the most dangerous anarchists in the world are now on their way to the United States, and that at this time there is no law on the statute books which prohibits the landing of an anarchist in this country," warned Congressman Charles Boatner (D-LA).[87] Over the course of these debates, however, some members of Congress were reluctant to pass anti-anarchist legislation. The main problem was that the bill did not include the definition of an "anarchist." Hill insisted that one was unnecessary, but others disagreed.[88] Some expressed concern about so much power and discretion left in the hands of individual immigration officials tasked with enforcing the provisions of the Hill Bill. They worried that, without an explicit definition included in the statute, officials could exclude anyone they considered or labeled an "anarchist," including nonviolent socialists and philosophers, who posed no actual threat to Americans or to their government.[89]

Senator George F. Hoar (R-MA) questioned the legitimacy of excluding anarchists, describing such exclusion as arbitrary and contrary to American values of freedom, including the right to travel and to emigrate. He declared, "It is one of the chief glories of the Republic itself . . . that a human being anywhere might lay down one nationality and take upon himself another. . . . The pending bill says . . . not that a man has done anything, not even that he has said anything, but that he is a character defined by the vague, indeterminate word 'anarchist,'" and because of this "he shall be excluded and sent back to the country whence he came."[90]

Yet, when an amendment to the Hill Bill added a definition of "anarchist," it raised more questions and concerns. According to Congressman John De-Witt Warner (D-NY), who refused to support the Hill Bill, the amendment's language was overbroad, barring all anarchists and all persons who objected to any particular government. He, too, was apprehensive about too much power and discretion held by immigration officers to determine who was an anarchist. "No amount of panic can scare the 'gentleman from New York' into putting into the hands of an administrative officer the detection and punishment of a crime which is not even defined in the measure which proposes to punish it by deportation."[91] Other members of Congress disagreed on whether there was a distinction between "violent" and "philosophical" anarchists, and if a distinction should be incorporated into the Hill Bill to exclude only violent anarchists.[92]

Some warned that if Congress passed the Hill Bill without a proper definition, it would have to deal with the consequences. Senator John M. Palmer (D-IL) cautioned his colleagues, "This measure is in the spirit of our fears rather than in the exercise of wise judgment. We are agreed to punish anarchists; but it must be remembered that in our eagerness to punish the guilty we ought not to subject the innocent to danger."[93] Hill argued that if Congress did not pass it, those consequences might include the anarchist violence in Europe on American soil.[94] While the Hill Bill passed in the Senate, it expired without final vote in the House of Representatives.[95]

After McKinley's assassination, one of the main criticisms of the United States government was that Congress had not passed protective legislation to prevent the spread of anarchism and anarchist violence until it was too late.[96] Many, including Senator Julius C. Burrows (R-MI), specifically called for a revival of the Hill Bill.[97] In 1903, Congress passed the Alien Immigration Act, which barred "anarchists, or persons who believe in or advocate the overthrow by force or violence of the Government of the United States or of all government or of all forms of law, or the assassination of public officials" from entry to the United States.[98]

There was little doubt of the successful passage of anarchist exclusions, but to ensure it, members of Congress insisted that the new immigration bill include a more specific definition of "anarchist" that the Hill Bill had lacked:

> A person who disbelieves in or who is opposed to all organized government, or who is a member of or affiliated with any organization entertaining and teaching such belief in or opposition to all organized government, or who advocates or teaches the duty, necessity, or propriety of the unlawful assaulting or killing of any officer or officers, either of specific individuals or officers generally, of the Government of the United States or of any other organized government, because of his or their official character.[99]

Congress designed the act not only to exclude foreign anarchists from entering the United States, but also to bar their naturalization and to allow deportation of foreigners found to have been anarchists upon their entry within three years of their landing.[100]

The Alien Immigration Act of 1903 and its ideological exclusion provisions would join a litany of explicit immigration restrictions already in place. The legal precedent and plenary power doctrine established by the Supreme Court in the nineteenth century gave legislators confidence in passing new exclusion provisions, and paved the way for ideological restrictions.[101]

The Alien Immigration Act, however, did not satisfy all of those concerned about the anarchist threat. The act's language and definition of "anarchist" was broad, and it did not distinguish between philosophical and violent anarchists. Some did not think the explicit ideological exclusion and deportation provision went far enough and suggested that the United States should help organize all nations in an international effort to round up all anarchists and deport them to an island, where they could then live together without any type of organized government.[102] Others believed such a law would be ineffectual and prove problematic. The *Nation* magazine considered it ridiculous to question anarchists and try to identify them on Ellis Island. An anarchist could simply lie during interrogations and easily evade exclusion.[103]

THE UNRESTRICTED DUMPING-GROUND.

The image of President McKinley in the left-hand corner floats above the open
border, linking his assassination and anarchist violence in the United States
to emigration from Europe. "The Unrestricted Dumping Ground"
by Louis Dalrymple, published in *Judge*, Vol. 44–45, 1903
From the author's collection.

The Turner Case

John Turner, an English trades unionist and founder of the Shop Assistants'
Union in London, was the first foreign anarchist to be excluded under the
Alien Immigration Act. Like Goldman, Turner had become an anarchist
because of the Haymarket Affair.[104] In 1896, Turner had traveled to the United
States and delivered lectures on philosophical anarchism and trades unionism
in San Francisco, New York, and Chicago.[105] At the time, the *Washington Post*
lamented that despite exclusions of criminals, lunatics, and paupers, there
were no current immigration laws to bar Turner and his dangerous rhetoric
from the United States.[106]

In 1903, Isaak and Goldman invited Turner for another lecture tour and
began raising money to pay his passage.[107] It is unclear if they invited Turner

in order to test the Alien Immigration Act.[108] Using the new act to exclude Turner appears to be exactly what immigration officials had in mind, and they were paying close attention. After learning of Turner's upcoming visit, William Williams, commissioner of immigration for the Port of New York, stopped John Turner and detained him on Ellis Island for questioning.[109] But it was the wrong Turner; this one was just a visiting Englishman who shared the same name.[110] Upon his release, Williams devised a plan that when the actual anarchist Turner arrived, he would be allowed to enter the United States in order for officials to gather evidence to use to demonstrate his inadmissibility and justify his subsequent deportation back to England under the Alien Immigration Act.[111]

Turner arrived in October 1903 and had already commenced his lecture tour in New York City when Secretary of Commerce and Labor George B. Cortelyou issued a warrant for his arrest.[112] On the evening of October 23, immigration inspectors, warrant in hand, arrested Turner after he delivered a speech entitled "Trades Unionism of the General-Strike" at the Murray Hill Lyceum.[113] They took Turner to Ellis Island, where he was detained as a foreigner who was illegally in the United States and barred from entry under the Alien Immigration Act.[114]

Commissioner Williams chaired the Board of Special Inquiry hearing, where the immigration inspectors who arrested Turner presented evidence that he was an anarchist. Inspector John McKee testified that during his speech, Turner had identified himself as an anarchist.[115] Inspector Joseph Weldon testified that he had executed the warrant and arrested Turner, whereby he confiscated a copy of *Free Society*, which Turner had in his pocket.[116] Williams then questioned Turner, who explained that he was a visitor to the United States and intended to stay for only a few months. He also identified himself as an anarchist.[117] Weldon, a member of the board, moved to have Turner excluded as an anarchist; the entire board agreed. Williams then informed Turner, that as an anarchist, he was barred from the United States. Turner would be held on Ellis Island pending his deportation back to England.[118]

The Free Speech League rushed to Turner's aid and filed a writ of *habeas corpus* on his behalf to challenge his detention and the deportation order in federal court and called for Turner's release.[119] While Turner was free to voluntarily leave and return to England, Goldman asked if he would remain in detention on Ellis Island in order to challenge the constitutionality of his ideological exclusion under the Alien Immigration Act.[120] Turner agreed. He strongly believed he would lose the case, but stated, "I would gladly stay here till I rot ... if by so doing I can assist my American friends in their fight for the vital principle of liberty involved."[121]

The Free Speech League worked to raise money for Turner's legal defense, establishing a defense fund, holding rallies, and delivering speeches on how Turner's exclusion threatened freedom of speech.[122] The League then asked Clarence Darrow to represent Turner in his appeal.

By 1903, Darrow had gained a reputation not only as one of the leading labor attorneys in America, but also as one willing to represent radicals and anarchists.[123] Based in Chicago, Darrow was a progressive liberal who began his career as a lawyer working for the government and then for the railroads, but in 1894, Darrow switched sides, defending Socialist Eugene V. Debs, who faced federal prosecution for leading the Pullman Strike.[124] Darrow was not an anarchist, but he was sympathetic to philosophical anarchism. He was disturbed by what he considered a prejudiced trial and unjust conviction in the Haymarket Affair and had encouraged Governor John Peter Altgeld to pardon the anarchists in 1893.[125]

While Darrow and his law partner, an attorney and poet named Edgar Lee Masters, appealed Turner's case to the Supreme Court, Darrow attempted to get Turner released on bail.[126] Darrow collected numerous affidavits attesting to Turner's good character and to his identity as a nonviolent, philosophical anarchist, who posed no threat to the United States. The affidavits included statements from those who had met Turner during his 1896 visit.

Samuel Gompers, president of the American Federation of Labor, attested that Turner had never called for the use of force, violence, lawlessness, or revolution.[127] Louis F. Post, a lawyer and editor of the liberal, progressive Chicago newspaper the *Public*, described Turner as a man "of very high character," who expressed "the most peaceable theories and principles concerning labor conditions."[128] Former New York Congressman John DeWitt Warner, who had strongly objected to the Hill Bill, admitted that he had never met Turner, but now wished to intervene "solely because of the importance to the rights of every citizen of the questions of law involved therein."[129] Warner denounced the exclusion procedure under the Alien Immigration Act as being more arbitrary than Russia's "administrative process" and founded on the "irresponsible" and reviled French monarchy's practice of arbitrary and absolute power exhibited in its *lettres de cachet*.[130] He declared that not since the Alien Friends Act and Sedition Act of 1798 had the federal government attempted to interfere with political opinions as it now had by excluding Turner.[131]

On February 29, 1904, the Supreme Court accepted Turner's bail application and ordered his release on a $5,000 bond, pending hearing his case a month later.[132] There were no restrictions on Turner's release, so he resumed his lecture tour. Turner attracted even larger crowds and raised money for his defense and bond by recounting his arrest, his detention on Ellis Island, and his constitutional challenge to his exclusion.[133] In his first public speech, Turner declared that in its efforts to exclude a foreigner based on his belief, "America has made itself ridiculous."[134]

On April 6, 1904, the Supreme Court heard arguments in *United States ex rel. Turner v. Williams*. In his 187-page brief submitted to the court, Darrow made a number of arguments but focused primarily on the unchecked and absolute power of immigration officials and on the First Amendment violation of free expression and belief applied to Turner, a philosophical anarchist. Darrow claimed that the Alien Immigration Act violated the First Amendment and had turned federal officials into censors, thereby posing a threat not only to anarchists but to all Americans' freedom of speech and belief.[135] Darrow did not defend anarchism as an ideology, but instead argued that the suppression of *any* belief or ideology was a threat to *every* thought or belief. To exclude Turner for his mere belief in anarchism, absent advocacy of violence, undermined America's purported identity as a nation tolerant of free thought and expression. Comparing the Alien Immigration Act to the Alien Friends Act of 1798, Darrow declared that both acts ultimately sought to eliminate dissent by authorizing the expulsion of foreigners.[136]

James Clark McReynolds, a future Supreme Court justice, was the government attorney who represented Commissioner Williams and defended the constitutionality of the Alien Immigration Act. McReynolds dismissed Darrow's First Amendment argument stating that, as a foreigner, Turner had no First Amendment rights. Turner lacked "standing" (the legal ability to challenge the act's constitutionality), because he could not claim a violation of a constitutional right he did not possess.[137] McReynolds insisted that Turner's exclusion was strictly an immigration issue, and thus, only immigration law applied. Citing the legal precedent establishing the plenary power doctrine, McReynolds declared Turner's exclusion a constitutional exercise of America's inherent right as a sovereign nation to self-preservation.[138]

While the Turner case would gain public attention and galvanize anarchists to work to preserve and protect free expression, Turner's prediction was correct: he lost. On May 16, 1904, two weeks after Turner left the United States to return to England, the Supreme Court, in a unanimous decision, upheld Turner's exclusion and the constitutionality of the Alien Immigration Act. Writing for the court, Chief Justice Melville Fuller deferred to Congress's plenary power to exclude any foreigners it wished, including anarchists:

> We are not to be understood as depreciating the vital importance of freedom of speech and of the press, or as suggesting limitations on the spirit of liberty, in itself unconquerable, but this case does not involve those considerations. The flaming brand which guards the realm where no human government is needed still bars the entrance; and as long as human governments endure they cannot be denied the power of self-preservation, as that question is presented here.[139]

Agreeing with McReynolds, Fuller insisted that foreigners wishing to enter the United States had no claim to rights under the Constitution, including the First Amendment right to free speech.[140] Thus, as a foreign visitor, Turner could not claim that the Alien Immigration Act violated his First Amendment rights, because "those who are excluded cannot assert the rights in general obtaining in a land to which they do not belong as citizens or otherwise."[141]

Fuller could have just dismissed Turner's challenge on standing, judicial deference to the plenary power, and the right to exclude, but in a significant turn within his opinion, he also dismissed any distinction between philosophical and violent anarchists. Fuller noted Congress's determination that anarchism advocated in any form presented a bad tendency that was "so dangerous to the public weal that aliens who hold and advocate them would be undesirable additions to our population, whether permanently or temporarily, whether many or few."[142]

While Fuller had applied immigration law to decide the Turner case, his reference to bad tendency implied that the First Amendment's protection of free speech was in some way implicated in Congress's decision to ideologically exclude or deport foreigners and in its constitutionality. Fuller would defer to Congress's determination, but such a determination was constitutional as long as courts held that anarchist expression was unprotected speech under the bad tendency test.

Despite the Supreme Court's application of immigration law and interpretation of Turner's exclusion as a constitutional exercise of the plenary power, members of the Free Speech League believed it was a violation of free speech under the First Amendment. "The decision of the Supreme Court against John Turner destroys even the faintest hope for free speech in this country, until a radical change in public sentiment is brought about," James F. Morton Jr.

wrote. "This now becomes the paramount issue, and the only possible hope for our civilization. Without free speech a country is not fit to live in; and all hope of progress is destroyed."[143] He concluded, "This does not concern only Anarchists, but all decent Americans. Now is the time to get to work. Join the Free Speech League at once; and help it all you can."[144]

Free Speech Defenders

Despite his loss in the Supreme Court, Turner had helped to garner sympathy for anarchists, and his exclusion raised new criticisms of America's War on Anarchy as counterproductive. The ideological exclusion of a philosophical anarchist helped to shift the perspective of the War on Anarchy from preventing violence to suppressing dissent and free expression. Louis F. Post wrote that governmental repression "[had] done more to advertise and propagate anarchist doctrines than ten thousand undisturbed lectures could have done; for these attempts to deport a thinker and to suppress a meeting have aroused to some extent the traditional believers in free speech in America."[145]

In the five years following the Turner case, anarchists continued to hold meetings, attend lectures, and read anarchist newspapers. Law enforcement, however, also continued to infiltrate meetings, prevent lectures, and shut down newspapers.[146] Yet, these efforts to repress anarchism largely backfired. Instead, they drew attention to the importance of protecting free speech and transformed anarchists' identities as dangerous, foreign criminals into free speech defenders.

Goldman recognized the propagandistic power of the political repression of anarchists and started to use it to draw attention to anarchism and crowds to her lectures. Beginning with the Turner case, Goldman began to work with the Free Speech League, challenging suppression of her speeches within the law, rather than solely promoting anarchism and the abolition of law. Writing to Goldman shortly after Turner's arrest, Prince Peter Kropotkin questioned her efforts. He wrote to her explaining that he did not consider working within the system as consistent with being an anarchist. "As to repealing these laws, it is not our business to ask it. Let those who believe in legislation & 'honest laws' do it."[147]

As Goldman assumed a position as a free speech defender and the suppression of anarchist speech continued, members of the public and the press questioned the use of the bad tendency test to determine if anarchism lacked protection under state constitutions and the First Amendment. In 1904, Ernst

Freund, a professor at the University of Chicago Law School, published a lengthy treatise on government restrictions on liberty and property entitled *The Police Power: Public Policy and Constitutional Rights*. Freund argued that espousing anarchism was not in itself a crime and dismissed the bad tendency test. State laws, such as New York's Criminal Anarchy Law, were "inconsistent with the freedom of speech and press, unless carefully confined to cases of solicitation of crime"; moreover, expression that "may have a tendency to arouse the public conscience should not in itself be held to constitute a crime." Only expression "to incite directly to the commission of violence and crime" was unprotected and could be prohibited. Freund admitted that anarchist expression often made it difficult to "draw the line" between "discussion or agitation" and incitement, but that line must be drawn.

Freund severed the association of anarchism with violence. He argued that anarchist expression did not necessarily lead to anarchist violence, and that not every listener would become an assassin. While not explicitly mentioning Czolgosz or his assassination of McKinley, Freund wrote, "Not even the fact that an adherent of the doctrine commits a crime is conclusive that the teaching of that doctrine amounts to incitement; for the crime may as well have been induced by a morbid brooding over conditions which are the cause of social discontent, and some of the most notable of recent anarchist crimes must probably be accounted for on the latter theory." Freund concluded that the Alien Immigration Act was constitutional under the plenary power doctrine and that foreigners did not hold constitutional rights, but he also argued that "it is impossible to strike at anarchism as a doctrine without jeopardizing valuable constitutional rights."

In his section on anarchist speech, Freund articulated the value of free expression as the "essence of political liberty," regardless of whether the "toleration" of free expression "may create disaffection or other inconvenience to the existing government." Such toleration was not "generosity," but rather operated under a principle that "ideas are not suppressed by suppressing their free and public discussion." Freund believed that free discussion, and not suppression, was the way to disarm radical speech and prevent acts of violence or illegality encouraged by suppression.[148]

Freund was not alone in questioning the bad tendency test and constitutionality of the suppression of anarchists under it. Members of the press and the public began to question it, too. In 1906, Charles J. Bonaparte, secretary of the Navy in the Roosevelt administration and great-nephew of Napoleon Bonaparte, called for the government to automatically impose the death penalty for any anarchist who directly or indirectly sought to take a life, including for any calls for the death of a president or a monarch. He suggested imprisonment and flogging as a deterrent and as a punishment for becoming an anarchist.[149]

While such suggestions might have been entertained in those days of anti-anarchist fervor after McKinley's assassination, by 1906, Bonaparte's views were swiftly dismissed. The *New York Times* challenged the constitutionality of convicting philosophical anarchists for their beliefs or for the bad tendency of their expressions. "Unless we take away the presumption [of innocence] we shall find it very difficult to convict an anarchist unless there has been some actual overt act in the way of an attempt at murder, or at least a direct incitement and instigation to a particular murder. One can hardly imagine the conviction of an anarchist simply for being an anarchist under laws, which would not abridge freedom of speech and of the press."[150]

Perhaps it was this public questioning of the bad tendency test and of the targeted suppression of anarchism that failed to distinguish philosophy and expression from action and violence that led to unsuccessful prosecutions of anarchists. The cases against anarchists arrested under New York's Criminal Anarchy Law often never continued past indictment. If the grand jury did indict, the courts frequently held the case for "further examination" or dismissed it for lack of evidence. None of the cases of anarchists arrested proceeded to trial.[151] According to Goldman, judges did not want to risk the embarrassment of a jury acquitting an anarchist.[152]

On April 26, 1908, Goldman delivered a lecture in San Francisco, which she began by asking, "What is patriotism?" She proceeded to denounce militarism in the United States and described the Army and the Navy as representing "the people's toys."[153] Army Private William Buwalda attended (in uniform), and afterward, he thanked Goldman for her speech and shook her hand. Audience members cheered.[154] Buwalda, however, was placed under military arrest and tried in a court-martial for a violation of the Sixty-Second Article of War for his applause and implied approval of Goldman's "attack and criticism on government."[155] Buwalda was convicted and sentenced to five years in Alcatraz, later commuted to three years. Describing the Buwalda case, the *Nation* magazine wrote to its readers that "unless the court wishes to make an anarchist out of him ... the case stands as another example of our national hysteria over what is a state of mind, and not in itself a crime."[156]

William Dudley Foulke, a progressive reformer and commissioner of the Civil Service, wrote to Bonaparte, now the attorney general. Foulke argued that people "have as good a right to be anarchists as you and I have to be

Republicans."[157] He also warned that "legislation against any class of opinions, short of incitement to crime, may be made the entering wedge for the gradual extension of the suppression of free speech on other subjects."[158] In June, Commanding Army Brigadier General Frederick Funston, who had reduced Buwalda's sentence to three years, convinced President Roosevelt to grant Buwalda clemency. Funston insisted that Buwalda was "too good a man to have his life ruined" and made assurances that "it is safe to say that it will be many a year before he or any other soldier participates in an anarchist meeting or applauds abuse of the government to which he had sworn allegiance."[159]

In January 1909, a few days after his release and discharge, Buwalda wrote to the War Department returning the medal he had received for service in the Philippines. Upon hearing of his release, Goldman sought to raise $1,000 to assist Buwalda if he could not find work because of his dishonorable discharge from the Army.[160] He told the press that he had never been an anarchist, but his conviction had "set me thinking."[161] Buwalda met with Goldman and explained that his experience had only raised his consciousness of the importance of free speech and reinforced her criticisms of militarism.[162] Agreeing to join Goldman on the platform during one of her speeches, Buwalda was arrested with Goldman as they walked to the lecture hall.[163] Goldman wrote that the whole Buwalda affair had been quite beneficial to the anarchist cause. "Nothing helps a movement like suppression."[164]

Denaturalizing Emma Goldman

With the suppression of anarchists drawing more attention to the fight for free speech, the federal government intensified its quest to muzzle Goldman and sought to rid the United States of her, permanently. Since McKinley's assassination, Goldman had been under constant surveillance by local or federal officials.[165] In 1907, Goldman left for a lecture tour and to attend the International Anarchist Congress in Europe. Immigration officials took note of her departure and plotted to prevent her reentry to the United States under the Alien Immigration Act.[166]

However, the watched were watching the watchers. When Goldman arrived in London, where she would lecture alongside John Turner, she received information that the federal government was seeking to keep her out of the country. "The first thing to greet us on our arrival were press dispatches from America reporting that the Federal authorities were planning to keep me out of the country under the provisions of the Anti-Anarchist Law."[167] Dismissing the reports as a "newspaper fabrication," Goldman soon learned from friends that the reports were true. "They informed me that Washington was determined to refuse me readmission, and they urged me to sail back as quickly and quietly as possible."[168]

Goldman decided to take her friends' advice to cut her trip short and return to the United States. Attempting to avoid immigration inspectors, Goldman entered through Canada. She encountered no trouble on her train journey from Montreal to the New York state border, which she helped secure with a generous tip to the Pullman porter when he collected her ticket.[169]

Goldman's entry into the United States, however, proved a bit more eventful. Immigration Commissioner-General Frank P. Sargent had ordered officials to stop and question Goldman in order to exclude her under the Alien Immigration Act.[170] At the border, an immigration inspector ordered Goldman off the train and questioned her regarding her right to enter the United States.[171] She was prepared. Goldman declared that she could not be excluded because she was an American citizen by marriage. Unable to refute her, the inspector reluctantly allowed Goldman to enter.[172] As long as Goldman was a citizen, the United States could not exclude or deport her. Undeterred, immigration officials sought to strip her of her citizenship.[173]

Goldman had obtained her citizenship automatically through her marriage to Jacob Kersner, a naturalized citizen.[174] This form of naturalization was "derivative" citizenship, based on a foreigner's relationship to a citizen. Under the Naturalization Act of 1855, "Any woman who is now or may hereafter be married to a citizen of the United States, and who might herself be lawfully naturalized shall be deemed a citizen."[175] Kersner's citizenship was itself derivative, also obtained under the Naturalization Act, but under a provision that automatically granted citizenship to minor children if their fathers were citizens.[176]

While Congress had regulated naturalization since 1790, it had never addressed the revocation of citizenship. In 1906, Congress passed a law that for the first time provided for denaturalization. The act authorized the revocation of citizenship, declaring it null and void if obtained through fraud, misrepresentation, or deception.[177] Goldman's marriage was legal, and thus, so was her derivative citizenship. Immigration officials agreed that the key would be to examine Kersner's citizenship. If they could prove that his citizenship was obtained through fraud or misrepresentation, they could denaturalize Kersner, and therefore, extinguish Goldman's citizenship; one could not derive citizenship from a noncitizen.[178]

Inspectors began to investigate Kersner. Upon learning of their investigation, Kersner fled, leaving inspectors to question his family in order to gather evidence of fraud or misrepresentation in his naturalization. Goldman grew increasingly concerned and careful. She remained in the United States, restricting her travels and not risking exclusion again.[179]

In 1909, immigration officials determined that Kersner had lied about his age during the naturalization process. He was not a minor when he claimed derivative citizenship through his father.[180] Therefore, under the Naturalization Act, Kersner's citizenship was obtained fraudulently, and therefore, he had never become an actual citizen.[181] Immigration officials issued a denaturalization order for Kersner.[182] They intentionally did not include Goldman in the order, attempting to prevent her knowledge of the denaturalization.[183] Denaturalizing Kersner was sufficient to eliminate Goldman's citizenship; notifying her was irrelevant.[184]

Of course, even without formal notification, Goldman had heard about Kersner's denaturalization, and thus, she knew that she could no longer claim American citizenship. Under the Alien Immigration Act of 1903, Goldman was ineligible to become a naturalized citizen because she was an anarchist, but immigration officials could not deport her because she reentered as a citizen and had been living and "permanently domiciled in the United States for 32 years."[185] After stripping Goldman of her citizenship, the federal government would now have to find a way to deport her.

In the aftermath of the murder of the president of the United States by a self-proclaimed anarchist and lone-wolf assassin, fearful Americans called on their government and turned to the law to protect them. As the United States entered the War on Anarchy, it adopted some European anti-anarchist tactics including exclusion and the suppression of anarchist speech. Yet, these tactics to silence and repress anarchists backfired. Instead, they served to unite and galvanize anarchists and others in a common recognition that such suppression and ideological exclusion threatened free speech, and that this was a freedom worth fighting to protect. This suppression led to the creation of the Free Speech League and helped transform the identities and public perception of anarchists such as Emma Goldman from dangerous, foreign criminals into free speech defenders. Repression also led to sympathy for anarchists and interest in anarchism, as well as public questioning of the bad tendency test and the suppression of expression under it.

Between the years 1904 and 1916, a total of twenty anarchists were barred under the Alien Immigration Act.[186] This low number might be due to the bilateral and multilateral international police efforts to combat anarchism in Europe, which resulted in anarchists being prevented from traveling to the United States. After the Anti-Anarchist Conference in Rome in 1898 and the St. Petersburg Protocol of 1904, European nations agreed to share and exchange information, as well as to coordinate with each other regarding deportation and extradition of anarchists and national suppression tactics.[187]

Perhaps this number also reflects the inability of US immigration officials to exclude or deport anarchists under the Alien Immigration Act at the time of entry or three years later. Tracking anarchists and determining who was an anarchist upon entry was difficult and required national and international communication and coordination of law enforcement. The United States had not participated in the conference or the protocol, having been reluctant to enter into any treaties with other nations and because it lacked a national police force.[188] Local law enforcement in police departments, detective agencies, and the US Postal Service suppressed anarchist meetings, communication, and publications. The Secret Service protected the president and government officials and enforced counterfeiting laws.[189]

This changed in 1908, when President Roosevelt directed Attorney General Bonaparte to create an investigative service within the Justice Department. On July 26, 1908, after Congress rebuffed his requests for funding, Bonaparte used Justice Department funds to establish a new investigative division with thirty-four special agents. In 1909, the division was named the Bureau of Investigation and received funding from Congress, designated "for the detection and prosecution of crimes against the United States." In 1910, Congress expanded the bureau's designation to include "for other investigations regarding official matters under the control of the Department of Justice as may be directed by the Attorney General."[190]

Despite their dubious efficacy, New York's Criminal Anarchy Law and the Alien Immigration Act remained on the books. Questions raised regarding the suppression of dissent under the breadth of the bad tendency test and the value of free speech to a democracy, as well as the interpretation of the language of the explicit ideological exclusion and deportation provisions in the Alien Immigration Act, would remain relevant over the course of the next decade. Immigration officials had succeeded in stripping Goldman of her citizenship, and with the Bureau of Investigation, the bad tendency test, and the constitutionality of ideological restrictions under federal immigration law established by the Supreme Court in *United States ex rel. Turner v. Williams* (1904), the seeds were sown for the repression of dissenters, radicals, and labor agitators during and after World War I.

In an essay entitled, "A Woman Without a Country," Goldman taunted the United States. "Were she an American citizen, we might some day hang or electrocute her," she wrote. "But an alien—what's left for us to do but to deport her. The trouble is, where, oh where can we send her?"[191] A decade later, she would find out. In 1919, in the wake of World War I, the Russian Revolution, and the Red Scare, the United States would successfully deport 249 foreign radicals to a new Communist country. Goldman would be among them.

3

Making Democracy Safe in America

IN THE YEARS THAT followed the anti-anarchist aftermath of President William McKinley's assassination, a new labor organization grabbed the nation's attention and became the next target of suppression and ideological restrictions. The Industrial Workers of the World (IWW) was founded by William "Big Bill" Haywood in 1905 as an international, radical labor union that was inclusive of all industrial labor (skilled and unskilled) and used new tactics to put pressure on employers and to achieve better conditions and protections for workers.

The IWW participated in direct action, strikes, sit-down and slow-down strikes, and sabotage by damaging equipment or property. Law enforcement arrested IWW speakers under local "disturbing the peace" statutes, which spurred IWW members ("Wobblies") to participate in free speech fights. Wobblies engaged in civil disobedience, increasing the number of those who delivered provocative speeches with the intention of getting arrested, clogging the jails, and slowing down the judicial system.[1] Free Speech League lawyers came to their aid, as well as Emma Goldman, who had participated in her own free speech fights in various cities throughout 1909.[2] Beginning with Idaho in 1917, many states began to pass "criminal syndicalism" laws in an effort to suppress the IWW. These laws prohibited the advocacy of the overthrow of the government, destruction of property, sabotage, or violence to bring political or industrial reform.

To many in the United States, the IWW represented the biggest threat to the nation's institutions and industries.[3] President Woodrow Wilson placed the blame for labor agitation on foreigners within the United States, and especially those who had become naturalized citizens. He believed they were primarily responsible for radicalism and the IWW strikes and labor agitation in America, and that they posed the "gravest threat against our national peace and safety."[4]

In his third annual message to Congress in 1915, Wilson remarked, "There are citizens of the United States, I blush to admit, born under other flags but welcomed under our generous naturalization laws to the full freedom and opportunity of America, who have poured the poison of disloyalty into the very arteries of our national life; who have sought to bring the authority and good name of our Government into contempt, to destroy our industries wherever they thought it effective for their vindictive purposes to strike at them, and to debase our politics to the uses of foreign intrigue." Wilson called for action by Congress to "enact such laws at the earliest possible moment and feel that in doing so I am urging you to do nothing less than save the honor and self-respect of the nation. Such creatures of passion, disloyalty, and anarchy must be crushed out."[5]

During World War I, the Russian Revolution, and the Red Scare that followed, denaturalization and ideological deportation served to suppress the threat of dissent within the United States, including labor agitation, violence, radicalism, and opposition to the war and US foreign policies. The United States continued to view foreigners as a source of subversion, which led many Americans, including politicians and public officials, to treat foreigners as scapegoats and targets for suppression. These officials turned to New York's Criminal Anarchy Law, the Naturalization Act of 1906, and the Alien Immigration Act of 1903 as their tools of repression. Congress also passed new laws, which revised explicit ideological restrictions in order to denaturalize, detain, and deport more foreign-born residents. Free speech advocates, judges, legal scholars, deportees, and public officials challenged efforts to deport and denaturalize foreigners. They pushed for more speech-protective legal standards and raised concerns about lack of due process protection and the damage done to America's free speech values and democracy.

World War I and the Russian Revolution

After running for reelection on the campaign slogan "He Kept Us Out of War," President Wilson would lead the United States into World War I in 1917. He argued that America's entrance into the war would help make "the world safe for democracy." Many followed him, giving their support to the war effort. The government created a special independent agency, the Committee on Public Information, in order to influence public opinion on the war and generate pro-war propaganda. This propaganda and promotion of patriotism included vilifying Germany: anti-German sentiment was high and states banned German language books and teaching German in schools. Opposition to the war was significant, and ranged from radicals, who opposed the war's motivations, to pacifists and antimilitarists, who opposed all war. Among the dissenters were socialists and anarchists, who argued that the war was about imperialism and capitalist interests. They created and joined organizations to express their opposition to the war and urge its end.[6]

As the United States entered World War I, Russia was in the midst of a revolution. In May 1917, the Bolsheviks, led by Vladimir Lenin and Leon Trotsky, stormed the Imperial Palace and took control. In October, they faced resistance and ousted the opposition, plunging Russia into a civil war, pitting the Bolshevik Red Army against the White Army of anticommunist counter-revolutionaries. In 1918, Russia had taken itself out of World War I, and the United States had intervened in its civil strife, sending troops to Siberia and supporting the White Army and anti-Bolshevik Czechs. Radicals in the United States saw hope in this revolution and threw their support behind the Bolsheviks. In addition to protesting the United States' involvement in World War I, many also championed the Bolsheviks and opposed the United States' military intervention to stop their revolution.[7]

Entry into World War I brought federal legislation that sought to eliminate internal subversion and to deport foreign radicals. Once Congress declared war with Germany, Wilson issued Proclamation 1364, which revived the dormant Alien Enemies Act of 1798.[8] Wilson declared German residents alien enemies and required their registration with the government.[9] The Justice Department kept records and created a list of enemy aliens. Citing concerns of espionage and internal subversion from Germans who gave their loyalty to Germany and not to their new homeland, the United States used the Alien Enemies Act to arrest 6,300 foreigners and intern 2,300.[10]

Congress also passed a wartime measure in 1918 referred to as the "Travel Control Act," which delegated power to the president to regulate entry to or departure from the United States.[11] Wilson issued a proclamation requiring documentation for anyone leaving or entering the United States. To receive a passport, US citizens had to have "adequate reasons" for departure or entry and such departure or entry could not be "prejudicial to the interests of the United States."[12] In 1926, Congress passed the Passport Act, delegating authority to issue and validate passports to the secretary of state under the direction of the president.[13]

In May 1917, Congress passed the Selective Draft Law, establishing the draft and punishment for those who sought to obstruct it.[14] And in June,

Congress passed the Espionage Act.[15] The Espionage Act made it a federal crime during wartime for anyone who "shall willfully cause or attempt to cause insubordination, disloyalty, mutiny, or refusal of duty, in the military or naval forces of the United States, or shall willfully obstruct the recruiting or enlistment service of the United States, to the injury of the service or of the United States."[16] During public hearings before the House Judiciary Committee, Free Speech League attorneys Gilbert Roe and Harry Weinberger had voiced their concerns about Congress passing the Espionage Act.[17]

Roe described protecting dissent as the essence of free speech. "One thing that we in the Free Speech League stand for is the right of our opponents to express their views just as freely as we claim the right to express our own, and that is really the test of whether you believe in free speech or not."[18] Weinberger cautioned against the Espionage Act's suppression of free speech. He did not believe the United States government had to sacrifice the rights of its citizens and undermine its democracy to make the world safe for it. Weinberger stated "I am pro-American and against all autocracy. But must the United States give up all the rights of democracy to overthrow autocracy?"[19]

Congress was unpersuaded, and after passing the Espionage Act, it added an amendment in 1918, the Sedition Act, that punished anyone who "shall willfully utter, print, write, or publish any disloyal, profane, scurrilous, or abusive language" about the United States and its institutions, government, or military.[20] Throughout the war, the Justice Department and federal law enforcement used these new laws to suppress radicalism, as well as antiwar sentiment and protests in public speeches and in the press.

IWW strikes and suppression efforts continued during World War I. In the wake of an IWW strike against the copper mining companies of Bisbee, Arizona, the sheriff, Harry Wheeler, deputized 2,000 men, creating an anti-union organization called the Citizen's Protective League. On July 12, 1917, the sheriff ordered the league to round up over 1,000 men. They put them on a train to New Mexico, left them in the desert, and then barred them from Bisbee.[21] After a public outcry, a Presidential Mediation Commission was established to investigate the "Bisbee Deportation." On November 6, 1917, the commission issued its report and found "the deportation was wholly illegal and without authority in law, either State or Federal."[22]

Wartime legislation, including the Espionage Act, provided the federal authority to suppress the IWW through arrests, imprisonment, and censorship through post office restrictions on IWW mail and materials. Wobblies continued to hold demonstrations and strikes during World War I, and the Justice Department continued to use the Espionage Act to suppress them.[23]

Free Speech League lawyers defended World War I dissenters against their prosecution under this new legislation. Socialist presidential candidate Eugene V. Debs spoke out against the war in 1918, and he was arrested and convicted under the Espionage Act.[24] Roe submitted an *amicus curiae* brief in his defense, and Debs continued to protest the war and run for president while in prison.[25] Roe also represented socialist Max Eastman, editor of *The Masses*, a popular radical journal that published pieces by Emma Goldman, Alexander Berkman, and John Reed. Eastman had been enjoined from circulating *The Masses* through the mail under the Espionage Act, because he published subversive cartoons, critical of conscription and World War I, and a poetic tribute to Goldman and Berkman.[26] Federal law enforcement also used the Espionage Act against Bolshevik supporters. Weinberger represented anarchists including Jacob Abrams and Mollie Steimer, who were convicted under the Espionage Act for throwing pro-Bolshevik leaflets that were critical of the United States off the roof of a New York building.[27]

Goldman was of course an outspoken critic of the war and conscription. She had openly condemned militarism since she delivered a speech in front of Private William Buwalda in 1908. In 1917, Goldman and Berkman founded the "No-Conscription League," and they gave lectures and organized events against the war and in opposition to the draft.[28] The police arrested them for conspiracy to obstruct the draft in violation of the Selective Draft Law. Goldman and Berkman were convicted and sentenced to two years in prison.

During the trial, Goldman addressed the jury and described the hypocrisy of her prosecution. "We say that if America has entered the war to make the world safe for democracy, she must first make democracy safe in America."[29] Weinberger represented Goldman and Berkman and appealed their conviction. He believed the jury was under the influence of "war hysteria" and had convicted them solely for their views and opposition to the war.[30] Goldman and Berkman lost their appeal and prepared for prison.[31] Both bid friends and supporters farewell and urged them to keep up the fight against the war.[32]

While federal law enforcement arrested radicals and dissenters, Congress passed legislation to further restrict foreigners from entering and residing in the United States. In the Immigration Act of 1917, Congress barred entry from the Asiatic Barred Zone, encompassing most Asian countries, and all other foreigners had to pass a literacy test to enter.[33] While the anarchist exclusion provision remained in place since its passage in 1903, the 1917 act now barred foreigners who were "anarchists, or persons who believe in or advocate the overthrow by force or violence of the Government of the United States, or of all forms of law, or who disbelieve in or are opposed to organized government" any time after entry to the United States.[34] It also included those "who advocate or teach the unlawful destruction of property," in order to incorporate anti-syndicalist efforts aimed at Wobblies.[35] The act extended the time limit for post-entry deportation of foreigners who fell under these explicit provisions from three years of entry to five years.[36]

In addition to prosecutions under the Espionage Act, the Justice Department worked with the Labor Department to use denaturalization and deportation as tools to suppress radicals and dissenters. In 1918, a US district court in Oregon ordered the denaturalization of a Wobbly from Germany named Carl Swelgin. Swelgin had joined the IWW in 1911, and in 1913, he had applied for and was granted American citizenship.[37] Under the Naturalization Act of 1906, in addition to listing misrepresentation, fraud, or deception as reasons to strip someone of his or her citizenship, the government could also revoke citizenship if it could demonstrate the individual's lack of attachment to the principles of the Constitution at the time of naturalization. The district court held that Swelgin's membership in the IWW, which it characterized as "antipatriotic" and "anarchistic," indicated that Swelgin lacked an attachment to the principles of the Constitution.[38] The district court concluded that Swelgin had fraudulently misrepresented his attachment when he took the naturalization oath, and then it voided his naturalization.[39]

The July 1918 issue of the *U.S. Immigration Service Bulletin*, a Labor Department publication under the direction of the commissioner of immigration, included the full district court decision in the Swelgin case. The *Bulletin* also instructed immigration officials to take note of the decision to denaturalize, as well as its importance to the enforcement of the new ideological deportation provision in the Immigration Act of 1917 and to the removal of foreign anarchists and Wobblies.[40] Immigration officials within the Labor Department did indeed use the expanded deportation provision in this manner, and ideological deportees brought legal challenges to their ejection from the United States.

In 1918, Frank Lopez, an anarchist from Spain, challenged his deportation under the Immigration Act of 1917. Like John Turner, he claimed he was a philosophical anarchist. When asked if was an anarchist, Lopez replied, "I believe in anarchy but not in the way you explain it, or the way newspapers say it is." He declared he was "against killing and against destruction," and described himself as "free thinking" and believing in "teaching, education, and telling the people to better their conditions." Lopez argued that he did not fall under the definition of an anarchist in the Immigration Act's exclusion provision, and he should not be deported.[41]

A US district court in New York and the Second Circuit Court of Appeals upheld Lopez's deportation order, dismissing any distinction between philosophical and violent anarchists.[42] "The fact that he is only a philosophical anarchist, and not an advocate of a resort to force and revolution, makes him, in the opinion of Congress, none the less a dangerous presence," wrote Circuit Court Judge Henry Wade Rogers. "His theories, if they could be put in practice, would end the government of the United States, and to that government he recognizes no allegiance, never having become a citizen of the United States." Rogers then reaffirmed Congress's right to ideologically deport under its plenary power. "If the government considers his presence undesirable, because of his advocacy of a doctrine which it regards as inimical to civilization, it must have the power to send him out of the country, and back to the country whence he came."[43]

In 1918, Congress passed the most restrictive ideological law since the Alien Immigration Act of 1903. The Anarchist Exclusion Act included revisions to the explicit ideological exclusion and deportation provisions, which the secretary of labor and the Justice Department devised to close perceived loopholes in the statute and to enable the Anarchist Exclusion Act to serve as a stronger tool to ideologically exclude and deport more foreigners.[44]

The comma after "anarchists" in the Immigration Act of 1917 could be interpreted to imply that the clause that followed the comma was the definition of an anarchist.[45] Thus, a person could argue that he or she did not fall under that definition and should not be excluded or deported from the United States. Clarifying the punctuation would eliminate any potential argument from philosophical anarchists such as Lopez, challenging their deportation through this ambiguity in the provision. The revision in the Anarchist Exclusion Act replaced the comma with a semicolon.[46] If a foreigner self-identified as an anarchist or immigration officials determined that the foreigner was an anarchist, he or she fell under this provision. Even if the US district courts were not willing to entertain the argument, this change in punctuation removed the ambiguity and relevancy of the philosophical versus violent anarchist distinction and thus eased the exclusion and deportation process.[47]

The Anarchist Exclusion Act's provisions also would target Wobblies, barring those who advocated the "unlawful destruction of property" and "sabotage," and used guilt by association, excluding or deporting anyone who was "a member of or affiliated with an organization" that advocated the overthrow of government by force or violence.[48]

Yet, the most significant change was that the Anarchist Exclusion Act completely eliminated the deportation time limit, permitting the deportation of those deemed excludable at *any time after entry*.[49] Even if foreigners were not anarchists when they entered, they were still subject to deportation if they became anarchists after entry, no matter how many years they had resided in the United States.

A month after Congress passed the Anarchist Exclusion Act, World War I was over, but the war against foreign radicals had only just begun. These more restrictive provisions in the act provided the new attorney general, A. Mitchell Palmer, and a young up-and-comer in the Justice Department named J. Edgar Hoover with the legal basis to conduct mass arrests of Wobblies, Communists, and anarchists, and to deport foreigners, including Goldman and Berkman.

The Red Scare

In September 1918, just before the end of World War I, Congress launched its first investigative committee into subversive activities within the United States. Chaired by Senator Lee Slater Overman (D-NC), a special subcommittee within the Senate Judiciary Committee held a series of hearings to investigate German propaganda and activities within the United States. In early 1919, the Overman Committee shifted its focus from German subversion to Bolshevism. From February to March, the committee held hearings on the potential threat of Bolshevism and its links to labor agitation and radicalism within the United States. In June, the Overman Committee issued its final report on "un-American" activities in the United States. It recommended efforts to assimilate and Americanize, including suppressing foreign newspapers, patriotic anti-radical campaigns, strict enforcement of deportation laws, and passage of a peacetime sedition law.[50]

While prosecutions under criminal syndicalism laws, the Espionage Act, and deportations had damaged the IWW, Wobblies continued to organize labor strikes. In February 1919, the Seattle General Strike, calling for better wages and hours for shipyard workers, increased law enforcement's concern over radicalism and the IWW.[51] The press and local officials blamed Bolshevism for this "revolution" and contributing to labor militancy in the United States.[52]

In March, the New York legislature formed a committee, chaired by state Senator Clayton R. Lusk, to investigate "seditious activities." The Lusk Committee focused its attention on radical organizations and the influence of

Bolshevism, and it used New York's Criminal Anarchy Law as the legal basis for law enforcement to conduct a series of raids on IWW headquarters, the Russian Soviet Bureau, and the socialist Rand School of Social Science.[53]

In April and June, bombs were mailed to the offices or homes of industrialists, legislators, and state and federal officials, including Seattle Mayor Ole Hanson, Secretary of Labor William B. Wilson, Postmaster General Albert Burleson, and Commissioner General of Immigration Anthony Caminetti. Many of those targeted had been involved in passing or enforcing immigration or antiradical laws, used to suppress anarchists and Wobblies.

On June 2, 1919, a bomb exploded at Attorney General Palmer's home; his family was present, but they were unharmed in the explosion.[54] In the wake of the bomb explosion, Palmer launched his war on radicals. Palmer called on Congress to appropriate $500,000 to go after anarchists,[55] but Palmer was not waiting for Congress to deal with the "Red Scare." Two days after the bombing, Palmer appointed William J. Flynn, considered at the time to be the "foremost authority in the country on anarchists and their activities," to head the Justice Department's Bureau of Investigation.[56] Flynn led the bureau in hunting the anarchists responsible for the bombings, while conducting raids, arresting radicals, and arranging to deport them.[57]

Flynn's investigation eventually traced the bombings to Italian anarchist Luigi Galleani and his followers. Galleani had been an active anarchist in the United States and a leader in the Italian anarchist community. In 1903, he founded *Cronaca Sovversiva* (Subversive Chronicle), one of the leading Italian-language anarchist newspapers in the United States.[58] The Justice Department used the Espionage Act to shut down *Cronaca Sovversiva* in 1918.[59] While Galleani was not a citizen, he had lived in the United States for fifteen years. Under the old immigration restrictions, the United States could not deport him because of his long-term residency and the post-entry deportation limits under the Immigration Act of 1917 and Alien Immigration Act of 1903. The new Anarchist Exclusion Act had eliminated those limits and provided the legal basis to enable the United States to deport Galleani and his followers.[60]

In August, Palmer created the General Intelligence Division of the Bureau of Investigation, known as the "Radical Division," which was devoted to the surveillance and investigation of radicals.[61] Palmer appointed J. Edgar Hoover in charge of this division. During World War I, Hoover had been the head of the Bureau's Enemy Alien Division, supervising the detention of foreigners under the Alien Enemies Act and generating long lists of suspected subversives in addition to Germans.[62] He had brought the classification and cataloging skills he had acquired as a former clerk at the Library of Congress to

Copyrighted 1919 by The Philadelphia Inquirer Company

PUT THEM OUT AND KEEP THEM OUT

----Morgan in the Philadelphia Inquirer

The dual threat of anarchy and Bolshevism under "Reds" are presented as a
foreign threat that requires stricter enforcement of ideological deportation
and exclusion laws in "PUT THEM OUT AND KEEP THEM OUT" by Fred Morgan,
published in *Literary Digest* vol. 63, no. 4, October 25, 1919
Columbia University Libraries.

his job at the Enemy Alien Division, and now he brought his experience with
investigating, arresting and detaining foreigners, along with his lists, to the
Radical Division.[63] Over the next six months, Hoover focused on conducting
raids of radical organizations, mass arrests, and deportations of foreigners.
He targeted not only anarchists and Wobblies, but also members of the
new Communist organizations that had formed in 1919. Yet, Hoover's
number one target was Emma Goldman. He sought to expel her from the
United States.[64]

Goldman and Berkman had just finished serving their prison sentences
when they were arrested under a warrant for deportation and brought before
a Board of Special Inquiry, which found them deportable under the Anarchist

Exclusion Act. Hoover had arranged for their arrest, and questioned both.[65] Berkman had never become a citizen, and, after the Alien Immigration Act of 1903, as an anarchist, he could never be naturalized. In 1909, Goldman had been denaturalized upon losing the derivative citizenship through her husband Jacob Kersner when his citizenship was revoked.[66] Harry Weinberger represented Berkman and Goldman in their deportation hearings, but he was unsuccessful in preventing their deportation.[67] They were not citizens, and they were anarchists, and no matter how long they had lived in the United States, under the Anarchist Exclusion Act, they could now be deported at any time.

At their hearing on October 27, 1919, Goldman made an impassioned plea to stay, arguing that the suppression of dissent was the prime objective of the Anarchist Exclusion Act and the deportations under it, and that these deportations violated freedom of speech and undermined America's foundational values and principles as a democracy. "Ever since I have been in this country—and I have lived here practically all my life—it has been dinned into my ears that under the institutions of this alleged Democracy one is entirely free to think and feel as he pleases." Goldman then asked, "What becomes of this sacred guarantee of freedom of thought and conscience when persons are being persecuted and driven out for the very motives and purposes for which the pioneers who built up this country laid down their lives?"[68]

On the morning of December 21, 1919, Berkman and Goldman joined 247 other foreign-born radicals being deported, bound for Soviet Russia on the SS Buford, referred to as the "Soviet Ark." Hoover arrived at the harbor in New York City just after midnight to see them off.[69] In her autobiography, Living My Life, Goldman recalled her departure from the United States as the ship left the harbor. "Through the port-hole I could see the great city receding into the distance, its skyline of buildings traceable by their rearing heads. It was my beloved city, the metropolis of the New World. It was America, indeed, America repeating the terrible scenes of tsarist Russia! I glanced up—the Statue of Liberty!"[70]

Over a month before Goldman and Berkman were deported, Hoover had assisted Palmer in conducting the first of what would be referred to as the "Palmer Raids." On November 7, 1919, Hoover orchestrated a massive raid to coincide with the second anniversary of the Bolshevik Revolution. He helped local law enforcement and federal officials raid offices of the Union of Russian Workers in twelve cities. There were over 600 arrests after warrantless searches and destruction or seizure of material.[71] More raids and arrests of Wobblies would take place in the next few days.

On January 2, 1920, Palmer and Hoover directed federal agents to raid "radical hangouts," including meeting halls, pool halls, cafes, and bowling alleys in over thirty cities. Over 6,000 arrest warrants were issued, and agents arrested about 4,000 radicals, including leaders and members of the Communist Labor Party and Communist Party of America.[72] The Palmer Raids represented a great show of force by the Justice Department and revealed its focus on foreigners and the use of the Anarchist Exclusion Act to deport them. Approximately, 10,000 radicals (citizens and noncitizens) were detained or arrested in the Palmer Raids; 3,000 radicals were held in detention on Ellis Island pending deportation, but only 556 of them were eventually deported under the Anarchist Exclusion Act.[73]

The standard deportation procedure for foreign noncitizens involved immigration officials gathering and evaluating evidence to support deportation and obtaining a warrant for arrest from the commissioner general of immigration. Those arrested would have a deportation hearing before the Board of Special Inquiry, which would decide if the foreigners were deportable, and, if so, issue a deportation order, which deportees could appeal to the commissioner. The Immigration Bureau fell under the Labor Department, and so it was the secretary of labor who reviewed the case and made the final decision to approve or cancel the deportation order. Deportation hearings were still not open to the public, and while deportees were allowed to have legal counsel at the hearings, they were not provided with legal counsel and there was no constitutional right to counsel as these were considered administrative hearings.

Hoover worked closely with Anthony Caminetti, the commissioner general of immigration, to expedite deportation proceedings against foreign radicals, including obtaining a revision to Rule 22 in the *Immigration Laws and Rules*, which informed those arrested for deportation that they could have access to legal counsel. Under this revision to Rule 22, immigration officials were not required to present the deportee with the warrant of arrest and evidence used to support deportation or to provide the deportee with information about access to counsel before or during the deportation hearing.[74]

Nevertheless, Palmer, Hoover, and Caminetti did not hold the ultimate authority to deport; only the secretary of labor could authorize deportation. One man would present the main obstacle in their way: Louis F. Post. Post was the progressive, liberal lawyer and journalist who had submitted an affidavit in support of John Turner's admission and had condemned his exclusion in 1904. In 1913, the same the year the Immigration Bureau moved to the Labor Department, Post joined the Wilson administration and became

Portrait of Louis F. Post, Assistant Secretary of Labor
Library of Congress, Prints & Photographs Division,
Photograph by Harris & Ewing, LC-DIG-hec-17508.

assistant secretary of labor. Goldman later wrote in her autobiography that she was shocked and felt deeply betrayed when she learned that it was Post in the Labor Department who had signed her deportation order.[75] Yet, after the Palmer Raids, it was Post who used his position and his limited discretion to prevent as many deportations as he could under his interpretation of the Anarchist Exclusion Act.

"Deportations Delirium"

Secretary of Labor William B. Wilson was away from the Labor Department on a personal leave of absence after the Palmer Raids in January 1920, as was John W. Abercrombie, the solicitor for the Labor Department. During the following two months until their return, Post was left as the head of the Labor Department.[76] In his memoir, *The Deportations Delirium of Nineteen-Twenty: A Personal Narrative of an Historic Official Experience*, Post discussed the antiradical and antiforeigner fervor that had swept through the United States during the

75

Red Scare. Post described the vast numbers of American and foreign-born radicals arrested in the Palmer Raids, and the tremendous pressure that Palmer and Hoover put on the Labor Department to authorize deportations.[77] Despite this pressure, Post had refused to act as a rubberstamp. He insisted on examining every deportation case individually, evaluating the evidence to determine deportability, and carefully deciding whether to authorize the deportation order or dismiss it.[78]

According to Post, he had ultimate discretion to deport and could dismiss the order only if there was insufficient evidence to support the foreigner's deportation under the law.[79] Post explained that he did not have discretion to dismiss the order if there was sufficient evidence.[80] He cited Goldman's deportation as a case where he had to deport under the Anarchist Exclusion Act. There was no question that Goldman was an anarchist, and, as such, she was deportable under the law. Post argued that he could not prevent it once Hoover had orchestrated her deportation.[81] Post canceled deportations by using his interpretive discretion—his authority to interpret the law—which he did so narrowly. For instance, Secretary Wilson had decided that membership in the Communist Party of America fell under the Anarchist Exclusion Act, but Post required sufficient proof of membership, and deemed that such membership must be intentional and in the interest of furthering the party's goals, not just to participate in a social club. He also canceled orders for those deportees who had resigned and were no longer members. Post estimated he canceled 2,700 of the arrest warrants out of 3,700 to 4,000 "red" cases.[82]

Because of his careful interpretation of the statute and evidence, Post canceled nearly 3,000 arrests for deportation in the months following the Palmer Raids, a number that prompted Palmer to urge President Wilson to fire Post and Congress to initiate impeachment proceedings against him. Congressman Albert Johnson (R-WA), chairman of the Committee on Immigration and Naturalization, charged Post with the "flagrant and unwarranted abuse of power," saying that he had "hindered, delayed and prevented" the deportation of foreigners who sought to overthrow the government.[83] In April and May 1920, Post testified before the House Rules Committee.[84] Post calmly withstood Palmer's testimony that he had thwarted the Justice Department's efforts to rid the United States of radicals, as well as Palmer's accusation that Post had a "perverted sympathy for criminal anarchists in the country."[85] Describing his evaluations and determinations in deportation cases, Post successfully defended his actions under the rule of law.[86] In the end, the House Rules Committee dismissed the charges and did not impeach Post.[87]

Outside of the committee hearings, Palmer also faced harsh criticism in response to his raids. In May 1920, the National Popular Government League, an organization seeking to improve government administration, issued a report entitled "To the American People: a Report upon the Illegal Practices of the United States Justice Department." Written by lawyers and legal scholars, including Ernst Freund, Roscoe Pound, and a future Supreme Court justice, Felix Frankfurter, the report praised Post's "courageous re-establishment of American constitutional law in deportation proceedings," and condemned the Palmer Raids as "brutal" as well as unconstitutional.[88] The report described a series of civil liberties violations and misconduct by the Justice Department and its agents, including physical beatings and threats of violence, warrantless arrests and detentions, lack of access to counsel, and the gathering and use of evidence from illegal searches and seizures against those arrested.[89]

Critics of the Justice Department also included First Circuit Court of Appeals Judge George Weston Anderson. In *Colyer v. Skeffington*, Anderson dismissed the arrest of twenty foreign radicals and their deportation orders for being members of the Communist Party of America or Communist Labor Party, prior to Post's review.[90] Anderson granted their applications for a writ of *habeas corpus* and released them.[91] Post and Wilson had determined the Communist Labor Party fell outside the Anarchist Exclusion Act's provisions, because it did not include advocacy for revolution by force or violence in their organizational principles, and so Post dismissed the orders for deportation for Communist Labor Party members. Judge Anderson found that there was insufficient evidence that either of these Communist organizations fell within his interpretation of the explicit provisions of the Anarchist Exclusion Act, and thus, the United States could not deport based on the foreigners' mere membership alone.[92]

Anderson's ruling was later overturned, but his criticisms remained salient. He had rebuked the Justice Department, characterizing the Palmer Raids as conducted under "terrorizing conditions" and describing the attempts to prevent foreigners from having access to legal counsel during their deportation hearings under the Rule 22 revision.[93] While Anderson had upheld Congress's right to exclude and deport under the plenary power doctrine, he insisted that foreigners facing deportation were entitled to equal protection under the law against the civil liberties and constitutional violations exhibited by the Justice Department. He also voiced concern over the power of the Justice and Labor Departments in effecting deportations without judicial review and oversight absent a writ of *habeas corpus* in a US district court.[94]

By June 1920, Palmer no longer garnered the same support to suppress radicals that he had the year before in the wake of the 1919 Red Scare. Palmer had predicted violent, radical May Day strikes, assassinations, and riots, which then failed to materialize.[95] A few days later, Congress refused to grant Palmer's request for $500,000 to continue his campaign against radicalism in the United States.[96] It also became increasingly difficult to deport radicals.

Deportation is a bilateral process. In order to deport, the receiving country must open its borders to accept the deportee. Geopolitics and international tensions and agreements among and between nations complicated this process. In 1919, the United States could deport individuals to Soviet Russia only with the permission of its new government, the Russian Soviet Federative Socialist Republic (RSFSR), which it refused to recognize. State Department officials engaged in a series of diplomatic negotiations with neighboring Latvia and then with Finland to help transport the "Soviet Ark" deportees to Soviet Russia, after negotiations between the Soviets and Finland were conducted through the assistance of Estonian officials. The United States continued to work with third-party nations to effect deportations after the Palmer Raids until Soviet Russia closed its borders in 1921.[97] Lacking support from Congress and the public, and now with the inability to deport foreign radicals to what would become the Soviet Union, the deportations delirium ended.

In 1920, Palmer ran for president, but he lost the Democratic Party nomination. In 1921, he resigned his position as attorney general and left the Justice Department. Hoover remained, and, in 1924, he became head of the Bureau of Investigation. He continued his surveillance and investigations of suspected internal subversives, compiling information and lists of individuals to potentially arrest or deport; his focus on foreigners as the source of subversion never waned.

The Palmer Raids and continuous arrests had significantly damaged the IWW.[98] Released on bail in his Espionage Act case, Big Bill Haywood had smuggled himself out of the country, after being invited to become an advisor to the Soviets.[99] By the mid-1920s, without a strong leader, the IWW had fractured, and Communist organizations had taken its place. In 1921, the Soviet Comintern officially recognized the Communist Party of the USA as the Communist Party in the United States. Members of various Communist organizations associated or affiliated with this Communist Party would also become the main focus of governmental suppression and ideological restrictions.

As for Goldman and Berkman, they were devastated by their deportation, but the Russian Revolution gave them hope.[100] Unfortunately, they were soon disappointed. Goldman and Berkman became disillusioned and concerned that the repression they had experienced in the United States was now emerging in the new Soviet Union, particularly, the suppression of dissenters and of anarchists.[101] Goldman and Berkman would leave, and in 1925, Goldman entered a marriage of convenience with Scottish anarchist James Colton in order to gain British citizenship to travel through Europe freely.[102]

In the 1930s, Goldman was involved in anti-Fascist activities and served as the director of the English-speaking propaganda campaign for the Iberian Anarchist Federation during the Spanish Civil War.[103] In 1934, the Labor Department allowed Goldman to enter the United States for a three-month visit to promote her autobiography.[104] She later wrote that being forced to leave after such a short stay was worse than her deportation in 1919; she missed the United States too much.[105] Two years later, Goldman would also experience the pain of losing her long-time comrade, when Berkman committed suicide in 1936.[106]

Once considered the most dangerous woman in America, Goldman died in Toronto, Canada in 1940. After her death, she was granted her wish to return to the United States and was interned in Chicago's Waldheim Cemetery, in a grave near to where the Haymarket martyrs were buried, so she could be close to those whose death had led her to become an anarchist.[107]

"Clear and Present Danger"

In the aftermath of World War I and the Palmer Raids, the Supreme Court evaluated the constitutionality of federal and state restrictions used to suppress radicals and dissenters, while the American Civil Liberties Union and a professor at Harvard Law School articulated new understandings of free expression and its value, and applied them to ideological deportation.

During World War I, while the Free Speech League handled many cases of those prosecuted under the Espionage Act, it was soon joined by another legal organization, the National Civil Liberties Bureau (NCLB). The NCLB grew out of an organization called the American Union Against Militarism (AUAM) founded in 1914. Roger Baldwin, who was a social worker in St. Louis specializing in the juvenile court system, had come to New York and joined the AUAM.[108] In 1917, Baldwin and the AUAM's executive secretary, Crystal

Eastman, a labor lawyer and the sister of Max Eastman, became concerned about the Espionage Act and Selective Draft Law and the prosecution of dissenters and radicals under them.[109] Eastman and Baldwin established the NCLB as a legal organization separate from the AUAM in order to challenge these laws and to provide legal support for and advocate on behalf of those prosecuted under them, including IWW members, antiwar protesters, and conscientious objectors.[110]

After World War I, the NCLB debated disbanding, but the Palmer Raids helped to push it to become a permanent civil liberties organization.[111] On January 12, 1920, Baldwin founded the American Civil Liberties Union (ACLU), which had joined the National Popular Government League in condemning the Palmer Raids and publishing the report denouncing the Justice Department's "utterly illegal acts, which have been committed by those charged with the highest duty of enforcing the laws."[112] By the 1920s, the ACLU had replaced the Free Speech League as the leading free speech organization in the United States.

While Baldwin described Emma Goldman and the Free Speech League as the most significant influences in the formation of the ACLU, the ACLU differed from the Free Speech League in a few ways. Whereas the Free Speech League addressed only free speech issues, the ACLU's mission was broader and more inclusive. In addition to freedom of speech, press, and assembly, the ACLU's platform included issues concerning fair trials, search and seizure protections, liberty in education, the right to strike, racial equality, and immigration and deportation.[113] Yet, even as its focus was wider than that of the Free Speech League, the ACLU's approach toward free speech protection was a bit narrower and more conservative.[114]

Some members of the Free Speech League, such as Theodore Schroeder, asserted that free speech was derived from individual liberty and that every person had the right to express whatever he or she wished as a free individual, without government infringing upon that right.[115] The ACLU focused on political and economic speech. It viewed free speech not just as part of individual liberty, but as essential to democratic self-government. For the ACLU, the value of free speech was not just the expression of the individual, but its contribution to public discourse and to political and economic thought.[116] The ACLU's approach reflected a new interpretation of free speech and its value articulated in legal scholarship and emerging in Supreme Court opinions in response to the prosecutions under the Espionage Act and to the suppression after the Red Scare.

By 1917, the federal courts began hearing challenges to prosecutions under the Espionage Act and other federal wartime legislation, and in 1919, these challenges had made their way to the Supreme Court. While the court upheld the constitutionality of the Espionage Act and the prosecutions under it, some jurists struggled with the lack of free speech protection under the bad tendency test and began to shift away from applying it to these cases. Echoing the criticisms of the bad tendency test and its breadth when it was used to suppress anarchists a decade earlier, a new free speech test emerged from this struggle: the "clear and present danger" test. Articulated with this new test was the value and purpose of free speech—contributing to the marketplace of ideas and truth-seeking.

In *Masses Publishing Co. v. Patten* (1917), New York US District Court Judge Learned Hand granted a request for an injunction against the postmaster's refusal to permit Max Eastman's *The Masses* to be distributed through the mail under the Espionage Act.[117] Hand dismissed the use of the bad tendency test, replacing the "tendency to produce natural and probable" danger with a new, more speech-protective test, "direct incitement" to violent resistance.[118] The Second Circuit Court of Appeals reversed Hand's decision, sticking with the bad tendency test and upholding the postmaster's refusal to mail *The Masses*.[119] Yet, Hand's "direct incitement" test did not go unnoticed by his colleagues or by legal scholars.

In *Schenck v. United States* (1919), the Supreme Court unanimously upheld Charles Schenck's conviction under the Espionage Act for mailing over 15,000 anti-conscription leaflets to men drafted to fight in World War I.[120] Writing for the court, Justice Oliver Wendell Holmes Jr. upheld Schenck's conviction, but not under the bad tendency test. Instead, Holmes introduced a new speech test. "The question in every case is whether the words used are used in such circumstances and are of such a nature as to create a clear and present danger that they will bring about the substantive evils that Congress has a right to prevent."[121] Describing the application of the "clear and present danger" test as "a question of proximity and degree," Holmes insisted that one must take into account the circumstances and context of the speech at the time it is expressed in order to determine its constitutional protection.[122] "The most stringent protection of free speech would not protect a man falsely shouting fire in a theatre and causing a panic," Holmes wrote.[123] He concluded that while Schenck's leaflets might be constitutionally protected free speech during peacetime, the anti-conscription leaflets constituted a "clear and present danger" to the government in wartime.[124]

A week after issuing its decision in *Schenck v. United States*, the Supreme Court unanimously upheld Eugene V. Debs's conviction under the Espionage Act. In *Debs v. United States* (1919), Justice Holmes, once again, wrote the court's opinion. This time he did not apply his new clear and present danger test. Instead, Holmes returned to the bad tendency test and upheld Debs's conviction because his speech was "so expressed that its natural and intended effect would be to obstruct recruiting."[125] Holmes then endorsed the use of the bad tendency test, declaring that the jury members were properly instructed to convict Debs if "the words used had as their natural tendency and reasonably probable effect to obstruct the recruiting service."[126]

Three months later, in June 1919, Zechariah Chafee Jr., a legal scholar and civil liberties advocate who was a professor at Harvard Law School, wrote an article, "Free Speech in Wartime," published in the *Harvard Law Review*. In this article, Chafee reviewed the Supreme Court's decisions in the Espionage Act cases, comparing the Espionage Act to the Sedition Act of 1798.[127] Calling for the end to the bad tendency test as a threat to freedom of speech, Chafee praised Judge Hand's "direct incitement" test and Justice Holmes's "clear and present danger" test as being more speech-protective and suitable replacements for bad tendency.[128] He then rebuked Holmes for his return to the bad tendency test in his opinion in *Debs v. United States*.[129] Chafee described the value of free speech as essential to its most important purpose for society—namely, "the discovery and spread of truth on subjects of general concern."[130] This search for truth in a sea of falsehoods, opinions, and arguments could take place only in a society that protected free and open discussion.

Chafee also argued that the First Amendment protects two interests in free speech: individual and social. The social interest concerned the "attainment of truth, so the country may not only adopt the wisest course of action but carry it out in the wisest way. This social interest is especially important in wartime."[131] Chafee described Holmes's neglect of the social interest in free speech as "regrettable."[132] According to Chafee, the problem with Holmes's approach to the Espionage Act cases was that he focused on the individual interest, "which must readily give way like other personal desires the moment it interferes with the social interest in national safety."[133] Chafee concluded that in evaluating the constitutionality of restrictions such as those included in the Espionage Act, the Supreme Court should weigh the public safety concerns against only the social interest in free speech.[134]

After reading critiques of his opinions, including Chafee's law review article, Holmes changed his approach to the Espionage Act and embraced his new clear and present danger test and Chafee's social interest value of free speech.[135] In *Abrams v. United States* (1919), a 7–2 decision, the Supreme Court upheld the conviction of Jacob Abrams, Mollie Steimer, and three others under the Espionage Act for throwing critical, pro-Bolshevik leaflets off a rooftop.[136] The court relied on the bad tendency test to uphold their conviction, but this time Holmes did not write the court's opinion.[137] Instead, Holmes wrote a dissenting opinion, joined by Justice Louis D. Brandeis, in which he rededicated himself to the clear and present danger test, and dismissed Abrams and Steimer as "puny anonymities," who posed no actual clear and present danger threat.[138] He also incorporated Chafee's view of the value of free speech as the search for truth. "When men have realized that time has upset many fighting faiths," Holmes wrote, "they may come to believe even more than they believe the very foundations of their own conduct that the ultimate good desired is better reached by free trade in ideas—that the best test of truth is the power of the thought to get itself accepted in the competition of the market, and that truth is the only ground upon which their wishes safely can be carried out."[139]

By the mid-1920s, the Supreme Court began to hear legal challenges from radicals arrested during the Palmer Raids and convicted under New York's Criminal Anarchy Law and California's Criminal Syndicalism Act. These cases upheld the use of these state laws to suppress radicalism in the United States and represented the shift from using these laws to suppress the IWW and anarchists to Communists and members of the Communist Labor Party.

In *Gitlow v. New York* (1925), a 7–2 decision, the Supreme Court upheld the conviction of Benjamin Gitlow, a founding member of the Communist Labor Party, under New York's Criminal Anarchy Law for distributing the "Left Wing Manifesto," printed in copies of the *Revolutionary Age*, a radical periodical.[140] New York law enforcement, under the direction of the Lusk Committee and in coordination with the Justice Department, had arrested Gitlow during the Palmer Raids in November 1919. Clarence Darrow joined ACLU attorneys in challenging the constitutionality of Gitlow's arrest and conviction. Writing for the majority, Justice Edward Sanford applied the bad tendency test, insisting that the "Left Wing Manifesto" was an incitement that presented a "sufficient danger of substantive evil." The New York legislature was within its constitutional rights to prevent its circulation as part of its police power to keep the state safe.[141] Sanford dismissed the application of the clear and present danger test as too burdensome and risky. "A single revolutionary spark may kindle a fire that, smoldering for a time, may burst into a sweeping and destructive conflagration," he wrote.[142]

While Sanford refused to apply the clear and present danger test and maintained the majority of the court's adherence to bad tendency, his opinion in *Gitlow v. New York* represented a seminal moment in First Amendment law and history. He upheld Gitlow's conviction under New York's Criminal Anarchy Law and declared that law to be a constitutional exercise in New York's police power. Sanford then incorporated the First Amendment into the Fourteenth Amendment's protections to apply to the states. He used the Fourteenth Amendment's due process clause prohibiting deprivation of "liberty," which included the fundamental rights included in the First Amendment, and guarantee of equal protection under the law.[143] The First Amendment was a prohibition on Congress and applied to federal laws, but through the Fourteenth Amendment, that prohibition applied to state legislation, as well. Now, a state law, and an individual's conviction under it, could face a legal challenge under the First Amendment and judicial review in a federal court under Supreme Court legal precedent, including the "clear and present danger" test.

Two years later, in *Whitney v. California* (1927), the Supreme Court unanimously affirmed guilt by association, when it confronted the constitutionality of Charlotte Anita Whitney's arrest in 1919 and conviction under California's Criminal Syndicalism Act for assisting in organizing a California chapter of the Communist Labor Party and for being a member of that organization.[144] Writing for the court, Justice Sanford cited his opinion in *Gitlow v. New York* and upheld the constitutionality of California's Criminal Syndicalism Act as a legal exercise of the state's police power and Whitney's conviction for membership and organization under it.[145]

Justice Brandeis wrote a concurring opinion in the court's decision, joined by Justice Holmes. Both had dissented in *Gitlow v. New York*, but Brandeis distinguished this case. While Gitlow had been convicted of distributing a newspaper, Whitney had been convicted of helping to organize and being a member of the Communist Labor Party. According to Brandeis, mere membership in the Communist Labor Party was insufficient to prosecute Whitney, but there was evidence of a conspiracy by members the IWW to commit crimes; where the conspiracy would be "furthered" by the activity of Whitney's organization, it was this furtherance in a conspiracy that pushed Brandeis to uphold Whitney's conviction as constitutional.[146]

Despite upholding Whitney's conviction, Brandeis spent the majority of his concurrence warning against fear driving the suppression of free speech and insisting that the clear and present danger test must be applied to speech restrictions and prosecutions. "Fear of serious injury cannot alone justify suppression of free speech and assembly. Men feared witches and burnt women. It is the function of speech to free men from the bondage of irrational fears," he wrote.[147] Brandeis concluded with a discussion of the social interest of free speech and value in exposing truth with more expression. "If there be time to expose through discussion the falsehood and fallacies, to avert the evil by the processes of education, the remedy to be applied is more speech, not enforced silence. Only an emergency can justify repression."[148]

Ideological Deportation

In 1920, Chafee expanded his law review article into a book entitled *Freedom of Speech*.[149] He included extensive analysis and discussion of the Espionage Act, specific cases such as *Abrams v. United States*, and the use of New York's Criminal Anarchy Law and state criminal syndicalism laws. He also reiterated his approach toward free speech and its value, dismissing the individual interest in free speech and emphasizing the social interest and its contribution to self-government and democracy.

Most notably, Chafee devoted an entire chapter to deportation during the Palmer Raids. In *Colyer v. Skeffington*, Chafee and Felix Frankfurter had assisted the court as counsel for the deportees, representing William T. Colyer and Amy Colyer, and Chafee had joined Frankfurter as one of the authors of the National Popular Government League's report. Chafee did not consider these ideological deportations of foreign radicals as solely an immigration issue, but rather as a free speech issue. He identified these deportations as tactics used to suppress dissent and radical speech in the absence of a sedition law, and, under the plenary power doctrine, without the constitutional restraints and judicial review.[150]

Comparing the Anarchist Exclusion Act to the Alien Friends Act of 1798, Chafee declared the Anarchist Exclusion Act to be worse because it was permanent.[151] He dismissed the insulation of ideological restrictions from due process and free speech protections as "unsound."[152] Neither the Fifth nor the First Amendment excluded foreigners. The Fifth Amendment applied to any "person," and the First Amendment stated that "Congress shall make no law" infringing on freedom of speech—it did not specify that "no law" only applied to citizens.[153]

Chafee argued that ideological deportation fell under the First Amendment, and therefore, First Amendment legal standards such as the new clear and present danger test should apply. He also contended that the presence of foreigners within the United States contributed to the social interest and search for truth. "Persons already here are seriously affected if they are denied the privilege of listening to, and associating with a foreign thinker," he wrote. "Furthermore, the progress of the country as a whole may be gravely retarded. Truth is truth, whether it comes from a citizen or an alien, and the refusal to admit a wise foreigner, especially if there is a postal censorship on books, may simply result in our remaining ignorant."[154]

Warning that ideological deportation would damage the United States' reputation abroad, Chafee also insisted that deportations made the United States appear hypocritical. He argued, "After priding ourselves for a century on being an asylum for the oppressed of all nations, we ought not suddenly to jump to the position that we are only an asylum for men who are no more radical than ourselves." Citing a few examples including England, which permitted anarchist Prince Peter Kropotkin to live there, Chafee contended that America's deportation policy would undermine its identity as a refuge and a democracy and would prove to be an international embarrassment. "We shall soon be in the shameful position of seeing political offenders from this country demanding asylum in the very lands from which men once fled to be free to think and talk on our shores."[155]

Chafee also denounced the Palmer Raids and subsequent deportations as serving only to increase interest in anarchism and Communism and as the primary cause behind foreigners' contempt for the United States and its government. "The raids have become a text for more agitators, who speak to men and women who now have a real reason for wanting to get rid of the existing form of government. It is not the soap-box orators, but Mr. Palmer with his horde of spies and midnight housebreakers, that have brought government into hatred and contempt."[156]

As Ernst Freund had argued in 1904 in his discussion of free speech and the suppression of anarchism, so Chafee also posited that tolerance was the best way to deal with radicalism in the United States. "Men cannot be forced to love this country. They will love it rather because it does not employ force except against obviously wrongful overt acts. They will love it as the home of wise tolerance, of confidence in its own strength and freedom."[157]

Chafee concluded his chapter on deportation with a discussion of American nativism emerging in times of crisis and with recommendations for deportation policy in the future. Chafee sought to answer the question of why these ideological deportations after World War I occurred and why many Americans supported these deportations. He described the national insecurity during the Red Scare and how xenophobia and nativism tend to emerge during such anxious times. He wrote, "Most of us have a hidden emotion which comes to the surface in a time of excitement, the wish that we did not have in our midst these foreigners who are so different from ourselves. The basis of dislike is normally unlikeness."[158] He claimed that "this instinct is normally controlled by a recognition of what immigration has done for the United States," but that those controls are loosened or broken in times of crisis.[159]

Chafee then asked, does American citizenship "give us the moral right after a man is admitted to prescribe what he shall think, under penalty of banishment from his new home, and perhaps forcible return to the secret police from whom he fled?"[160] Chafee answered, no. He suggested the only way to prevent such banishment was to make deportation subject to a judicial proceeding instead of an administrative one. Chafee also recommended that the secretary of labor should hold prosecutorial discretion to decide whether to expel a foreigner who is within a deportable class under the law or not, to prevent abuse during times of national insecurity.[161]

During and after World War I, Congress passed new ideological restrictions, revised old restrictions to incorporate new groups, and eliminated ambiguities in these restrictions in order to deport more foreign radicals. Public officials and judges also interpreted the text of the explicit ideological exclusion and deportation categories and evaluated evidence to prevent deportations.

The Justice Department relied on existing laws to suppress dissent and urged the passage of new ones, as it shifted its focus from anarchists and the IWW to supporters of Bolshevism and members of Communist organizations. However, it was the secretary of labor, and not the attorney general, who held the authority to deport under these laws. Ideological deportations rose and fell depending on who was the secretary of labor at the time and on his use of ultimate and interpretive discretion. The deportations delirium and Louis F. Post's account revealed how the political dynamic produced by this use of power and discretion led to tensions between the Labor Department, Justice Department, and Congress, specifically in ideological deportation cases.

The Free Speech League and its successor, the ACLU, challenged this governmental suppression of radicals and fought to protect foreigners from ideological deportation. Professor Chafee and Justice Holmes developed a speech-protective First Amendment legal standard, and they emphasized the contribution of free speech to democracy and its value in the search for truth in a marketplace of ideas. Chafee also interpreted ideological deportation as a First Amendment issue and argued that such deportation should be subject to First Amendment legal standards and not be insulated from due process protections and substantive judicial review under the plenary power doctrine. This approach toward free speech and interpretation of ideological deportation paved the way for future legal challenges. Chafee's concerns about the consequences of ideological restrictions and the damage to America's values and reputation abroad would also reappear in Supreme Court opinions and public criticisms throughout the twentieth century.

The 1920s saw anarchist violence and new immigration legislation. On September 16, 1920, a bomb blast killed thirty-eight people and seriously wounded 143 on Wall Street in New York City's financial district. The Bureau of Investigation's director, William J. Flynn, and J. Edgar Hoover investigated what became known as the "Wall Street Bombing," but the perpetrators were never identified. Allegedly Galleanists were responsible for planting the bomb, specifically Italian anarchist Mario Buda, as an act of revenge in response to the indictment of two Italian anarchists, Nicola Sacco and Bartolomeo Vanzetti, for murder and armed robbery in Massachusetts.[162]

The Wall Street Bombing did not lead to another Red Scare, but it did expand the role of the Bureau of Investigation, as well as furthering J. Edgar Hoover's career and deepening his desire to pursue and deport foreign radicals.[163] The Sacco and Vanzetti case became a cause célèbre. Like the Haymarket Affair, this case inspired sympathy for anarchists, as well as drawing attention to governmental repression and the anti-anarchist prejudice and nativism displayed during the jury trial. Sacco and Vanzetti's conviction and death sentence resulted in mass protests in the United States and abroad after their execution in 1927.[164]

During these years, antiradical, religious, and racial nativism merged and resulted in new immigration restrictions based on national origin.[165] Immigration restrictionists cast southern Italians and eastern European Jews as the source of radicalism and criminality in the United States. Restrictionists also used scientific racism and eugenics to support their efforts to push Congress to restrict the flow of "inferior" and "degenerate" immigrants.[166]

In 1921, Congress passed the Emergency Quota Act, which established a national origins quota system and annual numerical restrictions, admitting 3 percent of the number of residents living in the United States from the same country at the time of the 1910 census.[167] This discriminatory scheme was designed to favor immigration from northern and western Europe and lower the numbers from southern and eastern Europe. In 1924, Congress passed the National Origins Act, referred to as the "Johnson-Reed Act," which reduced the annual number of immigrants to 2 percent and used the 1890 census as the basis for the quota system.[168]

The Johnson-Reed Act also established the "consular control system," which required foreigners to obtain a valid visa from an American consulate abroad prior to admission to the United States. The State Department and Bureau of Immigration would share control of immigration and entry to the United States. Thus American consular officials abroad would serve as the primary gatekeepers, instead of immigration inspectors on Ellis Island.

Judicial deference to immigration officials administering the law under the plenary power doctrine also applied to the decisions made by consular officials to grant or deny visas to enter the United States. This doctrine would become known as the doctrine of "consular non-reviewability." Consular officials' decisions were final and not subject to judicial review.

During the 1930s, fear of subversion through labor agitation and Communist organizations in the United States would lead to a renewed focus on denaturalization and on ideological deportation of foreigners under the Anarchist Exclusion Act. Guilt by association and interpretation of the provisions of the Anarchist Exclusion Act, including questions of what constituted membership in or affiliation with Communist organizations, and whether these organizations fell under the act's provisions would also become the focus of discussion in Congress and the Supreme Court. Chafee's recommendation that the secretary of labor should have prosecutorial discretion, and that ideological deportation should not be insulated from due process and judicial review, became contentious issues that would lead to tensions between the Labor Department and Congress and another secretary of labor threatened with impeachment.

4

Denaturalization, Detention, Deportation, and Discretion

THE STOCK MARKET crash in 1929 plunged the United States into the Great Depression. During the early 1930s, with mass unemployment and labor strikes across the country, some members of Congress, as well as President Herbert Hoover and his administration, viewed deportation as part of the solution to the nation's economic woes and increased labor strikes and labor union organizing. The rise of Fascism in Europe brought new challenges to ideological deportation, including arguments to prevent deportation to countries where deportees faced persecution or death under Fascist regimes. In response, the American Civil Liberties Union (ACLU) would help create a new legal and advocacy organization to represent these deportees and challenge their deportations, denaturalizations, and detentions.

Throughout the 1930s, Congress continued its investigations of subversion within the United States, which began after World War I. Fear of internal subversion from Communists within labor unions and New Deal programs, as well as fear of Communist-front organizations in the United States (created, substantially dominated, or directed by the Communist Party), led to the use of guilt by association as a way to suppress dissent, which became an essential tool used in denaturalization and ideological deportation efforts.

By 1933, immigration and naturalization matters fell under a new agency within the Labor Department, the Immigration and Naturalization Service (INS). Under the secretary of labor, INS officials would continue to deport and denaturalize under the Anarchist Exclusion Act and Naturalization Act of 1906. The Board of Special Inquiry had become the Board of Review in the 1920s, and it now also fell under the INS. The focus on Communists and Communist organizations, which were not explicitly listed in these acts, would continue to present challenges. Judges and public officials deferred or dismissed deportations and denaturalizations through their use of interpretive discretion and authority to determine the meaning of explicit restrictions and their evaluations under their interpretations. In response, Congress sought to pass new, more restrictive laws to denaturalize, deport, and detain foreigners.

Doak and Perkins

In September 1930, President Hoover directed his administration to strictly enforce the likely to become a "public charge" (LPC) exclusion used by officials to restrict immigration based on economic resources since its introduction in the Immigration Act of 1882. In evaluating the admissibility of immigrants to the United States, US consuls were now instructed to determine whether immigrants would be likely to obtain employment in the United States based on current economic conditions; if not, they would be likely to become a public charge. In the first five months, President Hoover reported 96,883 immigrants were denied visas under this change, and within a year, the number of visas issued had been reduced by 60 percent.[1]

In December, Hoover appointed William N. Doak as secretary of labor. As the nation sank further into the Great Depression, Doak's answer to unemployment was to engage in deportation drives to expel foreign noncitizens in order to provide jobs for American citizens.[2] In January 1931, Doak announced to Congress that he estimated that there were 400,000 "illegal" immigrants in the United States. Out of these 400,000, he believed 100,000 could be deportable under current immigration laws.[3] Doak asked Congress for an increased budget and for stricter immigration laws to deport even more.[4]

Doak was relentless in his drive to deport immigrants from the United States. Doak continued and increased Mexican Removal. Often referred to as "repatriation," the practice of deporting Mexicans, or coercing them to "voluntarily" depart under the threat of deportation, had begun in the 1920s. There was no visa requirement to enter from Mexico, and thus, no documentation of legal presence in the United States, which aided in depicting Mexicans' presence in the United States as "illegal." Many Mexicans had children who were born in the United States and faced separation from their families if deported. Doak used scare tactics and deportation campaign public announcements to induce Mexicans to leave, and he arranged for the Southern Pacific railroad to transport them to Mexico City. Doak championed this use of force and fear as his method to alleviate unemployment.[5] By early

1931, the *Los Angeles Times* reported that over 12,500 Mexicans had been deported.[6] Yet the numbers remain unclear because of so many voluntary departures and so few formal deportations. It is estimated that 400,000 to one million Mexicans and Mexican Americans left the United States during the 1930s.[7]

Doak also authorized INS and Labor Department officials to raid homes, union halls, and workplaces, round up everyone, and then determine who were foreigners and whether they were in the United States in violation of the law. In February, INS officials raided the Seaman's Church Institute in New York City, interrogating 4,000 people and arresting over 100 foreigners, who were then sent to Ellis Island for deportation hearings.[8] A few days later, Labor Department officials raided a dance held at the Finnish Workers' Education Association in New York City. They demanded that the 1,000 dancers present produce documentation or other evidence to prove they were residing in the United States legally.[9] Eighteen dancers, unable to prove their legal status, were arrested and sent to Ellis Island for deportation hearings.[10] Roger Baldwin condemned these raids, and the Finnish dance raid in particular, describing the raids, and not the people, as "illegal."[11]

One deportation case that received press attention concerned a Chinese student attending New York University referred to as Li Tao Hsuan. Doak wanted to deport him because of his anti-imperialism and Communist "radical leanings."[12] Hsuan fought to stay in the United States or to be deported to the Soviet Union, claiming that if he was deported to China, he would face persecution because of his beliefs. Doak was unsympathetic and refused his voluntary departure, arguing that since the Soviet Union had closed its borders to foreign radicals whom the United States sought to deport, an exception should not be made for Hsuan until other radicals could join him.[13] There were protests against Hsuan's deportation, including from Columbia University Professor John Dewey, who urged Doak not to deport the student to China.[14] After receiving telegrams from all over the United States protesting Hsuan's deportation, Doak relented and allowed Hsuan to voluntarily depart to the Soviet Union, which had agreed to accept him.[15]

In May 1931, the Wickersham Commission, a national commission on "law observance and enforcement" appointed by President Hoover, released a "Report on the Enforcement of the Deportation Laws of the United States."[16] The commission was disturbed by Doak's response to the Li Tao Hsuan case, and others, and condemned his deportation drives, as well as the quasi-judicial administrative immigration system as "unconstitutional, tyrannic, and oppressive."[17]

The report noted the effect deportation and this system had on foreign-born noncitizens within the United States. It cited the permanent separation of deportees from their American families, "with results that violate the plainest dictates of humanity." The commission was particularly concerned with the lack of independence in deportation hearings, in which inspectors served as prosecutors and judges, as well as the lack of the same due process protections afforded to citizens and the unchecked power held by the Labor Department and the executive branch, subject to judicial deference and limited review. The commission described the adverse effects of this system and how it "deepens the immigrant's sense of insecurity and delays his mental and moral stabilization in the country which he is seeking to adopt."[18]

The commission issued recommendations including the creation of an independent "Board of Alien Appeals" consisting of men of "judicial caliber" appointed by the president to evaluate deportations and publish their findings. All deportees should have access to counsel, no matter their economic status, and the board should cooperate with legal aid and philanthropic societies and assist them in finding attorneys to represent the deportees. This board would also have the discretion to prevent deportation if expulsion would "result in unnecessary hardship" and allow deportees to voluntarily depart to a safe country that would accept them.[19]

Doak dismissed the report and depictions of his actions as secretary of labor.[20] He also had been quick to dismiss criticism of ideological deportations. He called those who objected to his tactics "un-American," and he considered the legal organizations seeking to prevent foreigners' deportation "unpatriotic."[21] In his annual report to Congress, Doak further responded by declaring 20,000 foreigners would be deported in 1932 and urging Congress to pass stricter immigration and naturalization laws.[22]

In 1932, 35,576 people immigrated to the United States, and 103,295 were deported or left "voluntarily."[23] For the first time in American history, the number leaving exceeded the number entering the country. Although there was no evidence linking these statistics to employment and job growth, Doak declared success. He viewed this decrease in immigration and the increase in departures as a victory for the United States and the employment of the American worker.[24]

In 1933, Franklin Delano Roosevelt brought a New Deal to the American people. As president, he also brought hope to foreigners with a new secretary of labor named Frances Perkins. Perkins was a progressive reformer and the first woman to serve in a presidential cabinet. She started her career as executive secretary of the New York City Consumers League, investigating

Portrait of Frances Perkins, Secretary of Labor
Library of Congress, Prints & Photographs Division, Photograph by
Harris & Ewing, LC-DIG-hec-21647.

sweatshops and calling for increased protections for workers, minimum wage, and shorter work hours. In 1911, Perkins witnessed the Triangle Shirtwaist Factory fire, and subsequently served as the executive secretary to a Committee on Safety, investigating the fire and making workplace safety recommendations. Before joining Roosevelt's administration, she chaired the New York State Industrial Commission.[25]

As secretary of labor, Perkins took almost exactly the opposite approach to immigration and deportation from her predecessor. Instead of declaring how many deportations she intended to authorize, Perkins launched an investigation of conditions on Ellis Island and the findings of the Wickersham Commission.[26] She did not consider deportation the solution to unemployment in the United States and sought to "humanize" deportation law, focusing on preventing hardship and the separation of families.[27] While Doak had pushed for stricter laws to allow him to deport more foreign noncitizens, including radicals, Perkins pushed for more lenient deportation laws that would provide more protection for foreigners in the United States and would give the secretary of labor the authority and discretion to cancel deportation in spite of the law.[28]

The American Committee for Protection of Foreign Born

During the Doak deportations, the ACLU was overwhelmed by the number of deportations and the need for assistance to try to prevent them. In 1933, Baldwin, in collaboration with the International Labor Defense (ILD), a Communist-front legal organization founded in 1925 to defend civil rights and liberties and provide representation to workers and radicals in the United States, formed an organization called the American Committee for Protection of Foreign Born (ACPFB). The ACPFB worked exclusively on behalf of foreign-born citizens and noncitizens, challenging deportations and obstacles to naturalization, as well as discriminatory legislation and employment practices. The ACPFB became the primary legal organization preventing and challenging denaturalizations, detentions, and deportations over the next three decades.[29]

The ACPFB was particularly concerned with the rise of Fascism in Europe and the vulnerability of anti-Fascist and Jewish foreign noncitizens deported to countries where they faced persecution or death. The ACPFB worked to prevent such deportations, arguing that deportees should be allowed to stay in the United States or be deported to other, safer countries.[30]

It was the ACPFB's efforts on behalf of these deportees that inspired its future executive secretary, Abner Green, to join the organization. Working as a journalist in New York, Green wrote a magazine article about a man named Alfred Miller.[31] Miller had immigrated to the United States from Germany in 1929 and had become the executive secretary of the United Farmers' Protective Association in Eastern Pennsylvania. In 1934, Miller was living in Montana when he was arrested for being a member of the Communist Party and ordered deported under the Anarchist Exclusion Act.[32] When Green met Miller, he was detained on Ellis Island pending his deportation to Germany.[33] Miller told Green about other radicals who opposed the Nazis who were being detained and who also feared for their lives if deported to Hitler's Germany, given their views or Communist Party membership. Green later wrote, "It was the law [that put that man on Ellis Island] and I realized that I was a part of that law . . . sending him to his death so long as I kept quiet. I should be able to help and I wasn't helping." Green explained that this experience on Ellis Island had pushed him to take action and join the ACPFB.[34]

Green soon became the driving force behind the organization. He started as the head of publicity and education and eventually became the ACPFB's executive secretary in 1941. Green was an active fundraiser and participant in legal cases and wrote articles about the ACPFB and its advocacy for its newsletter, the *Lamp*. From the moment he joined the ACPFB in 1934, Green dedicated the rest of his life to the organization and its fight to protect the foreign-born.

Green, however, was not an attorney, so he could not represent the ACPFB's clients in court. The lead attorney for the ACPFB was Carol Weiss King. Born in New York in 1895 and raised in an upper-middle-class Jewish family, King was the daughter of a lawyer, Samuel Weiss. Her brothers were also lawyers, and Louis's firm eventually became the international law firm Paul, Weiss, Rifkind, Wharton & Garrison. She married author Gordon King in 1917; he died of pneumonia in 1930, leaving Carol to care for their five-year-old son, Jonathan.[35]

While an undergraduate at Barnard College, King volunteered to work at the International Ladies Garment Workers Union, and after college, she worked at the American Association for Labor Legislation, focusing on workers' health, safety, and compensation for workplace injuries. King graduated from New York University Law School in 1920, and in 1921, began her legal career as an associate in the New York law firm of Hale, Nelles, Shorr, and Brodsky, which had represented those prosecuted under the Espionage Act during World War I and those arrested and ordered deported during the Palmer Raids. Both Walter Nelles and Isaac Shorr served as counsel to the ACLU, and Joseph Brodsky served as counsel to the ILD.[36]

King worked on a variety of cases with the law firm, including appeals in the Sacco and Vanzetti case and the Scottsboro Boys case. She edited the ACLU's *Law and Freedom Bulletin* from 1924 to 1931, and in 1931, she founded the International Juridical Association, conceived as a "legal research group that would hold forums on current legal problems, draft new social legislation, write briefs in pending cases, and publish a monthly legal bulletin on labor and civil rights law."[37] In 1937, King was one of the founding members of the National Lawyers Guild, a legal association created as a progressive, liberal alternative to the more conservative and anti-New Deal American Bar Association. By 1941, King had not only become the ACPFB's general counsel, but also was considered the nation's top expert on immigration law and deportation.[38]

As a young attorney at the law firm, King found her legal niche and a growing list of her own clients out on Ellis Island representing foreigners who were detained and ordered deported.[39] She soon was a fixture on the island, familiar with all the INS officials and staff who worked there. King became the go-to attorney to represent clients and began to hone her skills as an immigration lawyer. Like most attorneys representing deportees within the administrative immigration system, she was rarely victorious in her cases.[40] She decided that while she might not be able to save her clients from deportation, she could get them released on bail and out of detention while their deportation cases were pending by filing a writ of *habeas corpus* in the US District Court in New York, where the court would review the detention.[41] If she was unable to get her clients released on bail, King tried to improve their lives on Ellis Island, for instance by using her connections to get officials to call a doctor for an ill client.[42] By the 1930s, King had become an expert in deportation, and with Doak's deportation drives, she was in high demand. On behalf of the ILD, King had represented Li Tao Hsuan when he challenged his deportation.[43]

Another one of King's cases that received quite a bit of public attention was the deportation of Otto Richter. An anti-Fascist and outspoken critic of Adolf Hitler, Richter had been beaten on the night of the Reichstag fire and fled Germany. He jumped ship in Canada and entered the United States illegally.[44] In 1934, Richter was arrested during the San Francisco General Strike, and, due to his illegal entry, the Labor Department ordered him to be deported to Germany.[45] By 1936, the twenty-one-year-old Richter was married to an American citizen and was detained on Ellis Island pending his deportation. Richter asked "Why don't they just shoot me instead of sending me back to Germany to be tortured to death?" The ACPFB sought to prevent Richter's deportation by directly appealing to the Labor Department; it unsuccessfully petitioned for Richter to be able to reenter legally from Canada.[46] It also sought to draw public attention to and support for his case and held a mass rally to protest his deportation.[47] The ACPFB was able to get Richter released on bail and was successful in preventing Richter's deportation to Germany. It arranged to have Richter voluntarily depart to Mexico, which granted him asylum, as it would do for Alfred Miller.[48] Richter subsequently crossed the border and reentered the United States.[49]

In 1936, Green wrote a letter to the *New York Times* describing Richter's plight and that of three other anti-Nazi men detained on Ellis Island pending their deportation to Germany. He rebuked the Labor Department for ordering their deportation and placing the burden on them to arrange for voluntary departure, or face death or imprisonment if deported. He noted that because it was extremely difficult to obtain visas to come to the United States, some came illegally; the problem was compounded by the fact that it was also difficult to obtain passports from the German consulate to depart to another country. Some deportees had American-born spouses and children and faced separation from them either way.[50]

Green then rebuked the Labor Department for claiming that the deportation of these men was mandatory and for its failure to use its discretion to interpret the law to prevent it. Green cited Assistant Secretary of Labor Louis F. Post as an example of someone who used his interpretation of the law to find a way to prevent the deportation of Mexican anarchist Enrique Flores Magon, who he knew faced death if deported to Mexico in 1920 and was the father of American-born children. Post knew that if Magon said he was an anarchist, he automatically fell under the Anarchist Exclusion Act and deportation was mandatory. So, Post examined Magon's interview with an immigration inspector and found Magon did not fit his interpretation of an anarchist. Rather, he was a governmentalist, a believer in government, and not opposed to all government, which led Post to cancel Magon's warrant of arrest. Post could have deported him during the "deportations delirium," but had chosen not to do so.[51]

Green's mention of Post, and his use of interpretive discretion, were both apt and prescient. Like Post, Perkins was using her interpretive discretion and understanding of the law in the midst of a crisis. Perkins worked with the commissioner of immigration, Colonel Daniel MacCormack, to find ways to use the law to admit German Jewish refugees into the United States. They pressured the State Department to issue tourist visas, as well as to relax LPC restrictions and visa requirements, including a new instruction to US consuls to evaluate applicants under the assumption that those with family members in the United States would not be likely to become a public charge. Perkins also attempted to prevent LPC exclusions by using her discretion to accept public charge bonds for those admitted, thereby ensuring they would not become a public charge.[52]

Also like Post, Perkins faced tremendous pressure to deport and heavy criticism for being too soft on deportation and on antiradicalism. Many members of the public and legislators agreed with Doak and believed that deportation of illegal immigrants was the solution to unemployment and was necessary in order to prevent internal subversion from Communists and their activities within the United States.[53] For instance, while Post had authorized Emma Goldman's deportation in 1919, Perkins had authorized Goldman's brief return to the United States in 1934, despite J. Edgar Hoover's objections.[54] The Labor Department held the authority to admit someone who had been deported. Perkins had decided to admit Goldman, but on a conditional visa that limited her stay to three months to visit family and promote her autobiography, *Living My Life*. It also restricted Goldman to lecturing on nonpolitical subjects.[55]

Perkins drew praise by some and ire from others.[56] Expressing his disapproval in a letter to Perkins, George Rosenberger, a resident of Queens, New York, wrote that Goldman "caused enough trouble before and should not be allowed to put her feet on our land." He added, "I am for stricter immigration laws—we have about Three Million illicit immigrants in this Country—*Deport Them*—it will help solve the unemployment. Then American born can get a job."[57]

The late 1930s saw an anti-Communist delirium in Congress. Like Post, Perkins would face impeachment for her interpretation and use of the law to guide her decision not to deport.

1930s—Anti-Communism

By 1930, with increased labor union organizing and strikes, members of Congress focused their fear of internal subversion on the Communist Party and its infiltration of organizations, especially of labor. They viewed Communist-dominated organizations as being responsible for labor agitation, and they cast foreigners as the importers and conduits of Communism, bringing revolution to America. This fear and the exploitation of fear led to investigations, ideological deportations and denaturalizations, and the passage of new laws and revisions of old ones.

Congress established a new House Judiciary subcommittee to investigate Communist propaganda and Communist infiltration of American industry. Chaired by Congressman Hamilton Fish, Jr. (R-NY), the Fish Committee also held hearings, investigating labor unions and legal organizations such as the ACLU.[58] In 1931, the Fish Committee issued its final report, which recommended the suppression of Communist organizations, including the deportation of Communists.[59]

In 1932, after the Fish Committee's final report, Congress established a special subcommittee of the House Committee on Immigration and Naturalization to hold hearings on the "Exclusion and Expulsion of Communists."

Congressman Martin Dies Jr. (D-TX) presided over the hearings, which focused on revisions to the Immigration Act of 1917 and to the Anarchist Exclusion Act in order to exclude or deport Communists as well as anarchists from the United States.[60] During the hearings, there was quite a bit of discussion over the definition of "Communists" and whether to include Communists in any revision to the immigration restrictions.[61]

In his testimony, Assistant Commissioner of Immigration Edward G. Shaughnessy encouraged the subcommittee members to include "Communists," but without a definition. Shaughnessy's argument recalled the precise reasoning behind the Anarchist Exclusion Act's punctuation change from a comma to a semicolon to separate "anarchists" from its construed definition in the Immigration Act of 1917. He insisted that including a definition would only serve to provide a loophole for foreigners to slip through by arguing they did not fall under that definition.[62] Shaughnessy also emphasized the importance of guilt by association as an effective tool to ideologically deport foreigners. He claimed that once INS officials had proof that a foreigner was a member of or affiliated with a proscribed organization under the Anarchist Exclusion Act, definitions did not matter; the foreigner could be deported.[63] Congress simply had to revise the act to include Communist organizations, and INS officials would be able to deport without having to make difficult determinations under definitions.[64]

In 1935, Dies sponsored a new immigration measure referred to as the "Dies Bill." The Dies Bill severely restricted newcomers to the United States by reducing immigration by 60 percent and requiring that all immigrants declare their intention to become citizens within one year after entry and to become citizens after six years, or face deportation.[65] It precluded the Labor Department from issuing work permits to foreigners unless the foreigner or employer could demonstrate that there was no American citizen "able or willing" to "accept or hold the job or position," and it also denied issuance of work permits to foreigners who were engaged in "subversive political agitation or conduct."[66] The Dies Bill incorporated the Anarchist Exclusion Act categories and addressed Communists by including language that provided for the admission of foreigners from countries "not under the control of Communists" and the exclusion of foreigners from countries establishing a "'proletarian dictatorship' or a system based upon common ownership of property and abolition of private property."[67] The Dies Bill also eliminated the secretary of labor's discretionary power to refuse to deport under the law.[68]

The Dies Bill had a rival. Crafted with the Wickersham Commission's report in mind, another bill with the opposite approach to immigration was sponsored by Congressman John H. Kerr (D-NC) and Senator Marcus A. Coolidge (D-MA). The Kerr-Coolidge Bill eased immigration restrictions, particularly in regard to ideological deportation and in light of family unification and undue hardship.[69] Unlike the Dies Bill, the Kerr-Coolidge Bill did not restrict employment of foreigners or explicitly include Communists in its provisions, and it gave more discretionary power to the secretary of labor to refuse to deport foreigners under the law.[70]

In a public radio address, Dies urged his listeners to embrace the slogan, "America for Americans," and to support employment discrimination against foreigners and more restrictive immigration legislation. Dies blamed immigrants for mass unemployment during the Great Depression and insisted that deportation would provide more jobs for Americans.[71] Dies also described Communism as a foreign ideology and immigration restriction as necessary to protect the United States from the Communist threat.[72] Dies ardently defended his bill, praising its lack of discretionary power to refuse to deport. In a veiled criticism of Perkins, he declared, "I am not willing that discretionary power shall be vested in some Secretary of Labor, who may or may not be sympathetic to restriction, to deport or not deport as he or she sees fit."[73]

Neither the Dies Bill nor the Kerr-Coolidge Bill passed in the Senate, but those who supported one or the other bill had revealed their position on immigration. Perkins had been an outspoken supporter of the Kerr-Coolidge Bill, and Dies was an outspoken critic of Perkins's approach toward deportation and use of authority and discretion. His criticism would also draw public attention to Perkins's position and power as Secretary of Labor in one particular case.

Harry Bridges

In 1938, Congress created the House Un-American Activities Committee (HUAC) to investigate "un-American" propaganda and external and internal subversion within the United States.[74] Dies served as chairman of HUAC from 1938 to 1944, and it became known as the "Dies Committee." He turned the committee's attention to internal subversion within the United States, which was referred to as the "fifth column." He was particularly concerned with the spread of Communism and its "Trojan Horse" campaign to infiltrate American government and its institutions, as well as labor organizations in the United States.[75] Dies launched an investigation of Roosevelt's New Deal programs, including the Federal Theatre Project in the Works Progress Administration, which he claimed had been infiltrated by Communists.[76] Dies then focused on Communists in labor unions, and specifically the West Coast labor leader Harry Bridges.

Harry Bridges was born in Australia in 1901 and had become a merchant seaman at the age of sixteen. He arrived in the United States in 1920 and joined the IWW in 1921. Bridges worked as a longshoreman and joined various unions. In 1934, he led the San Francisco General Strike, which was part of the West Coast longshoremen strike that lasted for almost three months. Bridges was elected president of the International Longshoreman's Union, which included Communists. A popular and influential labor leader, Bridges was featured on the cover of *Time* magazine in 1937, and then became the West Coast director of the Congress of Industrial Organizations.[77]

To Dies, Bridges was a Communist labor agitator and troublemaker who posed a threat to American institutions, capitalist employers, and industry. He could not throw Bridges in jail, but as a foreign noncitizen, Bridges was vulnerable to deportation. Dies pressured the Roosevelt administration and Perkins to begin deportation proceedings against Bridges, but Perkins and Roosevelt did not want to deport Bridges without sufficient legal justification.[78] A Seattle immigration official presented Perkins with dubious, unsubstantiated evidence of Bridges's membership in the Communist Party; Bridges denied the membership under oath. While the INS began deportation proceedings against Bridges in March 1938, Perkins deferred action in moving forward with his deportation.[79] Dies was not pleased.

In early January 1939, the Dies Committee issued a report regarding its investigations of "un-American" activities in the United States and cited the Labor Department as an example for its laxity on deporting foreign radicals. "We believe that the failure of the Labor Department to carry out the laws with respect to deportation is a contributing factor to the widespread activities and propaganda carried on by un-American elements in the United States."[80] The Dies Committee also rebuked Perkins for her failure to deport Bridges, and, within a month after issuing its report, members of the committee pushed Congress to impeach her.[81]

Congressman J. Parnell Thomas (R-NJ) introduced Resolution 67 in the House of Representatives to impeach Perkins for conspiring with federal officials to violate immigration laws.[82] Thomas focused on Perkins's refusal to deport Bridges.[83] He charged Perkins with having "failed, neglected, and refused to enforce" immigration restrictions and accused her of having "defrauded the United States by coddling and protecting from deportation certain aliens illegally within the United States in violation of the statutes in such cases made and provided."[84]

It had been nearly twenty years since Post had testified before a congressional committee under a similar impeachment resolution, which had accused him of abusing his discretionary power by canceling deportation orders and having "hindered, delayed, and prevented" the deportation of foreign radicals under the law. Now, it was Perkins's turn to testify before Congress and to defend her decisions. In her testimony before the House Judiciary Committee, Perkins stated she was confident in her use of her authority in deportation cases and that an examination of her record as secretary of labor would reveal her exercise of discretion, not as arbitrary or lawless, but as promoting fairness and democratic ideals.[85] Perkins flatly denied any sympathy toward Communists or Communism, but she was clear that she did not believe the United States should simply round up Communists or members of Communist organizations and deport them.[86]

Echoing Zechariah Chafee Jr.'s view that First Amendment legal standards should apply to ideological deportation, Perkins testified that the United States should deport anyone who posed a "clear and present danger" to the nation, which was consistent with a "truly American viewpoint in regard to freedom of thought."[87] As for deporting Bridges, Perkins denied that she was unwilling to deport Bridges, and, like Post, she insisted that her decision to deport foreigners was guided by the law and the interpretation of the law.[88] Perkins argued that she had not refused to deport Bridges, but that she had postponed her decision pending the outcome of a deportation case under the Anarchist Exclusion Act currently before the Supreme Court, and this case directly pertained to the constitutionality of deporting Bridges.[89] Perkins's assurances that she intended to follow and adhere to the law successfully prevented her impeachment.[90]

The Supreme Court decision that Perkins awaited was *Kessler v. Strecker* (1939). In addition to representing Bridges, Carol King also represented Austrian-born Joseph George Strecker.[91] Strecker had arrived in the United States in 1912 and ran a restaurant in Hot Springs, Arkansas.[92] In 1932, he had joined the Communist Party, but his membership lapsed when he stopped paying membership dues six months after joining.[93] In 1933, Strecker applied for naturalization, and, during his examination, he admitted that he was a member of the Communist Party for six months the previous year.[94] Immigration officials then arrested Strecker and sought to deport him as a member of an organization seeking to overthrow the government by force or violence. Strecker was set for deportation in 1934, but King obtained a writ of *habeas corpus* to challenge the legality of his deportation under the Anarchist Exclusion Act in federal court.[95]

Frances Perkins testifies before the House Judiciary Committee under threat of impeachment, charged by Congressman J. Parnell Thomas (R-NJ) that she failed to enforce the law and order the deportation of Harry Bridges, February 8, 1939
Library of Congress, Prints & Photographs Division, Photograph by
Harris & Ewing, LC-DIG-hec-26018.

In June 1939, the Supreme Court issued its decision in the Strecker case. It was a watershed decision in the interpretation of the Anarchist Exclusion Act's provisions, and King and Perkins knew that the Supreme Court's decision would determine whether Bridges could be deported.[96] In *Kessler v. Strecker*, a 7–2 decision, the Supreme Court held in favor of Strecker.

Writing for the majority, Justice Owen J. Roberts held that under the Anarchist Exclusion Act, a foreign noncitizen could be deported only if he or she was *presently* a member of or affiliated with an organization advocating the overthrow of the government by force or violence.[97] Because Strecker was no longer a member of the Communist Party at the time he was arrested, he did not fall under the act's ideological deportation provision, and thus, he could not be deported. Roberts rejected the government's argument that membership "at any time" after entry meant past membership, calling such an interpretation an "unnatural and strained" reading of the Anarchist Exclusion Act provision.[98] "If Congress meant that past membership, of no matter how short duration or how far in the past, was to be a cause of present deportation the purpose could have been clearly stated. This section does not bear this import," he wrote.[99]

Ironically, the Anarchist Exclusion Act was crafted precisely to eliminate interpretation loopholes in the Immigration Act of 1917 that could prevent the deportation of radicals, and now the Supreme Court's interpretation of the act had revealed a very important and significant loophole. The Court's decision was a narrow one, though. It did not address whether the Communist Party did in fact constitute an organization advocating the overthrow of the government by force or violence under the Anarchist Exclusion Act. Nevertheless, the Supreme Court's decision was a huge victory for Strecker and King, and subsequently for Bridges.

Immediately after the decision, Perkins initiated a deportation hearing for Bridges.[100] She appointed John Landis, dean of Harvard Law School and former chairman of the Securities and Exchange Commission, as an independent special officer to conduct the deportation hearing, held on Angel Island in San Francisco Bay, to determine whether Bridges was presently a member of or affiliated with an organization seeking to overthrow the government by force or violence.[101] King was pleased with the decision to choose Landis; he had knowledge of the law and respected due process. His understanding of corporate power, corruption, and greed might also make Landis sympathetic to Bridges's efforts to help dockworkers form unions.[102]

Landis heard eleven weeks of testimony concerning Bridges's activities and affiliations. Bridges emphatically denied ever being a member of the Communist Party.[103] Eventually, in the fall of 1939, Landis determined that Bridges was "energetically radical," that he had friends and associates who were Communists, and that he had refused to discriminate against Communists in his longshoreman union.[104] Yet, despite these associations, Bridges was not a member of or affiliated with the Communist Party.[105] Like the Supreme Court, Landis kept his decision narrow, explicitly stating that he would not address whether the Communist Party was an organization that advocated the overthrow of the government by force or violence.[106] This did not matter to Perkins. In light of Landis's decision and the court's interpretation

Harry Bridges accompanied by his daughter, Jacqueline Betty Bridges (left),
and his counsel, Carol King (right), en route to his deportation
hearing held on Angel Island, July 10, 1939
San Francisco History Center, San Francisco Public Library.

of the Anarchist Exclusion Act in *Kessler v. Strecker,* Perkins canceled Bridges's
deportation warrant.[107]

If Martin Dies was upset by the Landis decision, J. Edgar Hoover was in-
furiated. In 1935, Hoover had become the first director of the Federal Bureau
of Investigation (FBI). Hoover continued to focus his investigations on radicals and foreigners since the Palmer Raids in 1920, and in the 1930s, he had
launched investigations into subversion in the United States including Fascism and Communism. One of those investigations was the Communist control and infiltration of labor unions, including Harry Bridges's International
Longshoreman's Union. Hoover created a special squad operating out of San
Francisco devoted to uncovering Communists in this union and, in particular,
finding evidence to prove Bridges was a Communist in order to deport him.[108]
The FBI's report on Bridges was 2,500 pages. Hoover also investigated Carol
King in order to prove she was a Communist to discredit her and Bridges.[109]

Hoover continued to amass long lists and files on subversives and to clas-
sify them. He began to develop a "custodial detention" list beginning in 1939,

which included organizations and individuals classified in different categories based on their threat of subversion and danger to the United States, and the names of those who would be detained during a national emergency. The information in the files contained evidence obtained through surveillance, wiretaps, informants, and mail interception, as well as secret searches without a warrant. In 1943, when Attorney General Francis Biddle learned of the list, he called it "impractical, unwise, dangerous, illegal, and inherently unreliable" and ordered Hoover to destroy it. Hoover simply changed its name to the "Security Index" and concealed it from the Justice Department.[110]

Hoover would continue to investigate subversion and Communism within the United States and work with members of Congress, attorney generals, commissioners of immigration, and INS officials to use his investigations to suppress dissent and to deport and exclude over the next thirty years. Soon, he would get a second chance to help deport Bridges from the United States.

Landis's decision in the Bridges case had thwarted Dies's and Hoover's efforts to deport Bridges; *Kessler v. Strecker* provided protection for foreign radicals and presented a major legal obstacle to ideological deportation. A day after Landis issued his decision there was speculation that Congress would take action.[111] The House of Representatives passed a bill 330 to 42 to authorize the deportation of Harry Bridges to Australia, but it was unconstitutional as he was found not to fall under the Anarchist Exclusion Act and thus was not deportable. The Senate did not pass the bill. Instead, Congress passed legislation so that he could be deported under the law.

The Smith Act

In May 1940, the State Department, and specifically Under Secretary of State Sumner Welles, who was the president's foreign policy advisor, pressured Roosevelt to transfer the INS to the Justice Department and away from Perkins. Tensions had arisen between the State and Labor Departments. State Department officials had been reluctant to issue visas to the German Jewish refugees Perkins had pushed to admit, and Perkins had opposed measures such as fingerprinting foreigners as a security measure.[112] Roosevelt also had become increasingly fearful of potential fifth column infiltration of government agencies and internal subversion by German refugees.[113] Hoover had opposed efforts to admit Jewish refugees and sent memoranda to Roosevelt claiming that Nazi Germany and the Soviet Union had planted spies and agents among the refugees.[114]

In June, Congress approved Roosevelt's Reorganization Plan V, which moved the INS under the Justice Department.[115] After this transfer, the attorney general reconstituted the Board of Review and created the Board of Immigration Appeals (BIA). The BIA would serve as an independent body within the Justice Department with the authority to review and decide immigration case appeals.[116] The attorney general and the BIA, and not the secretary of labor, would now have control over ideological deportation.

The transfer of the INS from the Labor Department to the Justice Department also reflected an official shift in perception of foreigners in the United States. Under the Labor Department, foreigners were both a source and concern of employment and labor. Under the Justice Department, foreigners were a criminal concern or those who posed a security threat.

In his message to Congress, Roosevelt did not mention this tension between Welles and Perkins when he discussed the transfer of the INS to the Justice Department, but instead focused on World War II in Europe and the Nazi-Soviet Pact in 1939. Recent events had "necessitated a review of the measures required for the Nation's safety" and the "pressing need" to make the transfer.[117] Roosevelt argued that while leaving the INS in the hands of the Labor Department in "normal times" was sufficient, under "existing conditions," it was best for the nation if the INS was "closely integrated with the activities of the Department of Justice."[118] He clarified that while the transfer was "designed to afford more effective control over aliens," the transfer did not intend "to deprive them of their civil liberties or otherwise to impair their legal status."[119]

In June, Congress passed the Alien Registration Act, referred to as the "Smith Act" after its conservative, anti-Communist sponsor Congressman Howard W. Smith (D-VA).[120] The Smith Act addressed both Americans and foreigners. It was a permanent sedition act that included prohibitions against expression in New York's Criminal Anarchy Law and California's Criminal Syndicalism Act. Just like the Anarchist Exclusion Act, the Smith Act was purposefully designed to restrict and close any loopholes standing in the way of implementing ideological deportation, and specifically those standing in the way of deporting Harry Bridges.[121]

The Smith Act restricted advocacy and association in the United States by making it a federal crime to (1) "knowingly or willfully advocate, abet, advise, or teach the duty, necessity, desirability, or propriety of overthrowing or destroying any government in the United States by force or violence"; (2) "print, publish, edit, issue, circulate, sell, distribute, or publicly display any written or printed matter advocating, advising, or teaching the duty, necessity, desirability, or propriety of overthrowing or destroying any government in the United States by force or violence"; or (3) "organize or help to organize any society, group, or assembly of persons who teach, advocate, or encourage the overthrow or destruction of any government in the United States by force or violence; or to be or become a member of, or affiliate with, any such society, group, or assembly of persons, knowing the purposes thereof."[122]

The Smith Act did not explicitly include "Communists," "Communist organizations" or advocacy of "Communism," but the provisions were broad enough to be applied to Communism and Communist organizations, if so interpreted. The act also penalized "conspiracies" to overthrow or destroy the government by force or violence.[123]

In *Kessler v. Strecker*, the Supreme Court had interpreted the Anarchist Exclusion Act as allowing deportation only if the foreigner was a present member of a radical organization. The Smith Act now amended the Anarchist Exclusion Act to include the deportation of any foreigner who "shall be or shall have been" a member of or affiliated with an organization advocating the overthrow of the government by force or violence, "at the time of entering the United States, or has been at any time thereafter."[124] This provision included past and present membership or affiliation as grounds for deportation, no matter how brief the membership or affiliation.

The Smith Act also incorporated a registration requirement for foreigners, similar to the one first introduced in the Naturalization Act of 1798 but including more information. It required all foreign noncitizens, fourteen years old or older, to be fingerprinted and register at a US post office. This registration would be under oath and required the foreigner to disclose his or her: (1) date and place of entry to the United States; (2) activities engaged in or intended to be engaged in; (3) length of time expected to remain in the United States; (4) criminal record, if any; and (5) any additional information prescribed by the INS, with the approval of the attorney general.[125] This provision required foreigners to notify the government and confirm their residence every three months. Penalties for violation included fines up to $1,000 and six months in jail.[126]

While the government justified the Smith Act as necessary in order to protect the nation against internal subversion, it depicted registration as good for the foreign-born.[127] It was a patriotic act for foreigners to register and would protect them from potential deportation.[128] Of course, the Smith Act's registration requirement enabled the government to keep track of not only foreigners, but also their political activities. The registration records would provide the Justice Department and FBI with information the government could use to orchestrate another deportation drive or to subject foreigners to criminal prosecution under the Smith Act.

A few months after the Smith Act, in October 1940, Congress addressed citizenship and passed the Nationality Act of 1940. The act incorporated all of the categories in the Smith Act, including past and present membership in or affiliation with an organization advocating for the overthrow of the government by force or violence, as a bar to naturalization.[129] Under the act, past membership or affiliation extended to ten years prior to a foreigner's filing an application for naturalization.[130]

World War II

With its entry into World War II after the attack on Pearl Harbor in 1941, the United States once again declared enemy aliens within the nation and required their registration. Italians, Germans, and Japanese noncitizens were now the internal threat during wartime, presumed to be disloyal to the United States and a source of subversion within the nation. On February 19, 1942, President Roosevelt signed Executive Order 9066, authorizing the secretary of war to designate military zones to intern individuals in the name of national security.

Approximately, 120,000 Japanese and Japanese Americans on the West Coast were relocated to and incarcerated in internment camps. ACLU attorneys helped to challenge the constitutionality of internment in the case of Fred Korematsu, a Japanese American citizen, born in Oakland, California, who defied the relocation order. In *Korematsu v. United States* (1944), a 6–3 decision, the Supreme Court, deferring to the executive branch and military leaders on national security matters, upheld Japanese internment despite a lack of evidence that Korematsu posed any threat to the United States beyond his race and ancestry.[131] Justice William "Frank" Murphy had previously served as Attorney General in the Roosevelt administration and established the Civil Liberties unit in the Justice Department in 1939. In his dissenting opinion, Murphy argued that the court should not defer to military decisions when those decisions are based on racial discrimination and xenophobia. Disloyalty cannot be inferred by race, ethnicity, or citizenship, and discrimination did not support the deprivation of civil liberties in the name of national security, even in wartime.[132]

During World War II, the ACPFB did not join ACLU attorneys in challenging the internment of Japanese Americans, but instead it focused its efforts on jobs and discrimination, pushing the Roosevelt administration and employers not to discriminate against foreigners for employment opportunities.[133] The ACPFB encouraged foreigners to support the war and display their patriotism and loyalty, while it promoted the image that foreigners were contributors to the war effort and not subversive.[134] The anti-Communism of the late 1930s was put on hold when the Nazis invaded the Soviet Union and the Hitler-Stalin pact was broken. By late 1941, the Soviets and the Americans had become allies, coordinating their efforts to defeat the Nazis.

The ACPFB and Carol King celebrated two major legal victories in the Supreme Court during World War II and the United States' temporary alliance with the Soviet Union. The first victory concerned denaturalization. In 1939, a Russian immigrant named William Schneiderman faced denaturalization based on his membership in the Workers Party of America (a predecessor to the Communist Party) when he became a citizen in 1927.[135] The INS argued that Schneiderman had obtained his naturalization through fraud, because his membership in the Workers Party revealed his lack of attachment to the principles of the Constitution of the United States.[136] A US district court agreed and revoked Schneiderman's citizenship, and in 1941, the Ninth Circuit Court of Appeals upheld his denaturalization.[137]

Schneiderman retained King to represent him in his Supreme Court appeal. King successfully petitioned the court to hear his case, but she would not argue it. In fact, King had never argued before the Supreme Court. Convinced she could not overcome the prevalent sexism in the courtroom and that it would place her clients in jeopardy, King consistently found male colleagues and the best attorneys she thought could argue her cases and win them.[138] This time, she asked the 1940 Republican nominee for president, Wendell Willkie. It was a strategic decision. Willkie would bring prestige and attention to the case, and his corporate background and conservatism would provide a contrast and balance to Schneiderman's radicalism. Also, Willkie had yet to argue a case before the Supreme Court, so he was likely to agree to do so now.[139]

Willkie said he took Schneiderman's case because it was a "vital test case" concerning "the individual liberties of an American citizen, and not the Communist Party."[140] He declared Schneiderman's denaturalization struck at the heart of free speech and its value to discussion on political and economic rights.[141] Willkie argued that the First Amendment protected expression and advocacy, including "Communistic doctrines," and that by stripping Schneiderman of his citizenship for lack of attachment to the principles of the Constitution, the lower courts had undermined those principles and "the most fundamental rights guaranteed by the Constitution, to wit, the right to criticize freely the Constitution and every principle therein and to advocate a change thereof."[142] Willkie described his denaturalization as discriminatory, as well as unconstitutional. "It would be an astounding doctrine to deny an alien admitted to our shores and about to become a citizen that freedom of speech which a native born citizen enjoys."[143]

In *Schneiderman v. United States* (1943), a 5–3 decision, the Supreme Court agreed with Willkie. The Court rejected the government's argument and dismissed Schneiderman's denaturalization. Writing for the majority, Justice Murphy held that the government had not carried its burden of proof in the case, having been unable to demonstrate by "clear, unequivocal, and convincing" evidence that Schneiderman's membership in the Workers Party revealed a lack of attachment to the principles of the Constitution.[144] He argued that while the evidence showed that in 1927 the Workers Party had advocated nationalization and "the dictatorship of the proletariat," this evidence did not prove that the party wanted change through the use of force or violence or that the party's expressions showed any lack of attachment to the Constitution. Advocacy for political and societal change was not incompatible with "general political philosophy" of the Constitution.[145]

Describing the Constitution as amendable to free expression and advocacy, Murphy wrote that "the constitutional fathers, fresh from a revolution, did not forge a political straitjacket for the generations to come."[146] He cited Abraham Lincoln's Emancipation Proclamation and supporters of the Thirteenth Amendment as examples of those who were attached to the principles of the Constitution while also advocating for fundamental societal change.[147] According to Murphy, such advocacy should be perceived not as an impediment to naturalization, but rather as a reflection of American values. "In view of our tradition of freedom of thought, it is not to be presumed that Congress, in the Act of 1906 or its predecessors of 1795 and 1802, intended to offer naturalization only to those whose political views coincide with those considered best by the founders in 1787, or by the majority in this country today."[148]

Two years later, the ACPFB would celebrate a second victory in the Supreme Court. This case concerned another attempt to deport its client Harry Bridges. In 1940, with the Smith Act in place and the INS under the Justice Department, Attorney General Robert Jackson, under pressure from Congress, had initiated deportation proceedings against Bridges. In this new case, the question before the Supreme Court would not focus on whether Bridges was currently a member or affiliated with the Communist Party; instead, the question would be whether Bridges had *ever* been a member of or affiliated with the Communist Party.

New York Court of Appeals Judge Charles B. Sears conducted the second set of deportation hearings regarding Bridges's affiliations. Sears held that the Communist Party was an organization that fell under the Anarchist Exclusion Act, amended by the Smith Act, and that Bridges was affiliated with and a member of the Communist Party.[149] Sears recommended deportation. The BIA heard Bridges's deportation case and found that Bridges had not been a member of or affiliated with the Communist Party since he entered the United States, and thus, should not be deported.[150] In 1942, Jackson was now a Supreme Court justice, and his successor, Attorney General Francis Biddle, reviewed the decision, concurred with Sears, and ordered Bridges deported.[151] King was livid. She immediately petitioned Biddle for a hearing and reconsideration of his decision.[152] Biddle refused and sought to deport Bridges as soon as possible.[153] King was able to file a writ of *habeas corpus* just in time and was able to obtain a stay of Bridges's deportation while a US district court in California reviewed his case.[154] The district court denied King's petition and allowed Bridges's deportation order to stand; the Ninth Circuit Court of Appeals affirmed.[155] Only the Supreme Court could save Bridges from deportation. King filed a writ of *certiorari*, which the Supreme Court granted.[156]

In *Bridges v. Wixon* (1945), the Supreme Court, in a 5–3 decision, held that Bridges had never been a member of or affiliated with the Communist Party, and thus, he could not be deported under the Smith Act.[157] Writing for the majority, Justice William O. Douglas evaluated the evidence presented in both of Bridges's hearings, the reports issued by Dean Landis and Judge Sears, and Biddle's deportation order. Addressing membership, Douglas dismissed the unsworn and the "highly speculative" testimony Biddle used to support his finding that Bridges was a member of the Communist Party as so "untrustworthy, contradictory, or unreliable" that Biddle should have rejected it.[158] Douglas agreed with the BIA, which described the evidence as "too flimsy" to support a finding of Bridges's membership in the Communist Party.[159]

Turning to Bridges's affiliation with the Communist Party, Douglas held that "affiliation" was broader than membership and narrower than mere sympathy with a proscribed organization.[160] Douglas concluded that Sears's and Biddle's findings to support Bridges's deportation were based on "too loose" an interpretation of affiliation.[161] According to Douglas, "affiliation" under the Smith Act "indicates an adherence to or a furtherance of the purposes or objectives" of an organization, not "mere cooperation with it in lawful activities," and that one's actions should demonstrate "a working alliance to bring the program to fruition."[162] The evidence in both of Bridges's hearings did not prove he had such an affiliation with the Communist Party. Douglas also emphasized that "cooperation" was not affiliation, providing the United States during the war as an example. "Individuals, like nations, may cooperate in a common cause over a period of months or years though their ultimate aims do not coincide," he wrote. "Certainly those who joined forces with Russia to defeat the Nazis may not be said to have made an alliance to spread the cause of Communism."[163]

Chief Justice Harlan Stone wrote a dissenting opinion, joined by Justice Owen Roberts and Justice Felix Frankfurter. Stone asserted that Biddle's deportation order for Bridges should have been sustained.[164] Describing the court's role as a "very limited one," Stone argued that under the plenary power doctrine, the judiciary should defer to Congress and administrative officers in deportation cases.[165] Congress passed laws regarding whom to exclude and deport, and it delegated the power to determine which foreigners fell under these laws to the attorney general in the Justice Department. According to Stone, "only in the exercise of their authority to issue writs of *habeas corpus* may courts inquire whether the Attorney General has exceeded his statutory authority or acted contrary to law or the Constitution."[166] The court is "without authority to disturb his finding if it has the support of evidence of any probative value."[167] In this case, the evidence against Bridges was sufficient and the court should defer to Biddle.[168]

Douglas did not address the plenary power doctrine, but Justice Murphy did. In his concurring opinion, Murphy not only agreed with Douglas's assessment of the evidence and interpretation of "affiliation," but also took the opportunity to directly attack the plenary power doctrine and call for substantive judicial review and the application of First Amendment constitutional standards to ideological deportation cases.

Addressing the effort to deport Bridges, Murphy wrote, "The record in this case will stand forever as a monument to man's intolerance of man. Seldom if ever in the history of this nation has there been such a concentrated and relentless crusade to deport an individual because he dared to exercise the freedom that belongs to him as a human being and that is guaranteed to him by the Constitution."[169] Like Zechariah Chafee Jr. articulated twenty-five years earlier, Murphy rejected the assumption that Congress's plenary power to deport was not subject to the Bill of Rights and the constitutional protections of freedom of speech and due process under the First and Fifth Amendments. He wrote that the Bill of Rights did not make any distinction between foreigners and citizens, and if those protections did not apply to foreigners then "an alien who merely writes or utters a statement critical of the Government, or who subscribes to an unpopular political or social philosophy, or who affiliates with a labor union, or who distributes religious handbills on the street corner, may be subjected to the legislative whim of deportation."[170]

It was inherently contradictory to deny substantive judicial review and due process protections to foreigners in deportation proceedings. "The alien would be fully clothed with his constitutional rights when defending himself in a court of law, but he would be stripped of those rights when deportation officials encircle him," Murphy wrote. "I cannot agree that the framers of the Constitution meant to make such an empty mockery of human freedom."[171]

Ideological deportation struck at the heart of freedom of speech in the United States. Murphy insisted that the Smith Act and ideological deportations under it should be subject to First Amendment constitutional standards and protections, which to him included judicial review under the clear and present danger test.[172] He warned that such deportations were tools to suppress dissent and would damage the nation and undermine its values as a democracy. This damage posed more of a threat to the United States than the presence of foreign radicals who expressed their beliefs or joined the Communist Party. "Congress has ample power to protect the United States from internal revolution and anarchy without abandoning the ideals of freedom and tolerance," he wrote. "We, as a nation, lose part of our greatness whenever we deport or punish those who merely exercise their freedoms in an unpopular though innocuous manner. The strength of this nation is weakened more by those who suppress the freedom of others than by those who are allowed freely to think and act as their consciences dictate."[173]

Murphy concluded his opinion by noting the significance of this case for foreigners in the United States, who, "like many of our forebears, were driven from their original homelands by bigoted authorities who denied the existence of freedom and tolerance. It would be a dismal prospect for them to discover that their freedom in the United States is dependent upon their conformity to the popular notions of the moment."[174] Ideological deportation was not the answer to establishing America's freedom and security; that would be accomplished only "by zealously guarding the rights of the most humble, the most unorthodox, and the most despised among us."[175]

Upon hearing the Supreme Court's decision and his huge victory, Bridges immediately announced his intention to apply for naturalization. "Naturally I welcome the decision because American citizenship is a priceless possession," he wrote.[176] On September 17, 1945, Bridges became an American citizen.[177] Carol King sent him a telegram: "To Harry Bridges: You may be a good client, but your lawyers are no slouches. Congrats. Carol."[178]

The Supreme Court's decision in *Bridges v. Wixon* was also a huge victory for foreigners residing in the United States. While the decision did not strike down the use of guilt by association in ideological deportation cases, Justice Douglas's definition of "affiliation" and scrutiny of evidence pertaining to membership provided foreigners with more protection against the use of their associations and political activities as a basis for deportation. Furthermore, the decision demonstrated the importance of the writ of *habeas corpus* and of substantive judicial review in a federal court as the most effective recourse in challenging and preventing the ideological deportation of foreigners. Justice Murphy's concurring opinion also revealed that at least one member of the Supreme Court believed that foreigners in the United States were protected under the First Amendment and supported judicial review and the application of First Amendment legal standards to ideological deportation cases, despite the plenary power doctrine.

The ACPFB celebrated its Supreme Court victory and produced a pamphlet for its members, reprinting Murphy's concurring opinion with an introduction written by King.[179] After praising Murphy and the Supreme Court's decision in favor of Bridges, King wrote, "While the Bridges case is won, the basic democratic issues are not settled."[180] The Smith Act was still the law, the ideological deportation provision remained in place, and both were ready to be used by the Justice Department and future attorney generals. "The ACPFB must rally all Americans to secure the repeal of this un-American provision in our deportation laws," declared King.[181]

During the Great Depression, two secretaries of labor presented two different perspectives on immigration and uses of their authority. William N. Doak viewed deportation as a solution to the unemployment crisis, and he used his discretion to deport as many as possible. His successor, Frances Perkins, did not view immigrants as a threat to the United States or its economy, and she tried to change the law and to use the law to increase refugee admissions. Both faced public criticism, and members of Congress, such as Martin Dies, sought to eliminate the discretionary power held by the secretary of labor to decide how to interpret and enforce the law.

Overwhelmed by deportation and asylum cases, Roger Baldwin helped create the ACPFB. Led by Abner Green and Carol King, the ACPFB attempted to prevent denaturalizations and deportations and brought legal challenges in federal court. While members of Congress focused on Communist influence and identifying Communists, King focused on the interpretation and application of the Anarchist Exclusion Act to defend her clients and found ways to directly and indirectly bypass the plenary power doctrine's insulation of deportation from substantive judicial review. King was successful in the Supreme Court, where members of the court such as Justice Murphy viewed ideological restrictions, including denaturalization and deportation, as violations of the First Amendment. They sought to push through the barriers to judicial review under the plenary power and argued for due process protections for deportation.

These successes, especially in preventing Harry Bridges's deportation, resulted in a legislative backlash from Congress. The Supreme Court could not deter the forces of anti-Communism within the federal government, and it could also not prevent Congress from passing new laws like the Smith Act to close loopholes and circumvent the court's decisions. Congress would continue to investigate and hold hearings on Communism within the United States through HUAC, focusing on Communists in government, entertainment, labor, education, and legal advocacy organizations.

The ACLU had been under investigation for being "closely affiliated with the Communist movement in the United States" since the Fish Committee in 1930, and HUAC had continued investigations through the late 1930s. While Baldwin identified himself as a Democratic Socialist, he was sympathetic to Communism, championed Communist ideology and revolution, and visited the Soviet Union in 1927.[182] When the ACLU was mentioned six different times during HUAC hearings on Communist and Communist-front organizations in 1938–1939, the ACLU's image was damaged, and the organization became concerned.

Baldwin led the charge in responding to accusations and attempting to prevent the ACLU from being labeled as a Communist or Communist-front organization. By 1937, influenced by Stalin's "show trials," Baldwin began to turn away from Communism and sever his affiliations with Communist-front organizations.[183] The ACLU had split into two camps: anti-Communist and Communist or Communist-sympathetic, and by 1939, the Nazi-Soviet Pact had "pushed Baldwin solidly into the anti-communist camp."[184] The leadership was also split between anti-Communists Morris Ernst, Norman Thomas, and John Haynes Holmes, and Communist Elizabeth Gurley Flynn and "fellow travelers" Harry Ward and Corliss Lamont.

In a meeting arranged by J. Edgar Hoover, Ernst met informally with Dies, who, in late 1939, issued a public statement "clearing" the ACLU.[185]

In 1940, the ACLU expelled Flynn from its board and passed a resolution barring anyone from being an ACLU board or staff member "who is a member of any political organization which supports totalitarian dictatorship in any country, or who by his public declarations indicates his support of such a principle." It included the Communist Party and organizations with "obvious anti-democratic objectives or practices."[186] Ward resigned as chairman of the board and left the ACLU.[187] Some ACLU members denounced the resolution, and Chicago, Massachusetts, and California affiliates pushed to have the resolution rescinded.[188]

Unlike the ACLU, the ACPFB did not purge its Communist members or staff and did not denounce Communism. Neither Green nor King was a Communist, but they worked with Communists and Communist organizations and represented clients who were Communists.[189]

Before and throughout World War II, the ACPFB enjoyed public popularity and increased membership. New York City Mayor Fiorello LaGuardia published a pamphlet with the ACPFB called "Non-Citizen Americans in the War Emergency," which described the loyalty and patriotism of foreigners in the United States and explained how these foreigners could help the war effort.[190] Both President Roosevelt and First Lady Eleanor Roosevelt publicly praised the ACPFB for its efforts on behalf of foreigners. In his greeting to the ACPFB's annual conference in 1941, Roosevelt wrote that the ACPFB "has undertaken the task of assuring fair play to the foreign born within the United States. Every American wishes it success."[191]

Hollywood actor Edward G. Robinson, an emigrant from Romania who supported the ACPFB and assisted in its fundraising efforts, declared, "It seems to me that the American committee has made an incalculable contribution to our unity and national morale by promoting integration of the foreign born in our society. It has consistently encouraged greater participation by the foreign born in our social, economic, and political life. It has strengthened our democracy by its activity in encouraging and making possible the naturalization of non-citizens."[192]

Yet, the respite from anti-Communism and the embrace of the ACPFB were short-lived. By the end of World War II, a new war had begun, the Cold War. In the late 1940s, HUAC and the anti-Communist fervor of the late 1930s would return with a vengeance. The Justice Department, armed with the Smith Act and with assistance from Hoover, would arrest and prosecute Communist Party leaders and launch deportation and denaturalization drives against foreign Communists and labor organizers. In the 1950s, Congress would pass restrictive laws focusing on guilt by association, granting the attorney general ultimate discretion to exclude or deport, and explicitly proscribing Communist organizations to ease deportation efforts, as suggested by Assistant Commissioner of Immigration Edward G. Shaughnessy in 1932.

During the Cold War, King would continue to use the writ of *habeas corpus* to help foreigners swept up in these deportation drives, but these more restrictive laws and adherence to the plenary power doctrine would thwart her efforts and end her legal victories. Green and the ACPFB would work tirelessly to defend foreigners from deportation and governmental suppression, but they soon discovered that they would also have to work to defend themselves.

5

An Iron Curtain of the West

TWO YEARS AFTER the end of World War II, the United States entered the Cold War with the Soviet Union. The United States focused on projecting an anti-Communist identity as a free, liberal democracy through its foreign policies and containment of Communism abroad. It also sought to address the threat of Communism and internal subversion through the suppression and elimination of Communism in the United States. During the late 1940s, these efforts focused on exposing Communists or alleged Communists in government and on guilt by association with alleged Communists or Communist organizations. It also included loyalty oaths requiring employees to profess that they were not Communists, the creation of "blacklists" of those associated with or accused of being Communists, and the purging of Communists and suspected Communists from influential professions, including those working in Hollywood and academia.[1]

As anti-Communist repression spread, a public hysteria and fear of Communist infiltration and corruption of the United States and its institutions led to persecution and accusation, the suppression of free speech and association, intimidation, fear, and self-censorship, as well as the barring and expulsion of foreigners from the United States. Political cartoonist and satirist Herb Block ("Herblock") depicted this hysteria and fear, resulting in actions that threatened to extinguish America's image and identity as a free and welcoming nation, in his cartoon "Fire!" published in the *Washington Post* on June 17, 1949.[2]

A year later, Block would coin the term "McCarthyism" in a cartoon inspired by the accusations of Communist infiltration in the State Department and subversives in the United States made by Senator Joseph McCarthy (R-WI).[3] "McCarthyism" would soon become the ubiquitous term used to

"FIRE!" by Herb Block, published June 17, 1949
A 1949 Herblock Cartoon, © The Herb Block Foundation.

describe the increasing paranoia and pervasive fear that the mere presence of Communists would destroy the United States. The term would also be used to describe the trampling of First Amendment freedoms in the name of national security.[4]

Yet, as popular as the term "McCarthyism" was and continues to be to describe this period of repression, McCarthyism was more than McCarthy and his efforts. The repression associated with McCarthy and his investigations in the early 1950s was a continuation, intensification, and extension of anti-Communism in the late 1930s.[5] Relying on existing laws, such as the Smith Act, and passing new ones, legislators, bureaucrats and public officials worked to suppress free speech through criminal prosecutions, registration requirements, investigations establishing guilt by association, and the detention, denaturalization, and deportation of foreign-born residents and visa denials to foreign visitors.

To many in the United States and abroad, the ideological exclusions and deportations the United States insisted were necessary during the Cold War to prevent subversion that was capable of destroying the nation's institutions and corrupting its ideals, undermined those institutions and ideals by turning the attorney general and consular officials into censors. Those skeptical of McCarthy and his allies argued that the exclusion of foreign scientists, writers, and artists based on their beliefs or associations damaged an image of the United States as a confident, democratic, freedom-loving nation, in contrast to the Soviet Union, and revealed an insecure, repressive nation that was fearful of foreigners and freedom of speech.

The Return of Anti-Communism

The anti-Communist efforts to denaturalize, detain, and deport foreigners in the 1930s had returned by the late 1940s. In 1945, Congress made the House Un-American Activities Committee (HUAC) a permanent, standing House committee, which would investigate the infiltration of subversives and Communists in American society and government. In 1946, Attorney General Tom C. Clark and the Justice Department launched its first deportation drive.

Clark, a lawyer from Dallas, Texas, who had joined the Justice Department in 1937, had quickly advanced in the Criminal Division to become assistant attorney general. During World War II, Attorney General Francis Biddle appointed Clark to be the civilian coordinator of the Alien Enemy Control Program, which would implement and oversee the internment of Japanese and Japanese Americans. In 1945, President Harry Truman appointed Clark to succeed Biddle as attorney general. Clark was an ardent anti-Communist, who was eager to suppress Communism and zealous in his prosecutions of Communists and alleged Communists. To Clark, Communists posed a serious threat to American institutions by dividing the nation, infiltrating labor unions, and creating civil unrest. He turned to existing law as a tool to suppress this threat.[6]

Like Secretary of Labor William N. Doak, who used existing law to implement his deportation drive in 1931, Clark used his authority under the Smith Act to deport as many foreign-born Communists as he could, arresting any foreign noncitizen who "at the time of entering the United States . . . or at any time thereafter" was a member of an organization "advocating the violent overthrow of the government."[7] Initially, Clark's Justice Department focused primarily on those who had been members of the Communist Party and labor organizers. Immigration officials were able to arrest forty-one foreigners for deportation under the Smith Act's past and present membership provision.[8] By 1949, that number would swell to 135 foreigners arrested for deportation.[9] J. Edgar Hoover and the Federal Bureau of Investigation (FBI) provided lists of names and information to Clark and immigration officials to conduct the deportation drives.[10] Clark also called on Congress for a stronger anti-Communist law that would enable him to arrest and deport the 2,100 foreign Communists he claimed resided in the United States.[11]

The American Committee for Protection of Foreign Born (ACPFB) was the main organization representing those foreigners who were arrested and detained during Clark's deportation drives, and Carol King and Abner Green worked to get them released from detention and prevent their deportations. Peter Harisiades was one of their clients. Harisiades was an emigrant from Greece who had lived in the United States since he was thirteen years old. In 1925, he was working in a textile mill in Massachusetts when he decided to join the Communist Party. During the 1930 textile strike, immigration officials issued a warrant for Harisiades's arrest in order to deport him along with other foreign noncitizens in the Textile Workers Union, but he was not deported at that time.[12]

In the 1930s, Harisiades led the Greek bureau of the Communist Party in New York, but in 1939, the party discontinued his membership. In October 1946, during its first deportation drive, the Justice Department arrested Harisiades for deportation because of his past membership in the Communist Party. In 1949, the Board of Immigration Appeals (BIA) upheld his deportation order under the Smith Act; the Justice Department sent Harisiades to Ellis Island to deport him to Greece. Carol King immediately filed a writ of *habeas corpus* to prevent his deportation and bring his case before a federal court.[13] Harisiades would serve as a "test case" for the ACPFB, which challenged the constitutionality of the Smith Act and his deportation for past membership.[14]

Throughout the 1940s, the Justice Department continued its efforts to arrest, detain, and deport.[15] In many cases, foreign noncitizens who were detained pending deportation were released on bail. The average bail amount was $500, but the Justice Department would insist on increasing that amount to $10,000 or even $25,000.[16] Those who could not make bail, or were not granted bail, were sent to Ellis Island and detained pending deportation. Such detention could be quite lengthy; some deportees were detained for over two years. In 1948, Charles Doyle, Gerhart Eisler, Irving Potash, Ferdinand Smith, and John Williamson protested their detention at Ellis Island without bail by staging a hunger strike. After thousands of telegrams, as well as protest demonstrations across the United States, the strikers were released after five days.[17]

King had used bail applications and writs of *habeas corpus* as her main weapons to prevent detention and deportation since she began representing deportees held on Ellis Island in the 1930s. The Justice Department was now directly attacking one of her strategies, so King decided to attack the Justice Department. King turned to a new law passed in 1946 called the Administrative Procedure Act (APA), which sought to promote fairness and public transparency in governmental agencies and prevent decisions that were "arbitrary, capricious, an abuse of discretion, or otherwise not in accordance with the law."[18]

King argued that the APA and its provisions requiring "impartial" judges in administrative hearings applied to the Justice Department and deportation hearings.[19] Not much had changed since the Wickersham Commission's report in 1931 had criticized the lack of independence of adjudicators in deportation hearings. Immigration officials presiding over these hearings were also often the same officials who gathered evidence against foreigners arrested for deportation. Acting as both prosecutor and judge, these officials were in no way "impartial."[20]

King believed that if she could persuade a federal court that the APA applied to deportation hearings, and that those hearings violated the APA, she could stop the Justice Department from continuing its deportation drives. King was overjoyed when in *Wong Yang Sung v. McGrath* (1950), the Supreme Court held that the hearings in deportation cases had to conform to the APA and its requirement for a separate, impartial adjudicator.[21] The Immigration and Naturalization Service (INS) announced that all deportation hearings since June 3, 1947, were invalid (estimated at 14,000 hearings).[22] In 1951, Congress responded by passing the Supplemental Appropriations Act, which exempted the deportation hearings from the APA.[23]

While King focused on Clark's deportation drives, he was focused on denaturalizing and deporting her client Harry Bridges. Three years after King had congratulated Bridges on becoming an American citizen, the Justice Department persuaded a federal grand jury to indict Bridges for committing fraud and perjury during his naturalization process. In 1949, a California jury convicted Bridges, and his citizenship was revoked.[24] The Justice Department attempted to deport Bridges, but in *Bridges v. United States* (1953), the Supreme Court reversed his conviction and denaturalization because his indictment fell outside the three-year statute of limitations.[25] The Justice Department made one last attempt to denaturalize Bridges in civil court in 1955, but finally gave up when the court ruled in Bridges's favor.[26]

The Justice Department also used the Smith Act to prosecute leaders and members of the Communist Party within the United States, as well as to deport them. In 1948, the Justice Department charged eleven leaders in the

Communist Party for conspiracy and for membership in an organization that advocated the violent overthrow of government under the Smith Act. In 1949, they were convicted, and in *Dennis v. United States* (1951), the Supreme Court upheld the constitutionality of the Smith Act and their conviction under it. The court also replaced the bad tendency test, used to determine whether expression was protected under the Constitution, with another one: "whether the gravity of the 'evil,' discounted by its improbability, justifies such invasion of free speech as is necessary to avoid the danger."[27] The court held that the gravity and threat of Communism to the United States justified restriction of free speech and association.

By 1950, Clark was no longer attorney general. Truman had nominated Clark to the Supreme Court to replace Justice Frank Murphy, who had died in 1949, and he was confirmed by the Senate in a vote 73–8. Prior to his confirmation, King had testified before the Senate Judiciary Committee opposing Clark's nomination and describing his deportation drives.[28] Clark's successors, J. Howard McGrath, James P. McGranery, and Herbert Brownell Jr., continued his anti-Communist efforts. They also had new legislation to assist them. In 1948 and 1949, members of HUAC introduced bills that included a requirement that all Communist organizations and all Communist-front organizations register as such with the attorney general.[29] A sponsor of one of these bills was Richard M. Nixon (R-CA), a junior congressman who had been involved in the investigation of Alger Hiss. Both bills failed to pass in the Senate, but there was one man, the most powerful anti-Communist legislator in the United States, who would successfully lead Congress in passing this type of legislation: Senator Patrick McCarran (D-NV).

McCarranism during McCarthyism

In 1950, the Justice Department used new laws to root out Communists and subversives by suppressing expression and punishing association, as well as by barring Communists from entering the United States and deporting foreign subversives from its shores. The politician largely responsible for the successful passage of these laws in Congress was not Senator McCarthy, but rather Senator McCarran. One of the most influential members of Congress, McCarran sponsored two acts containing ideological restrictions that would last for decades. The term "McCarranism," used to describe these laws and McCarran's investigations of Communists, often appeared alongside "McCarthyism" in newspapers and popular rhetoric.[30]

Patrick McCarran was born in Reno, Nevada in 1876 to Irish Catholic immigrant parents. He arrived in Congress in 1933 at the beginning of the Roosevelt administration, but he was one of the Democrats who opposed the New Deal. McCarran was also a fervent anti-Communist. One of Congress's conservative cold warriors, he was outspoken in his belief that Communists would subvert American ideals and institutions.[31] By 1950, McCarran had become chairman of both the Senate Judiciary Committee and the Senate Appropriations Subcommittee. He reveled in the committees' importance and in the power he wielded through them.[32]

McCarran held nativist views that helped shape his belief that Communism was a foreign ideology imported to the United States by immigrants and spread through foreign influence.[33] In 1950, McCarran chaired a special subcommittee of the Senate Judiciary Committee, which produced a 900-page comprehensive report on immigration regulation. The report characterized foreigners as posing a national security threat and declared, "The protection of the public safety requires the exclusion from the United States of those aliens who bring with them their alien ideologies which are subversive to the national security and contrary to our constitutional form of government."[34] Describing Communism as an "alien force," the report then turned its attention to the Communist threat. "It is inconceivable that the people of the United States would, of their own volition, organize or become part of a conspiracy to destroy the free institutions to which generations of Americans have devoted themselves."[35] The committee recommended broadening ideological restrictions and adding "Communists" to the list of exclusion and deportation categories included in the Smith Act.[36]

Shortly after the United States entered the Korean War, Congress passed the Internal Security Act of 1950 ("McCarran Act").[37] The act passed in the House 286–48 and in the Senate 57–10 and over Truman's veto. With an upcoming election, members of Congress feared red-baiting and felt pressure to pass it.[38] The McCarran Act, like the Smith Act, devoted half of its provisions to the suppression of subversives within the United States and restrictions on American citizens. In its own form of ideological "containment," the McCarran Act denied the issuance of passports to any member of an organization that Washington deemed a "Communist organization."[39] Also, all Communist and Communist-front organizations had to register with the attorney general and provide membership lists and documents relating to their activities and finances.[40] The act established the Subversive Activities Control Board (SACB), which was charged with carrying out this registration process through investigations of those refusing to register.[41] Such registration left these organizations and their members vulnerable to governmental and public scrutiny, as well as blacklisting, prosecution, passport denial, denaturalization, and deportation.

The McCarran Act included all of the previous ideological exclusion and deportation categories created since the Alien Immigration Act of 1903 and added Communists, as well as members and those affiliated with organizations that teach, advocate, advise, publish, or distribute the "economic, international, and governmental doctrines of world communism"[42] or of "totalitarianism."[43] It also placed no exceptions on membership in such organizations, even if membership had long been terminated or had been entered into under coercion, duress, or necessity.

The McCarran Act gave ultimate discretion to the attorney general to admit, exclude, or deport. Similar to the Alien Friends Act of 1798, which gave President John Adams discretion to deport, the McCarran Act included an implicit restriction authorizing the attorney general to exclude any foreigner and to arrest, detain, and deport any noncitizen who he deemed would be "prejudicial to the public interest or would endanger the welfare or safety of the United States."[44] The attorney general could keep the reason and evidence confidential if he considered disclosure of them to be "prejudicial to the public interest, safety and security" of the United States.[45]

Tasked with implementing the McCarran Act's provisions, immigration officials and the State Department's consular officials were completely unprepared and overwhelmed. The lack of bureaucratic procedures in place to support these new exclusionary policies wreaked havoc on the immigration and visa system.[46] Ellis Island had to shut down for almost a month, and the State Department temporarily stopped issuing visas to foreign visitors and immigrants, because it could not effectively conduct the pre-entry interviews and exclusions.[47] Immigration officials detained 13,000 seaman on their ships pending a determination that they posed no security threat, and officials excluded 2,400 foreigners seeking admission as suspected subversives. Only 156 of these seamen were eventually found to be legally excludable under the McCarran Act.[48]

Much of the national and international press coverage of the ideological exclusions under the McCarran Act concerned those excluded under the totalitarian organization provision, the category that included Fascists and Nazis. This provision disproportionately affected Italians and Germans seeking entry in 1950; almost all of them at one point had been members of Fascist or Nazi organizations, even if this membership was coerced or necessary for survival.[49]

Newspapers were filled with articles describing foreigners caught up in these exclusion provisions and detained on Ellis Island pending investigation, including world-renowned musicians and opera singers.[50] Conductor Arturo Toscanini was briefly questioned on his way back from a European tour,[51] and Joseph Szigeti, a fifty-eight-year-old Hungarian-born violin virtuoso was detained for five days while being questioned about his affiliations.[52] The Metropolitan Opera lamented that its performances were being disrupted.[53] Friedrich Gulda, a twenty-year-old pianist from Austria, was detained on Ellis Island due to a mandatory membership in Hitler Youth when he was a child. Attorney General McGrath used his authority and discretion to permit Gulda's brief release to perform at Carnegie Hall.[54]

Such exclusions and detentions also led to international tension. Italian ambassador Alberto Tarchiani contacted the State Department to protest the detention of Italian passengers and ship crews under the McCarran Act. He argued these exclusions and detentions were a direct violation of the US-Italian treaty of friendship and commerce.[55] The *Christian Science Monitor* reported that Austrian and other European Communists had been using these exclusions and detentions, especially Gulda's, as propaganda against the United States.[56] The visa denials had angered Western Europeans, driving a wedge between them and America, which these Communists sought to exploit.[57] The reporter concluded that the McCarran Act undermined America's security efforts by "alienating foreigners instead of safeguarding the United States."[58]

While much of the criticism and concern regarding the McCarran Act's categories of exclusion focused on its lack of exceptions for former members of Fascist organizations, the Communist exclusions gained some public attention. In 1952, British author Graham Greene encountered difficulty when the State Department delayed issuing him a visa because of Greene's month-long membership in the Communist Party in 1922 as a teenage "prank" when he was eighteen years old.[59] McGrath authorized the State Department to issue Greene a conditional, restricted visa, which limited Greene's stay in the United States to thirty days.[60]

While Greene characterized his visa delay and entry limitation as "comical," he was not laughing when he described the impression these restrictions left in Europe, remarking "America's allies are beginning to wonder if their concept of democracy is the same as yours."[61] After describing a number of exclusions of artists, scientists, and writers under the McCarran Act, the *New York Times* echoed Greene's concern. "What we are worried about is the attempt of Senator McCarran and his friends to create a futile intellectual *cordon sanitaire* about the United States—an attempt which has seriously damaged our reputation as a liberal democracy abroad and has encouraged the forces of reaction, parochialism and xenophobia at home."[62]

In 1952, Senator McCarran and his colleague Congressman Francis E. Walter (D-PA), a fellow cold warrior and immigration restrictionist, sponsored the most comprehensive and exclusionary law ever enacted. It remains the current immigration law in the United States. Resembling a Russian *matryoshka* nesting doll, the Immigration and Nationality Act of 1952 ("McCarran-Walter Act") not only combined all previous immigration and naturalization laws into one statute, but also represented the culmination of ideological exclusion and deportation.

The McCarran-Walter Act attempted to avoid the bureaucratic chaos and national embarrassment that arose during the McCarran Act's initial implementation in 1950.[63] It left the Communist and world Communism provisions intact, but revised the totalitarian provision. The revised provision did not include Fascist and Nazi organizations and now added an exception for foreigners who had terminated membership in totalitarian organizations within five years of the visa request.[64] It also included an exception for an "innocent joiner" of such organizations.[65]

"Seldom has a bill exhibited the distrust evidenced here for citizens and aliens alike—at a time when we need unity at home and the confidence of our friends abroad."[66] Truman included this sharp rebuke to Congress before it passed the McCarran-Walter Act over his veto. In addition to expressing his disgust that the act maintained the discriminatory national origins quotas established by the Johnson-Reed Act of 1924, Truman characterized the ideological exclusion provisions as a form of "thought control" and "inconsistent with our democratic ideals," and he emphasized the detrimental effects of such restrictions to America's self-professed image as a free and welcoming nation.

Under the McCarran-Walter Act, consular officials' decisions to deny visas continued to be nonreviewable, and these officials were not required to provide the visa applicant with a reason for the denial or the evidence used to support it.[67] Truman also argued that conferring unlimited power and ultimate discretion to the attorney general to exclude or deport was akin to the power and discretion given to President Adams under the Alien Friends Act of 1798. Truman chastised Congress for turning the attorney general into a censor and providing no standards or definitions "to guide discretion in the exercise of powers so sweeping."[68]

The McCarran-Walter Act had also strengthened the attorney general's control and ultimate discretion over which foreigners he could admit or exclude. The Attorney General could admit someone deemed inadmissible if that person's entry would be in the public interest.[69] The act also included a provision permitting the attorney general to bar a foreign noncitizen, legal resident who had left the United States, if reentry would be contrary to the nation's interests.[70] James P. McGranery, the new attorney general, sought to use his authority and discretion under this provision to bar renowned silent film star Charlie Chaplin from reentering the United States.

Eventually subpoenaed but never called to testify about his politics, Chaplin sent a preemptive and taunting telegram to HUAC in 1947: "While you are preparing your engraved subpoena I will give you a hint on where I stand. I am not a Communist. I am a peace-monger."[71] Two years later, Senator Harry Cain (R-WA) called to deport Chaplin. He submitted a statement to the Senate Judiciary Committee listing Chaplin's alleged "connections with Communist fronts and Communist-dominated organizations." Cain also cited a telegram Chaplin sent to Pablo Picasso in 1948. He asked Picasso to organize a rally of French artists in front of the US embassy in Paris to protest against the deportation of Hanns Eisler, a Vienna-born former Hollywood composer and Communist, from the United States. Cain described Chaplin's request as one that "skirts perilously close to treason."[72] The FBI had been investigating Chaplin since the 1920s, and by 1949, the INS and J. Edgar Hoover were working together to find sufficient evidence to support grounds to deport or exclude Chaplin based on his subversive affiliations and beliefs.[73]

In September 1952, a few months after the passage of the McCarran-Walter Act, Chaplin sailed to London on a European tour to promote his new film, *Limelight*. After consulting with Hoover and the INS, McGranery seized the opportunity once Chaplin, a foreign noncitizen, was out of the United States, and revoked his reentry permit.[74] Accusing Chaplin of a "leering, sneering attitude toward the country whose gracious hospitality has enriched him," McGranery insisted Chaplin submit to an interview regarding his views, morals, and associations in order to "prove his worth and right to enter the United States."[75] Chaplin refused, and in April 1953, he announced that he and his family would not return.[76] He was sad and angry, describing his treatment as the "object of lies and vicious propaganda by powerful reactionary groups who by their influence and by the aid of America's yellow press have created an unhealthy atmosphere in which liberal minded individuals can be singled out and persecuted."[77]

Graham Greene penned an open letter to Chaplin published in the *New Republic*. Greene denounced Chaplin's exclusion as another one of the nation's "ugly manifestations of fear." He wrote, "To our pain and astonishment you paid the United States the highest compliment in your power by settling within her borders, and now we feel pain but not astonishment at the response—not from the American people in general, one is sure, but from those authorities who seem to take their orders from such men as McCarthy." Greene described Chaplin's treatment as a "disgrace," and he insisted that condemnation of his exclusion and of McCarthyism were matters of international importance. "Intolerance in any country wounds freedom throughout the world."[78]

Perhaps the most compelling critique and description of the implementation and effect of ideological exclusion under McCarranism appeared in the October 1952 special issue of the *Bulletin of the Atomic Scientists: A Magazine for Science and Public Affairs* entitled "American Visa Policy and Foreign Scientists."[79] A number of eminent scientists contributed to the issue, including British and French scientists who had applied for visas to come to the United States and had faced delays, interrogations, and denials due to their affiliations. Albert Einstein, himself an immigrant from Germany, cautioned against such visa denials as having a damaging effect on scientific discovery, asserting that "the free, unhampered exchange of ideas and scientific conclusions is necessary for the sound development of science as it is in all other spheres of cultural life."[80] Hans A. Bethe, a professor of physics at Cornell University, emphasized the importance of the oral communication of scientific results and the sharing of ideas and experiments in person by traveling to and working in other laboratories abroad.[81]

Victor F. Weisskopf, a professor of physics at the Massachusetts Institute of Technology, found that at least sixty scientists had been barred from the United States under the McCarran Act. He described a visa application process that had bewildered, annoyed, angered, and embarrassed the scientists. The delay in the time between visa application and receipt, stretching from four months to over one year, made it difficult for American scientists to plan meetings, as well as for foreign scientists to attend them. Political activities, present and past, appeared to have been the reason behind many visa denials, despite evidence of anti-Communist attitudes.[82]

Visa applicants were required to fill out a questionnaire, under oath, listing all the organizations they had been associated with in the past fifteen years. Applicants found this procedure repugnant, and many feared that if they could not remember a particular organization, the consular official could interpret this omission as error or perjury. Finally, there was an oral interview with the consular official, who asked the applicant detailed questions regarding his or her political affiliations, beliefs, and attitudes, including questions such as "What do you think of the United States' policy in Korea?" and "What's your stand on NATO?"[83]

Edward Shils, a professor of social sciences on the Committee of Social Thought at the University of Chicago, described the "ineptitude" of consular officials who lacked the knowledge, time, and training necessary to assess the applicants' written work and its significance, as well as the nature of the applicants' political affiliations. Shils depicted officials as insecure and fearful to issue visas. There was no risk to the official to delay or deny a visa, but great risk if the official admitted the "wrong" applicant. While their decisions were nonreviewable by superiors or the courts, they were reviewable by Congress, which was more likely to question an official's decision to grant rather than to deny a visa. According to Shils, the xenophobia inherent in the McCarran-Walter Act also led officials to justify the law and their role enforcing it, and provided additional motivation for them to exclude.[84]

Shils mentioned applicants' reluctance to request a waiver, an exception to their exclusion, from the State Department and granted by the attorney general in order to be admitted to the United States; such a request added to their humiliation and implied guilt. He declared, "Nearly every refusal of a visa, every unnecessary prolongation of the bureaucratic labyrinth through which a visa applicant must pass, embarrasses a Western friend of the United States and the Western alliance." It gave the impression that there was no difference between the United States and the Soviet Union and that Europeans should avoid "involvement in a quarrel between the two paranoid, freedom-hating, barbarian regimes with which they have no common interests."[85]

M. Louis LePrince Ringuet, a French physicist and professor at L'Ecole Polytechnique in Paris, echoed Shils's sentiments, describing the difficulties and frustration in obtaining a visa to come to the United States. He explained that the vast majority of French scientists, "irrespective of their political opinions," belonged to the Association des Travailleurs Scientifique, and that membership in this association had inexplicably served as the basis for visa denials and effectively barred most French scientists. Ringuet wrote of the deplorable effect visa denials had on French opinion of America, adding, "I have even had occasion to see the expression 'Iron Curtain of the West' quite widely applied to the United States."[86]

Deportation, Detention, and Denaturalization
under McCarranism

While foreign visitors faced visa denials, preventing them from entering the United States, foreign-born residents faced denaturalization and deportation, preventing them from staying in the United States. The McCarran-Walter Act had provided the attorney general not only with absolute, unlimited discretionary power to exclude, but also with discretionary power to arrest, detain, and deport noncitizens from the United States.

Under the McCarran-Walter Act, the deportation hearings remained only "quasi-judicial." Where one or more INS officers served as "investigator, prosecutor, and judge," they also lacked impartiality. The fact that deportation hearing officers were under the immediate supervision of an INS district director provided an incentive for the officers to tailor their decisions to meet their supervisor's expectations and focus on enforcement of the law. Hearing officers were poorly paid and recruited through promotion within the INS. In 1952, there were 119 full-time hearing officers, 74 of whom were former immigration inspectors, 21 of whom had law degrees, 32 of whom had college degrees, and 60 percent of whom had no college education or legal training.[87] The attorney general's approval of a deportation hearing decision and his deportation order were final. The McCarran-Walter Act exempted consular officials' decisions and deportation hearings from the APA, but later in *Shaughnessy v. Pedreiro* (1955), the Supreme Court held the act did not exempt the attorney general's orders from conformity to and review under the APA.[88]

The threat of deportation affected not just foreign noncitizens within the United States but also naturalized immigrants who faced the threat of denaturalization. Once stripped of their citizenship, these foreigners could also be subject to deportation. By 1950, the Justice Department had included denaturalization drives with its deportation drives, announcing it had planned to deport 3,000 foreigners due to their affiliations and to denaturalize 1,000.[89] In 1953, the Justice Department announced it would deport 12,000 and denaturalize 10,000.[90]

The actual numbers of foreigners deported and those denaturalized were far lower than these declarations. Between 1950 and 1956, 788 foreigners were ideologically excluded from the United States, but only 231 foreigners were deported on ideological grounds, 26 were denaturalized, and 91 were denied naturalization for lack of attachment to the principles of the Constitution due to their beliefs or associations with subversive organizations.[91] Yet, while many foreigners were not deported or denaturalized, it was the threat and the fear of deportation and denaturalization and the potential detention pending deportation that took their toll physically and psychologically on foreign-born residents. Fear, intimidation, and inhibition served as the most significant tools of McCarthyism and McCarranism.

ACPFB staff members also became targets of the Justice Department, including efforts to denaturalize with the intent to deport. An emigrant from Russia, Rose Chernin became a citizen in 1928. She was active in the International Labor Defense in the early 1930s. In 1934, she joined the Communist Party and was arrested under California's Criminal Syndicalism law. In 1951, Chernin, who was also the founder and executive director of the Los Angeles chapter of the ACPFB, was indicted and later convicted under the Smith Act.[92]

In 1952, the Justice Department initiated proceedings to revoke Chernin's citizenship in order to deport her once she had served her sentence under the Smith Act.[93] In order to denaturalize an individual, the Justice Department had to present evidence of a concealment of material fact or willful misrepresentation during the naturalization process. In these cases, naturalized foreigners were accused of failing to disclose membership in certain subversive or Communist organizations during the naturalization process, which thus invalidated their citizenship. The Justice Department was unsuccessful in its efforts to denaturalize Chernin, but did succeed in curtailing her work for the ACPFB while she fought to protect her citizenship.[94]

The McCarran-Walter Act added a new ground for revocation of citizenship: refusal to testify as a witness in a congressional committee concerning his or her subversive activities or for being convicted of contempt of Congress for such a refusal within ten years of naturalization.[95] American-born citizens could refuse to testify under the Fifth Amendment's privilege against self-incrimination and face a year in jail for contempt. But, if foreign-born citizens refused to testify, they could be stripped of citizenship and face subsequent deportation.

Refusing to testify before a congressional committee could also lead to deportation. Cedric Belfrage, a British journalist and co-founder of the independent, left-wing journal the *National Guardian*, had resided in the United States for twenty-seven years. In 1953, Belfrage refused to answer questions regarding his activities and affiliations when he was called to testify before HUAC. Edward J. Shaughnessy, the district director of Immigration in New York, immediately issued a warrant to deport Belfrage, who was sent to Ellis Island. In 1954, the BIA affirmed Belfrage's deportation order for his alleged prior membership in the Communist Party in 1937.[96] In 1955, Belfrage was forced to leave the United States and return to England.[97]

Two years later, Belfrage published an account of his detention and deportation in *The Frightened Giant: My Unfinished Affair with America*. He concluded with his press statement upon his departure in 1955. "I leave with a clear conscience and a heart less heavy than it might have been, since I know two things as definitely as I ever knew anything," he wrote. "The Walter-McCarran Act under which I am being deported is as unconstitutional as a counterfeit dollar, as Harry Truman said in stronger terms when he vetoed it; and that the people will eventually repeal it just as they ash-canned the Alien and Sedition laws 150 years ago."[98]

By 1954, 340 foreign-born noncitizens had been arrested for deportation.[99] The deportees included men and women, mostly over the age of fifty, many who had lived in the United States for decades and had American-born spouses and children. Those who faced deportation included Russian-born Alexander Bittelman, aged sixty-one, who had resided in the United States for thirty-nine years, Italian-born Francesco Costa, aged eighty-three, who had been a resident for fifty years, and Ukrainian-born Rose Nelson, aged fifty, who had been a resident for forty years.[100] Russian Polish-born Benny Saltzman, aged fifty-six, who had resided for thirty-eight years, worked as a house painter in the Bronx in New York City. He was ordered deported for his past membership in the Communist Party in 1936. "This is the home, the land that I love. Everything is here," he said. Saltzman's American-born son had been killed fighting in World War II and was buried in the United States.[101]

While these foreigners were ordered deported, many never left the United States. In fact, Saltzman remained in the Bronx, unable to be deported because no country would accept him.[102] The Soviet Union had closed its borders after briefly reopening them in the 1930s, so many deportees who had emigrated from Russia remained unless another country agreed to accept them. In 1952, a Finnish journalist with Canadian citizenship named Knut Heikkinen was ordered deported for past membership in the Communist Party, but Canada sought to denaturalize him and Finland had yet to agree to accept him. He was arrested and convicted in 1953 for failing to apply for travel documents to self-deport.[103] The Supreme Court later overturned his conviction.[104] Even if deportees' countries of origin were willing to accept them, some faced persecution upon arrival. In 1952, Korean journalist Sang Rhup Park was ordered deported for alleged membership in the Communist Party. A critic of South Korean President Syngman Rhee, Park argued he would suffer physical persecution if deported to South Korea. A federal judge enjoined the Justice Department from deporting him.[105]

Initially, foreigners who were ordered deported from the United States were either detained on Ellis Island on the East Coast or Terminal Island on the West Coast after Angel Island closed in 1940. The ACPFB struggled to get detainees released on bail. The McCarran-Walter Act included a provision allowing the attorney general, at his discretion, to deny bail and keep the deportee in custody.[106]

Under the act, if the deportee posted bail, or after six months of detention pending deportation, he or she would be placed on supervisory parole. This conditional release required the deportee to remain within a fifty-mile radius, report periodically to an immigration officer, submit to psychiatric and medical examinations, terminate any membership or affiliation with Communist or subversive organizations proscribed by the attorney general, and give information, under oath, on his or her friends, habits, associations, and activities. If the deportee failed to comply with any of these conditions, he or she faced a $1,000 fine and/or one year in jail.[107] While the deportee was no longer detained on Ellis Island or Terminal Island, the supervisory parole requirements exploited the deportee's desire to avoid or escape detention, and these requirements effectively turned him or her into an informer for the Justice Department.

While orchestrating the ACPFB's legal challenges to the McCarran Act and McCarran-Walter Act, Carol King traveled across the United States, working to prevent denaturalizations, deportations, and detentions. Over two decades representing deportees, King had focused her efforts on detention and bail, especially when she could not prevent deportation. King continued to argue against prolonged detention and pushed for deportees' release on bail.[108]

In her last case, King represented John Zydok, a Russian immigrant, who had been a member of the Communist Party when he was arrested for deportation in 1949 and released on $2,000 bail. In 1950, Zydok was rearrested and ordered deported under the McCarran Act.[109] This time, the attorney general did not release Zydok on bail, and he was detained for five months. King filed a writ of *habeas corpus* and argued that the denial of bail was arbitrary and capricious and that the attorney general was abusing his discretion in detaining Zydok, as well as violating the APA, Zydok's Fifth Amendment right to due process, and his Eighth Amendment right against cruel and unusual punishment.[110] King could find no one willing to argue on Zydok's behalf on his appeal in federal court. So, on November 26, 1951, after thirty years of practicing law as the leading immigration attorney in the United States, King argued her first case before the Supreme Court.[111] Two months later, King died of cancer at the age of fifty-six.

Fighting McCarranism while under Attack

As foreign visitors and long-time residents found themselves facing ideological exclusion or deportation, denaturalization, and detention, familiar organizations came to their aid. The American Civil Liberties Union (ACLU) handled visa denials, in addition to challenging the constitutionality of prosecutions under the Smith Act and the McCarran Act. Unfortunately, there was little the ACLU could do beyond contacting the State Department and directly appealing to consular officials and the secretary of state to issue a visa and admit the foreigner to the United States.[112] While the ACLU participated in efforts to challenge deportation and detention, it was the ACPFB that took the lead in these cases. While the ACLU and ACPFB defended foreign-born non-citizens against McCarranism, they found that they also had to defend themselves. Unlike the ACLU, the ACPFB never purged Communists from the organization. The purge had split and damaged the ACLU, but the purge, as well as a close relationship between its legal director, Morris Ernst, and J. Edgar Hoover, had successfully prevented the ACLU from being labeled a Communist-front and had saved it from demise. The ACPFB would not be so lucky.

After the 1940 resolution and purge, the ACLU's anti-Communist leadership remained in place for the next fifteen years. While it would challenge some aspects of the anti-Communist fervor during McCarthyism, including loyalty oaths, blacklisting, visa denials, and Smith Act prosecutions, it was cautious. During these years, the ACLU would often submit *amicus curiae* briefs during the appeals in constitutional challenges in lieu of direct representation, and it was reluctant to work too closely with groups that the Justice Department had designated as Communist-fronts. One ACLU staff member expressed reluctance working with a Midwest branch of the ACPFB on an exclusion case. He remarked, "It looks like a possible civil liberties case, but I am not enthused with the prospect of playing footsie with these people."[113] By 1955, the leadership had departed, the tide of McCarthyism had turned, and the ACLU began to openly and vigorously challenge anti-Communist measures and free speech suppression.[114]

In 1951, philosopher and civil libertarian Corliss Lamont founded the Emergency Civil Liberties Committee (ECLC), a legal organization focused primarily on defending those prosecuted under the McCarran Act. Lamont had grown increasingly disappointed and frustrated with the ACLU since the 1940 resolution and especially with its cautious approach toward challenging McCarranism and McCarthyism. The State Department not only sought to prevent Communists from entering the United States, but also American Communists from leaving it. It withheld or revoked passports from anyone it had "reason to believe" was a member of a Communist organization, anyone whose "conduct abroad is likely to be contrary to the best interest of the United States," or anyone who would "engage in activities which will advance the Communist movement."[115] The ECLC became the main organization representing Americans whose passports were withheld by the State Department. ECLC clients included the actor, singer, and activist Paul Robeson and the artist Rockwell Kent. The ECLC's legal challenges to the withholding of passports, however, also turned the ECLC into a target, and it soon had to start handling its own passport cases, when the State Department revoked Lamont's passport.[116]

From the first deportation drive in 1946, the ACPFB did not hesitate in bringing legal challenges on behalf of the deportees, arguing for release and reasonable bail, appealing deportation orders, and calling for an end to supervisory parole. Abner Green worked tirelessly to raise funds to support legal counsel for deportees and to publicize their accounts in calling for reform, support, and protest. A prolific writer, Green continued to produce the ACPFB newsletter, the *Lamp*, and pamphlets comparing anti-Communist efforts to the Alien Friends Act and Sedition Act, the Palmer Raids, and the Doak deportation drives, while publicizing deportees' accounts and providing legal analysis of the McCarran-Walter Act's provisions.[117]

When the anti-Communism of the late 1930s returned in the late 1940s, so did accusations that the ACPFB was a Communist-front organization. The ACPFB continuously and consistently denied it was a Communist-front, publicly and privately, before Congress and the courts. Anti-Communist members and those who feared blacklists and guilt by association dealt a significant blow to ACPFB sponsorship when many of them resigned or denied their sponsorship in an effort to disassociate themselves from a perceived Communist organization.

ACPFB sponsorship began to drop, and Green received dozens of letters asking him to cancel the sender's sponsorship, or to remove the sender from any record of him or her as a contributor or from ACPFB letterhead or sponsorship lists.[118] Green received one such letter from actor Edward G. Robinson, who had publicly supported the ACPFB during World War II and

"Should Miss Liberty Be DEPORTED?" A pamphlet produced and distributed by the American Committee for Protection of Foreign Born in 1950, describing the Statue of Liberty as a "foreigner," born in France, who immigrated to the United States and represents "ideas of freedom and equality" threatened by the Justice Department's deportation drives. It discusses Peter Harisiades's case and asks for contributions to "fight against the deportation hysteria and to provide defense and assistance to those non-citizens who are under attack." New York Public Library, http://digitalcollections.nypl.org/items/3b3f91f0-d5f4-0134-b40b-00505686a51c.

assisted in its fundraising efforts. In 1950, Robinson was called to testify before HUAC and presented with evidence of his alleged affiliations with Communist organizations, including the ACPFB. Seeking to clear his name and avoid being blacklisted because of such affiliations, Robinson wrote to Green requesting that he "immediately discontinue the usage of [his] name in connection with your association" or in connection with any of the ACPFB's activities and to remove his name from any ACPFB mailing lists.[119]

While some wrote to Green to cancel their sponsorship, others wrote to Green to inquire whether the ACPFB was indeed a Communist-front. They cited the ACPFB's almost exclusive representation of Communists and former Communists in its legal challenges. Green responded that the ACPFB's defense of the foreign-born remained the same, but the Justice Department's "attitude toward citizens and non-citizens" had changed. The Justice Department, and not the ACPFB, had made the choice to focus its attention on Communists.[120] Green categorically denied that the ACPFB was a Communist-front. "We never inquire into the political beliefs of those non-citizens who apply to us for assistance," he wrote. "In deportation and naturalization the most important principle question is whether non-citizens who are members of or former members of the Communist Party can become citizens of the United States. Our organization maintains that political beliefs cannot serve as the basis for the denial of citizenship of the United States. At the same time, we find that many who are not members of the Communist Party face serious difficulties in naturalization because of their progressive or labor activities."[121]

During the 1950s, Abner Green and the ACPFB became targets of the attorney general and the Subversive Activities Control Board (SACB). After twenty years of defending foreigners from governmental suppression, the ACPFB now had to defend itself. When Green was called before the SACB, he refused to "name names" and provide information about ACPFB sponsorship. Green served six months in prison for contempt after again refusing to disclose the names of ACPFB sponsors and contributors to a New York grand jury.[122] In 1953, the attorney general petitioned the SACB to order the ACPFB to register as a Communist-front organization.[123] Protesting and refusing to register, Green appealed the SACB's order following a hearing in 1955.[124]

The most damage to the ACPFB came from the New York State attorney general. Designating the ACPFB as a charitable organization, it ordered Green to turn over the committee's records, sponsorship lists, and activities under the New York Social Welfare Law.[125] Green was not giving up or giving in, and he refused to disclose the lists. He denied that the ACPFB was a charitable organization and identified it as a political one, which was thus not subject to the Social Welfare Law. The attorney general then enjoined the ACPFB from soliciting funds pending Green's appeal of the charitable organization designation.[126] By 1958, the ACPFB was hobbled, unable to fund legal challenges to deportations and denaturalizations in the courts.[127] The indefatigable Green persisted in his battle against the designations and to prevent disclosure of ACPFB sponsorship lists until his death from a brain tumor in 1959.

Ira Gollobin would continue his fight. Gollobin was a lawyer who had joined the ACPFB in 1936 and, with King, represented foreigners facing deportation. He became the ACPFB's general counsel after King's death and not only challenged ideological deportations, but also the ACPFB's designation as a Communist-front and registration with the SACB. Litigation lasted until the mid-1970s.[128] As the Supreme Court would eventually declare guilt by association and registration with the SACB unconstitutional, the SACB vacated the order for the ACPFB to register as a Communist-front.[129] Through the late 1960s and early 1970s, the ACPFB shifted its focus from deportation to assisting refugees to the United States and helping immigrants from Mexico, Haiti, and Latin America.[130] In 1982, the ACPFB agreed to be absorbed by the ECLC as part of a special immigrant rights division of the legal organization dedicated to working on foreign-born issues and visa denials.[131]

A Conflicted Supreme Court

In a series of decisions in the early 1950s, the majority of the Supreme Court consistently upheld the constitutionality of ideological restrictions under the plenary power doctrine. Yet, some members expressed their growing concern over judicial deference under the doctrine, as well as the insulation of ideological exclusion and deportation from substantive review and due process protections, the use of confidential evidence by the attorney general, and his ultimate discretion to detain, deport, and exclude based on such evidence in the name of national security.

In *United States ex rel. Knauff v. Shaughnessy* (1950), a 4–3 decision (Justices Tom C. Clark and William O. Douglas did not take part in the decision), the Supreme Court upheld the attorney general's discretion to exclude Ellen Knauff, the German wife of an American citizen, based on confidential evidence that her entry would be "prejudicial to the interests of the United States."[132] Writing for the majority, Justice Sherman Minton cited the plenary power doctrine and its legal precedent, characterizing the admission of foreigners to the United States as "a privilege granted by the sovereign United States Government."[133] Affirming the constitutionality of the attorney general's use of confidential evidence and his discretion to determine whom to exclude, Minton described this authority as "final and conclusive."[134] "It is not within the province of any court, unless expressly authorized by law, to

141

review the determination of the political branch of the Government to exclude a given alien," he wrote.[135] Minton also declared "any procedure authorized by Congress for the exclusion of aliens is due process," and thus, foreigners facing exclusion were not entitled to a fair hearing or constitutional protections.[136]

In his dissenting opinion, Justice Robert Jackson expressed his apprehension and discomfort with the attorney general's use of confidential evidence to bar Knauff's entry to the United States. "Security is like liberty, in that many are the crimes committed in its name," Jackson warned. "The plea that evidence of guilt must be secret is abhorrent to free men, because it provides a cloak for the malevolent, the misinformed, the meddlesome, and the corrupt to play the role of informer undetected and uncorrected."[137] Jackson upheld Congress's plenary power to exclude, but he expressed concern over the lack of due process for Knauff. "I do not question the constitutional power of Congress to authorize immigration authorities to turn back from our gates any alien or class of aliens," he wrote. "But I do not find that Congress has authorized an abrupt and brutal exclusion of the wife of an American citizen without a hearing."[138]

ACPFB client Peter Harisiades, the Greek immigrant who had been arrested under the Smith Act during the 1946 deportation drive, had already voluntarily left the United States. Fearing persecution if deported to Greece, Harisiades was granted asylum in Poland and left the United States in 1952, just when his test case finally came before the Supreme Court.[139]

In *Harisiades v. Shaughnessy* (1952), a 6–2 decision (Justice Clark recused himself), the Supreme Court affirmed the order to deport Harisiades. Writing for the majority, Justice Jackson deferred to the legislative and executive branches and their authority to determine whom to deport under the plenary power doctrine.[140] "That aliens remain vulnerable to expulsion after long residence is a practice that bristles with severities. But it is a weapon of defense and reprisal confirmed by international law as a power inherent in every sovereign state. Such is the traditional power of the Nation over the alien, and we leave the law on the subject as we find it."[141]

Jackson acknowledged calls for judicial intervention in deportation cases. "There is no denying that, as world convulsions have driven us toward a closed society, the expulsion power has been exercised with increasing severity, manifest in multiplication of grounds for deportation, in expanding the subject classes from illegal entrants to legal residents, and in greatly lengthening the period of residence after which one may be expelled," he wrote. "This is said to have reached a point where it is the duty of this Court to call a halt upon the political branches of the Government."[142] Yet, Jackson refused to call a halt, insisting "nothing in the structure of our Government or the text of our Constitution would warrant judicial review by standards which would require us to equate our political judgment with that of Congress."[143]

Addressing Congress's judgment, Jackson wrote, "Congress received evidence that the Communist movement here has been heavily laden with aliens, and that Soviet control of the American Communist Party has been largely through alien Communists. It would be easy for those of us who do not have security responsibility to say that those who do are taking Communism too seriously, and overestimating its danger."[144] Congress had not only refused to repeal the Smith Act, but had passed even stricter provisions in the McCarran Act. Jackson cited *Dennis v. United States* (1951) upholding the Smith Act's provisions as not violating the First Amendment. He insisted only Congress, and not the courts, could change the law. "We, in our private opinions, need not concur in Congress's policies to hold its enactments constitutional. Judicially, we must tolerate what personally we may regard as a legislative mistake."[145]

Carol King's last case was decided by the Supreme Court in *Carlson v. Landon* (1952). In a 5–4 decision, the Supreme Court upheld the attorney general's discretionary authority to refuse bail to those foreign noncitizens who were detained pending deportation.[146] Writing for the majority, Justice Stanley Reed reaffirmed the attorney general's authority under the plenary power doctrine and also described foreign noncitizens as subject to deportation at Congress's discretion. "When legally admitted, [foreigners] have come at the Nation's invitation, as visitors or permanent residents, to share with us the opportunities and satisfactions of our land," he wrote. "So long, however, as aliens fail to obtain and maintain citizenship by naturalization, they remain subject to the plenary power of Congress to expel them under the sovereign right to determine what noncitizens shall be permitted to remain within our borders."[147]

"Detention is necessarily a part of this deportation procedure," Reed wrote. "Otherwise, aliens arrested for deportation would have opportunities to hurt the United States during the pendency of deportation proceedings."[148] Since some foreigners would pose such a threat to the United States, Congress placed the discretion to grant or deny bail in the hands of the attorney general.[149] As the purpose of the McCarran Act was "to deport all alien Communists as a menace to the security of the United States," he held that "the discretion as to bail in the Attorney General was certainly broad enough to justify his detention to all these parties without bail as a menace to the public interest."[150] Reed concluded that the "refusal of bail in these cases is not arbitrary or capricious, or an abuse of power" and that "there is no denial of the due process of the Fifth Amendment under circumstances where there is reasonable apprehension of hurt from aliens charged with a philosophy of violence against this Government."[151]

In *Shaughnessy v. Mezei* (1953), a 5–4 decision, the Supreme Court affirmed the denial of reentry to the United States to a foreign noncitizen under the attorney general's discretionary authority.[152] Hungarian immigrant Ignatz Mezei had lived in the United States for twenty-five years. After leaving the United States to visit his family, he was subsequently denied reentry. The attorney general ordered Mezei's "temporary exclusion to be made permanent without a hearing before a board of special inquiry" on the basis of "confidential" evidence, which he refused to disclose because it "would be prejudicial to the public interest."[153] All other countries, including Hungary, refused to admit him, so Mezei was left stranded on Ellis Island for nearly two years, unable to leave, while also prevented from entering the United States.

Writing for the majority, Justice Clark upheld Mezei's denial of reentry and the attorney general's discretion under the plenary power doctrine. Clark acknowledged that if Mezei was being deported, he was entitled to a hearing, but he insisted that Mezei was not being *deported*; rather, he was being *excluded* from the United States. Congress did not provide for a hearing in exclusion cases; exclusion was left to the discretion of the attorney general. "That exclusion by the United States plus other nations' inhospitality results in present hardship cannot be ignored," Clark wrote. "Whatever our individual estimate of that policy and the fears on which it rests, respondent's right to enter the United States depends on the congressional will, and courts cannot substitute their judgment for the legislative mandate."[154]

Justice Jackson wrote a scathing dissenting opinion. "It is inconceivable to me that this measure of simple justice and fair dealing would menace the security of this country. No one can make me believe that we are that far gone."[155] Referring to the use of confidential evidence, Jackson added, "This man, who seems to have led a life of unrelieved insignificance, must have been astonished to find himself suddenly putting the Government of the United States in such fear that it was afraid to tell him why it was afraid of him."[156]

Jackson acknowledged that the law placed "more restrictions on the alien than on the citizen," but he insisted that the "basic fairness in hearing procedures does not vary with the status of the accused. If they would be unfair to citizens, we cannot defend the fairness of them when applied to the more helpless and handicapped alien."[157] Jackson also expressed his concern over the use of national security and fear of Communism as means to justify any ends. "I have not been one to discount the Communist evil," he wrote. "But my apprehensions about the security of our form of government are about equally aroused by those who refuse to recognize the dangers of Communism and those who will not see danger in anything else."[158]

Rolling back McCarranism

By the end of 1954, Senator McCarthy had been publicly discredited and censured by the Senate, and Senator McCarran had died. Under Chief Justice Earl Warren, the Supreme Court began to roll back anti-Communist restrictions under McCarranism and help bring an end to McCarthyism. The court also focused its attention on ideological deportation, as well as detention. It clarified previous decisions and definitions of "membership" and provided more procedural steps for the government and more safeguards for foreigners within the United States.

While it did not overturn *Carlson v. Landon,* the Supreme Court curbed the use of supervisory parole of deportees as informers under the conditions of their parole. In *United States v. Witkovich* (1957), a 6–2 decision (Justice Charles Whittaker did not take part in the decision), the court held that immigration officials could no longer inquire as to the deportees' activities, associations, and habits. Writing for the majority, Justice Felix Frankfurter rejected the government's contention that "the eloquent breadth" of the supervisory parole clause in the McCarran-Walter Act granted the attorney general unlimited, absolute discretion in information inquiries from parolees.[159] "Congress did not authorize that official to elicit information that could not serve as a basis for confining an alien's activities," he wrote. "In providing for the release of aliens convicted of willful failure to depart, [Congress] specifically requires courts to inquire into both the effect of the alien's release upon national security and the likelihood of his continued undesirable conduct."[160] Thus, immigration officials were allowed to gather only information relevant to the deportee's parole, including whereabouts for the purposes of supervision and security, and the location to effect eventual deportation.[161]

Also in 1957, the Supreme Court dismissed a deportation order for former membership in the Communist Party. Charles Rowoldt, a German citizen, had joined the Communist Party in 1935 during the Great Depression.[162]

Rowoldt had joined the party, not because he did not like living under a democracy, but instead, because of widespread unemployment. "We had to fight for something to eat and clothes and shelter," he stated. "We were not thinking then—anyways the fellows around me—of overthrowing anything. We wanted something to eat, and something to crawl into."[163] Rowoldt said that the few Communist meetings he attended in 1935 did not discuss overthrowing the government. "All they talked about was fighting for the daily needs. That is why we never thought much of joining those parties in those days."[164]

In *Rowoldt v. Perfetto* (1957), a 5–4 decision, the Supreme Court dismissed Rowoldt's deportation under the McCarran Act. Writing for the majority again, Justice Frankfurter distinguished this case from *Galvan v. Press* (1952), where he had upheld the deportation of Juan Galvan, a Mexican citizen and former member of the Communist Party, under the McCarran Act. Frankfurter had argued that, while Galvan had not advocated the violent overthrow of government, he was "aware that he was joining an organization known as the Communist Party which operates as a distinct and active political organization," and that this awareness when joining was sufficient grounds for deportation.[165] In this case, Frankfurter held that Rowoldt's membership in the Communist Party was devoid of any "political implications." Rowoldt's description of the motivation for his membership lacked a "meaningful association" with the Communist Party, which Frankfurter declared was required in order to deport.[166]

This new "meaningful association" requirement was reminiscent of Louis F. Post's interpretation of membership during the deportations delirium in 1920, which he had used to prevent deportations. This requirement now provided a significant hurdle to ordering ideological deportations for brief memberships in the Communist Party and Communist-front organizations, which had served as the basis for deportation orders throughout the past decade.

The Supreme Court further clarified "meaningful association" in *Gastelum-Quinones v. Kennedy* (1963). Writing for the majority, in a 5–4 decision, Justice Arthur Goldberg dismissed Jose Maria Gastelum-Quinones's deportation order for lack of a "meaningful association" with the Communist Party. Evidence of dues payments and meeting attendance was insufficient.[167]

Goldberg required the government to prove that the foreigner had a meaningful association with the Communist Party "either directly, by showing that he was, during the time of his membership, sensible to the Party's nature as a political organization, or indirectly, by showing that he engaged in

Party activities to a degree substantially supporting an inference of his awareness of the Party's political aspect."[168] Goldberg concluded by stating, "Deportation is a drastic sanction, one which can destroy lives and disrupt families," and "the ultimate burden [of proof] in deportation cases such as this is on the Government," not on the foreigner.[169]

Gastelum-Quinones v. Kennedy would mark the beginning of the end to the Justice Department's fifteen-year crusade to deport foreigners for past membership in the Communist Party or Communist-front organizations. In 1954, sixty-one were deported; then the number dropped to thirty in 1955, to seven in 1959, and to four in 1960.[170] This judicial curb on ideological deportation also coincided with the Supreme Court beginning to strike down restrictions on fundamental rights including travel, advocacy, and association, and its establishment of more speech-protective legal standards for expression.

In *Yates v. United States* (1957), the Supreme Court declared the conviction of a group of Communist Party members under the Smith Act unconstitutional under the First Amendment. Overturning *Dennis v. United States*, the court held that merely advocating or teaching Communism was protected speech under the First Amendment and could not be restricted.[171] The ECLC celebrated a victory in *Kent v. Dulles* (1958), when the court declared refusing to issue US passports based on alleged beliefs or past or present Communist Party membership violated American citizens' fundamental right to travel under the Fifth Amendment.[172] During the 1960s, the court continued to chip away at the suppression of Communist speech and free expression and association. The court struck down loyalty oaths,[173] and in *Albertson v. Subversive Activities Control Board* (1965), it held that the McCarran Act's registration requirement was a violation of the Fifth Amendment's privilege against self-incrimination.[174]

In *Lamont v. Postmaster General* (1965), the Supreme Court expanded its interpretation of First Amendment protections to include the right to receive information and ideas when it struck down a restriction on the delivery of Communist material and propaganda through the mail.[175] In *Red Lion Broadcasting Co. v. FCC* (1969), the court included the public's right to hear as well as to speak.[176] The court also extended First Amendment protections to American public schools, holding that neither "students [nor] teachers shed their constitutional rights to freedom of expression or speech at the schoolhouse gate."[177] American universities had been targets of McCarthyism. Professors faced anti-Communist investigations, firings, and blacklists.[178] The court now characterized academic freedom as a special concern of the

First Amendment. "The vigilant protection of constitutional freedoms is nowhere more vital than in the community of American schools."[179] It declared that "the nation's future depends upon leaders trained through wide exposure to that robust exchange of ideas."[180]

The Supreme Court also finally severed belief and advocacy from calls to action and actual threats of violence and provided First Amendment protection to radical expression and association. In *Brandenburg v. Ohio* (1969), the court returned to the syndicalism acts passed to crush the Industrial Workers of the World and used to suppress Communist speech and association. The court struck down an Ohio syndicalism statute's advocacy and association provisions as unconstitutional under the First Amendment. It explicitly overturned *Whitney v. California* (1927) and established a speech-protective advocacy test. Combining Justice Oliver Wendell Holmes Jr.'s "clear and present danger" test and Judge Learned Hand's "direct incitement" test, the court issued its new test to determine whether advocacy was protected. The government could no longer restrict mere advocacy, but only speech "directed to inciting and producing imminent lawless action and is likely to incite or produce such action."[181]

Within a decade, the Supreme Court had provided speech and association protections and created significant burdens of proof for the government to meet in order to ideologically deport. Yet, the court had not included ideological exclusion in this period of revision and reform. Visa denials under the McCarran-Walter Act continued. In the 1960s, a new president and his administration sought to end ideological exclusion with the promise of transforming the United States from a closed society into an open one. The vestiges of McCarranism stood in his way.

Attempting to Open a Closed Society

"I'm fed up with the image we have as a police state. I keep seeing reports about excluding visitors because of their political views. We act like a closed society," remarked President John F. Kennedy to Abba Schwartz in 1962.[182] The president had just appointed Schwartz, a liberal Washington lawyer specializing in refugee policy and law, to become the new head of the Bureau of Security and Consular Affairs, created by the McCarran-Walter Act to issue passports and visas within the State Department. Kennedy was an outspoken critic of the McCarran-Walter Act and had opposed its passage, and while in the Senate, he wrote *A Nation of Immigrants*, celebrating immigrants' contribution to the United States.[183] As president, Kennedy advocated for the elimination of national origins quotas, an increase in refugee admissions, and an easing of the foreign relations tensions and national embarrassment due to ideological exclusions.[184]

After World War II, Congress passed legislation addressing admission of refugees, including the Displaced Persons Act of 1948 and the Refugee Relief Act of 1953. The provisions within these acts were narrow, including specific countries and numerical quotas, and they focused on admitting those who had faced persecution under the Nazis and those fleeing Communism. Communists were excluded from entry under these acts, as well as under the McCarran-Walter Act, and refugees were required to undergo screenings and evaluations to ensure they posed no threat to the United States, including an ideological threat. Passed during the Cold War, these acts sought to project to the world, and to the Soviet Union, an American identity as an anti-Communist nation and a refuge to those seeking freedom.[185]

Kennedy had fought for admission of refugees while in the Senate, and now as president, he focused his efforts not just on admission, but on passing refugee policy and legislation to address resettlement and asylum in order to provide assistance to these newcomers once they arrived in the United States and to set them on the path to becoming American citizens who would contribute to American society. Kennedy also pushed to broaden refugee legislation to reflect not just an anti-Communist nation to the world, but also an open society.[186]

One of his first acts as president was to establish the Cuban Refugee Program in 1961. It provided additional funds to support resettlement for refugees who fled Cuba, including employment opportunities and health services. The Migration and Refugee Assistance Act of 1962 provided funds for the president to administer to support refugees for the "essentials of life" and included resettlement and asylum protection for those fearing persecution if they returned. The act did not define refugees as specifically those who fled Communist countries, but rather included all those who, "because of persecution or fear of persecution on account of race, religion, or political opinion, fled from a nation or area in the Western Hemisphere."[187]

In his book *The Open Society*, Schwartz wrote that the President had not just focused on refugees but had also directed Schwartz to eliminate visa restrictions and denials to foreign visitors with unorthodox political views. Kennedy, like Truman, considered ideological exclusion a form of "thought control."[188] According to Schwartz, Kennedy believed that such visits could be mutually beneficial. "It was all the more important, he said, for the anti-American foreigner, whether he be a scientist, writer, lecturer, educator, artist or politician 'to exchange ideas and information with our public and to be exposed to our free society.'"[189]

Yet, bureaucrats in the State Department did not share Kennedy's perspective or embrace his impetus for change. According to Schwartz, those offices still contained anti-Communist senior officers who were appointed to satisfy and appease McCarthy or who had close connections with conservatives in Congress.[190] He also described the fear that had pervaded the State Department since the beginning of the Cold War, which he called its "repressive McCarthy hangover."[191] Firings and investigations of alleged Communists had plagued the department and created an atmosphere in which bureaucrats overcompensated in demonstrating their anti-Communism by denying passports and refusing to grant visas.[192]

The McCarran Act had helped turn the visa office into a gatekeeper responsible for keeping the United States safe from foreign Communists. This security function within the visa office led to "security neuroses" and to the automatic refusal of visas to most of the applicants who fell under ideological exclusion provisions because of past membership, without considering any other factors or the purpose of their visit.[193] HUAC and the Senate Internal Security Subcommittee (SISS) also took a special interest in visa denials, and to some bureaucrats, granting a visa to a foreigner was not worth having to endure testifying and being questioned before Congress and potentially losing their jobs.[194] Schwartz's observations were consistent with Edward Shils's critiques in the *Bulletin of the Atomic Scientists* in 1952.

Schwartz decided to use his power and discretion under the law to prevent ideological exclusion and visa denials. The McCarran-Walter Act included a waiver provision, enabling a foreigner to obtain a visa despite inadmissibility, if admission was in the national interest and if it would not pose a threat to national security. The foreign visitor could request and receive a waiver for temporary admission to the United States, with a recommendation from the secretary of state and approval from the attorney general.[195] Schwartz and Attorney General Robert F. Kennedy worked together to recommend and grant waivers. Cultural exchange agreements made during the Eisenhower administration ensured that visas from the Eastern Bloc were typically not a problem.[196] Trouble arose with those from other countries and critics of US foreign policy.

Just before Schwartz's appointment, the State Department had refused to issue a visa to Mexican novelist and essayist Carlos Fuentes to come to the United States to participate in a televised debate on the Alliance for Progress program in Latin America.[197] It claimed that Fuentes was ineligible to receive a visa "on security grounds"; because he might be a Communist, it would not "be in the national interest" to allow him to visit the United States.[198] Schwartz believed the real reason for the denial was that the State Department feared Fuentes would publicly criticize the Alliance for Progress program and embarrass the American government during his visit.[199] Scholars and writers denounced his exclusion and rebuked the State Department. They warned that barring Fuentes would damage the nation's reputation among intellectuals abroad and would serve only to undermine the Alliance for Progress program.[200] Schwartz recalled a professor of Latin American history in the United States who wrote to the State Department, "If this is the sanctimonious pomposity which guides the Department of State, I fully understand why the crowds of Lima and Caracas spat on our Vice-President and why Fidel Castro has remained in power so long. I think the facts of the matter indicate that the granting of a visa to Mr. Carlos Fuentes IS decidedly in the national interest. No reply required."[201]

In 1964, Fuentes applied for another visa to visit the United States.[202] Fuentes was still deemed inadmissible under the McCarran-Walter Act, but now Schwartz was in the administration. He recommended a waiver, Kennedy granted it, and Fuentes was admitted.[203]

Schwartz was then called to testify before HUAC and SISS regarding his recommendation of waivers to foreigners deemed inadmissible under the ideological exclusion provisions of the McCarran-Walter Act. He would now join Louis F. Post and Frances Perkins on the list of public officials who had to defend their exercise of discretion in refusing to deport or to exclude foreigners based on their beliefs, associations, or expressions before Congress. Schwartz speculated that HUAC took a special interest in visas not only because its members wanted to continue the State Department policies of the 1950s, but also because they were anxious about their role and were trying to stay relevant amidst the end of McCarthyism.[204]

Like Perkins, Schwartz also found himself the target of a conservative, anti-Communist congressman's critique and calls for termination from his position. Congressman Michael A. Feighan (D-OH) had succeeded Francis Walter as chairman of the House Subcommittee on Immigration. Feighan had been an outspoken critic of Kennedy's and Schwartz's efforts. According to Schwartz, in 1964, Feighan was livid when Schwartz refused to revoke a visa granted to British actor Richard Burton on grounds that, if admitted to the United States, Burton would "imperil the morals of American youth." Feighan later wrote to President Lyndon Johnson and asked him to fire Schwartz for committing perjury in testimony before his subcommittee or for "gross and inexcusable incompetence in discharge of his official responsibilities."[205]

In 1966, Schwartz learned that the Johnson administration had developed a reorganization plan that included abolishing the Bureau of Security and Consular Affairs, and thus would eliminate Schwartz's position in the State Department.[206] While the administration stated that cutting the Bureau was a cost-saving measure made for budgetary reasons, Schwartz speculated that, given the timing of the approval of the plan, the bureau's elimination was due to a deal struck between Johnson and Feighan for votes in the House and Senate to ensure the successful passage of the Hart-Celler Act of 1965, which eliminated the discriminatory national origins quotas passed in the Johnson-Reed Act of 1924.[207] Rather than wait for Congress to pass the reorganization plan and lose his job, Schwartz resigned. The plan was never passed.[208]

The Cold War revived and continued the anti-Communist repression of the late 1930s, as the United States presented an anti-Communist identity to the world through its domestic and international policies and its use of ideological exclusion and deportation to suppress dissent and prevent Communist subversion within the country. Public officials used old laws such as the Smith Act and new ones such as the McCarran Act of 1950 and McCarran-Walter Act of 1952 to criminalize Communist expression and establish guilt by association. The detention, denaturalization, and deportation of foreign-born residents and visa denials to foreign visitors under these laws did not result in large numbers of expulsions or exclusions, but they did serve to intimidate and strike fear in foreigners, who were under the threat of being barred or ejected from the United States, and many Americans shared their fear, as well as their humiliation.

The McCarran-Walter Act granted the attorney general, as well as immigration and consular officials, tremendous discretion to exclude or deport, which renewed perpetual questions and criticism about ultimate discretion and authority to admit, bar, or expel held by the executive branch and resulted in congressional interrogations of those who used their discretion and authority to refuse to deport or exclude. The motivations behind and implementations of ideological restrictions faced increased scrutiny by the public as well. Some argued these restrictions did not protect the United States from subversion but rather were a form of subversion themselves, undermining the nation's values and identity as a free democracy, damaging its reputation abroad, and inhibiting free exchange, inquiry, and scientific progress at home.

By the late 1960s, the United States was still entrenched in the Cold War, and it was continuing its efforts to fight Communism abroad. While anti-Communism persisted in American culture, government, and foreign relations, McCarthyism had not returned. While Abba Schwartz had worked to reduce visa denials to foreign visitors in his determination to fulfill President Kennedy's vision of an open society, ideological exclusion did not end, and the law did not change. The Hart-Celler Act had abolished the discriminatory national origins quotas, but it had also left the McCarran-Walter Act's ideological restrictions intact.

The Supreme Court provided more protections against ideological deportation and denaturalization and abuse of power in detention, but it had also upheld the constitutionality of ideological exclusion and deportation under the plenary power doctrine. Now, the court found itself at a crossroads. For the first time, free speech standards and First Amendment legal precedent would protect the expression and associations that had served as the basis for ideological exclusion and deportation under federal immigration restrictions. In *United States ex rel. Turner v. Williams* (1904), Chief Justice Melville Fuller had referred to Congress's determination that anarchist speech presented a "bad tendency" and upheld John Turner's exclusion under the Alien Immigration Act of 1903. In *Harisiades v. Shaughnessy* (1952), Justice Jackson lamented upholding Harisiades's deportation, because Congress and the court had determined Communism posed a grave danger and threat to national security. The Warren Court had replaced bad tendency with the speech-protective incitement test, and the restrictions on Communist expression and association had been held unconstitutional. When faced with a new constitutional challenge to ideological exclusion, would the court choose to apply First Amendment standards, or would it continue to interpret ideological exclusion as an immigration issue and insulate it from substantive judicial review under the plenary power doctrine?

In 1968, Richard M. Nixon was elected president of the United States. A month after his inauguration in 1969, Carlos Fuentes was en route to Mexico on a passenger ship, when he was denied permission to land in Puerto Rico, because he was deemed "undesirable" by the Justice Department and excludable under the McCarran-Walter Act.[209] An editorial in the *New York Times* denounced his exclusion: "One sure way to tarnish the United States is for some bureaucrat to decide that a writer, painter or other artists is an 'undesirable alien' because of his work or beliefs. Politicizing literature is a common practice for authoritarian governments; it should not become one for this country."[210]

Three years after his resignation from the Johnson administration, Abba Schwartz reflected on his public service and his push to help create an open society. Commenting on Fuentes's exclusion by the Nixon administration, he hoped it was "an isolated instance" and not a return to the restrictive policies of the 1950s.[211] Schwartz's hopes would soon be dashed.

6

The Return of McCarranism

IN SEPTEMBER 1969, a forty-six-year-old Belgian Marxist economist named Ernest Mandel applied for a visa to visit the United States. Students at Stanford University had invited Mandel to attend a conference on "Technology and the Third World" in October and to participate in a debate with renowned Canadian-born Keynesian economist and Harvard University Professor John Kenneth Galbraith. While Mandel awaited his visa, other colleges and universities invited him to speak on their campuses, including Amherst College, Princeton University, Columbia University, the New School for Social Research, and the Massachusetts Institute of Technology. Mandel accepted these invitations. Yet, Mandel would never receive a visa to attend the Stanford conference and debate Galbraith, or to speak at those universities and colleges. Under the Nixon administration, Mandel was ideologically excluded and barred from entry to the United States.

The presidency of Richard M. Nixon, who rose to prominence in the McCarthy era, marked the return of McCarranism and the use of ideological exclusion to suppress the threat of dissent. The motivations behind the Nixon administration's decisions and use of ultimate discretion to exclude or deport, including in the case of Ernest Mandel, were political and self-interested. These exclusions and deportations were part of the Nixon administration's abuse of power and use of retaliation to stifle critics, punish perceived enemies, win supporters, and secure Nixon's reelection in 1972.

The return of McCarranism under the Nixon administration did not go unnoticed. It revived past arguments against ideological exclusion as a form of censorship, infringing on First Amendment rights, undermining values of free speech and democracy, and depicting the United States as a fearful, insecure nation. The Supreme Court once again confronted the question of

155

whether to evaluate the constitutionality of explicit ideological restrictions under immigration or First Amendment legal precedent. While Mandel was not the only one who faced exclusion under the Nixon administration, his case resulted in the most important and influential legal strategies and constitutional challenges to ideological exclusion in the United States.

Ernest Mandel

Ernest Ezra Mandel was born in Frankfurt, Germany, in 1923 and raised in an educated, secular Jewish family in Antwerp, Belgium. As a teenager, Mandel joined Antwerp's branch of the Trotskyist Revolutionary Socialist Party and then the Belgian resistance movement in World War II. During the German occupation, Mandel was arrested for distributing anti-Fascist, anti-capitalist leaflets to German soldiers in 1944. Deported to Germany, Mandel passed through "half a dozen prison and work camps" before being liberated by the Americans in 1945. As a "resistance fighter, a Jew and a Trotskyist, despised by Stalinist fellow prisoners," Mandel believed that luck played a role in his survival, but he credited his ability to communicate and talk politics with his German guards, in addition to other prisoners, as the key to his self-preservation.[1] These experiences convinced Mandel of the power of free exchange and to become an ardent internationalist.[2]

In the 1950s and 1960s, Mandel was a leader in the Trotskyist Fourth International. He was a passionate lecturer and a prolific writer, publishing dozens of articles on Marxism and economics and editing the Belgian Socialist newspaper *La Gauche* (the Left). Mandel wrote *Marxist Economic Theory*, published in French in 1962 and in English in 1968. The two-volume book described and promoted the theory and received international attention and praise.[3]

In the late 1960s, Mandel served as a generational bridge between members of the Old and New Left, encouraging antiwar activists to unite with workers in a common cause for reform and revolution. In support of the May 1968 protests in France, Mandel participated in demonstrations and spoke to students and to protest leader Daniel Cohn-Bendit. Like Cohn-Bendit, Mandel was expelled and barred from France because of his involvement in the protests.[4]

Mandel traveled to the United States twice in the 1960s, first in March 1962, under a "working journalist" visa, and again in September 1968, with his wife Gisela, under a "tourist" visa.[5] During his 1968 visit, Mandel delivered lectures at over a dozen universities and colleges. At the International As-

Ernest Mandel, 1973
Sueddeutsche Zeitung Photo / Alamy Stock Photo.

sembly of Revolutionary Student Movements, sponsored by the Columbia University Students for a Democratic Society (SDS), Mandel addressed 600 people. In his lecture, "The Revolutionary Student Movement: Theory and Practice," Mandel urged students to broaden their protests beyond their campuses by including working-class demands and to ground their activism in Marxism.[6]

During both visits, Mandel was able to enter and leave the United States freely (albeit under surveillance), and, while there was some press coverage of his lectures, there was no protest, violent riot, or campus unrest in response to his remarks. So Mandel was shocked when his visa application was denied in September 1969. Mandel soon learned that he had become ensnared in the ideological exclusion provisions of the McCarran-Walter Act. Mandel was ineligible to receive a visa under two provisions within Section 212(a)(28) of the McCarran-Walter Act: (1) foreigners who "advocate the economic, international, and governmental doctrines of world communism"; and (2) foreigners who "write or publish . . . the economic, international, and governmental doctrines of world communism."[7] Unbeknownst to Mandel, the visas he had received in 1962 and 1968 were obtained under waivers of inadmissibility for temporary admission. He had received these waivers with a recommendation from the secretary of state and the approval from the attorney general, which was at his discretion.[8] This time, in 1969, the new Nixon administration had refused to grant a waiver and had excluded Mandel.

"The Pragmatist"

During his campaign, Nixon pledged to bring an honorable end to the Vietnam War and "law and order" to the United States.[9] Nixon had attempted to appeal to all Americans, including those who opposed the Vietnam War. Yet, almost a year into his presidency, Nixon dismissed these vocal critics and protesters in the streets and on college campuses as a minority, and he now claimed to represent the "Silent Majority," whom he called upon to support him.[10]

Nixon chose his close friend and campaign manager, John N. Mitchell, as his attorney general. Mitchell, a fifty-six-year-old New York municipal bonds lawyer, took a tough stance against student protesters, as well as leftist organizations and their leaders.[11] Mitchell would soon come to embody Nixon's "law and order" campaign promise, which he immediately sought to fulfill.[12]

Mitchell had little patience or sympathy for the student protesters and antiwar demonstrators on and off college campuses and called for their arrest. The Black Panthers, the Weathermen, and members of the New Left disgusted Mitchell. He authorized surveillance of these groups and pushed for the use of warrantless wiretaps in the interest of "national security" and to thwart "domestic subversion."[13] While his predecessor, Ramsey Clark, had chosen not to file charges against the leaders of the protests outside the Democratic National Convention in 1968, Mitchell worked with US attorneys in Chicago to prosecute eight men for conspiracy and incitement to riot, including Students for a Democratic Society (SDS) leader Tom Hayden, Black Panther Bobby Seale, and Abbie Hoffman and Jerry Rubin, founders of the Youth International Party (known as the "Yippies").[14] The "Chicago Eight" were indicted by a federal grand jury on March 20, 1969. Mitchell personally announced their indictment.[15]

In December 1969, a few weeks after the massive antiwar Vietnam Moratorium demonstrations, Newsweek published a short profile of Mitchell entitled "The Pragmatist." It described Mitchell as the "chief architect of Richard Nixon's victory" and the one cabinet member who had Nixon's "ear and confidence." The profile mentioned Mitchell's reverence for "the virtues of pragmatism." When describing his Justice Department, he advised, "Watch what we do instead of what we say."[16]

Pointing to his delays on desegregating schools in Mississippi and his tough stance on antiwar demonstrators, Mitchell's critics viewed his Justice Department as "tinged with more politics than pragmatism." Recounting a television interview with Mitchell's wife, Martha, in which she stated that her husband would like to take "some of the liberals in this country and change them for the Russian Communists," *Newsweek* quoted Mitchell's amendment: "Transpose the word 'liberal' into 'violence-prone militant radicals.' I would be delighted to change them for some of the academically inclined Marxist Communists." Noting Mitchell's recent visa denial to Belgian Marxist economist Ernest Mandel, *Newsweek* added, "But as the Attorney General urges, Mitchell's actions bear more watching than his words."[17]

Under the McCarran-Walter Act, neither the secretary of state nor the attorney general was required to disclose the reason behind refusing to recommend a waiver or refusing to grant one. Mandel's Immigration and Naturalization Service (INS) file, obtained under the Freedom of Information Act (FOIA), includes statements from State and Justice Department officials providing the reasons for Mandel's receipt of waivers in 1962 and 1968. In an internal report on Mandel in 1962, the US embassy in Brussels described Mandel's reputation in Belgium as a "left-wing anti-communist Socialist who is hated and feared by Belgian communists." It also noted that many pro-American Socialists in the government were associated with *La Gauche* and many prominent intellectuals and politicians had made "positive statements" regarding Mandel.

The report urged an immediate waiver for Mandel, asserting that the "denial of visa would result in most adverse public relations and would severely damage U.S. prestige in socialist and intellectual circles in Belgium and West Europe in general." In granting the waiver, the Justice Department added, "It is clearly in the U.S. interest to avoid the unfortunate publicity that would be caused by a denial of the waiver."[18] In 1968, Mandel received a waiver for the same reasons.[19] Yet, in 1969, Attorney General Mitchell and the Justice Department apparently did not share these concerns over adverse public relations and tarnishing America's prestige.

In communication with Alta Fowler, the administrator of the Bureau of Security and Consular Affairs in Brussels, Mandel claimed that he was unaware that he had previously obtained visas in 1962 and 1968 through the McCarran-Walter Act's waiver provision.[20] During his 1968 visit, Mandel had attended and spoken at a cocktail party, where the hosts had raised funds for the legal defense of participants in the May 1968 student protests in France. Mandel insisted he was not directly involved in the fundraising.[21] According to Fowler, upon receiving a waiver, a foreign visitor received a conditional visa, which required the visitor to adhere to special restrictions on travel activities while in the United States. Mandel had violated these restrictions by deviating from his itinerary and engaging in activities beyond the stated purpose of his trip. Therefore, Secretary of State William P. Rogers had recommended that Mandel not receive a waiver of inadmissibility.[22]

Mandel attempted to assuage the State Department's concerns.[23] He explained that since he did not know that he had received his previous visas through the waiver provision, he was also unaware of the special restrictions on his activities during his visit to the United States. While Mandel wrote, "Personally, I believe that such promises are inappropriate and contrary to the elementary principles of liberty," he promised Fowler that if he received a visa, he would disclose his full itinerary to the State Department and would not to stray from it.[24]

In light of this new information, the State Department changed its mind. "In view of [Mandel's assurances that he will now follow the waiver requirements] in the interest of free expression of opinion and exchange of ideas, we recommended a waiver for Mr. Mandel."[25] The attorney general would now have to grant the waiver for Mandel to obtain a visa. While in most cases granting a waiver upon the secretary of state's recommendation was *pro forma*, it was not in this case. Mitchell refused to grant the waiver. A few weeks later, Mitchell appeared in a television interview. When asked if he had discussed the Mandel case with Rogers, Mitchell snapped, "Hell no!"[26]

Leaks to the press attributed to sources within the State Department described a rift between Mitchell and Rogers over the Mandel case.[27] Rogers and Under Secretary of State Elliot Richardson had sent a recommendation to the Justice Department to grant a waiver, which, they argued, was "in the national interest."[28] After Mitchell rejected their recommendation, these State Department sources added, "It was clear in advance that the Attorney General did not share their opinion on how the visa-granting power should be used."[29]

The State Department publicly announced Mitchell's final decision to deny the waiver for Mandel, while the Justice Department refused to comment. The *New York Times* reported that in announcing Mitchell's decision, the State Department "took the unusual step of disassociating the Secretary of State from it, stating that the department had recommended that Dr. Mandel be allowed to make his scheduled visit."[30] There was no attempt to "paper over the differences among two Cabinet members, as is usually done once a decision is made final."[31] One State Department staffer commented, "It's not up to us to take the blame for their argument."[32] In the *Newsweek* profile of

Mitchell, another State Department staffer recalled that when discussing Mandel's exclusion, Rogers had asked, "Why should we be afraid of this man and his ideas?"[33]

While initially refusing to comment, the Justice Department would not stay silent forever. When asked about Mandel a few days after the State Department's announcement, Mitchell replied, "I don't think we need to import any more trouble than we have." Citing Mandel's exclusion from France, Mitchell described him as having "quite a track record in this country," and went on to state that it "would be most appropriate that [Mandel] remain in Belgium and not return to this country to carry out some of the activities he did on his previous trips."[34]

INS Associate Commissioner James F. Greene answered most of the inquiries regarding the reasons for Mandel's exclusion on behalf of the Justice Department. Greene insisted that Mandel's straying from his itinerary during his 1968 visit when he attended the cocktail party fundraiser justified his exclusion and represented "a flagrant abuse of the opportunities afforded him to express his views in this country." Greene claimed that Mandel had "sought to obtain money for the assistance of those involved in the student-labor riots in France during the Spring of 1968, responsibility for inciting which lies heavily on him, and for which he has been barred from readmission by that country." While Mandel was an academic and had presented his ideas, Greene wrote, "He spent as much or more of his time in covert association with individuals and organizations dedicated to the promotion of violence and the systematic undermining of our social and political systems."[35]

Greene insisted that Mandel's exclusion was not a form of censorship and a threat to free expression and that the Justice Department had denied only two waivers out of "over a thousand such requests involving the same or similar grounds of inadmissibility" since January 1969.[36] "The mere recital of these figures serves to rebut any charge that we seek to erect a barrier against the free interchange of ideas and the advocacy, within proper bounds and by proper means, of social, economic, and political philosophies which vary from our own and which are repugnant to the vast majority of our people."[37]

Greene's responses were not only defensive, but also disingenuous. Mandel was excluded, not because he had strayed from his itinerary in 1968, but because of his beliefs and associations and a fear of what he might say and to whom on college campuses. Mitchell did not want to "import any more trouble than we have," and Greene's emphasis on Mandel's alleged "covert" activities and incitement of protests in France revealed a deep concern over

Mandel's return. The Justice Department did indeed "seek to erect a barrier against the free interchange of ideas" between Mandel and students and professors in the United States. And this barrier was part of the Nixon administration's efforts to suppress dissent on and off college campuses.

"Silly, Stupid, Irrational and also Grievously Bad Politics"

Critics of the Nixon administration's use of the McCarran-Walter Act to exclude Mandel compared it to McCarthyism in the 1950s and a sign of a return of McCarranism. They reiterated previous arguments that ideological exclusion was censorship, and it reflected a nation that lacked confidence in its people and undermined its ideals. The attorney general's refusal to admit Mandel was an abuse of governmental power that threatened academic inquiry and exchange and would damage the international reputation and credibility of the United States.

The American professors who had invited Mandel to speak at their institutions and participate in conferences were outraged by his exclusion, but they were determined to hear Mandel. The Stanford students who had organized the conference on "Technology and the Third World" did not cancel the event. Instead, they arranged for Mandel to tape-record the lecture and mail it to them. In lieu of a debate, Mandel responded to Galbraith via a trans-Atlantic telephone call; the call lasted thirty minutes and cost $100.[38]

Before he rebutted Mandel's argument that "Western capitalism was responsible for the undeveloped state of most nations of the Southern Hemisphere,"[39] Galbraith addressed Mandel's exclusion: "It seems to me that the failure to give Ernest Mandel a visa is silly, stupid, irrational and also grievously bad politics. It angers everyone involved. It angers the Belgians. It angers the Americans and so far as I can see doesn't please anybody."[40] Galbraith urged the audience to write to the State Department condemning this "stupid action."[41] A letter to the *New York Times*, signed by Noam Chomsky, Arno Mayer, Richard Poirier, S. E. Luria, Richard Falk, Susan Sontag, Robert Paul Wolff, and Robert Heilbroner, characterized Mandel's exclusion as an "egregious violation of academic freedom." As Galbraith had instructed his audience, the letter signers encouraged readers to write to the State Department to protest Mandel's visa denial.[42]

By then, the State Department had recommended a waiver for Mandel and the Justice Department had refused to grant the waiver. Academics then shifted their protests and petitions from the secretary of state to the attorney general. In a letter addressed to Mitchell, Princeton University President

Robert F. Goheen wrote to express his "distress" over Mitchell's decision to exclude Mandel.[43] Identifying Princeton as one of the universities that had invited Mandel to speak on its campus, Goheen argued that excluding him would do "grave injury to the very idea of the free society which we prize."[44] He contended that allowing Mandel to come and speak was in "keeping with the tradition of open inquiry and free expression which has long been a keystone of the intellectual life of the Western world, as well as a basic tenet of our nation."[45]

Alan Simpson, the president of Vassar College, also wrote a letter to Mitchell protesting Mandel's exclusion. He argued that Mitchell's action "strikes at the heart of the freedom of an academic institution to provide an open forum for the free interplay of ideas." Simpson characterized Mitchell's use of power and discretion as "inappropriate" and an echo of the McCarthy era. Simpson wrote that this old approach would "not only discredit our political system but will very likely increase the alienation so many of our college students and faculty already feel toward their government."[46]

Professors, students, teaching fellows, administrative staff, and employees from the Massachusetts Institute of Technology, Boston University, and Harvard University signed a petition protesting Mandel's exclusion.[47] They called on Mitchell to permit Mandel to enter the country to speak at a conference scheduled for December 4, 1969.[48] There were 210 signatures.

While many American academics focused their protests against Mandel's exclusion as a violation of academic freedom and free exchange and expression, some also voiced concern about the damage it would do to the nation's reputation by depicting the United States as a fearful, insecure nation. In a long letter to Mitchell, Yale University President Kingman Brewster Jr. urged Mitchell to reconsider his decision. He argued that when "the nation's senior legal officer shows a fear of freedom, I fear for the freedom of the nation. When the freedom at issue is freedom of thoughtful expression, my concern is especially deep." Brewster insisted that only when Mandel is permitted to enter the United States "will the credibility of our government's willingness to take the risk of freedom of thought and expression be restored among the international community of scholars, on the nation's campuses, and to the citizens of the United States."[49]

Norman Birnbaum, a professor of sociology who had invited Mandel to speak at Amherst College, wrote to Mitchell describing his exclusion of Mandel as another step in his "campaign against dissent in America" and a reflection of "a mentality more appropriate to a police state than to American democracy." Birnbaum suggested that Mitchell would have much in common with his counterparts in the Soviet Union, where "politicians are free of the tiresome burdens of criticism from either an opposition party, from universities, or from press or television."[50]

The *New York Times* characterized Mandel's exclusion as an "idiotic decision" that undermined the "credibility of the United States as the defender of freedom of speech and ideas" and proved that "the bad old days of censorship by visa are not yet over." It described the "empty chair" at the Stanford conference as an "embarrassment suffered by this country as a result of this triumph of police over diplomacy, of fear over freedom and of ideological rigidity over democratic common sense."[51] In "McCarranism Revisited," the editors argued that Mitchell had ignored "the damage thus inflicted on the image of America as the defender of freedom of ideas."[52] The *Chicago Daily News* described Mitchell's refusal to grant a waiver as a "fearful policy" and rebuked the Justice Department for trying to "fight the war of ideas with denial and repression."[53] It insisted that the country would only lose in that kind of fight, which would depict the United States as weak and fearful, as opposed to a confident and free nation. "America and Americans, we believe, are secure and strong enough, and correct enough in their ideals, to withstand an ideological onslaught from any quarter. Mitchell evidently thinks otherwise."[54]

While almost all national newspapers supported Mandel's entry to the United States, one exception was the *Chicago Daily Tribune*. It described Mandel as a dangerous radical who was responsible for the May 1968 protests in France and who would encourage revolt and bring revolution to college campuses if allowed entry. It rebuked the State Department for recommending a waiver, while it praised Mitchell's refusal and his exclusion of Mandel.[55]

The press coverage of Mandel's exclusion captured the public's attention, and many concerned citizens wrote to their representatives. In a letter to Congressman Howard W. Robison (R-NY), William Faris wrote that while he was sure that he would disagree with Mandel's point of view, "many Americans, myself included, feel that we should never be prevented from hearing and discussing with advocates of various positions, even if they are foreigners."[56] Faris asked, "Is it now Justice Department policy that there are points of view that it is afraid to let us hear?"[57]

In a telephone interview, Mandel expressed his surprise "at the great interest this visa issue has aroused since I am not at all an international celebrity." He added, "It shows that public opinion in the United States is very much alive to the dangers that threaten our basic freedom."[58]

On November 29, the Socialist Scholars Conference held in New York played a tape-recorded lecture entitled "Revolutionary Strategy in the Imperialist Countries," which Mandel had intended to deliver in person. Mandel stated that his visa denial "demonstrates a lack of confidence on the part of the Nixon administration in the capacity of its supporters to combat Marxism on the battleground of ideas."[59] He assured the audience that he would not have brought "high explosives" into the United States, "but only, as I did before, my revolutionary views which are well known to the public."[60] Mandel asked why the Nixon administration was so afraid of him and his ideas when his books are freely sold in America. "In the nineteenth century the British ruling class, which was sure of itself, permitted Karl Marx to live as an exile in England for almost forty years," Mandel explained. "Times have certainly changed when the most powerful of capitalist governments today refuses a brief visit to an exponent of his doctrines!"[61]

Leonard Boudin

Leonard Boudin, the general counsel for the Emergency Civil Liberties Committee (ECLC), now called the National Emergency Civil Liberties Committee (NECLC),[62] agreed to represent Mandel and challenge his ideological exclusion in court.[63] One of the nation's most prominent civil liberties attorneys, the fifty-seven-year-old Boudin had worked tirelessly to challenge the constitutionality of McCarranism in the 1950s and 1960s.[64]

Boudin's triumphs in the Supreme Court included Kent v. Dulles (1958), which established the right to travel as a fundamental liberty held by American citizens and declared the refusal to issue US passports to US citizens based on their past or present membership in the Communist Party or alleged Communistic beliefs or associations was unconstitutional.[65] Boudin also won in Lamont v. Postmaster General (1965), which established the right to receive information under the First Amendment and struck down a provision authorizing the postmaster to detain "communist political propaganda" sent through the mail.[66]

Boudin's losses in the Supreme Court included Zemel v. Rusk (1965). In this case, the court upheld the secretary of state's refusal to issue a passport to a US citizen who wanted to visit Cuba to "gather information." Distinguishing the case from Kent v. Dulles, the court held that the refusal was based not on the passport applicant's views or associations, but rather on foreign policy and national security concerns, which outweighed the right to travel.[67]

By 1969, Boudin was representing critics of the Vietnam War, such as Dr. Benjamin Spock and civil rights activist Julian Bond, and, like William Kunstler, he would become an important attorney for the New Left. Boudin was appalled to learn of the Nixon administration's return to McCarranism. In a telephone interview, Boudin called Mandel's ideological exclusion under the McCarran-Walter Act as "pure cold-blooded politics" and "an affront to the academic community."[68] He remarked, "It has a Neanderthal quality about it that just isn't 1969."[69]

David Rosenberg started working for Boudin's law firm, Boudin, Rabinowitz, and Standard, as a delivery boy and then as an attorney after he graduated from New York University Law School in 1967. He later formed his own firm and then became a professor at Harvard Law School. Rosenberg devised the legal strategy that challenged Mandel's exclusion under the First Amendment. He relied on the successful legal precedent Boudin had helped establish in *Kent v. Dulles* and *Lamont v. Postmaster General*, while avoiding unsuccessful arguments and the precedent set in *Zemel v. Rusk*. He also used recent Supreme Court decisions articulating the value of academic inquiry and freedom under the First Amendment and establishing a right to hear to bolster his argument that Mandel's exclusion was unconstitutional.[70]

The biggest challenge was *United States ex rel. Turner v. Williams* (1904), which upheld the constitutionality of ideological exclusion under the plenary power doctrine and had stated that foreigners seeking entry did not hold constitutional rights, including under the First Amendment. To overcome this obstacle, Rosenberg decided that Boudin and the NECLC would not only represent Mandel, the foreigner seeking entry, but also the American professors in the United States who had invited him to speak at their campuses. Boudin would argue that the exclusion of a foreigner invited to the United States was a form of censorship and that, by refusing to grant the waiver to Mandel, Mitchell had unconstitutionally violated Americans' right to receive information and to hear under the First Amendment.[71]

Boudin and Rosenberg asked some of the American professors who had invited Mandel to come to the United States to join him in a lawsuit.[72] Boudin also asked the NECLC to create the Ernest Mandel Legal Defense Fund to raise money for the case, as well as public awareness, especially on college campuses.[73] On March 19, 1970, Boudin filed a legal Complaint against Attorney General Mitchell and Secretary of State Rogers in the US District Court for the Eastern District of New York, challenging the constitutionality of the McCarran-Walter Act's ideological restrictions and Mandel's exclusion. In addition to Mandel, the "American Plaintiffs" included Norman Birnbaum from Amherst College, Wassily Leontief from Harvard University, Robert Heilbroner from the New School for Social Research, Robert Paul Wolff from Columbia University, and David Mermelstein and Louis Menashe from the Polytechnic Institute of Brooklyn.[74] A few months later, the NECLC added Noam Chomsky from the Massachusetts Institute of Technology and Richard Falk from Princeton University to this list.[75]

In the Complaint, Boudin argued that the ideological exclusion provisions unconstitutionally restricted and abridged Americans' First Amendment rights. This exclusion acted as a prior restraint on their right "to exercise their freedom of academic inquiry by engaging Mandel in an open and face-to-face

"DO AMERICANS HAVE THE RIGHT TO HEAR?" Pamphlet produced and distributed by the National Emergency Civil Liberties Committee discussing the legal challenge to Ernest Mandel's exclusion and requesting donations to the Mandel Case Legal Defense Fund. National Emergency Civil Liberties Committee Records Columbia University Rare Book & Manuscript Library.

exchange of information and opinions."[76] Boudin claimed that the provisions were void on their face and as applied to Mandel because they predicated inadmissibility on the foreigner's mere belief in or advocacy of unpopular political viewpoints and in the absence of any evidence that the foreigner would engage in unlawful speech or conduct. He argued that the waiver provision that gave the attorney general "unbridled discretion" to exclude failed to provide any "procedural safeguards" or "adequate or ascertainable standards" for making the determination to grant or deny a waiver violating Americans' Fifth Amendment right to due process.[77]

At the end of the Complaint, Boudin requested a declaratory judgment and a preliminary and permanent injunction to invalidate sections of the McCarran-Walter Act and to restrain the State Department and Justice Department from enforcing them in Mandel's visa application for admission to the United States. Boudin also requested that a three-judge panel be convened to review the case, as required by federal statute upon bringing a constitutional challenge to an act of Congress.[78] The US district court granted this request, and a three-judge panel was designated and heard arguments in *Mandel v. Mitchell* on the afternoon of June 24, 1970.[79]

Shirley Graham Du Bois

The NECLC Press Release announcing the designation of the three-judge panel in the Mandel case had mentioned another ideological exclusion under the Nixon administration.[80] In May 1970, news broke that the Justice Department had refused to grant a waiver of inadmissibility to Shirley Graham Du Bois, the seventy-four-year-old widow of the renowned scholar and civil rights activist, W. E. B. Du Bois.[81] Graham Du Bois was deemed inadmissible under the McCarran-Walter Act due to her alleged beliefs and affiliations with Communist organizations.[82] The Justice Department also had refused to grant a waiver despite the State Department's recommendation.[83] Yet, by August, the Justice Department would reverse its decision.

During the 1950s, W. E. B. Du Bois had become a target of McCarranism due to his political associations. In 1961, outraged by the Supreme Court's decision to uphold the constitutionality of the McCarran Act,[84] Du Bois joined the American Communist Party, and he and Graham Du Bois left the United States, moved to Accra, Ghana, and became citizens of Ghana.[85] When her husband died in 1963, Graham Du Bois remained in Ghana until she fled during a coup d'etat in 1967 and moved to Cairo, Egypt.[86] In February 1970, Graham Du Bois, a writer and political activist who championed civil rights, pan-Africanism, women's liberation, and anticolonialism, received invitations to come to the United States to speak at Fisk University and other college campuses. No longer an American citizen, Graham Du Bois obtained a Tanzanian passport and applied for a tourist visa, but was deemed inadmissible under the McCarran-Walter Act, and the Justice Department now refused to grant a waiver.[87]

Graham Du Bois's exclusion was widely reported and condemned in the national and international press.[88] Roy Wilkins, executive director of the National Association for the Advancement of Colored People (NAACP), sent a telegram to Mitchell referring to his refusal to grant Graham Du Bois a waiver as a "monstrous error" and stating that he found it "inconceivable that the presence in this country of Mrs. S. G. Du Bois widow of the late W. E. B. Du Bois, can be regarded by sane men as a menace to the national security."[89] Congresswoman Shirley Chisholm (D-NY) protested Graham Du Bois's exclusion "in the name of all black Americans."[90] New York Assemblyman Charles Rangel also expressed his outrage and argued that barring Graham Du Bois was "part of Mr. Mitchell's invidious campaign against black people in the United States—as shown by the Justice Department's past repressive actions against the Black Panthers and other militant Black leaders."[91]

Graham Du Bois was angry and disappointed by her visa denial and appreciated the support and press coverage of her plight to enter the United States. She, too, viewed her exclusion as part of the Nixon administration's repressive approach to activism, as well as being consistent with the McCarranism that had led her and her husband to leave the United States.[92]

In late May, Daniel Patrick Moynihan, the counselor to the president for urban affairs, sent Nixon a memorandum discussing the Justice Department's refusal to grant a waiver for Graham Du Bois. Nixon responded suggesting it might be a "good case for clemency" and to explore the possibility of letting Graham Du Bois in the country.[93] Yet, others disagreed.

In June, INS Commissioner Raymond F. Farrell responded to Nixon's suggestion, and sent a memorandum to Egil "Bud" Krogh Jr., deputy assistant to the president for domestic affairs. Farrell stated that the purpose of visa restrictions was "to protect the national interest and the continuing good order and well-being of the nation." He argued that allowing Graham Du Bois to enter the United States would "not be in the best interests of this country," despite the State Department's favorable recommendation on her behalf.[94] Farrell stated that Graham Du Bois "has been affiliated with over thirty Communist-controlled organizations," and she had served in "leadership positions" in many of them. He also claimed "there was no evidence of any change in her views." Farrell explained that the Justice Department refused to grant a waiver because Graham Du Bois's primary reason for visiting was to speak at Fisk University and at a number of college campuses and that those activities "did not outweigh, from a national interest view, the factors in her background which compelled the initial denial of the visa."[95]

Three days later, Bud Krogh sent a memorandum to Kenneth R. Cole Jr., an assistant to John Ehrlichman, the White House counsel. Krogh reiterated Farrell's justification for excluding Graham Du Bois and then added:

> While much has been written on campuses that the government should not prevent a speaker—regardless of political views—from coming on to campus, I do not think we gain anything in the present climate by permitting Mrs. Du Bois to come back and lecture throughout the country. Clemency is not an issue here; it is simply whether or not we are going to grant her a visa to come back and talk to young people who currently are star-struck by representatives of the Third World and the hard-core Communist revolutionaries. In addition, I don't see what benefit we will really gain either in the academic community or the liberal domain at large by permitting Mrs. Du Bois to return. I do see a real disadvantage among our supporters—if I can use such a loose term—by letting such a renowned Communist back into our country.[96]

At the end of his memorandum, Krogh suggested Ehrlichman recommend the administration should not permit Graham Du Bois to enter the United States,[97] which is what he did.[98]

Krogh's comments revealed not only the political motivations in keeping Graham Du Bois out—namely, to appease Nixon's base support, his "Silent Majority"—but also the calculus. The decision was not about free exchange of ideas or speech, but about what Nixon would lose or gain in permitting Graham Du Bois to enter the United States. The Nixon administration had readily assumed the role of a censor, making the decision based on whether her entry was in its best interests.

In August, the Justice Department reversed its decision to exclude Graham Du Bois. She now stated she wished to come to the United States to settle some personal business and to attend a dedication of the Black Hall of Fame in New York. The State Department once again recommended a waiver, and, in light of Graham Du Bois's new reasons for her visit, the Justice Department granted the waiver.[99] Apparently, as long as Graham Du Bois had no intention of visiting American colleges and universities and speaking her mind to students on these campuses, she was free to return to the United States, temporarily.

Prior to the Justice Department's reversal, Graham Du Bois had contacted Abdeen M. Jabara, a lawyer in Detroit, Michigan, to help her challenge her visa denial. Jabara had been hired to obtain a visa for Tariq Ali, a twenty-six-year-old British Pakistani political activist, as well as a friend of Mandel's and fellow Trotskyist.[100] Ali was denied a waiver in December 1969 after appearing in a photograph with a burning American flag during a protest demonstration in front of the US embassy in London.[101]

Jabara told Graham Du Bois that her exclusion from the United States was "part of a developing pattern here." He described Mandel's waiver denial and Boudin's legal challenge, which Jabara was watching very closely. Jabara explained he would adopt Boudin's First Amendment argument to challenge Graham Du Bois's ideological exclusion.[102] This plan proved unnecessary when the Nixon administration permitted Graham Du Bois to come to the United States. Mandel, however, remained excluded. The fate of his entry was left to the US district court.

Mandel Wins in US District Court

On March 18, 1971, the three-judge panel in the US district court issued a 2–1 opinion in favor of Mandel and the American professors. In *Mandel v. Mitchell*, Second Circuit Court of Appeals Judge Wilfred Feinberg and US District Court Judge John Dooling Jr. declared the ideological exclusion provisions within the McCarran-Walter Act to be unconstitutional, violating the First Amendment, and the waiver provision to be unconstitutional, violating due process under the Fifth Amendment.[103] They ordered a preliminary injunction against enforcing the exclusion provisions against Mandel, which had prevented the issuance of his entry visa.[104]

Writing for the majority, Dooling held that Mandel's exclusion fell under First Amendment law and the American professors' right to receive information and therefore was subject to current First Amendment standards and protections, including evaluation under "strict scrutiny" by the court. Under strict scrutiny, a restriction on fundamental rights, including those under the First Amendment, must be narrowly tailored to further a compelling governmental interest, or it is unconstitutional. Dooling concluded that the ideological exclusion provisions were unconstitutionally overbroad.

The teaching or advocating of "world communism" was now considered protected expression under the First Amendment, and thus, the government's exclusion based on this expression could not be considered furthering a compelling interest.[105] Dooling also noted that "Mandel's visit is in general to be limited to the academic community," and deserved First Amendment protection because it "gives particularized enhancement to the values for the self-governing process that are jeopardized by such exclusions as this case presents."[106]

Drawing on the past, Dooling included references to the Sedition Act of 1798 and James Madison's observation that "the censorial power is in the people over the Government, and not in the Government over the people."[107] He argued the people were sovereign and that the attorney general's absolute and unchecked discretion had turned him into a censor, exercising prior restraints on speech he found unacceptable for Americans' ears. Dooling concluded that Mandel's exclusion was the kind of censorship the First Amendment was designed to prevent.[108]

US District Court Judge John Bartels issued a dissenting opinion. He wrote that Mandel's exclusion fell under immigration law and the plenary power doctrine. Bartels asserted that the federal government was sovereign and held the right to exclude was a matter of foreign policy and national security.[109] Therefore, the judiciary must defer to the legislative and executive branches and their determinations on whom to exclude or admit and why. The district court could not and should not question the McCarran-Walter Act's exclusionary provisions or the attorney general's discretion and authority to enforce them.[110] Citing *Zemel v. Rusk*, Bartels concluded, "And, if the right to speak and publish does not carry with it the unrestrained right to gather information and ideas for American audiences, then the right to hear does not carry with it the unrestrained right to have foreign citizens orate those ideas in the United States."[111]

While Boudin and the NECLC celebrated their victory, Dooling's opinion and Bartels's dissent revealed a fundamental conflict in interpreting ideological restrictions as a question of First Amendment or immigration law, and national sovereignty as held by the people or by the federal government.[112] The American professors renewed their invitations to Mandel, but he remained excluded from the United States. The government had appealed the three-judge panel decision to the US Supreme Court, which would now have to confront this conflict in interpretation of ideological exclusion and to determine which legal precedent should apply to Mandel's case.

The Mandel Case at the Supreme Court

The government's brief to the Supreme Court reiterated Judge Bartels's arguments in his dissent and his application of the plenary power doctrine, which as such required judicial deference to Congress and the attorney general.[113] It emphasized that the ideological exclusion provisions under the McCarran-Walter Act concerned the admission of foreigners and were a regulation of "action, not speech." These provisions did not place restraints on communication with Mandel or access to his ideas or publications, but rather on his physical presence within the United States.[114] The government insisted that a challenge to the explicit exclusion categories within these provisions was a political question—one not for the courts, but for Congress to address.[115]

In their brief to the Supreme Court, Boudin and Rosenberg insisted Mandel's exclusion "concerns the rights of American citizens" and "has seriously impaired the First Amendment right of citizens to hold academic discussions and to receive information. Planned meetings were disrupted and specific invitations or contemplated discussions were precluded."[116] Boudin and Rosenberg also focused on the attorney general's unlimited discretion to grant or deny a waiver of inadmissibility "on a case by case basis" under the McCarran-Walter Act. They did not challenge the constitutionality of the act, but rather they argued that Congress intended for the waiver provision to provide temporary admission of foreigners in the "public interest," which included free exchange and inquiry in the United States protected under the First Amendment. They insisted that Mitchell had abused his discretion and not proffered a "legitimate" reason "in the realm of national security, foreign relations or otherwise" for why he had denied a waiver to Mandel.[117]

Boudin and Rosenberg most likely shifted the emphasis of their argument to focus on the attorney general's use of discretion and adopted a more narrow, careful approach, because they were concerned that a majority of the Supreme Court justices might be reluctant to follow Dooling's lead and apply First Amendment law and strict scrutiny to Mandel's exclusion. Attempting to align the case with *Kent v. Dulles*, which curbed the State Department's unbridled discretion to issue or deny passports to American citizens, Boudin and Rosenberg provided a pathway for the court to conclude that Mandel's exclusion was unconstitutional, without the justices thinking they would have to strike down the McCarran-Walter Act or overturn the well-established plenary power doctrine and decades of legal precedent to do so.

The Supreme Court heard oral arguments on April 18, 1972. Representing the government, Deputy Solicitor General Daniel Friedman noted the shift in emphasis in Boudin and Rosenberg's brief focusing on the attorney general's discretion and his reason for denying the waiver to Mandel. He insisted the plenary power doctrine applied to the case, and not the First Amendment, and framed the constitutional question as one considering whether Americans could force the United States to admit entry to anyone they wished. Friedman argued that while "the people in this country admittedly have a First Amendment right to listen to speaking that is going on, they do not, we think, have a right to overrule the settled power of the Congress and force the admission of an alien who belongs to a category that Congress has said is not to be admitted."[118]

Boudin framed the constitutional question as one considering the First Amendment rights of Americans to hear and to receive information. He argued that the plenary power doctrine did not give the attorney general the absolute power and unlimited discretion to violate these rights. He also described Mandel's visit as essential to academic freedom and intellectual inquiry, which the court had previously held was an important First Amendment value.[119] At the end of his argument, Boudin distinguished this case from *United States ex rel. Turner v. Williams* by emphasizing that this case concerned American litigants asserting their First Amendment rights. He described "poor Mr. Turner" as a man who had challenged his ideological exclusion by arguing that being barred violated his First Amendment rights, which, as a foreigner, he did not possess. "I would like to re-argue Turner against Williams, but it's too late." Boudin told the court. He then added sheepishly, "and if Clarence Darrow failed, I would certainly fail."[120]

Just before oral arguments, attorneys Melvin Wulf and David Carliner filed an *amicus curiae* brief on behalf of the American Civil Liberties Union (ACLU) in support of Mandel's entry.[121] They not only insisted First Amendment law should apply, but also viewed the case as a chance to challenge the plenary power doctrine's reliance on legal precedent upholding immigration restrictions such as Chinese exclusion. Wulf and Carliner suggested the Supreme Court reexamine "these precedential pages of history" in light of the development of antidiscrimination laws.[122] They urged the court to question the continued use of exclusions passed at the height of McCarthyism and racist legal relics such as the Chinese Exclusion Case. "If 'writing upon a clean slate,' this Court would strike down a statute of Congress which required the expulsion, for example, of all aliens who are Jews or black, or who advocate the smoking of tobacco or the practice of birth control," they wrote, "there appears to be no reason not to correct a page of history which should never have been written." Their brief cited *Brown v. Board of Education of Topeka* (1954) as an example.[123]

In a preliminary conference meeting of the justices, the breakdown of votes was 7 to 2 in favor of reversing the US district court's decision and upholding Mandel's exclusion. While Justice William O. Douglas and Justice William J. Brennan found Judge Dooling's opinion persuasive, the other justices believed the court was not 'writing on a clean slate,' and instead was bound by significant legal precedent and the plenary power doctrine.[124] Justice Thurgood Marshall was initially assigned to write the majority opinion, but, after oral arguments, he switched sides. Marshall wrote to Chief Justice Warren E. Burger that he could no longer write for the majority:

> While I appreciate the assignment of this opinion to me and have worked on it almost continuously since that time, I sincerely regret that I find myself unable to write it. As a matter of fact, I am convinced that my vote was in error. You will remember that my vote was to agree because 'we had come too far to turn back.' However, my further research convinces me that I am not in accord with *The Chinese Exclusion Case* and do not agree that the Constitution gave to either Congress or the Executive the broad power they assert. As I said before I am sorry, but I will have to go down as a 'backslider.'[125]

The vote was now 6 to 3. Burger reassigned the majority opinion to Justice Harry Blackmun.[126]

A "Facially Legitimate and *Bona Fide* Reason"

Justice Blackmun did not ask any questions during oral arguments, but an examination of his notes on the case reveals some of his reservations and concerns, which were later reflected in his opinion. Regarding the attorney general's refusal to grant the waiver, Blackmun wrote, "I may not like the rules but are they unconstitutional?" He did not want to challenge the plenary power doctrine or overturn legal precedent. "I must leave immigration and entry to Congress," Blackmun added. "I do not want to reexamine old decisions on absolute Congressional power." Describing Boudin's approach as "one on slippery ground," Blackmun appeared worried that some Americans would have the power to "force" the entry of any foreign visitor, despite the government's objections or a compelling interest. "Who could we stop?" he asked. "Would this mean the American Nazi party could force to invite Hitler? Or Chinese Americans Chairman Mao?"[127]

On June 29, 1972, the Supreme Court reversed the US district court decision. In *Kleindienst v. Mandel*, the court upheld the constitutionality of the McCarran-Walter Act's ideological exclusion provisions and Mandel's exclusion under them.[128] Blackmun began his opinion with a description of the case and provided a brief summary of the history of Congress's exclusion of foreigners since 1875, citing the exclusion of anarchists and then of Communists as a part of that history.[129] Blackmun then adopted the government's framing of the constitutional question as "whether the First Amendment confers upon the Appellee professors, because they wish to hear, speak, and debate with Mandel in person, the ability to determine that Mandel should be permitted to enter the country, or, in other words, to compel the Attorney General to allow Mandel's admission."[130]

Blackmun rejected the government's assertion that excluding Mandel involved no restriction on First Amendment rights.[131] "The rights asserted here, in some contrast, are those of American academics who have invited Mandel to participate with them in colloquia, debates, and discussion in the United States," he wrote. "In light of the Court's previous decisions concerning the 'right to receive information,' we cannot realistically say that the problem facing us disappears entirely or is nonexistent because the mode of regulation bears directly on physical movement."[132] Blackmun also rejected the contention that books, tapes, and "telephone hook-ups" were sufficient to convey Mandel's message in lieu of his physical presence on American campuses, which he argued "overlooks what may be particular qualities inherent in sustained, face-to-face debate, discussion and questioning."[133]

Blackmun then turned to Boudin's argument. He focused on Boudin's claim that the attorney general's discretion to refuse to grant a waiver was unconstitutional because of its breadth and its lack of standards and procedures.[134] Boudin insisted that, absent a reason for the attorney general's denial of a waiver, First Amendment protections should apply and prevail. Blackmun rejected this argument out of concern that "either every claim would prevail, in which case the plenary discretionary authority Congress granted the Executive becomes a nullity or courts in each case would be required to weigh the strength of the audience's interest against that of the Government in refusing a waiver to the particular alien applicant, according to some as yet undetermined standard."[135] Yet, Blackmun also rejected the government's argument that Congress had delegated the decision to grant or deny the waiver to the attorney general, who had "sole and unfettered discretion" and did not have to provide any reason for his decision.[136]

Attempting to forge a middle path between the opposing arguments, Blackmun concluded by issuing a narrow holding and a new legal standard. First, Blackmun asserted that the attorney general had "validly" exercised his discretion and had provided a reason for Mandel's exclusion. "Previous abuses by Mandel [straying from his itinerary during his 1968 visit] made it inappropriate to grant a waiver again," he wrote. Second, Blackmun held that this reason was not "arbitrary or capricious," but instead, it was a "facially legitimate and *bona fide* reason" for the attorney general to deny a waiver to Mandel, and, as such, sufficient to be constitutional.[137]

Blackmun did not define or elaborate on what constituted this reason, but explained that under the plenary power doctrine, if the attorney general presented such a reason, "the courts will neither look behind the exercise of that discretion nor test it by balancing its justification against the First Amendment interests of those who seek personal communication with the applicant."[138] Blackmun then carefully dodged the question of how to proceed in cases where no reason is given, stating, "What First Amendment or other grounds may be available for attacking exercise of discretion for which no justification whatsoever is advanced is a question we neither address nor decide in this case."[139]

While Blackmun acknowledged that "First Amendment rights are implicated" in this case, he insisted these rights were not "dispositive of our inquiry here."[140] Blackmun deferred to Congress's plenary power to regulate foreigners' entry and its delegation of enforcement, including ideological exclusion provisions, to the executive branch.[141] According to Blackmun, national sovereignty was held by the federal government, and not by the people, and he refused to weigh First Amendment protections against a sovereign nation's right to control its borders and to self-preservation.[142]

Justices Douglas, Marshall, and Brennan dissented. They argued that ideological exclusion was a First Amendment issue and that the Attorney General's discretionary authority had to meet First Amendment legal standards. They rejected Blackmun's new "facially legitimate and *bona fide* reason" standard, as well as his determination that Mitchell's reason had satisfied it.

In his opinion, Douglas focused on the attorney general's discretion and authority to exclude. He asked if, under this authority, "one who maintains that the earth is round can be excluded? That no one who believes Darwinian theory shall be admitted?"[143] He wrote, "Congress never undertook to entrust the Attorney General with the discretion to pick and choose among the ideological offerings which alien lecturers tender from our platforms, allowing those palatable to him and disallowing others."[144] Douglas described the discretion to deny visas to certain foreign speakers as a form of "thought control," which turned the attorney general into "a censor."[145] Absent an actual threat to national security, Mandel's exclusion was unconstitutional.

In a separate opinion, Marshall, joined by Brennan, wrote, "I, too, am stunned to learn that a country with our proud heritage has refused Dr. Mandel temporary admission. I am convinced that Americans cannot be denied the opportunity to hear Dr. Mandel's views in person because their Government disapproves of his ideas." He continued, "The freedom to speak and the freedom to hear are inseparable; they are two sides of the same coin. But the coin itself is the process of thought and discussion. The activity of speakers becoming listeners and listeners becoming speakers in the vital interchange of thought is the 'means indispensable to the discovery and spread of political truth.'"[146]

Marshall sarcastically dismissed the government's use of such "milestones" as the legal precedent used to "exclude and expel Chinese aliens from our midst" but did not insist this legal precedent be overturned or reconsidered in order to hold Mandel's exclusion was unconstitutional.[147] As Marshall explained, the case concerned Americans' First Amendment rights, so First Amendment precedent and standards should apply. "Without any claim that Mandel 'live' is an actual threat to this country, there is no difference between excluding Mandel because of his ideas and keeping his books out because of their ideas. Neither is permitted."[148]

Marshall was also perplexed by Blackmun's new "facially legitimate and bona fide reason" standard, which he referred to as "unusual" and as too low to override constitutional rights.[149] Describing the court's deference to the attorney general as "unprecedented," Marshall declared, "Even the briefest peek behind the Attorney General's reason for refusing a waiver in this case would reveal that it is a sham."[150] The government did not produce evidence that Mandel had knowingly or willfully departed from his itinerary, and there was no "factual hearing" to see if Mitchell had "any support for his determination."[151] He concluded, "Nothing is served—least of all our standing in the international community—by Mandel's exclusion. In blocking his admission, the Government has departed from the basic traditions of our country, its fearless acceptance of free discussion."[152]

With the creation of the "facially legitimate and bona fide reason" standard, Blackmun had delivered a blow to the plenary power doctrine and the attorney general's ultimate discretion and the ability to use that discretion to make determinations to admit or exclude without disclosing the reason.

Albeit a low standard, it was a standard nonetheless, and future challengers to ideological exclusions and waiver denials would be able to hold the government to that standard. Yet, it was far lower than what would be applied in a First Amendment case.

A few months after the Supreme Court's decision, Mandel wrote to his friends and supporters at the NECLC, thanking all of those instrumental in challenging his exclusion, including Boudin and Rosenberg, and marveling at the widespread support for his admission to the United States. He noted, "We are living in an epoch of deep social crisis, when this principle [of free communication of ideas and of human beings] is all too often trampled upon."[153] Mandel also reflected on the lessons of history. "No revolutionary change was ever prevented by trying to suppress free circulation of ideas," he wrote. "If anything, such measures of suppression always in the end hasten radical social change rather than stopping it."[154]

Abuse of Power

While the Supreme Court had upheld the constitutionality of Mandel's ideological exclusion, the Nixon administration may not have been celebrating. The previous week, five men, with connections to Nixon's reelection campaign, were caught breaking into and attempting to wiretap the offices of the Democratic National Committee at the Watergate Hotel. Two days later, the Supreme Court struck down Mitchell's use of warrantless wiretaps he authorized in the name of "national security" as violating the Fourth Amendment.[155] While Nixon would win reelection in November, the public would soon learn of the abuse of power and illegality committed in order to make that possible.

One example of the Nixon administration's abuse of power during this time period that is often overlooked is the Justice Department's attempt to deport John Lennon from the United States. In 1968, Lennon was convicted of possession of cannabis resin in England. Lennon's drug conviction could have led to his exclusion under a provision in the McCarran-Walter Act, but, in 1970, Lennon was able to successfully obtain a visa under a waiver, authorized by Mitchell.[156] The popular British musician and his wife and collaborator, Yoko Ono, had become outspoken critics of the Vietnam War, and their participation in rallies, television interviews, and recording of "Give Peace a Chance" had attracted quite a bit of public attention.[157] In February 1972, citing Lennon's drug conviction, the Justice Department refused to renew Lennon's visa and, once it expired, ordered him to leave the United States.[158]

Although Lennon did not face deportation under an explicit or implicit ideological restriction, many, including Lennon, believed that his deportation was retaliatory. The Justice Department had used the drug conviction as a pretext to expel Lennon because of his beliefs and expressions.[159] "The real reason is that I'm a peacenik," Lennon replied, when asked why he thought he was being deported.[160] An article entitled "American Hospitality," published in *Newsday*, noted that the United States had welcomed Lennon when he was a member of "The Beatles," but it now sought to exclude him after becoming involved in the antiwar movement.[161] In "Love It and Leave It," the *New York Times* described the "official" reason for deporting Lennon as "suspicious," arguing it was because of his "unconventional views and radical statements," and recalled Charlie Chaplin's exclusion two decades earlier.[162] The comparison was apt, as well as ironic. In April, the Nixon administration had permitted Chaplin to return to the United States to receive an honorary Academy Award for lifetime achievement.[163]

Lennon hired New York immigration attorney Leon Wildes. Determined to keep Lennon in the United States, Wildes submitted a FOIA request, and subsequently filed a lawsuit to obtain documents he believed would reveal Mitchell's motivations behind the deportation order. Wildes discovered that the INS had a scheme that prioritized deportation and deferred action as part of its exercise of prosecutorial discretion. Lennon was not considered a high priority for deportation, but something had changed.[164] One of the documents was a letter Senator Strom Thurmond (R-SC) sent to Mitchell before Mitchell resigned to manage Nixon's reelection campaign. Thurmond noted, "Many headaches might be avoided if appropriate action be taken in time," and attached a memorandum on Lennon from the Senate Internal Security Subcommittee. According to a "confidential source," Lennon was affiliated with a group of New Left leaders, who were "strong advocates of the program to 'dump Nixon,'" and planned to hold rock concerts in primary election states to attract young voters and recruit them to disrupt the Republican National Convention, as the Democratic National Convention had been disrupted in 1968. The group intended to use Lennon "as a drawing card" to promote the concerts, which "will pour tremendous amounts of money into the coffers of the New Left." The source "felt that if Lennon's visa is terminated it would be a strategy counter-measure."[165]

After three years of investigation and litigation, in 1975, the Second Circuit Court of Appeals overturned Lennon's deportation order. It found that Lennon's conviction in England for possession of cannabis resin did not render him excludable under the McCarran-Walter Act's provisions.[166] In his argument before the court, Wildes also revealed Thurmond's letter and other documents demonstrating its influence on the decision to deport Lennon. Wildes remarked, "There is substantial reason to believe that official governmental action was based principally on a desire to silence political opposition squarely protected by the First Amendment."[167] The court agreed, insisting, "The courts will not condone selective deportation based upon secret political grounds."[168] It signaled the protection of noncitizens within the United States against public officials' application of viewpoint discrimination and retaliatory motivations behind their exercise of prosecutorial discretion to determine who to deport. The decision was a victory for Wildes and for Lennon, who obtained a "green card" granting him legal permanent residency in the United States in 1976. Wildes and Lennon had not only publicly revealed yet another instance of the Nixon administration's abuse of power, but also the political motivations behind the Nixon administration's use of immigration law to suppress dissent.

By 1969, many in the United States believed that the worst of the McCarthy era was behind them. Times had changed, legal precedent had changed, and the Cold War had changed. What had not changed were the ideological exclusion provisions under the McCarran-Walter Act. The return of Nixon marked the return of McCarranism and the use of these provisions as tools to suppress radicalism, stifle criticism, and attempt to gain political advantage. The exclusion of Ernest Mandel also marked the return of familiar arguments against ideological exclusion and its use as a form of censorship, undermining American values and threatening free speech.

While the Mandel case was over, Leonard Boudin was not done with the Nixon administration. He defended Daniel Ellsberg against criminal charges for theft, conspiracy, and espionage, brought by Mitchell, for Ellsberg's disclosure of the Pentagon Papers. Some of the White House advisors who had recommended excluding Shirley Graham Du Bois were involved in a covert investigative unit, which broke into Ellsberg's psychiatrist's office to gather information to discredit him and also sought to discredit Boudin.[169] The revelation of the Nixon administration's misconduct led to a mistrial and the dismissal of charges against Ellsberg in 1973 and a victory for Boudin.[170] The investigation of Nixon's abuse of power would result in the end of his presidency and prison sentences for members of his administration, including Mitchell. Mandel would spend the rest of his life continuing to publish, lecture, and advocate for radical and revolutionary change. In 1994, he received a visa and spoke in the United States one last time before he died in 1995.[171]

The Mandel case revived old arguments against ideological exclusion under the McCarran-Walter Act and its use as a tool of political repression, but the legal challenge brought by Boudin and David Rosenberg was new. It led to a significant change to the exercise of ultimate discretion to exclude and a pathway to challenge ideological exclusion cases in federal court. Justice Blackmun's opinion acknowledged Americans' First Amendment rights in exclusion cases and his "facially legitimate and *bona fide* reason" standard placed a limit on the government's discretionary power. Yet, his standard fell short of speech-protective standards and strict scrutiny applied in First Amendment cases and his opinion upheld the constitutionality of exclusion under the McCarran-Walter Act's ideological restrictions. These restrictions would remain intact and ready to be used by the next presidential administration.

7

One Door Closes, Another Opens

ON AUGUST 1, 1975, the United States signed the Helsinki Final Act. The act concluded a series of negotiations following the 1973 Conference of Security and Cooperation in Europe held in Helsinki, Finland. Referred to as the "Helsinki Accords," the act was not a treaty, but an international agreement signed by thirty-five nations, including the Soviet Union, to promote particular values and "ensuring conditions in which their people can live in true and lasting peace free from any threat to or attempt against their security."[1] The accords were part of détente and viewed as an important step in international efforts to ease Cold War tensions. The United States committed itself to the "freer movement" of individuals by easing security restrictions and facilitating travel and cultural exchange, as well as to "respect human rights and fundamental freedoms, including the freedom of thought, conscience, religion or belief."[2]

During President Jimmy Carter's tenure, the Helsinki Accords helped push Congress toward curbing ideological exclusion under the McCarran-Walter Act. In 1977, in an effort to resolve the discrepancy between ideological exclusion and the commitment to this international agreement, Congress passed an amendment to the Foreign Relations Authorization Act, sponsored by Senator George McGovern (D-SD). The "McGovern Amendment" applied to the ideological exclusion provisions in Section 212(a)(28) of the McCarran-Walter Act, which addressed past or present beliefs, advocacy, or membership in proscribed organizations that advocate anarchism, or the overthrow of government by force, or the "economic, international, or governmental doctrines of world communism."

The McGovern Amendment sought to prevent exclusions based on guilt by association by increasing oversight of denials of waivers of inadmissibility by the secretary of state and by limiting reasons for denials to national security concerns. Under the amendment,

> The Secretary of State should, within 30 days of receiving an application for a nonimmigrant visa by any alien who is excludable from the United States by reason of membership in or affiliation with a proscribed organization but who is otherwise admissible to the United States, recommend that the Attorney General grant the approval necessary for the issuance of a visa to such alien, unless the Secretary determines that the admission of such alien would be contrary to the security interests of the United States and so certifies to the Speaker of the House of Representatives and the Chairman of the Committee of Foreign Relations of the Senate.[3]

Two years later, in 1979, Congress added an exemption to the McGovern Amendment, which reflected US foreign relations and support of Israel, as well as terrorism fears. The exemption pertained to the Palestine Liberation Organization (PLO). The United States had refused to recognize the State of Palestine and the PLO until the PLO recognized the State of Israel. Members of Congress also expressed concern about admitting PLO members and officers associated with terrorism and violence abroad.[4] Now, the McGovern Amendment explicitly did not apply to admission for any PLO "member, officer, official, representative, or spokesman."[5]

Over the next decade, President Ronald Reagan's administration found ways to circumvent the McGovern Amendment and continued to use the McCarran-Walter Act's provisions to ideologically exclude and deport foreign scholars, writers, artists, officials, and activists. The administration defended its use of the act's provisions and justified these exclusions and deportations based on foreign policy interests and terrorism concerns.

Those excluded from the United States, as well as members of Congress, the press, and the public, condemned the Reagan administration's ideological exclusions and deportations as a form of censorship, which they said would damage the United States and its reputation. They dismissed the administration's foreign policy and terrorism reasons as a pretext to suppress dissent. The visa denials to these foreign visitors under implicit and explicit provisions in the McCarran-Walter Act were also retaliatory, based on the Reagan administration's disapproval of their affiliations and expressions criticizing US foreign policy. Leonard Boudin and the National Emergency Civil Liberties Committee (NECLC) joined American Civil Liberties Union (ACLU) attorneys to challenge these visa denials in federal court, using the Ernest

Mandel case strategy and arguing that such ideological exclusions violated Americans' First Amendment rights.

Lawmakers in Congress seized the opportunity presented by this public criticism and litigation to push to revise, reform, and repeal the explicit ideological exclusion provisions within the McCarran-Walter Act. While they were successful, their efforts led to exclusion and deportation based on membership in and material support of terrorist organizations. As the Cold War came to a close, this shift from Communism to terrorism opened the door to new forms of ideological exclusion and deportation, familiar arguments, and uses of guilt by association.

Ideological Exclusion under Reagan

The McGovern Amendment addressed the waiver provision, and thus, it did not apply to all of the exclusionary "security" provisions in the McCarran-Walter Act. Under Sections 212(a)(27) and (a)(29) visa applicants could not receive a waiver, and exclusion was mandatory.

Section 212(a)(29) excluded those who "probably would, after entry" engage in unlawful activities "relating to espionage, sabotage, public disorder, or in other activity subversive to the national security."[6] Section 212(a)(27) excluded those "who seek to enter the United States solely, principally, or incidentally to engage in activities which would be prejudicial to the public interest, or endanger the welfare, safety, or security of the United States."[7] This section was an implicit provision, similar to the Alien Friends Act of 1798, and it left tremendous discretion in the hands of the secretary of state and attorney general to exclude whoever they believed would pose a threat to the United States.

Former Security and Consular Affairs Bureau Chief Abba Schwartz recalled rarely using Sections 212(a)(27) and (a)(29) to exclude during his tenure in the 1960s. According to Schwartz, Section 212(a)(27) was "imposed only in cases of 'political' personages whose activities would be seriously embarrassing politically to the United States," or to "dictators themselves and their followers whose regimes we oppose, whose succeeding governments we have recognized, and who were likely to engage in activities on our soil which would prejudice our relationship with other governments."[8] His interpretation of the statute was narrow and applied to activities and not to membership in organizations under Section 212(a)(28).

In his State of the Union address in 1985, President Reagan declared, "We must not break faith with those who are risking their lives—on every continent from Afghanistan to Nicaragua—to defy Soviet aggression and secure rights which have been ours from birth."[9] Referred to as the "Reagan Doctrine," foreign policy during the Reagan administration focused on conducting the Cold War through containment and through support of anti-Communists abroad to counter and to reverse Soviet expansion and influence. While President Carter had eased tensions with Cuba, reaching an agreement with Fidel Castro to open diplomacy and exchange and admitting Cuban refugees during the Mariel Boatlift in 1980, the Reagan administration's approach led to increased tensions with Fidel Castro and Cuba.

Reagan administration policies included trade sanctions and embargoes, suspensions on travel to and from Cuba, and restrictions on emigration from Cuba. Other examples of the Reagan Doctrine included the support and funding of the Contras in their efforts to topple the Sandinista National Liberation Front Socialist government in Nicaragua and of the Mujahideen resistance fighters seeking to push back the Soviet invasion of Afghanistan.

Reagan also listed Cuba as a state sponsor of terrorism for its support of leftist groups in Central and Latin America. Castro dismissed the charge and described Reagan as "a madman, an imbecile and a bum."[10] While Reagan expanded his own definition of terrorism to suit his foreign policy, terrorist acts abroad had become a significant threat and resulted in the loss of American lives. Between 1981 and 1989, there were 600 terrorist attacks abroad including embassy bombings, airline and ship hijackings, and hostage-takings.[11] Reagan entered the White House in 1981 at the end of the Iran hostage crisis. This crisis was part of an anti-American response by supporters of the Iranian revolution to Carter's admission of Shah Mohammad Reza Pahlavi to the United States for medical treatment.

Admissions of certain foreign officials or public figures to the United States could lead to serious consequences for Americans abroad and US foreign policy, and the threat of potential terrorist attacks committed within the United States was also of great concern. Yet, these consequences and concerns did not appear to be the factors determining the Reagan administration's use of Section 212(a)(27) to deny visas to certain foreign visitors. Boudin and ACLU attorneys noticed that the State Department had started to use Section 212(a)(27) to exclude foreigners based on membership and associations, yet these exclusions should have fallen under Section 212(a)(28). They also noticed the use of Section 212(a)(27) to exclude foreigners based on their prior advocacy or criticisms of the United States and its policies. The State Department had started to abandon initial exclusions under Section 212(a)

(28) to avoid the national security reasons and oversight requirements for waiver denials under the McGovern Amendment. A handful of ideological exclusion cases demonstrated this strategic shift.

On March 3, 1983, the State Department denied a visa to Chilean Hortensia Bussi de Allende, the sixty-eight-year-old widow of Chile's first Socialist president, Salvador Allende, overthrown by a military coup led by Augusto Pinochet in 1973. After her husband's death during the coup, Bussi fled and lived in exile in Mexico. Her visa denial was reminiscent of Shirley Graham Du Bois's exclusion in 1970. Bussi had applied for a visa to come to the United States after receiving an invitation by the Northern California Ecumenical Council to deliver a lecture at an event for International Women's Week in San Francisco, as well as numerous invitations to speak from religious and educational institutions in California. She planned to speak about the political and social situation in Latin America, the role of women in human rights struggles, and United States policies in Latin America.[12]

The State Department claimed Bussi was a "highly placed and active member of the World Peace Council, which has a direct affiliation with the Communist Party of the Soviet Union."[13] The Reagan administration had criticized the World Peace Council for its opposition to deployment of US nuclear missiles in Europe and described the organization as an "instrument of Soviet foreign policy."[14] Bussi stated she had never been denied a visa to travel to the United States in the past, including most recently in 1981, when she attended an anti-apartheid meeting at the United Nations. While she had attended World Peace Council meetings, she was not a high official in the organization or a member of any political party, including the Communist Party. She described the State Department's decision as an "arbitrary action," and added, "I don't think I'm so dangerous at my age."[15]

Having initially barred Bussi under Section 212(a)(28) because of her affiliations, the State Department would have had to certify that Bussi posed a national security threat to the United States, as required by the McGovern Amendment. Under Secretary of State Lawrence Eagleburger did not consider the waiver for Bussi. Instead, he issued an advisory opinion sent to the US embassy in Mexico to deny Bussi's visa under Section 212(a)(27). He cited Bussi's membership in the World Peace Council and the speeches she would deliver. Eagleburger deemed Bussi's entry to the United States as "prejudicial to the public interest."[16]

Later that year, the Reagan administration used Section 212(a)(27) to deny visas to Cuban scholars Olga Finlay and Leonor Rodríguez Lezcano. In classified documents, the State Department described them as "two officers of the Federation of Cuban Women," considered an "instrumentality of the Cuban Communist Party."[17] Finlay and Lezcano had been invited to testify at hearings held by the New York City Commission on the Status of Women, on Cuban families and the Cuban response to juvenile delinquency. The State Department stated it would be prejudicial to the public interest for the two Cuban women to address an American audience. The State Department later granted Finlay a visa to attend the Pan American Health Organization in Washington, DC, on the condition she not speak to any American groups during her visit.[18]

In September 1983, Italian General Nino Pasti, a NATO vice air marshal and top nuclear strategist, was invited to deliver lectures on nuclear policy; Pasti supported nuclear disarmament. At the time, there was a debate within the United States regarding the deployment of nuclear missiles in Western Europe. Despite having obtained visas to visit the United States on five separate occasions, Pasti was barred by the State Department because of his views and association with the World Peace Council, like Bussi. Initially, Pasti was barred under Section 212(a)(28), but when he applied for a waiver of inadmissibility, the State Department switched its justification to Section 212(a)(27), describing Pasti's visit to the United States as "prejudicial to the conduct of the foreign affairs of the United States."[19]

The State Department also refused to disclose the reason behind its visa denial to Nicaragua's interior minister Tomás Borge, who was invited to come to the United States to speak on Nicaraguan policies. The Reagan administration opposed the Sandinista National Liberation Front and did not want to give Borge, one of its founders, a "propaganda platform in the United States."[20] Questions about Borge were directed to Secretary of State George P. Shultz. Shultz had previously served in the Nixon administration in various positions including as secretary of labor and secretary of the treasury. He was known for famously refusing President Richard Nixon's request to investigate and audit the individuals on Nixon's "enemies list."[21]

As secretary of state, Shultz had used his ultimate discretion to deny Borge's visa, because he objected to Borge's presence and what he might say. Shultz did not appear to consider the rights of those who had invited Borge to come to the United States and had wanted to hear him speak. When asked about the visa denial to Borge, Shultz replied, "As a general proposition I think we have to favor freedom of speech, but it can get abused by people who do not wish us well, and I think we have to take some reasonable precautions about that." While Shultz said he did not believe Borge was "going to overthrow the government or anything like that," he was concerned that

George P. Shultz, Secretary of State, testifies before the House Foreign
Affairs Committee on February 9, 1984
Mark Reinstein / Alamy Stock Photo.

his visit would distract from the Contadora group meeting held in Panama to
discuss conflicts in Central America.[22]

"Good grief," responded John Coatsworth, a professor of Latin American
history, who had arranged for Borge to speak at the University of Chicago
during his visit. "It's hard to know where to start responding to a statement
of that kind. . . . The notion that denying a visa to Borge will facilitate the Contadora peace-making process is not only absurd, it's preposterous." He remarked, "The First Amendment means nothing at all if it does not permit
American citizens to listen to views their government disapproves of."[23]

While the Reagan administration defended its use of the McCarran-
Walter Act's ideological exclusion provisions as an important foreign
policy tool, the press and members of the public continued to criticize these
visa denials, which some characterized as a "vestige of McCarthyism."[24]
Describing ideological exclusions as a form of censorship, they asked why
Americans should "fear foreigners' free speech" and be shielded from their
views.[25] Why was the Reagan administration was so afraid of Hortensia
Bussi de Allende and engaged in a "persistent pattern" of excluding foreigners based on their associations and critiques of US foreign policy?[26]
Such exclusions not only suppressed dissent, but also reflected a lack of con-
fidence in liberal democracy and free expression that would embarrass the
United States. They argued America was "making the world safe from democracy," and not safe for it.[27]

Barney Frank's Crusade

During the Reagan administration, Congressman Barney Frank (D-MA) was one of the most outspoken critics of ideological exclusion. Born in Bayonne, New Jersey in 1940, he graduated from Harvard College and Harvard Law School and served in the Massachusetts State Legislature before his election to the US House of Representatives in 1980. Frank vividly remembered watching the Army-McCarthy Hearings in 1954, when he was a teenager. He wrote in his autobiography that watching those hearings "inspired my fascination in government." He admired the Army's attorney Joseph Welch and was "glad to see Welch score heavily against the McCarthy side."[28] During his tenure in Congress in the 1980s, Frank pushed for AIDS funding, as well as the elimination of exclusion categories in the McCarran-Walter Act, including "psychopathic personalities," "sexual deviation," and "mental defect," which were used to bar homosexuals under immigration policy. In 1987, Frank came out publicly as homosexual. Frank described these exclusions, as well as ideological exclusions, as an "egregious example of bigotry" and motivated by a fear of admitting "undesirables."[29]

Frank was not the first to challenge the McCarran-Walter Act in Congress. In the 1950s, Senator Herbert Lehman (D-NY) was an outspoken critic of both the McCarran and McCarran-Walter Acts, but was not successful in his attempts to defeat their passage. He compared the McCarran Act to the Alien Friends Act and Sedition Act of 1798, and warned that its provisions would not "catch only those whose views you hate. All of us may become victims of the gallows we erect for the enemies of freedom."[30] Lehman described the McCarran-Walter Act as reflecting "fear, suspicion, and distrust of the foreigners outside our country, and of the aliens within our country." He joined Senator Hubert Humphrey (D-MN) in sponsoring competing legislation that offered liberal immigration provisions with more protections for those ordered excluded or deported.[31] Senator Patrick McCarran (D-NV) made sure the bill never made it out of the Senate Judiciary Committee, which he chaired.[32]

At the height of McCarthyism, many members of Congress reluctantly voted for the McCarran Act and McCarran-Walter Act out of fear of red-baiting from senators like McCarran, and subsequently losing elections.[33] There simply was no incentive to get rid of ideological exclusion or deportation provisions within these acts and seem weak on Communism. There were other attempts to repeal or revise the provisions, including when the Nixon administration barred Carlos Fuentes from disembarking in Puerto Rico in

1969. Critics of the exclusion, including editors at the *New York Times*, called on Congress to "re-examine and eliminate these purposeless restrictions which make the United States ridiculous rather than secure."[34] Congressman James Scheuer (D-NY) and Senator J. William Fulbright (D-AR), longtime chairman of the Senate Foreign Relations Committee, condemned Fuentes's exclusion and sought to repeal the provisions and revise the law, but they were unsuccessful.[35]

While the Reagan administration took a tough stance on Communism, times had changed, the Cold War had changed, and anti-Communism had changed. McCarthyism was over and, Frank hoped, so was the same fear that had led some to pass the McCarran-Walter Act. He now saw a chance to change the law, especially after public criticisms characterizing recent visa denials as a return of McCarthyism and a form of censorship.[36] Frank found the explicit ideological exclusions and deportations within the McCarran-Walter Act repressive, punishing protected speech and dissent, and reflecting anachronistic objects of fear and perceived sources of subversion within the United States. "The notion that somehow we are this pristine nation and we will be polluted from outside is crazy," he said. "What harm a philosophical anarchist is to the United States I do not understand. But this law keeps them out."[37]

In June 1984, the Subcommittee on Immigration, Refugees, and International Law of the House Judiciary Committee held a hearing to discuss two bills Frank had introduced.[38] H.R. 4509 and H.R. 5227 included repealing the ideological exclusion provisions under Sections 212(a)(28) and (a)(27). They also barred entry to anyone whom the attorney general or consular officer "knows or has reasonable ground to believe probably / likely would engage after entry in any activity (i) which is prohibited by the laws of the United States relating to espionage or sabotage, (ii) which endangers public safety or national security, or (iii) a purpose of which is the opposition to, or the control or overthrow of the Government of the United States by force, violence, or other unconstitutional means." The bills barred anyone "who is an active member of an organization that is engaged in violence or terrorist activities," unless entering as temporary visitors.[39]

Frank opened the hearing stating "I think we are going to be dealing today with one of the most fundamental questions that a society deals with; namely, the extent to which we as citizens trust ourselves and our own judgment. I think we have inherited a statutory scheme, which really puts the Government in a position of acting as a censor, puts the Government in the position of deciding what is and is not fit material for the American people to hear, and read, and talk about." Frank then addressed the United States' identity and values, as well as the importance of beginning the process to change this legislation, "which was wrong, in my judgment, when it was enacted, and has become progressively more embarrassing to this country." He declared, "One of the great strengths of this country, both domestically and internationally, is our commitment to freedom, our self-confidence, our view that we are strong enough and wise enough as a people to take on all comers." Frank concluded, "We have, I think, an unfortunate piece of legislation here which suggests that somehow we are not mature enough, we are not stable enough to take all ideas and all forms of debate and allow them to go forward."[40]

In her testimony, Joan Clark, assistant secretary for consular affairs in the State Department, rejected the characterization of the ideological exclusion and deportation provisions as "ideological censorship" and insisted that the United States did not exclude based on abstract belief or expression.[41] Clark also objected to any potential elimination of Section 212(a)(27), stating that the provision was not aimed at excluding based on ideology but was a foreign policy tool, reflecting the United States' views and assisting in foreign relations. "Denying a visa is a U.S. Government action, and is considered as an act of the U.S. Government," she explained.

Clark argued that a visa denial was a form of government expression and diplomacy. "For example there are bilateral relationships with other countries to be considered. If we are supporting one point of view, we certainly need to make the point known I think to the government that is concerned."[42] Frank questioned the legitimacy of excluding critics of the United States because such dissent would contradict the US government's positions.[43]

Clark argued that ideological exclusion provisions also had been used to exclude terrorists or those supporting terrorist organizations.[44] She mentioned terrorism in response to Frank's question regarding the exclusion of Italian playwright Dario Fo and his wife, Franca Rame, in August 1983, who had wanted to come to the United States to attend the New York Shakespeare Festival and lecture at the New York School of Arts and Yale Drama School. Frank referred to a *New York Times* article, which included quoted remarks from an officer in the Italian consulate regarding Fo's exclusion: "Nobody at State thinks Fo is going to foment revolution or throw bombs. . . . It's just that . . . Dario Fo has never had a good word to say about the [United States]."[45] Clark stated that Fo was excluded under Section 212(a)(28), because in an interview with his wife, the US embassy learned he had raised funds for Soccorso Rossa (Red Aid), which Clark described as an organization that "provides support for the Italian terrorist groups."[46]

Clark then discussed statistics. Between 1963 and 1982, 519 nonimmigrant visas were denied under Section 212(a)(27) out of over 70 million nonimmigrant visas issued during that period. The chairman of the committee, Congressman Romano Mazzoli (D-KY), noted that there were twenty-six visa denials under this provision in 1983. Under Section 212(a)(28), foreign visitors could overcome a visa denial through a waiver. Mazzoli cited 26,973 visa denials under this provision and 26,211 waivers permitting admission, leaving approximately 700 excluded from the United States. Frank was not reassured by this number and argued, "If the mayor of a town were to allow 26,000 requests to have speeches and deny 700, I think that would be outrageous." Even if one received a waiver, this process took time. Frank thought not much was accomplished if one applied for a visa to attend an event in the United States only to receive the visa after the event was over.[47]

In her testimony before the committee, Jeri Laber, the executive director of the US Helsinki Watch Committee, a nongovernmental organization monitoring human rights provisions under the Helsinki Accords, stated that ideological exclusions represented an "egregious" violation of the accords and urged repeal of the McCarran-Walter Act's exclusion provisions. Laber began her testimony by mentioning that under the Reagan administration, the Swedish author Jan Myrdal, the son of Nobel laureate Gunnar Myrdal, the author of the seminal work on race relations, *An American Dilemma: The Negro Problem and Modern Democracy* (1944), had received a restricted visa to come to the United States based on alleged Communist affiliations. It had generated a lot of discussion in the Swedish press, as well as anti-American sentiment.[48]

Laber described ideological exclusions as "shameful and embarrassing." They sent the impression to the world that "our Government is so fearful and defensive that it will not give foreigners who are critical of its policies an opportunity to express their views." She compared the humiliating experience of answering questions about political views and affiliations and visa denials to her own experience failing to obtain a visa to enter the Soviet Union. Laber noted that exclusions made the United States "extremely vulnerable" to criticisms of hypocrisy when American leaders accused other governments of violating the Helsinki Accords, "dedicated to encouraging the free exchange of ideas and the free movement of citizens across national borders."[49]

Listing a number of artists, scholars, and writers who had been excluded, including Dario Fo, Carlos Fuentes, and Nobel laureates such as the Chilean poet and politician Pablo Neruda and the Colombian novelist Gabriel García

Márquez, Laber described how Márquez had experienced difficulties obtaining a visa since 1963. In April, Laber wrote an article in the *New York Times* describing Márquez's failure to appear at an event in New York City to discuss US foreign policy in Central America. Due to his "political beliefs," the United States had issued Márquez a conditional visa under a waiver of inadmissibility, which he had declined. Márquez explained he had refused to travel to the United States on a visa that restricted his freedom during his visit for "reasons of principle and personal dignity."[50]

Morton Halperin, a foreign policy expert who had served in the Department of Defense during the Johnson administration and as a staff member for the National Security Council in 1969 during the Nixon administration, testified on behalf of the ACLU as the director of its Washington office and of the Center for National Security Studies. Halperin described such exclusions as Márquez's as a loss to American society, culture, and intellectual and political life. Responding to the recital of statistics, he remarked that if fifty of those 700 excluded were Nobel laureates, it is "a real loss, even if it is a small number." Halperin also noted the number does not include people who refuse to apply, no longer wanting to endure the indignity of answering questions about their beliefs and affiliations and the prolonged uncertainty, waiting to know if those affiliations or beliefs will be used to bar them from the United States.[51]

As someone who had worked in the government, Halperin appreciated that some expression might prove embarrassing and understood the State Department's desire to have foreign policy tools at its disposal to prevent it, but the price was too high with ideological exclusion. Avoiding embarrassment was not a sufficient justification for violating First Amendment freedoms and liberal democratic values, and Congress must step in and protect the right of Americans to communicate with foreigners about political, cultural, or intellectual issues.[52]

Halperin quoted President Harry Truman's veto of the McCarran-Walter Act and characterization of the "distrust" the act displayed for citizens and foreigners. He echoed Laber's statement that ideological exclusions violated the Helsinki Accords, and noted that exclusions contradicted Reagan's affirmation of those principles in recent remarks about how "expanding contact across borders and permitting a free exchange or interchange of information and ideas increase confidence; sealing off one's people from the rest of the world reduces it." Halperin also described the State Department's attempt to circumvent the McGovern Amendment requirements and reminded the committee that in 1983, the State Department had submitted a proposal to

Congress to revise the amendment to permit the secretary of state to consider "foreign policy factors" in addition to national security interests as a basis for denying waivers.[53]

Halperin urged the committee to view these ideological exclusions during the Reagan administration as part of the administration's concerted effort to restrict the free flow of information. He cited the administration's classification of Canadian films dealing with acid rain and nuclear war as political propaganda and regulating their distribution and screenings in 1983. According to Halperin, in 1982, after five years without restriction, the administration prohibited American tourists from traveling to Cuba under the International Emergency Economic Powers Act of 1977. In 1981, after almost twenty years without restriction, the government instituted an embargo on Cuban publications, including the newspaper Granma, sent to readers in the United States under the Trading with the Enemy Act of 1917.[54]

He believed Frank's bills "would strengthen our constitutional system by ensuring American's [sic] access to foreign people and ideas, making possible a more fully informed and politically sophisticated citizenry."[55] Halperin concluded his testimony with some suggestions for the bills and any future legislation seeking to eliminate ideological exclusions.

Halperin recommended a provision prohibiting exclusion based on "any past or expected speech, activity, belief, affiliation, or membership, which if held or conducted within the United States by a US citizen, would be protected by the First Amendment." The provision would also prohibit exclusion based on "the expected consequences of any activity" if conducted in the United States, if the activity would be protected by the First Amendment. Recognizing a potential for the abuse of discretion in exclusions based on "national security" grounds, he recommended limiting the government's discretion to exclude, and to extend it only to activity that was not protected by the First Amendment.[56] In 1977, the Supreme Court had reaffirmed its holding in Kleindienst v. Mandel (1972), including use of the lower "facially legitimate and bona fide reason" standard of review.[57] Thus, Halperin now urged Congress to take action by passing this legislation and not to wait for the courts to raise the standard of review for ideological exclusion cases to be consistent with First Amendment standards and protections.

He also recommended that Congress include a statutory "standing to sue" provision, which "would permit any person within the United States intending to communicate with a foreigner who is denied admission in violation of the statute to bring a civil action to enforce compliance with the law." While Kleindienst v. Mandel had established that individuals within the United

States had standing to sue in exclusion cases, a statutory provision would eliminate any potential barriers to litigation or lack of clarity in court decisions by preventing the government from arguing in each exclusion case that individuals lacked the standing to sue.[58]

As Frank predicted, the hearings were a good start to discussing ideological exclusion and deportation and how to end the practice through legislation. However, Frank's bills never made it out of the committee. According to Frank, as he was working on rewriting immigration law, Congress decided the best course of action was to divide the legislation into two parts. The first part focused on illegal immigration, including amnesty and employer sanctions, which became the Immigration Reform and Control Act of 1986. The second part would focus on legal immigration and exclusion categories.[59]

While Frank continued to fight to eliminate ideological restrictions from the McCarran-Walter Act, he was not alone. In addition to the ACLU, the PEN American Center had already joined his crusade.

PEN American Center

In 1921, British poet Catherine Amy Dawson Scott founded PEN International (Poets, Essayists, and Novelists, later broadened to include playwrights and editors) to unite writers after World War I. Eugene O'Neill, Willa Cather, Robert Frost, Ellen Glasgow, Edwin Arlington Robinson, and Robert Benchley, founded the PEN American Center in New York City a year later. One of the principles PEN stood for was "the unhampered transmission of thought within each nation and between all nations"; thus, "members pledge themselves to oppose any form of suppression of freedom of expression in the country and community to which they belong."[60]

William Styron, a Pulitzer Prize–winning novelist and author of *The Confessions of Nat Turner* and *Sophie's Choice*, testified on behalf of PEN American Center at the 1984 congressional hearings on Frank's bills to eliminate exclusions within the McCarran-Walter Act. Styron described how ideological exclusion undermined PEN's principles and mentioned the importance of "direct face-to-face discourse and confrontation" for writers. He dismissed arguments that access to works by authors who were barred from the United States provided sufficient free exchange of ideas and communication between these authors and Americans. Styron compared the argument to questioning the reason for universities if the country already had libraries. "Writers—just as other professionals, businessmen, and politicians—are charged with understanding the world as it is," he told the committee. "It is crucial to writers that they meet and talk with others who are grappling for the same sorts of expressions of truth."[61]

Styron also described how ideological exclusion damaged America's reputation abroad. The barring of writers, scholars, and artists depicted the United States as a nation that lacked confidence in its own values and freedoms, which appeared to be "more fragile than we claim they are." Styron recounted Gabriel García Márquez's choice between bureaucratic humiliation and visiting the United States, which Márquez considered his spiritual home and source of inspiration after reading works by William Faulkner. He also discussed the resentment felt by authors subjected to exclusion, such as British writer Graham Greene in 1952. He stated that Greene had developed a "pathological anti-Americanism, largely because of what I feel, what most people who followed his troubles and travels with the State Department felt was a gross mistreatment." Since his initial exclusion in 1952, Greene had traveled to the United States, but on a conditional visa granted by a waiver of inadmissibility due to his month-long membership in the Communist Party when he was a teenager. Styron added, if an influential man like Greene is "so soured on our way of life that he becomes an old grump, and known as the man who hates America, then I think we have done both him and us a disservice."[62]

In his testimony, Styron mentioned an event held on April 30, 1984, sponsored by PEN's Fund for Free Expression, where he joined writers E. L. Doctorow, John Irving, Susan Sontag, Arthur Miller, and Carolyn Forché to read works by authors who had been ideologically excluded from the United States, including Greene, Neruda, Márquez, Julio Cortázar, Dario Fo, Doris Lessing, Michel Foucault, Czeslaw Milosz, Dennis Brutus, Ángel Rama, and Alberto Moravia.[63] At the event, Forché commented, "I am puzzled as to why my government is afraid of a free exchange of ideas. I would hope that my country and its institutions are strong enough to endure freedom of expression." Irving described the exclusion provisions under the McCarran-Walter Act as "vestiges of McCarthyism" that "shame us today." Miller explained, "I doubt strongly that this law could have been passed before 1952, the wildest time of McCarthyism . . . but it's hung on the books because most people aren't aware of it."[64]

Carlos Fuentes had also attended the April 30 event. The State Department had recommended waivers and issued restricted visas to Fuentes to visit the United States since his exclusion in 1969. Fuentes had subsequently visited to speak and teach at American colleges and universities. Unlike Márquez, Fuentes chose not to decline a limited visa and to continue to travel to the United States. Refusing to visit and engage "would be giving in to the

Carlos Fuentes in Washington, DC, 1984
Miguel Sayago / Alamy Stock Photo.

negative and isolationist spirit of the law," he said. "And we would be denying our solidarity with those individuals and institutions in the USA that so steadfastly seek the removal of Section 28."[65]

A few months after the congressional hearings in 1984, the ACLU and PEN's Fund for Free Expression jointly convened a conference held on September 18, in Washington, DC. Entitled "Free Trade in Ideas," the one-day conference addressed the free exchange of scientific information inhibited by federal regulations, ideological exclusion of foreign visitors under the McCarran-Walter Act, access to foreign films restricted by the government, and travel to Cuba.

The American Association of University Professors, the American Association of Arts and Sciences, and the Federation of American Scientists, joined thirty-nine other organizations co-sponsoring the event, and speakers addressed an audience of 300 artists, writers, scholars, activists, and lawyers.[66] Speakers included First Amendment lawyer Floyd Abrams and Hodding Carter, assistant secretary of state for public affairs in Jimmy Carter's administration. Hodding Carter described the Reagan administration as "not uniquely evil," but its information control, secrecy, and intolerance of dissent as "the most virulent in my lifetime." He urged the organizations in the audience to focus on consistent and continuous advocacy against ideological exclusion and to forget about "a ritual denunciation or resolution at their yearly meeting." They "should be hitting it and hitting it and hitting it to the point of boredom."[67]

Audience members also heard from those excluded under the McCarran-Walter Act. Fuentes recounted his visa denials and waivers since the 1960s, describing exclusionary provisions as belonging to "the realm of sado-masochism, not to the legal ledgers of a self-respecting, powerful democracy." Nino Pasti and Dario Fo spoke live from Toronto, Canada, via satellite, and Márquez and Hortensia Bussi de Allende delivered prepared remarks on videotape, which were played for the audience. Márquez announced that the State Department had recently granted him an unrestricted visa to visit the United States, which he would accept. "It is a good precedent, not only for myself, but for all those who find themselves in the same situation."[68]

The increase in public pressure from organizations to end ideological exclusions under the McCarran-Walter Act and the press attention to their efforts prompted members of the Reagan administration to address the public to defend its policies and to defend themselves. In 1986, PEN International's Forty-Eighth Congress held the first of its annual meetings in New York City. Over 600 writers attended. PEN American Center hosted the meeting and its president, Norman Mailer, had chosen its theme: "The Writer's Imagination and the Imagination of the State." At the suggestion of John Kenneth Galbraith, Mailer had invited Secretary of State Shultz to deliver the keynote address at the meeting's opening plenary session, sparking protests from PEN members. E. L. Doctorow and Grace Paley were among the sixty-five signers of a public letter denouncing Mailer's decision to invite Shultz as "inappropriate," given Shultz's leadership in the State Department, which "has, in the past, excluded many writers from the United States using the McCarran-Walter Act." Paley called his invitation to speak "outrageous." She asked, "What is his relationship to us? Is he a writer? What has he got to do with us? There is no reason to have him here, and people resent it." On January 12, Shultz delivered his speech, "The Writer and Freedom," after receiving the letter and a "chorus of hisses and boos" from the audience.[69]

"I am so pleased and honored to be here," Shultz said. "It has been a long while since the International Conference of PEN has been held in the United States. America is proud to have you here. Diversity, debate, contrast, argumentativeness are what we as a people thrive on. So, as individuals, each of you is truly welcome here." Addressing the protests to his appearance at the conference, Shultz explained he had recently learned he had become "the latest PEN controversy," but in "Norman's world, it a high form of flattery—and that's how I take it. And I salute you for taking this decision in favor of free speech."[70]

Shultz praised the United States as a place where "writers can speak, write and publish without political hindrance," in contrast to other nations where writers "may be silenced, imprisoned even killed" if their work appeared to threaten the government or its leaders. To Shultz, a free society was vindicated by the "outspokenness, even the obstreperousness, and the self-evident vitality of the artists and intellectuals," which PEN and the audience demonstrated. He added, "And serious people know the difference between freedom and its absence."[71]

Shultz then addressed concerns about exclusions under the McCarran-Walter Act. "This Administration is committed, and I am personally committed, to protecting free expression of all political ideas," he declared. He insisted that the United States has never had an "approved policy" to deny visas to foreign visitors "merely because the applicant wants to say that he disapproves of the United States or one of its policies." Shultz announced a State Department policy change for exclusions under the McCarran-Walter Act: "When a writer or artist seeks a visa for the purpose of speaking or lecturing or performing in the United States, the administration of the Act now involves the strong presumption against denying access for foreign policy reasons."[72]

Yet, there was an exception to this "new" policy. Shultz emphasized that the United States would exclude foreigners "who aim to undermine our system through their actions, who are likely to engage in proscribed intelligence activities, or who raise funds or otherwise assist our enemies." He did not provide any further details or definitions of these activities or enemies.[73]

Shultz concluded his speech with praise for PEN members and a show of support from the administration. "The yearning for freedom is the most powerful political force all across the planet. You are among its champions," he said. "You can be proud of what you have done for that cause. And don't be so surprised by the fact that Ronald Reagan and I are on your side."[74]

Shultz's speech sparked conversation among the writers about the role of the state. Mailer, for one, declared it a "victory for free speech." Yet, Shultz did not quell concerns about ideological exclusions or rehabilitate his image or that of the State Department. Instead his speech renewed the push to end exclusions under the McCarran-Walter Act. An editorial in the *New York Times* noted that the State Department continued to exclude based on affiliations under Section 212(a)(28) and that not every applicant received a waiver. While Shultz proudly announced a new policy of a "presumption against denying access for foreign policy reasons," his State Department still used guilt by association to deny visas. "The thought is welcome, but a close reading of Mr. Shultz's text suggests considerably less change than meets the eye."[75]

Moynihan-Frank Amendment

John G. Roberts Jr.'s copy of Shultz's speech at the PEN International conference had marked the passages discussing exclusion under the McCarran-Walter Act.[76] Long before becoming the chief justice of the Supreme Court, Roberts had served as associate counsel to the White House from 1982 to 1986. During February 1986, Roberts was tasked with responding to a resolution sent to the Reagan administration by the American Bar Association (ABA), which called for revision to Section 212(a)(28) of the McCarran-Walter Act.

Under ABA Resolution 103, "An alien invited to the United States to speak or otherwise participate in an exchange of ideas should not be denied a visa solely on the basis of past or current political beliefs or political associations or on the basis of the expected content of the person's statements in the United States." The ABA's recommendation was narrow and conservative. It stated that this revision applied only to nonimmigrant visas under Section 212(a)(28) and would not preclude visa denials to those whose presence or activity in the United States the government believed would harm the interests of the United States, including foreign relations. It would also not prevent reciprocal visa denials used to gain entry for Americans to another country, or interfere with the ability of the government to continue to exclude terrorists, those who sought entry to engage in illegal activity, or those detrimental to the nation's security or interests. The ABA emphasized that its recommendation for revision to Section 212(a)(28) left intact the other exclusion provisions the administration could use for foreign policy, including presidential proclamation.[77]

The presidential proclamation the ABA referred to was under Section 212(f) of the McCarran-Walter Act, which provided that "whenever the President finds that the entry of any aliens or of any class of aliens into the United States would be detrimental to the interests of the United States, he may by proclamation, and for such a period as he shall deem necessary, suspend the entry of all aliens or any class of aliens as immigrants or non-immigrants, or impose on the entry of aliens any restrictions he may deem to be appropriate."[78]

At that time, Reagan had issued two proclamations. The first concerned refugees from Haiti and Cuba. Proclamation 4865, issued in 1981, suspended the entry of undocumented foreigners from the high seas and directed the interdiction of certain vessels carrying them.[79] The second explicitly pertained to foreign policy with Cuba and its government. Proclamation 5377, issued in 1985, suspended entry to Cuban officers, or employees of the Cuban government or members of the Cuban Communist Party holding official or diplomatic passports, and to individuals who were considered by the secretary of state to be officers or employees.[80]

State Department legal advisor Abraham D. Sofaer had asked Fred F. Fielding, counsel to the president, for comments regarding the ABA resolution. According to Roberts, Sofaer saw no issue with repealing Section 212(a)(28), as it would be consistent with State Department practice in its current administration of the provision. Sofaer had described the waiver process under Section 212(a)(28) as "time-consuming, expensive, and sterile."[81]

In his memorandum to Fielding, Roberts expressed skepticism that the provision served no purpose if a significant percentage did not receive waivers. He also recommended that Fielding insist administrators "guarantee that exclusion for foreign policy reasons would be just as readily available (and defensible in court) without [Section 212(a)28] as with it." Roberts noted that the elimination of this provision would mean that Section 212(a)(27) "must be fully usable for foreign policy exclusions." He dismissed the suggestion that the foreign policy presidential proclamation provision was sufficient as the presidential proclamation "is unworkable with respect to individual cases." He concluded by asking why the Reagan administration was "trailing after ABA on this." Roberts argued that, rather than "reacting" to the ABA's resolution, if Sofaer and the State Department thought repealing Section 212(a)(28) was wise, then "we should propose it and submit our own bill."[82]

In his response to Sofaer, Fielding incorporated Roberts's recommendations, including his last one regarding the ABA. He wrote, it "seems preferable to seize the initiative and submit our own proposals to Congress, stealing some thunder from those who hardly support the administration. This approach would also better enable us to control the specific statutory language of any repeal or modification."[83] In a follow-up for Sofaer, Roberts cautioned that Sofaer's proposed revision to the McCarran-Walter Act, excluding foreigners "who would be detrimental to the national security," was "a far cry from exclusion for foreign policy reasons, which he and the ABA have argued would be retained as a legitimate basis for exclusion."[84]

On June 23, 1987, the Subcommittee on Immigration, Refugees, and International Law, held a hearing to discuss H.R. 1119, a revised bill introduced by Congressman Frank and forty-six of his colleagues to repeal and replace the ideological exclusion and deportation provisions within the McCarran-Walter Act. The bill removed the security provisions, Sections 212(a)(27), (a)(28), and (a)(29), and replaced them with a provision that excluded foreign visitors whom the consular official or attorney general "knows, or has reasonable ground to believe, is likely to engage after entry in any activity which is prohibited by the laws of the United States relating to espionage or sabotage, any other criminal activity which endangers public safety or national security, any activity a purpose of which is the opposition to, or the control or overthrow of, the Government of the United States by force, violence, or other unconstitutional means, or any terrorist activity." It also barred any foreigner who has engaged in terrorist activity, which it defined as "organizing, abetting, or participating in a wanton or indiscriminate act of violence with extreme indifference to the risk of causing death or serious bodily injury to individuals not taking part in armed hostilities." These provisions also applied to deportation.[85]

Incorporating Morton Halperin's suggestions at the 1984 hearing, Frank's revised bill included judicial review within the statute and the "standing to sue" provision, based on *Kleindienst v. Mandel* (1972). A citizen or permanent resident "who intends to meet in person with, or hear in person, an alien, and who has been denied such opportunity because the alien has been denied the issuance of a visa or entry . . . may bring a cause of action for review of the denial in any District Court of the United States in which the individual resides or . . . intended to meet or hear the alien."[86]

In his testimony before the committee on behalf of the Reagan administration, Sofaer opposed the elimination of Section 212(a)(27) for foreign policy reasons. He suggested replacing the language of the statute, providing the executive with the authority to deny visas to persons whose admission to the United States would cause "potentially serious foreign policy consequences." Sofaer also opposed the inclusion of the judicial review provision and "standing to sue." He argued, "Foreign policy exclusions are essentially political decisions and should only be made by the branches of Government charged with this authority under the Constitution." The judiciary must defer to the legislative and executive branches and could not review political decisions. Sofaer expressed concern that litigation could require the government to reveal "sensitive information, including intelligence sources and methods, in order to prove its case." The administration would be forced to choose between damaging American diplomacy or the nation's intelligence operations.[87]

During the hearing, Frank and Congressman Mazzoli engaged in a discussion about the terrorism provisions with Dr. Juliana Geran Pilon, a senior policy analyst at the Heritage Foundation, a conservative public policy think tank. Pilon noted that H.R 1119 did not include a specific exclusion for members or officers of the PLO, which was included in the McGovern Amendment. Pilon expressed concern that absent a similar provision in the bill, the PLO would not be subject to exclusion.[88] Frank was emphatic that the PLO was implicitly included in the terrorist exclusion. Frank's response reflected Congress's categorization in the Anti-Terrorism Act of 1987, which designated the PLO as a terrorist organization and "a threat to the interests of the United States and its allies, and to international law." The committee also discussed whether fundraising activities fell under the terrorism provision. Frank insisted fundraising did, under the "abetting" language, and, according to Frank, this included raising funds for guns or food.[89]

This time, Frank was not waiting for Congress to pass another immigration act to address the exclusion provisions. Senator Daniel Patrick Moynihan (D-NY) joined Frank in his crusade against ideological restrictions, and, in December 1987, Congress passed Section 901 of the Foreign Relations Authorization Act, referred to as the "Moynihan-Frank Amendment." While it was a temporary measure with a one-year sunset provision, Section 901 prohibited exclusion and deportation from the United States "because of any past, current, or expected beliefs, statements, or associations which, if engaged in by a United States citizen in the United States, would be protected under the Constitution of the United States."[90] The Senate Committee on Foreign Relations described it as an "affirmation of the principles of the First Amendment."[91]

In 1988, Congress extended the Moynihan-Frank Amendment for two more years. It also included some restrictions and exceptions reflecting the concerns expressed in the 1987 hearings. Congress restricted the amendment to apply to nonimmigrant visitors, as opposed to immigrants. It included a foreign policy and national security reason for exclusion, but only if it did not conflict with the existing protections under the amendment. Congress also incorporated the PLO exception in the McGovern Amendment, excluding PLO members, officials, officers, representatives, or spokesmen, and H.R. 1119's definition of terrorist activity and its terrorist provision, but added membership in a terrorist organization. It barred anyone the attorney general or consular officer knew or had reason to believe had engaged in terrorist activity, as an individual or member of an organization, or was likely to engage in such activity after entry.[92]

The text of the Moynihan-Frank Amendment represented a significant moment in the history of ideological exclusion and deportation. The amendment effectively repealed the ideological restrictions based on expression, belief, and association within the McCarran-Walter Act and held foreign noncitizens inside the United States and those applying for visas to visit to the same First Amendment speech-protective standards and safeguards as US citizens.

The Moynihan-Frank Amendment closed the door on the ideological exclusions and deportations based on anarchist or Communist beliefs, associations, and expressions that had persisted within federal legislation for over half a century. Yet, the restrictions and terrorism provisions that remained would also open the door to future ideological exclusions and deportations through guilt by association with and material support to terrorist organizations.

Litigation

The ACLU and NECLC worked together and brought legal challenges on behalf of the organizations and individuals who had invited Borge, Pasti, Finlay, Lezcano, and Bussi to come to the United States, challenging their exclusion for violating Americans' First Amendment right to receive information. By 1988, the federal courts had determined the visa denials were unconstitutional. In *Abourezk v. Reagan*, Leonard Boudin joined Steven Shapiro, who led the ACLU attorneys challenging the exclusion of Borge, Pasti, Finlay, and Lezcano. In *Allende v. Shultz*, Shapiro joined Boudin who challenged Bussi's exclusion.

In 1984, DC District Court Judge Harold H. Greene granted summary judgment in favor of the government in *Abourezk v. Reagan*. Greene dismissed Shapiro and Boudin's argument that Section 212(a)(27) pertained to the activities of the foreigner and not merely presence within the United States. Greene cited the entry of the former Shah of Iran and his mere presence in the United States, which resulted in serious consequences for the United States, including the hostage crisis. He also rejected their argument that (a)(27) did not explicitly exclude based on foreign policy reasons, but rather for direct threat to national security and safety. In light of the executive's "substantial independent authority" in foreign relations and in the admission of foreigners, Greene located foreign policy implicitly within (a)(27)'s clauses regarding "prejudicial to the public interest" and "endangering the welfare."[93]

Yet, when he applied the "facially legitimate and *bona fide* reason" standard established in *Kleindienst v. Mandel* (1972), the government initially failed the test. Absent further details beyond the government's assertion the admission of Borge, Pasti, Finlay, and Lezcano "would have been prejudicial to the conduct of foreign affairs," Greene considered it reasonable to conclude that the State Department denied the visas because it "did not agree with or feared the content of whatever communication they might make while in this country." Under (a)(27), foreigners could not be excluded solely for the content of their speech.

The State Department then provided the court with a classified affidavit from Under Secretary Eagleburger, which Greene inspected *in camera* (privately), without disclosure to Shapiro, Boudin, or the plaintiffs. After this inspection, Greene reversed and concluded that the government did have a "facially legitimate and *bona fide* reason" to exclude. The reason was based not on what Borge, Pasti, Finlay, and Lezcano might say, but on their "personal status as officials of governments or organizations hostile to the United States." These organizations or governments might seek to acquire "legitimacy and respectability" through the admission of their officials to the United States.[94]

In *Allende v. Shultz* (1985), Massachusetts District Court Judge Andrew A. Caffrey held in favor of Bussi. Caffrey began his decision by upholding the right of the American invitees to bring a challenge to Bussi's exclusion in federal court, as a violation of their First Amendment right to receive information, citing *Kleindienst v. Mandel*. As Morton Halperin predicted in the 1984 hearings when he advocated for a statutory "standing to sue," despite the legal precedent set in *Mandel*, the government had argued the case should be dismissed because the American invitees lacked standing.[95]

Caffrey then declared that the government had failed to provide a "facially legitimate and *bona fide* reason" for excluding Bussi under Section 212(a)(27). The State Department had barred Bussi based on her membership in the World Peace Council, and (a)(27) did not include membership, but rather activities. The membership statute was under Section 212(a)(28) and subject to the McGovern Amendment's waiver requirement. The provisions were not interchangeable. The (a)(28) provision would be superfluous if (a)(27) encompassed the same reasons for exclusion. The State Department could not simply replace one provision with another to serve its needs or desire to circumvent statutory requirements. The government produced a classified affidavit from the State Department for the judge's *in camera* review, as it did in *Abourezk v. Reagan*. Unlike Greene, Caffrey declined to inspect the affidavit. Caffrey explained that the First Circuit Court of Appeals had ruled the court could not grant summary judgment based on evidence, which the opposing party (in this case the plaintiffs) was denied access to review.[96]

Shapiro and Boudin appealed Greene's ruling in *Abourezk v. Reagan* to the DC Court of Appeals, and in 1986, a three-judge panel (2–1) vacated Greene's decision and remanded the case for further review. Writing for the majority, future Supreme Court Justice Ruth Bader Ginsburg concluded that Greene had incorrectly analyzed Section 212(a)(27) when he granted summary judgment in favor of the government and that questions of material fact remained in the case. She also expressed concern regarding his reliance on classified evidence not disclosed to the plaintiffs to render his decision and justify exclusion, which she argued was unfair and undermined the adversarial system.[97]

Judge Ginsburg's interpretation was the same as Caffrey's. The provisions of Section 212(a)(27) and (a)(28) were not interchangeable, and thus required independent reasons to support exclusion. The government's concern about what Borge, Pasti, Finlay, and Lezcano might say in the United States stemmed from their membership in organizations or affiliation with governments and thereby fell under the (a)(28) category, and not from their anticipated activities or mere presence under (a)(27). According to Ginsburg, "A reason that is *in addition to* the fact of membership but not *independent of* that fact provides an insufficient bulwark against the possibility of Executive evasion of the will of Congress as expressed in the McGovern Amendment."[98]

After reviewing the legislative history of Section 212(a)(27) in the McCarran-Walter Act, which she described as "terse and tugs in more than one direction," Ginsburg concluded that while the text of (a)(27) explicitly listed "activities" and not mere presence within the United States, the interpretation of the statute had included presence in certain circumstances where the foreigner was a member or associated with a terrorist or criminal organization or brutal, authoritarian regime. Greene should have required the government to produce more examples of this interpretation of (a)(27) and provide the plaintiffs with the chance to refute them and offer counter-examples. Yet, visa denials based on a generalization about affiliations or membership in organizations was a "brand of guilt by association Congress sought to check" with the McGovern Amendment. Thus, Ginsburg held that the government could exclude under (a)(27) only if it established a reason independent from membership in and affiliation with an organization under (a)(28).[99]

Ginsburg concluded with a reminder that the plenary power doctrine required judicial deference to the executive branch, but it did not eliminate judicial review entirely. "The Executive has broad discretion over the admission and exclusion of aliens, but that discretion is not boundless," she wrote. "It extends only as far as the statutory authority conferred by Congress and may not transgress constitutional limitations. It is the duty of the courts, in cases properly before them, to say where those statutory and constitutional boundaries lie."[100]

In 1988, the DC District Court held that the government had not provided sufficiently independent reasons to justify exclusion of Borge, Pasti, Finlay, and Lezcano under Section 212(a)(27) and ordered the government to grant their visas to enter the United States. At this time, the Moynihan-Frank Amendment effectively changed the law and the evaluation of exclusions.[101]

A year later, the DC Circuit Court held that the Presidential Proclamation 5377, signed in 1985, which barred Cuban officers of the Cuban Communist Party could bar Finlay and Lezcano entry, as it constituted an independent reason under Section 212(a)(27). The court also held that Presidential Proclamation 5887, signed in 1988, which suspended entry to officers and employees of the government of Nicaragua would similarly bar Borge from entry to the United States.[102]

A few months before the DC District Court's decision, the First Circuit Court of Appeals affirmed Caffrey's decision in *Allende v. Shultz*. While the State Department had since granted Bussi's application for a visa, Boudin sought a declaratory judgment from the court that the government had exceeded its authority under Section 212(a)(27) and violated the plaintiffs' First Amendment right to receive information. The court agreed, arguing that (a)(27) pertained to activities and not membership or status, as did (a)(28). It noted that the State Department had conceded that its decision to exclude Bussi from the United States would have been different if she had intended to visit a sick relative rather than deliver speeches. The government's foreign policy concern did not change the fact that this concern "flows directly from anticipated content of [Bussi's] speech in the United States and anticipated reaction of American audiences." Under the Moynihan-Frank Amendment, this concern was not a legitimate basis for exclusion.[103]

The decision was a victory for Boudin and also his last major case. He died a year later, in 1989. His obituary in the *New York Times* discussed the celebrated civil liberties lawyer's impressive legal career, including his successful

Supreme Court challenge to ideological passport restrictions in *Kent v. Dulles* (1958), establishing the fundamental right to travel. It named some of his clients—Paul Robeson, Daniel Ellsberg, Julian Bond, and Dr. Benjamin Spock.

The obituary also included descriptions of his children. His son, Michael Boudin, was a deputy assistant attorney general in the antitrust division of the Justice Department. His daughter, Kathy Boudin, was a former member of the Weathermen serving a prison sentence for her involvement in the Brink's armored truck felony-murder in 1981 after living underground as a fugitive. She had fled an explosion in Greenwich Village killing three fellow Weathermen after their accidental detonation of a bomb in 1970.[104]

Yet, Boudin's obituary did not mention Ernest Mandel or Hortensia Bussi de Allende. It did not mention his other successes in the Supreme Court, including *Lamont v. Postmaster General* (1965), establishing the right to receive information under the First Amendment, or *Kleindienst v. Mandel* (1972), establishing the right of Americans to challenge the exclusion of foreigners as a violation of their First Amendment right to hear and receive information. These cases and clients are an important part of Boudin's significant legacy and of the history of ideological exclusion, immigration, and First Amendment freedoms in the United States.

In 1998, the NECLC was absorbed by the Center for Constitutional Rights (CCR), a human rights legal organization focusing on First Amendment, immigration, and civil liberties cases. Founded in 1966, CCR had consistently represented civil and human rights activists, protesters, and immigrants and immigrant activists. In the 1980s, CCR challenged human rights violations in Nicaragua and Federal Bureau of Investigation (FBI) surveillance of the US-based Committee in Solidarity with the People of El Salvador (CISPES). A lawyer named David Cole went to work for CCR shortly after graduating from Yale Law School in 1984. Cole's first trial was his defense of Margaret Randall, a poet, photographer, and activist who had lived in Mexico, Nicaragua, and Cuba. Randall was born in New York City in 1936, and when she returned in the 1980s, the Reagan administration sought to deport her under the McCarran-Walter Act for advocating the doctrines of "world communism." The administration unsuccessfully argued that Randall had forfeited her US citizenship when she obtained Mexican citizenship in the 1960s.[105]

Like Boudin, Cole would pursue a legal career in civil liberties and First Amendment law. Whereas Boudin's career traced anti-Communism from the late 1930s to the end of the Cold War, Cole's legal representation in the 1980s and 1990s and into the twenty-first century would follow the transition from Communism to terrorism as the object of fear within the United States.

The Shift toward Terrorism

In 1986, the Reagan administration created the Alien Border Control Committee as part of its counterterrorism strategy. The committee examined proposals for the deportation of those with links to international terrorism and visa restrictions to foreigners "likely to be supportive of terrorist activity within the United States," as well as for the Immigration and Naturalization Service (INS) to receive more access to Central Intelligence Agency data.[106] According to Cole, the committee developed a plan to selectively deport foreign activists who were critical of the United States and its foreign policy, specifically targeting activists "not in conformity with their immigration status" and deporting them by using existing law, including terrorism provisions, as well as secret, classified evidence.[107]

The Popular Front for the Liberation of Palestine (PFLP) was a Marxist-Leninist group affiliated with the PLO, which was critical of US foreign policy and of its support of Israel in the Middle East. Founded in 1967 by George Habash, the PFLP had been affiliated with the PLO since 1968, but maintained its autonomy. Beginning in the late 1960s, members of the PFLP had been responsible for a series of terrorist acts abroad, focusing on Israeli targets and often involving plane hijackings or airport and ground attacks.

In the 1980s and 1990s, Cole represented immigrants in the United States who were members of or linked to the PFLP. Two cases reveal the government's use of the McCarran-Walter Act and the Moynihan-Frank Amendment to deport based on guilt by association with the PFLP and the interpretation of these laws in federal courts that prevented their deportation. These cases raised questions regarding membership, affiliation, designation, support, and confidential evidence familiar from previous cases concerning alleged Communists and affiliations with Communist organizations. Judges also turned to legal precedent from the 1940s and 1950s to guide them in determining whether Cole's clients fell under the terrorist restrictions and if those restrictions were unconstitutional.

In 1986, the INS sought to deport Fouad Yacoub Rafeedie, a legal permanent resident who had emigrated from the West Bank in 1975 and was living with his family in Ohio. Rafeedie was an outspoken critic of the United States' support of Israel and its foreign policy in the Middle East and advocated for Palestinian rights, publishing articles and speaking on television and radio. He was also a member of Arab and Palestinian political and cultural organizations in the United States. Returning from a brief trip to Syria, he was stopped at the border by INS, which then pursued his deportation, deeming him excludable under the McCarran-Walter Act. Based on confidential information submitted to the DC District Court, the INS claimed that Rafeedie attended a meeting of the Palestinian Youth Organization (PYO) while in Syria and that PYO was an affiliate of PFLP. It alleged Rafeedie was a "high-ranking member" of the PFLP.[108]

In *Rafeedie v. INS* (1988), DC District Court Judge Joyce Hens Green held Rafeedie could not be deported under the Moynihan-Frank Amendment to the McCarran-Walter Act. Green determined that the PLO exception applied only to the PLO and not to alleged affiliates like the PFLP. Green then turned to the terrorist activity exception. The government's case was based on guilt by association. It had not shown that Rafeedie was likely to engage in terrorist activity ("organizing, abetting or participating in a wanton or indiscriminate act of violence") after entry or had engaged in such activity in the past, as an individual or as part of any organization.

The government claimed that Rafeedie had fundraised and recruited for the PFLP, but offered no evidence. Green looked to the conference report in Congress accompanying the Moynihan-Frank Amendment, which she found broadly interpreted the provision to include recruiting and financing or fundraising. Cole argued that such activity should be read as "activity specific" in the context of terrorist activities, to facilitate terrorism and not just to provide funds for the organization. Some activities might not pertain to terrorism. Green was skeptical.[109]

"Conceivably, under some circumstances, [Rafeedie's] fundraising and recruiting might be characterized as passive, innocent, or in furtherance of advocacy or speech," Green wrote. "On the other hand, the money may well have been raised directly for the PFLP's 'war chest' to finance its activities, including terrorist activities." Because the government did not provide a description of the evidence of Rafeedie's recruiting or fundraising, it was impossible to determine if his alleged activities "did in fact directly aid the PFLP in carrying out terrorist activities or whether they were clearly for nonterrorist purposes." Green ended with a discussion of which party bore the burden of proof. It might be impossible for both the government and Rafeedie to demonstrate that fundraising and recruiting directly supported terrorist activity or that it was solely used for innocent purposes. Green concluded that a foreigner "assumes this risk of proof when he becomes involved with a terrorist organization and does not clearly delimit his activities on its behalf."[110]

Rafeedie was not deported, but his case revealed how similarly situated immigrants were vulnerable to deportation based on their associations and memberships in organizations the government considered terrorist organizations and through material support such as recruiting or fund-raising. The same could also apply to exclusion cases. In her decision, Green did not address whether Rafeedie knew or had reason to know that the PFLP was considered a terrorist organization by the government, and that his association and activities could be used as grounds to deport him. Green did, however, raise the question and possibility of "innocent" support to a terrorist organization and limiting one's support to lawful as opposed to terrorist activities.

Reflecting this shift to terrorism, another case focused on affiliation and membership. The "Los Angeles Eight" (LA 8) case began in January 1987, when FBI and INS officials arrested seven Palestinians and one Kenyan immigrant in Los Angeles, California and charged them with being affiliated with the PFLP, which it claimed advocated the doctrines of "world communism" and thus made them subject to deportation under Section 212(a)(28) of the McCarran-Walter Act. The government abandoned those grounds, and a few months later switched to other provisions. Two of the Palestinians, Khader Musa Hamide and Michel Ibrahim Shehadeh (both legal permanent residents), were charged under a provision in the McCarran-Walter Act, Section 241(a)(6)(F)(iii), for being members of or affiliating with an organization that "advocates or teaches the unlawful damage, injury or destruction of property." The other six were charged under other provisions, not pertaining to advocacy or membership.[111]

While Hamide and Shehadeh were in the midst of administrative appeals of their deportation orders, the other six and the American-Arab Anti-Discrimination Committee (ADC) requested a declaratory judgment, challenging the constitutionality of this provision under the McCarran-Walter Act, which they argued posed an immediate threat of deportation and chilled their First Amendment right to free expression and association within the United States. They cited the government's efforts to deport those affiliated with the PFLP, including Rafeedie, and the government's switch to different provisions of the McCarran-Walter Act in order to deport. The INS had not disavowed its intent to deport these six on similar charges in the future.[112]

In *ADC v. Meese* (1989), California District Court Judge Stephen V. Wilson struck down the ideological deportation provisions in the McCarran-Walter Act as unconstitutionally overbroad and thus chilling speech and association protections and violating the First Amendment. In his decision, he directly confronted the question posed by ideological deportation and discussed by scholars, advocates, and jurists for nearly a century. Wilson held that non-citizens within the United States were entitled to the same First Amendment protections and safeguards as citizens and subject to the same standards of judicial review.[113]

Wilson then turned to the Supreme Court's decision in *Harisiades v. Shaughnessy* (1952). While the court had upheld deportation and deferred to Congress under the plenary power doctrine, the decision was consistent with the suppression of Communist expression and association under the prevailing First Amendment standard at the time, *Dennis v. United States* (1951). Wilson rearticulated Zechariah Chafee Jr.'s argument that the Bill of Rights did not distinguish between citizens and noncitizens, and then cited Justice Frank Murphy's concurring opinion in *Bridges v. Wixon* (1945), remarking on the disparity between rights held within the United States and within the deportation setting, which made such an "empty mockery of human freedom."[114]

Wilson concluded his opinion by applying the current First Amendment standard to the ideological deportation provisions in the McCarran-Walter Act, which they failed. Under *Brandenburg v. Ohio* (1969), the First Amendment protected advocacy unless it was directed to incite lawless activity that was imminent and likely to occur. The McCarran-Walter provisions were overbroad, encompassing protected advocacy, and thus violated the First Amendment.[115]

During President George H. W. Bush's administration, Congress finally passed immigration reform addressing the exclusion and deportation categories. The legislation focused on terrorism and closed perceived loopholes. The Immigration Act of 1990 amended the McCarran-Walter Act and simply did not include the ideological exclusion provisions in Sections 212(a)(27) and (28).[116] The 1990 act incorporated Sofaer's proposed text to replace (a)(27) by excluding foreigners if their entry or activities in the United States "would have potentially serious adverse foreign policy consequences for the United States."[117] It also incorporated the Moynihan-Frank Amendment, prohibiting exclusion or restrictions on entry based on past, present, and future expected beliefs, associations, and expressions.[118] This included foreign government officials. Addressing John Roberts's foreign policy concern, there was an exception for all nonofficials if the secretary of state determined the admission would "compromise a compelling foreign policy interest." The secretary was required to report the name and provide the reason for the exclusion to Congress.

While the 1990 act eliminated exclusions based on "world communism" or what would be "prejudicial to the public interest," it incorporated the Moynihan-Frank Amendment exception for anyone who "engaged in terrorist activity or is likely to engage in terrorist activity upon entry to the United States." The definition of terrorist activity focused on action (such as hijacking, sabotage, assassination, and use of biological weapons or explosives).[119] The terrorist activity provision also included anyone who knowingly provided "any type of material support" to an actor who that person "knows or has reason to believe has committed or plans to commit" terrorist activity. Such support included planning and preparation, communication, gathering information, recruiting, and funds, as well as the "soliciting of funds or other things of value" for a terrorist organization or terrorist activity.[120] The 1990 act excluded officers and high-ranking officials in the PLO and explicitly designated the PLO as a terrorist organization.[121]

Congress and President Bill Clinton felt increased public pressure to pass antiterrorism legislation after the World Trade Center attack in 1993 and after the Oklahoma City bombing in 1995.[122] The Antiterrorism and Effective Death Penalty Act of 1996 (AEDPA) left tremendous power and discretion in the hands of the secretary of state to designate a group a Foreign Terrorist Organization (FTO) and to determine if it "engages in terrorist activity." AEDPA criminalized "material support" to a designated FTO, and membership in and material support to a designated FTO were grounds for exclusion and deportation. In 1997, Secretary of State Madeleine Albright added Hamas, Hezbollah, and the PFLP to the FTO list. AEDPA authorized the use of classified, secret evidence in terrorist deportation cases without full disclosure to the deportee and provided for the immediate detention of deportees subject to special removal proceedings.[123]

The Moynihan-Frank Amendment and the Immigration Act of 1990 required the government to demonstrate that a foreigner was likely to engage or had engaged in terrorist activity either as an individual or in an organization in order to exclude. Under AEDPA, membership in a designated FTO was sufficient; it was guilt by association. In *Rafeedie v. INS*, Judge Green discussed whether foreigners could limit their material support to lawful activities and if the government was required to distinguish between support for terrorist and lawful activities. Green described foreigners as assuming the risk of exclusion by providing any support to an organization the US government deemed a terrorist organization. Under AEDPA, it appeared that no such delineation or limitation of support mattered. Any support to a designated FTO constituted material support.

During the 1980s, the Reagan administration sought to ideologically exclude foreign visitors from the United States and to circumvent the McGovern Amendment's requirement pertaining to explicit exclusions in Section 212(a)(28) under the McCarran-Walter Act by turning to Section 212(a)(27), an implicit exclusion that barred those engaging in activities prejudicial to the public interest or endangering the welfare, safety, or security of the United States. It argued that such exclusions were necessary to effect US foreign policy and were reflective of that policy. Those excluded, the public, members of Congress, and legal advocates dismissed this justification and argued that the Reagan administration used the law as a form of retaliatory exclusion of critics of its foreign policy and those who expressed dissenting views they sought to suppress. Congressman Barney Frank seized the opportunity to rid the United States of ideological exclusion and deportation under the McCarran-Walter Act and pushed to revise the law. When the ACLU and the PEN American Center joined him in calling for the end of ideological exclusions under the act, their arguments rearticulated those made in the past regarding the damage done to the United States and its reputation abroad and the depiction of the nation as fearful and lacking confidence in its own institutions, democratic values, and people.

The NECLC and the ACLU successfully challenged the Reagan administration's use of Section 212(a)(27) in federal courts and reaffirmed the ability of individuals and organizations within the United States to challenge exclusions based on the right to receive information and to hear under the First Amendment, as established in *Kleindienst v. Mandel* (1972). Judge Ruth Bader Ginsburg held the Reagan administration accountable for its attempts to evade statutory requirements by switching to another provision of the McCarran-Walter Act to suit its needs and to suppress criticism. She asserted that the executive branch did not hold limitless discretion to exclude and could not use its discretion to violate the Constitution. The DC Circuit Court agreed, but later upheld exclusions based on foreign policy and under Reagan's use of presidential proclamations to suspend entry to foreign nationals under Section 212(f) of the McCarran-Walter Act. The circuit court's opinion showed judicial deference to the president's exercise of ultimate discretion to suspend foreign nationals under this presidential proclamation power.

Although Frank succeeded in eliminating ideological exclusion under the McCarran-Walter Act through the Moynihan-Frank Amendment, and later in the Immigration Act of 1990, these laws paved the way for the shift of exclusions and deportations based on Communism to those based on terrorism. This shift and the designation of terrorist organizations and discussions of affiliation resembled the shift from suppression of radicalism and anarchism in the early twentieth century to Communism in the 1930s and into the 1950s. Members of Congress, as well as Labor and Justice Department officials, had parsed definitions and sought to revise statutes in order to ideologically exclude or deport Communists, as did those who challenged these exclusions and deportations. Once the McCarran Act and the McCarran-Walter Act explicitly included Communists and members of Communist organizations as excludable and deportable, as well as using guilt by association with designated Communist-front groups, it became harder to prevent deportations and exclusions based on belief and association.

Leonard Boudin observed the use of the McCarran-Walter Act from its passage at the height of McCarthyism to the Nixon administration and through the Reagan administration. He drew on his experiences challenging civil liberties and First Amendment violations to establish legal precedent that he and his colleagues would later employ in new challenges. Similarly, David Cole would take his experiences and perspective as a lawyer at CCR challenging the McCarran-Walter Act, including the LA 8 and Rafeedie cases, during this shift toward terrorism in the late 1980s, and use them to bring more legal challenges and develop his arguments.

During the 1990s, Cole joined the Georgetown Law Center faculty and continued to represent clients facing civil liberties violations and deportation. The government also remained determined to deport the LA 8. The INS charged members of the LA 8 with material support to a terrorist organization under the Immigration Act of 1990, but a district court ruled that the INS had selectively targeted the LA 8 for deportation based on their lawful activities and that this violated the First Amendment.

In 1995, the Ninth Circuit Court of Appeals affirmed the district court's ruling and noncitizens' entitlement to First Amendment protections. The INS tried again under the Illegal Immigration Reform and Immigrant Responsibility Act of 1996 (IIRIRA), arguing that its provisions stripped federal courts of judicial review of the attorney general's decision to commence action or execute removal orders, thus barring the court from review for selective deportation. The district court and court of appeals again held in favor of the LA 8 and their First Amendment claims.[124]

In *Reno v. ADC* (1999), a 8–1 decision, the Supreme Court held in favor of the attorney general and the INS. Writing for the majority, Justice Antonin Scalia argued that under the plenary power doctrine, Congress had the power to regulate immigration, which included stripping power from the courts to review decisions by the executive branch regarding selective enforcement claims, such as the LA 8's selective deportation claim under the First Amendment. Scalia then appeared to contradict Justice Murphy, Judge Wilson, and the Ninth Circuit's contention that noncitizens and citizens were entitled to the same First Amendment protection.[125]

"When an alien's continuing presence in this country is in violation of the immigration laws, the Government does not offend the Constitution by deporting him for the additional reason that it believes him to be a member of an organization that supports terrorist activity," he wrote.[126] Scalia appeared to be placing challenges to selective enforcement in deportation proceedings outside of First Amendment protections for foreign noncitizens, as well as dismissing First Amendment protection for lawful activities and associations if the government believed the foreign noncitizen was a member of an organization that provides support for terrorist activity. Scalia did not specify whether that organization was a designated FTO or if that support included lawful activities.

Scalia did not address whether lawful activities by members of a designated FTO or as material support to a designated FTO fell outside First Amendment protections for US citizens. This expanded the questions raised by Judge Green and Cole's defense of Rafeedie. A decade later, Cole would bring this question and a First Amendment challenge to the Supreme Court, and the United States would use material support provisions to ideologically exclude and suppress dissent. The Cold War had come to a close, and the new War on Terror had begun.

8

War on Terror

ON THE MORNING OF SEPTEMBER 11, 2001, nineteen members of the radical extremist Sunni Islamist and Salafi jihadist global terrorist organization, al-Qaeda, located in Afghanistan, hijacked four American passenger planes and deliberately crashed them into the World Trade Center towers in New York and the Pentagon in Virginia; one of the planes did not reach its target and crashed in Pennsylvania. Approximately 3,000 people died in what was considered the most devastating terrorist attack in American history. The hijackers were all of Middle Eastern descent, chosen by Osama Bin Laden, the leader of al-Qaeda. Their preparation included obtaining visas to come to the United States and training to fly commercial airliners.

Recalling the anti-anarchist fervor and violence that followed President William McKinley's assassination in 1901, the weeks after the attacks on "9/11" saw some seeking revenge by attacking individuals of Middle Eastern or South Asian descent, treating them as scapegoats or suspects.[1] The Justice Department coordinated efforts to interrogate, detain, and deport Middle Eastern immigrants or visitors on visas as "material witnesses" or as preventative measures, without due process or access to legal counsel.[2] Stunned by such a devastating terrorist attack within the United States, an anxious nation called on the government to protect it.[3]

On September 20, 2001, President George W. Bush addressed a joint session of Congress and the public and announced the United States' "War on Terror." This war "will not end until every terrorist group of global reach has been found, stopped, and defeated," he stated. "We will direct every resource at our command, every means of diplomacy, every tool of intelligence, every instrument of law enforcement, every financial influence, and every necessary weapon of war, to the disruption and to the defeat of the global terror network." Bush encouraged other nations to join the United States in its War on Terror, but his message was polarizing. There was no room for dissent in this war: "Either you are with us, or you are with the terrorists."[4]

A century earlier, the War on Anarchy had declared war on belief, association, and expression considered by many lawmakers, jurists, and members of the public to be inextricably linked to violence and the overthrow of government by force. Conversely, the War on Terror was a war on violence used to inflict harm and provoke fear, yet efforts to fight this war often focused on beliefs, associations, and expressions of dissent. The laws used to prevent terrorist attacks were broad and encompassed lawful advocacy and nonviolent activities and associations. The War on Terror also represented the completion of a shift toward ideological restrictions based on terrorism that began in the 1980s and had continued through the 1990s. If the 1980s and 1990s had opened a back door to guilt by association with terrorist organizations and suppression through material support provisions, the United States walked through that door after 9 / 11.

During the Bush and Obama administrations, and then into the Trump administration, laws and restrictions used and passed to fight the War on Terror in the name of national security raised familiar concerns, as did judicial deference under the plenary power doctrine and public officials' use and abuse of discretion to exclude or deport from the United States. Civil liberties lawyers brought legal challenges to ideological exclusions and organizations such as the American Civil Liberties Union (ACLU) took action through media campaigns and protests. They argued that civil liberties did not have to be violated to conduct the War on Terror and that national security concerns did not justify suppression of dissent and speech chilling or policies that discriminated based on race, ethnicity, religion, and viewpoint. Members of the public returned to comparisons with previous restrictions and historical examples of repression in the name of national security. They also reiterated arguments that exclusions reflected a fearful nation, undermining America's image as a democracy and identity as a nation of immigrants.

"Fear and Freedom Are at War"

President Bush's September 20 address included a declaration that "fear and freedom are at war." Americans were free, and the terrorists wanted to destroy that freedom and make them fearful and vulnerable to attack.[5] Thus, those in the United States were presented with a false dichotomy: freedom or security. You are either with us or against us. The rhetoric and choice between security and civil liberties were similar to the Federalists' rhetoric and defense of the Alien Friends Act in 1798.

Within days after the attacks, members of Congress proposed bills to strengthen security measures, incorporating many changes to criminal, immigration, financial, and intelligence law.[6] On October 26, 2001, Bush signed "The Uniting and Strengthening America by Providing Appropriate Tools Required to Intercept and Obstruct Terrorism Act" (USA PATRIOT Act).[7] This act removed barriers between foreign intelligence and law enforcement officials, and it included enhanced surveillance and information gathering and sharing from websites, "sneak and peek" warrants, and "roving wiretaps" of citizens and noncitizens.[8]

Congress swiftly passed the USA PATRIOT Act. It approved the 342-page omnibus bill, with a vote in the House of 357 to 66 and in the Senate of 98 to 1. The lone dissenter in the Senate was Russ Feingold (D-WI). Feingold argued the act posed a threat to civil liberties by eliminating constitutional protections for freedom of speech and due process and against illegal searches and seizures. He was particularly concerned about racial and religious profiling and surveillance.[9]

Attorney General John Ashcroft dismissed concerns and criticism of the USA PATRIOT Act during his testimony before the Senate Judiciary Committee on December 6, 2001: "We need honest, reasoned debate, not fear-mongering. To those who scare peace-loving people with phantoms of lost liberty, my message is this: Your tactics only aid terrorists, for they erode our national unity and diminish our resolve. They give ammunition to America's enemies and pause to America's friends. They encourage people of goodwill to remain silent in the face of evil."[10]

In 2002, a year after the attacks on 9/11, the ACLU launched a new public campaign, Keeping America "Safe *and* Free" as an alternative to what it perceived as the Bush administration's "Safe *or* Free" dichotomy and as a rebuke to Ashcroft.[11] Congress created a new agency, the Department of Homeland Security (DHS). In 2003, the Immigration and Naturalization Service (INS) was reorganized and divided into the US Citizenship and Immigration Services (USCIS), US Immigration and Customs Enforcement (ICE), and US Customs and Border Protection (CBP). In the years that followed, the War on Terror demonstrated that the lost liberties were not "phantoms."

Whistleblowers in the National Security Agency under DHS revealed the vast data-mining collection during the War on Terror and surveillance of noncitizens and citizens. Under the Bush and Obama administrations, CBP

Attorney General John Ashcroft depicted as a Puritan evocative of James Montgomery Flagg's iconic Uncle Sam "I WANT YOU FOR U.S. ARMY" recruiting poster in 1917 in "I WANT YOUR CIVIL LIBERTIES," by Ann Telnaes, published in *The American Prospect*, December 18, 2001

agents were authorized to check phones and laptops of any American citizen or foreign-born noncitizen entering the United States at the border. These phone and laptop checks raised privacy concerns, as well as questions of Fourth Amendment protections against unreasonable searches and seizures without probable cause and First Amendment protections against speech chilling and the suppression of expression.[12]

No-fly lists and terror watchlists also raised issues regarding rights and protections of American citizens and foreign nationals entering the United States. "Lookout" lists had been in effect since the early twentieth century in the State Department and passport office. Those who found themselves excluded did not know why or how they appeared on the list and had to challenge their exclusion, often through litigation and filing Freedom of Information Act (FOIA) requests. The lookout lists were consolidated after 9/11, and many found that they were on the no-fly list and prevented from traveling to or from the United States with no explanation.[13]

The conflation of terrorism with Middle Eastern and Muslim immigrants and Arab Americans was not new and did not start after 9/11. It began in the 1970s and 1980s with a string of terrorist attacks abroad, including hijackings and bombings during the Carter and Reagan administrations, as well as with the World Trade Center bombing in 1993. The attacks on 9/11 exacerbated and perpetuated existing stereotypes and presumptions that disloyalty and subversion were linked to nationality, ethnicity, or religion.[14] This resulted in surveillance of Arab American, Middle Eastern, and Muslim communities and profiling at airports and subway stations. The Countering Violent Extremism Task Force manifested a discriminatory focus on these communities, rather than on those espousing white nationalist and white supremacist extremism, as did the National Security Entry-Exit Registration System (NSEERS), which targeted foreign nationals from Muslim-majority countries for special screening and registration.[15]

The ACLU challenged civil rights and liberties violations, including those under the USA PATRIOT Act, in a fearful atmosphere of suspicion and surveillance that included guilt by association, intimidation, and speech chilling.[16] The ACLU and various organizations such as the Center for Constitutional Rights and the PEN American Center worked together to bring legal challenges in all areas, including ideological exclusion and material support to terrorism.

Ideological Exclusion and Material Support

Beginning in 2003 and continuing into 2007, the ACLU began to document a number of ideological exclusion cases and took the lead in challenging their constitutionality. In its report called "The Excluded: Ideological Exclusion and the War on Ideas," the ACLU detailed over a dozen such exclusions from the United States.[17]

The report began by describing ideological exclusion as a "discredited practice," recounting those ideologically excluded under the McCarran-Walter Act of 1952 such as Gabriel García Márquez, Pablo Neruda, and Carlos Fuentes, and the efforts to restrict, revise, or repeal the act, including the McGovern Amendment and the Moynihan-Frank Amendment.[18]

Noting that the Immigration Act of 1990 reduced the exclusion categories, the ACLU declared, "Ideological exclusion was thrown into the dustbin of history, which is where it should have remained." During the first six years of the War on Terror, the Bush administration had now revived ideological exclusion under the USA PATRIOT Act and existing terrorist provisions.[19]

According to the ACLU, a number of professors were among those excluded. Dora María Téllez, a former Sandinista and minister of health in Nicaragua, was a professor at the Central American University in Managua and had traveled to the United States on many occasions. In 2003, Téllez accepted a position as a visiting professor in Latin American Studies at Harvard University. In preparation, she sought to enroll in English training classes in the United States and applied for a student visa, but she was denied on the ground that she had previously engaged in "terrorist activity." After her exclusion, Téllez had to resign from her visiting professorship.[20]

Adam Habib, a South African scholar, political analyst, and human rights activist, found himself excluded from the United States in 2006. Habib had traveled to the United States a number of times since 9 / 11 and had previously lived there for three years while earning his PhD from the City University of New York. When he arrived at John F. Kennedy airport to attend some meetings in the United States, Habib was detained for seven hours. He initially assumed it was because he was a Muslim and the interrogation was a form of harassment, but Habib described being asked repeatedly about his political views and associations. Habib had publicly criticized US foreign policy and the war in Iraq. After the interrogation, which he compared to the questioning he had received in South Africa during apartheid, officials revoked his visa and put him on a plane back to South Africa. A few months later, visas for Habib's wife and two sons were revoked, causing his eldest son to miss a two-week long Junior Ambassadors Program in the United States. The ACLU noted that Habib might also have been excluded as part of a pattern of denying entry to other South African Muslims.[21]

After contacting the State Department, Habib learned that his visa had been revoked "prudentially" under a provision in the McCarran-Walter Act. He received no further explanation. Then, upon accepting an invitation to speak at an American Sociological Association (ASA) conference, he applied for another visa, but the status of his application remained pending, and he was unable to attend the conference. In 2007, the ACLU and ASA sued the State Department and DHS, and challenged the constitutionality of Habib's exclusion.[22]

During this time, the ideological exclusion of a professor that received the most public attention was the visa denial to Swiss scholar Tariq Ramadan under the USA PATRIOT Act. Tariq Ramadan was born in Geneva,

Switzerland in 1962 to a prominent Egyptian Muslim family; his grandfather, Hassan al-Banna, founded the Muslim Brotherhood in 1928. He studied philosophy and French literature at the University of Geneva, where he also received a PhD in Arabic and Islamic studies. A prolific writer and popular lecturer and commentator on Islam and the West, Ramadan was considered one of Europe's "most influential and provocative Muslim thinkers."[23] Ramadan promoted a liberal, reformist vision of Islam, in which Muslims integrated into Western society, but also retained their Muslim identity. He argued that Muslim women should not be forced to wear a *hijab*, but they should be free to wear one. Ramadan denounced terrorism and the characterization of Islam as a violent religion, but he was also a controversial figure. Ramadan expressed criticism of Israel, the War on Terror, and "Jewish French intellectuals," and he was accused of "double-talk" and criticized for views perceived to condone violence and extremism, reflect Islamic fundamentalism, and reveal anti-Semitism.[24]

In January 2004, the University of Notre Dame offered Ramadan a tenured professorship to teach Islamic studies in its Institute for International Peace and Justice. Ramadan accepted the position. Notre Dame submitted a work visa on Ramadan's behalf, which was approved in May 2004. Ramadan and his family made arrangements for their move to the United States, scheduled for early August, but on July 28, the US embassy in Bern revoked his visa without explanation.[25] The consulate advised Ramadan that he could reapply for a visa, which he did, on October 4, but when Ramadan had not received a response by December 13, he resigned from his position.[26]

Section 411 of the USA PATRIOT Act had added a provision to the McCarran-Walter Act that excluded foreigners who "have used [their] position of prominence within any country to endorse or espouse terrorist activity, or to persuade others to support terrorist activity or a terrorist organization, in a way that the Secretary of State has determined undermines United States efforts to reduce or eliminate terrorist activities."[27] A spokesman for DHS stated that Ramadan's visa had been revoked because he endorsed or espoused terrorist activity under Section 411.[28]

Ramadan was "shocked" by his visa revocation and by the reason. "I had consistently opposed terrorism in all of its forms, and still do," he wrote in "Why I'm Banned in the USA," published in the *Washington Post*. "And, before 2004, I had visited the United States frequently to lecture, attend conferences and meet with other scholars. I had been an invited speaker at conferences or lectures sponsored by Harvard University, Stanford, Princeton and the

William Jefferson Clinton Presidential Foundation. None of these institutions seemed to consider me a threat to national security."[29]

Ramadan's exclusion troubled many American scholars. "I worry about the implications for academic freedom and more generally for freedom of speech and openness of American society," said Scott Appleby, a professor at Notre Dame's Institute for International Peace and Justice. Describing the importance of Ramadan's views on Islam and foreign policy to American students, Appleby explained, "A secondary, more subtle level of concern is about how ready we are as a society to hear a discourse that is authentically Muslim, not an extremist discourse but one that is critical of U.S. policy."[30] "I fear for the future of American education," wrote Molly Greene, an Ottoman Empire scholar and professor at Princeton University. "Are we going to retreat from the world and deny our students access to anyone whose views, they, or the government, might find uncomfortable?"[31]

The ACLU and PEN American Center stepped in to help Ramadan challenge his exclusion. Using the legal strategy introduced in the Ernest Mandel case, they arranged for American institutions, including the American Association of University Professors (AAUP) and the American Academy of Religion (AAR) to invite Ramadan to deliver lectures and to attend conferences. On September 16, 2005, Ramadan applied for a visa to visit the United States to participate in these events. DHS officials did not proceed in answering Ramadan's visa request.

On January 25, 2006, the "American Plaintiffs"—the ACLU, AAUP, AAR and PEN—filed a Complaint in a US district court in New York challenging Ramadan's exclusion from the United States as violating their First Amendment right to receive information and to hear Ramadan and his views.[32] In September, DHS responded that Ramadan was excluded from the United States, not for "endorsing or espousing terrorist activity," but for providing material support to a terrorist organization under the REAL ID Act of 2005, which broadened existing statutes to include support to undesignated terrorist organizations that provided material support to designated terrorist organizations.[33] Similar to the Reagan administration's switch from using Section 212(a)(28) to using Section 212(a)(27) of the McCarran-Walter Act to deny visas in the 1980s, DHS had switched to another statutory provision in order to exclude Ramadan.

According to Ramadan, during an interview for his 2005 visa application, DHS officials questioned him about his political views and associations. Ramadan told them that, between 1998 and 2002, he had donated approximately $1,336 to the Association de Secours Palestinian (ASP).[34] In August 2003, the

US Treasury Department listed ASP as a fundraiser in Switzerland for Hamas, a designated terrorist organization, and listed ASP as a "Specially Designated Global Terrorist" organization.[35] Based on this 2005 interview, DHS had now barred Ramadan from the United States because his donations to ASP constituted material support to Hamas. It argued that Ramadan "reasonably should have known" that ASP funded Hamas, and therefore should have known his donations were providing support to a designated terrorist organization.[36]

To Ramadan, this contention was absurd. Characterizing ASP as a humanitarian organization assisting Palestinians, Ramadan asked how he could have reasonably known that ASP was funding a terrorist organization, when the United States did not designate it as such until a year after Ramadan had made his last donation. "I am increasingly convinced that the Bush administration has barred me for a much simpler reason: It doesn't care for my political views," Ramadan wrote in "Why I'm Banned in the USA."[37]

"In recent years, I have publicly criticized U.S. policy in the Middle East, the war in Iraq, the use of torture, secret CIA prisons and other government actions that undermine fundamental civil liberties," Ramadan explained. "I have called upon Western societies to be more open toward Muslims and to regard them as a source of richness, not just of violence or conflict." He asked, "What words do I utter and what views do I hold that are dangerous to American ears, so dangerous, in fact, that I should not be allowed to express them on U.S. soil?"[38]

"I fear that the United States has grown fearful of ideas. I have learned firsthand that the Bush administration reacts to its critics not by engaging them, but by stigmatizing and excluding them," wrote Ramadan. "Will foreign scholars be permitted to enter the United States only if they promise to mute their criticisms of U.S. policy? It saddens me to think of the effect this will have on the free exchange of ideas, on political debate within America, and on our ability to bridge differences across cultures."[39]

In 2007, the US district court in New York upheld Ramadan's exclusion. Citing *Kleindienst v. Mandel* (1972), Judge Paul Crotty held that DHS had presented a "facially legitimate and *bona fide* reason" to justify excluding Ramadan for material support to a terrorist organization.[40] Crotty explained that the REAL ID Act's material support provision applied retroactively to Ramadan, and included donations to ASP prior to its special designation as a charity funding Hamas, a designated terrorist organization. Under the doctrine of consular non-reviewability, Crotty deferred to the decision by DHS officials that Ramadan did not demonstrate that he did not know or should not have reasonably known that ASP was supporting Hamas, and therefore, Ramadan's donations to ASP were donations to Hamas.[41] The ACLU appealed.

In 2009, the Second Circuit Court of Appeals reversed Crotty's decision, but it did so narrowly. The court upheld the United States' right to exclude Ramadan for material support to a terrorist organization and the application of the REAL ID Act's material support provision to Ramadan, but it rejected Crotty's deference to the DHS officials and his holding.[42] Under this provision, the consular official "was required to confront Ramadan with the allegation against him and afford him the subsequent opportunity to demonstrate by clear and convincing evidence that he did not know, and reasonably should not have known, that the recipient of his contributions was a terrorist organization."[43] DHS officials did not give Ramadan this opportunity when they denied his visa application. Therefore, the court remanded the case to DHS for further proceedings, so Ramadan could produce such evidence in his defense.[44]

Ramadan and the ACLU celebrated this legal victory. Although, a narrow decision, the Second Circuit had given them hope that one day, Ramadan would be able to obtain a visa and come to the United States.[45] "I am very gratified with the court's decision," remarked Ramadan. "I am eager to engage once again with Americans in the kinds of face-to-face discussions that are central to academic exchange and crucial to bridging cultural divides."[46] Melissa Goodman, one of Ramadan's ACLU attorneys, called on the Obama administration to "immediately end Professor Ramadan's exclusion." She added, "We also encourage the new administration to reconsider the exclusion of other foreign scholars, writers and artists who were barred from the country by the Bush administration on ideological grounds."[47]

On January 20, 2010, Secretary of State Hillary Clinton signed orders rescinding the exclusions of Habib and Ramadan and authorizing the State Department to issue visas to both scholars. Clinton cited her discretionary authority under the McCarran-Walter Act.[48] After Clinton's order, both Ramadan and Habib obtained visas to visit the United States, but the McCarran-Walter Act, the USA PATRIOT Act, and the material support statutes remained law.

On April 8, 2010, Ramadan arrived at Newark Liberty International Airport with a visa.[49] Ramadan received a visa for a five-day visit, which included a series of meetings and lectures in Washington, Chicago, Detroit, and New York City.[50] His first stop was the stage in Cooper Union's Great Hall to participate in a panel discussion, "Secularism, Islam, and Democracy: Muslims in Europe and the West." A century earlier, Emma Goldman had delivered speeches on that stage condemning John Turner's exclusion under the Alien Immigration Act of 1903. While Ramadan would not share the same fate as Turner or Goldman, he would share the same stage and contribution to the history of ideological exclusion and deportation in the United States.

In the wake of the Second Circuit's opinion and significant publicity and public outcry, Clinton had used her ultimate discretion to admit the scholars, while DHS officials and the Bush administration had used their discretion to exclude them. The cases served as a reminder of the importance of discretion and of who holds that discretion to determine the fate of foreigners seeking to enter the United States, as well as the potential for abuse of discretion under the law.

The Ramadan case also illustrated how material support, including donations to organizations, could be used as grounds for exclusion. It raised questions about how restrictions on material support could be used to suppress free expression and association of individuals and organizations within the United States, and whether those restrictions were constitutional.

Since the 1990s, David Cole had continued to teach at Georgetown Law Center and to provide legal representation in civil liberties and terrorism cases. The US government had also continued to try to deport Cole's clients, Khader Musa Hamide and Michel Ibrahim Shehadeh, in the "Los Angeles Eight" (LA 8) case, until an immigration judge, Bruce J. Einhorn, dismissed the case in 2007. Einhorn revealed that the government had admitted long ago that it did not have evidence against Hamide and Shehadeh, and that the pursuit to deport them for their affiliations with the Popular Front for the Liberation of Palestine (PFLP) was intended to suppress dissent and their lawful activities and advocacy. Einhorn described the government's effort to deport these two men over the course of two decades as "an embarrassment to the rule of law."[51]

During the early years of the War on Terror, Cole wrote *Enemy Aliens: Double Standards and Constitutional Freedoms in the War on Terrorism* (2003). The book begins with a discussion of civil liberties violations after 9/11, and, in particular, the targeting of foreign-born noncitizens. He then proceeds to mention some of the historical antecedents throughout the twentieth century and to draw connections with twenty-first century violations, describing deportations, detentions, and government surveillance from the Red Scare to the Cold War to the War on Terror.[52] Cole also chose to turn to the past to help understand and inform the present when he revised and republished a 1999 book, *Terrorism and the Constitution: Sacrificing Civil Liberties in the Name of National Security* (2002, 2006), co-authored with James X. Dempsey. In the third edition, they discuss terrorism statutes and legal challenges in the 1980s and 1990s and make comparisons with those in the War on Terror, concluding that guilt by association with terrorist organizations continues to pose a threat to First Amendment protections as it did two decades earlier.[53]

A few weeks before Tariq Ramadan was able to enter the United States and take the stage at Cooper Union, Cole had stood before the Supreme Court on behalf of the Center for Constitutional Rights (CCR) and argued that the current material support statutes were unconstitutionally overbroad and violated the First Amendment. CCR represented the Humanitarian Law Project (HLP), a human rights organization based in Los Angeles, which held a consultative status with the United Nations. According to Cole, the HLP had focused on helping Turkey's Kurdish minority by "encouraging recognition of their basic human rights, and promoting a peaceful resolution of their conflict with Turkey's government." The HLP worked with the Kurdistan Workers' Party ("PKK"), "the principal political organization representing the Kurds in Turkey, specifically by training and assisting them in human rights advocacy." However, because "training" fell under material support, the HLP was concerned that its work with PKK had become a crime, when the secretary of state listed the PKK as a designated foreign terrorist organization (FTO). The HLP joined other American groups seeking to challenge the material support law, including the Sri Lankan Tamils who wanted to provide support to the Liberation Tigers of Tamil Eelam (LTTE), a designated FTO.[54]

The definition of material support, originally under the Antiterrorism and Death Penalty Act of 1996 (AEDPA) and then under an amendment by a 2004 law, the Intelligence Reform and Terrorism Prevention Act (IRTPA), included "service," "training," "expert advice or assistance," and "personnel." Cole argued those terms were unconstitutionally overbroad and vague, encompassing lawful activities and association. The HLP and the Tamils wanted to engage in lawful, nonviolent activity protected by the First Amendment, but potential criminal prosecution for providing material support to a designated FTO precluded their activities and advocacy.[55]

In *Holder v. Humanitarian Law Project* (2010), a 6-3 decision, the Supreme Court upheld the constitutionality of the statute and the definitions of material support.[56] Writing for the majority, Chief Justice John G. Roberts Jr. found the terms "training" and "expert advice" were sufficiently specific, and the statute had distinguished these terms from what could be considered "independent advocacy."[57] He also argued that material support could serve to "legitimate" a designated FTO and thus interfere with US foreign policy and alliances with other nations. Roberts was persuaded by the government's argument that providing material support to a designated FTO, even "seemingly benign" or lawful, "bolsters the terrorist activities of that organization."[58] He then provided some examples of hypothetical scenarios of such bolstering.

According to Roberts, the PKK could use training on "how to use humanitarian and international law to peacefully resolve disputes" in order to "pursue peaceful negotiation as a means of buying time to recover from short-term setbacks, lulling opponents into complacency, and ultimately preparing for renewed attacks." He continued, "A foreign terrorist organization, introduced to the structures of the international legal system might use the information to threaten, manipulate, and disrupt." Roberts added, "This possibility is real, not remote."[59]

Roberts dismissed the dissenting opinion, which "fails to address the real dangers at stake." He wrote, "In the dissent's world, such training is all to the good," but the legislative and executive branches of government "have concluded we live in a different world: one in which the designated foreign terrorist organizations 'are so tainted by their criminal conduct that any contribution to such an organization facilitates that conduct.'"[60]

Justice Stephen J. Breyer wrote the dissenting opinion, joined by Justice Ruth Bader Ginsburg and Justice Sonia Sotomayor. Breyer did not believe the government had met its burden of showing "that an interpretation of the statute that would prohibit this speech- and association-related activity serves the Government's compelling interest in combatting terrorism."[61] He insisted, "Not even the 'serious and deadly problem' of international terrorism can require *automatic* forfeiture of First Amendment rights."[62] Roberts's argument about bolstering presented "no natural stopping place" where lawful activities could be used to serve terrorist ends.[63] Mere coordination with a designated FTO was not sufficient to eliminate First Amendment protections. Breyer argued that the statute should be interpreted as prohibiting activity whereby one "purposefully intends it to help terrorism" or "knows (or willfully blinds himself to the fact) that the activity is significantly likely to assist terrorism."[64]

This distinction between knowingly supporting terrorist activities and supporting or engaging in lawful activities was a distinction for which Cole had advocated since the late 1980s. A week after the decision, Cole wrote an article in the *New York Review of Books* entitled "The Roberts Court's Free Speech

Problem," where he began by contrasting the Roberts Court's upholding of Congress's material support restrictions on forms of advocacy in *Holder v. Humanitarian Law Project*, while striking down a regulation of organizations' campaign spending as a restriction on a form of protected speech that violated the First Amendment a few months earlier in *Citizens United v. Federal Election Commission* (2010).[65]

Cole argued that the Roberts Court's decision in *Humanitarian Law Project* presented a serious threat to association and advocacy. He gave a series of examples, including former President Jimmy Carter's monitoring elections in Lebanon in June 2009, an action that could have led to prosecution under material support for "expert advice" to Hezbollah, a designated FTO. He also noted that when newspapers published opinion pieces by Hamas leaders, they were providing a "service," which could constitute material support for Hamas, a designated FTO.[66]

Cole was also disturbed by Chief Justice Roberts's supposition on how advising might be manipulated to serve terrorist activities, in contrast to the "heavy burden of justification on the government" and evidence he required in *Citizens United*. Cole observed that in *Humanitarian Law Project*, "Once the government invoked national security and the war on terror, the Court simply deferred to rank speculation," instead of requiring "hard evidence" and evaluating the restriction under strict scrutiny, as required for content-based restrictions on speech. Cole concluded, "When the Court allows unsupported speculation about 'terrorism' and disapproval of a speaker's viewpoint to justify making advocacy of human rights a crime, the First Amendment as we know it is in serious jeopardy."[67] The Roberts Court had chosen to uphold the government's use of material support laws to suppress speech and justify guilt by association.

In the years that followed, questions continued to arise over material support provisions and free expression and association. Scholars and analysts voiced concern over reports of making the Muslim Brotherhood a designated terrorist organization, warning of the consequences to foreign relations and the potential of provoking extremism, as well as the ramifications for research and academic exchange in the United States and throughout the Middle East, including speech chilling and potential prosecution.[68] The decision in *Humanitarian Law Project* also raised questions about liability and prosecution of social media platforms under antiterrorism laws for providing material support to designated terrorist organizations using their products.[69]

Extreme Vetting

In his farewell address in 1796, President George Washington had warned about the danger posed by foreign influence and partiality to one nation, as well as political factions for such factions "are likely, in the course of time and things, to become potent engines, by which cunning, ambitious, and unprincipled men will be enabled to subvert the power of the people and to usurp for themselves the reins of government." Washington also emphasized the importance of the separation of powers within the federal government and guarding against too much power held by one department without a check by others.[70]

The Trump administration would test Washington's warnings. Deep political divisions within the nation led to and have continued through the Trump presidency. Accusations of President Trump's abuse of power, obstruction, and partiality to Russia and its president, Vladimir Putin, have also persisted. Yet, it was the separation of powers that proved most salient during the first few years of the Trump administration. Trump's focus on immigration restrictions, including extreme vetting policies, demonstrated how much authority and ultimate discretion the executive branch holds, as well as the extent of judicial deference to that authority under the plenary power doctrine.

On June 16, 2015, Donald J. Trump, a New York real estate developer and reality television celebrity, announced his candidacy for president of the United States with a vow to "Make America Great Again." While he did not define what he considered the factors that would constitute a "great" nation, he did specify the source of subversion within the United States and what he believed was not making America great. In his announcement he referred to Mexican immigrants as "rapists" and "bringing crime" across the border.[71] At campaign rallies he told his supporters he would deport illegal immigrants, build a wall between Mexico and the United States to prevent illegal immigration, and have Mexico pay for the wall.[72] Trump also targeted Muslims in his remarks as the source of subversion and terrorism within the United States. Stating that he thought "Islam hates us," he suggested government surveillance of mosques and perhaps establishing a Muslim database, and he called for a "total and complete shutdown of Muslims entering the United States" in the wake of the mass shooting terrorist attack in San Bernardino, California by a Muslim couple in 2015.[73]

After becoming the Republican nominee, Trump gave a speech in Youngstown, Ohio, on August 15, 2016, in which he proposed what appeared to be a revised version of his Muslim ban to "temporarily suspend immigration from some of the most dangerous and volatile regions in the world that have a history of exporting terrorism." He also declared his intention to "Make America Great Again" by implementing a screening test for immigrants and visitors and to admit only "those who share our values and respect our people" into the United States. "In the Cold War, we had an ideological screening test," Trump said. "The time is long overdue to develop a new screening test for the threats we face today. I call it extreme vetting."[74]

With the election of Trump to the presidency, many were troubled by his campaign promises and concerned he would implement his policy proposals. Three days after the election, the New York Times published a letter from ACLU Executive Director Anthony Romero addressed to President-elect Trump. It included a list of Trump's campaign promises and described them as "un-American" as well as "unconstitutional." Romero warned, "If you do not reverse course and endeavor to make these campaign promises a reality, you will have to contend with the full firepower of the ACLU at your every step." He concluded, "Our staff of litigators and activists in every state, thousands of volunteers, and millions of supporters stand ready to fight against any encroachment on our cherished freedoms and rights."[75] Helping to lead this fight would be David Cole, the ACLU's new national legal director. The ACLU had also launched a new donation campaign with a picture of Trump and the words "See You in Court."[76]

Over the next three years, the Trump administration focused on restricting legal and illegal immigration through exclusion, detention, denaturalization, and deportation efforts. Using executive orders and changes to rules within the USCIS and DHS, the Trump administration attempted to eliminate asylum protections, temporary protected status, prosecutorial discretion and deferred action in deportation cases, and legal permanent residency for use of public assistance under the likely to become a "public charge" immigration exclusion first introduced in the nineteenth century. Stephen Miller, senior policy advisor to the president and a staunch immigration restrictionist, was largely responsible for orchestrating these efforts.[77]

Shortly after President Trump's inauguration, he began to fulfill his campaign promises, including implementing the extreme vetting he had mentioned on the campaign trail. This vetting included using social media to ideologically exclude and chill speech, as well as Trump's first initiative—the travel ban—designed by Stephen Miller. The ACLU would see Trump in court.

The Travel Ban

On January 27, 2017, Trump signed Executive Order 13769: "Protecting the Nation from Foreign Terrorist Entry into the United States," citing his authority under Section 212(f) of the McCarran-Walter Act. It was the foreign policy presidential proclamation provision that allowed the president to suspend the entry of any foreigner or class of foreigners or place restrictions on their entry if the president determines that entry would be "detrimental to the US interest."[78]

Trump cited visa issuance as crucial to national security and the failure of State Department policies to prevent the 9 / 11 terrorists from entering the United States. His executive order stated, "The United States must be vigilant during the visa-issuance process to ensure that those approved for admission do not intend to harm Americans and that they have no ties to terrorism." It continued, "In order to protect Americans, the United States must ensure that those admitted to this country do not bear hostile attitudes toward it and its founding principles. The United States cannot, and should not, admit those who do not support the Constitution, or those who would place violent ideologies over American law." It added, "The United States should not admit those who engage in acts of bigotry or hatred (including 'honor' killings, other forms of violence against women, or the persecution of those who practice religions different from their own) or those who would oppress Americans of any race, gender, or sexual orientation."[79]

Trump insisted that to ensure proper security screenings and verification of those admitted to the United States, he needed to lower admitted refugees from 110,000 to 50,000, bar refugees from Syria indefinitely, bar refugees from all other countries for 120 days, bar entry from Muslim-majority countries Iran, Iraq, Libya, Somalia, Sudan, Syria, and Yemen for ninety days, and prioritize admission of refugees from minority religions based on religious persecution. Trump claimed these countries currently did not have sufficient security screenings in place.[80]

The Trump administration had not provided any guidance to CBP agents or DHS officials regarding the implementation of this travel ban.[81] There was chaos at airports in the United States reminiscent of Ellis Island during the implementation of the McCarran Act of 1950. Foreigners who fell under the ban were in-flight, about to get on planes with visas in hand, or in the process of obtaining visas. Those within the United States were unsure about the status of relatives, friends, and colleagues subject to the ban or their own status if they left the country and tried to reenter. Lawyers rushed to the

Protesters rally against President Trump's travel ban in front of Tom Bradley
International Terminal at Los Angeles International Airport on
January 29, 2017
Christine Chew / UPI / Alamy Stock Photo.

airports to provide legal assistance to arrivals subject to the travel ban, and
thousands rushed to protest the ban and welcome arrivals.[82] Some held
signs stating "We are a nation of immigrants," "No hate no fear, refugees are
welcome here," and "No ban, no wall." Many recalled Trump's campaign
promise to ban all Muslims from the United States. To them, this executive
order was not just a travel ban; it was Trump's Muslim ban.[83]

On January 28, Romero and ACLU attorneys including Omar C. Jadwat,
the director of the ACLU Immigrants' Rights Project, and the deputy director,
Lee Gelernt, arrived at the US district court in Brooklyn, New York, to request

a stay of removal and restraining order to immediately stop the travel ban. Outside the courthouse a large crowd had gathered and chanted "A-C-L-U, We are here, We Stand with you!"[84] US District Court Judge Ann Donnelly issued the stay and a nationwide injunction stopping the travel ban. She held that the ban would cause "irreparable harm" if implemented and that there was a likelihood of success in establishing that the ban was unconstitutional insofar as it violated due process and equal protection rights.[85]

Over the course of the next month, more federal judges would issue temporary restraining orders or injunctions to stop the travel ban. There were more federal district court decisions, more appeals to the circuit courts, and more revisions to the travel ban in response to these decisions.[86] In March 2017, the Trump administration revised the travel ban; it removed Iraq from the list and added North Korea, Chad, and Venezuela. It changed the indefinite restriction on Syrian refugees to 120 days; removed the minority religions priority; exempted lawful permanent residents, dual nationals traveling on unrestricted country passports, and those already in the United States or already in possession of a valid visa; and expanded a waiver provision included within the travel ban to admit those foreign nationals with significant contacts or facing undue hardship due to the ban.[87]

On June 26, 2017, the Supreme Court issued a *per curiam* (from the court) opinion in which it agreed to hear appeals from cases in the upcoming term. It also granted a stay of the injunctions, which allowed the revised travel ban to go into effect, but only in regard to those who did not have a "*bona fide* relationship with an entity or person in the United States."[88] During the next few months, there were more rulings in the district and circuit courts, and the district court case in Hawaii headed for the Supreme Court. In 2018, DHS announced the implementation of "enhanced security procedures for refugees."[89]

The main legal arguments against the travel ban included a statutory and constitutional argument. The statutory argument contended that the travel ban exceeded the authority granted by Congress to the President, including overriding existing terrorist prevention schemes. It also contradicted the Hart-Celler Act of 1965, which prohibited preference or discrimination in the issuance of immigrant visas based on race, sex, nationality, place of residence, or place of birth. This was the provision that repealed the discriminatory national origins quotas in the Johnson-Reed Act of 1924. While Section 212(f) of the McCarran-Walter Act of 1952 gave Trump broad discretion to exclude, that discretion was bounded by congressional action and legislation.[90]

The constitutional argument charged that the travel ban was discriminatory because it violated the Establishment Clause under the First Amendment. The Establishment Clause prohibits the government from favoring or disfavoring one religion over another and from displaying religious animus. If the government action intended to disfavor a particular religion, it violated the Establishment Clause. The text of the first travel ban included all Muslim majority countries and a preference for religious minorities. Trump's statements during his presidential campaign calling for a Muslim ban could demonstrate this violation, but they raised questions about using campaign statements as evidence against presidential policies. Yet, Trump had not disavowed his campaign statements or the first travel ban, which he continued to embrace and identify as the strongest iteration of the ban.[91] Furthermore, when former New York City Mayor Rudy Giuliani, Trump's personal lawyer and advisor, appeared on television a day after Trump announced the travel ban, Giuliani explained that Trump had called him after his campaign announcement of the Muslim ban and asked Giuliani how to "do it legally."[92]

The main legal argument in defense of the travel ban was the president's broad, ultimate discretion under Section 212(f) and judicial deference to the President and Congress under the plenary power doctrine. Under *Kleindienst v. Mandel* (1972), Trump needed a "facially legitimate and *bona fide* reason" to exclude, and the court should not "look behind" his reason. On its face, the travel ban did not ban Muslims, not all Muslim majority countries were listed in the revised ban, and Trump had articulated his reason for the ban—or, more precisely, articulated what he claimed was a facially legitimate and *bona fide* reason: namely, national security.[93]

Once again, the Supreme Court would have to confront the plenary power doctrine and decide whether it would defer to the executive branch and apply the "facially legitimate and *bona fide* reason" standard or evaluate the executive's decision and use of discretion under strict scrutiny and First Amendment standards. It would also confront its own legacy upholding the constitutionality of discrimination against and internment of Japanese Americans in the name of national security. In that regard, there was one Supreme Court precedent that was mentioned repeatedly in federal court decisions and public discussions in comparison to the travel ban.

In *Korematsu v. United States* (1944), the court held that Executive Order 9066 authorizing internment did not violate equal protection under the Constitution and deferred to the judgment of Congress and the executive under their war power authority that those of Japanese descent were disloyal and posed an internal threat to the United States.[94] The solicitor general had misled the court regarding this threat and knowingly suppressed an official naval intelligence report, which described Japanese Americans as posing little risk to national security.[95] In 1983, a federal district court judge overturned Fred Korematsu's conviction in light of this deception, and in 1988, President Reagan signed the Civil Liberties Act, which paid reparations to individuals who were interned and issued a formal apology.[96] Yet, the decision in *Korematsu*, upholding the constitutionality of internment, remained and had never been overturned in the Supreme Court.

In his dissenting opinion in *Korematsu*, Justice Robert Jackson issued a warning about the consequences of the court's decision and violations of the nation's values and protections in the name of national security: "Once a judicial opinion rationalizes such an order to show that it conforms to the Constitution, . . . the principle then lies about like a loaded weapon, ready for the hand of any authority that can bring forward a plausible claim of an urgent need. Every repetition imbeds that principle more deeply in our law and thinking and expands it to new purposes."[97]

On June 26, 2018, in *Trump v. Hawaii*, a 5–4 decision, the Supreme Court upheld Trump's travel ban.[98] Writing for the majority, Chief Justice Roberts found that Trump had not exceeded his authority and broad discretion under Section 212(f) and that the court should defer to his authority and discretion to exclude. Roberts was familiar with Section 212(f) from his work in the Reagan administration and cited Reagan's use of the proclamation provision as part of US foreign policy efforts. He noted that other presidents had used Section 212(f) to bar from specific countries, that doing so was entirely within the scope of the statute, and that it did not violate the Hart-Celler Act's prohibitions. The travel ban was not discriminatory; it focused on inadequate information and security protocols within the countries listed in the ban. Accordingly, the ban's aim was to put pressure on those countries, while protecting the United States.

Roberts cited the inclusion of a waiver provision and case-by-case review as support for upholding the travel ban, and he rejected claims that Trump's findings of inadequate information and security protocols were insufficient and unpersuasive. Roberts insisted Section 212(f) required Trump to "make" a finding that entry would be "detrimental to the interests of the United States," not to "explain that finding with sufficient detail to enable judicial review."[99]

Roberts also held that the travel ban did not violate the Establishment Clause. He dismissed Trump's statements during his campaign and while president, and held that Trump had a "facially legitimate and *bona fide* reason" to exclude. Even applying a rational basis standard and looking behind the reason, he found "the entry policy is plausibly related to the Government's stated objective to protect the country and improve vetting processes."[100]

Roberts rejected comparisons with *Korematsu v. United States*: the "forcible relocation of US citizens to concentration camps, solely and explicitly on the basis of race, is objectively unlawful and outside the scope of Presidential authority." Trump's travel ban, by contrast, was a "facially neutral policy denying certain foreign nationals the privilege of admission. The entry suspension is an act that is well within executive authority and could have been taken by any other President." Roberts described *Korematsu* as "gravely wrong the day it was decided," and it "has been overruled in the court of history," with 'no place in law under the Constitution.'"[101]

In a dissenting opinion, Justice Sotomayor, joined by Justice Ginsburg, attacked the chief justice and the majority for blatantly ignoring the facts—namely, that Trump's campaign statements and those made after he became president revealed his intent and religious animus and that the travel ban vetting was a pretext used to enact a Muslim ban. "The United States of America is a Nation built upon the promise of religious liberty. Our Founders honored that core promise by embedding the principle of religious neutrality in the First Amendment," she wrote. "The Court's decision today fails to safeguard that fundamental principle. It leaves undisturbed a policy first advertised openly and unequivocally as a 'total and complete shutdown of Muslims entering the United States' because the policy now masquerades behind a façade of national-security concerns." Sotomayor described revisions to the travel ban as "repackaging," which did "little to cleanse" it "of the appearance of discrimination." She argued, based on Trump's own words, that "a reasonable observer would conclude that the Proclamation was motivated by anti-Muslim animus. That alone suffices to show that plaintiffs are likely to succeed on the merits of their Establishment Clause claim." Sotomayor charged Roberts and the majority with "turning a blind eye to the pain and suffering the Proclamation inflicts upon countless families and individuals, many of whom are United States citizens."[102]

Sotomayor rejected the use of the "facially legitimate and *bona fide* reason" standard applied to exclusion. As Justice Thurgood Marshall had argued in his dissenting opinion in *Kleindienst v. Mandel*, she argued for applying First Amendment standards of review to determine the constitutionality of an exclusion charged with violating the First Amendment. Sotomayor found Roberts's approach perplexing "given that in other Establishment Clause cases, including those involving claims of religious animus or discrimination, this Court has applied a more stringent standard of review."[103]

Sotomayor concluded by addressing *Korematsu v. United States*, which presented "stark parallels" with the reasoning in the court's holding. "As here, the Government invoked an ill-defined national-security threat to justify an exclusionary policy of sweeping proportion," she wrote of *Korematsu*. "As here, the exclusion order was rooted in dangerous stereotypes about a particular group's supposed inability to assimilate and desire to harm the United States." While Sotomayor appreciated Roberts's repudiation of *Korematsu*, it did not absolve the majority from its decision in this case. "By blindly accepting the Government's misguided invitation to sanction a discriminatory policy motivated by animosity toward a disfavored group, all in the name of a superficial claim of national security, the Court redeploys the same dangerous logic underlying *Korematsu* and merely replaces one 'gravely wrong' decision with another."[104]

Justice Breyer also wrote a dissenting opinion, joined by Justice Elena Kagan. Breyer focused on the waiver provision in Trump's travel ban, permitting case-by-case review and admission under exemptions to the ban. He believed this waiver system was an indicator of the intentions and constitutionality of the ban, since a review of its application should "make clear" that it did not intend to "deny visas to numerous Muslim individuals (from those countries) who do not pose a security threat." In his review of the implementation of the waiver system, Breyer found evidence that the government was "not applying the Proclamation as written."[105]

In the first month, only two waivers were approved out of 6,555 eligible applicants. While the government claimed that number increased to 430 in the first four months, Breyer found that number "miniscule" compared to the number of applicants. He noted a significant drop in number of student visas and nonimmigrant visas from countries affected by the ban, processing errors, as well as discrepancies between waiver determinations by consular officials in different countries. Officials did not receive guidance on how to exercise their discretion to enforce the ban and to issue waivers. Breyer wrote, "Given the importance of the decision in this case, the need for assurance that the Proclamation does not rest upon a 'Muslim ban,' and the assistance in deciding the issue that answers to the 'exemption and waiver' questions may provide, I would send this case back to the District Court for further proceedings."[106]

Breyer's concern about the waivers not only cast doubt on the travel ban's constitutionality, but also raised concern about the current and future implementation of the ban. His discussion of waivers recalled those under the McCarran-Walter Act for ideological exclusions under Section 212(a)(28) and the use and abuse of discretion to deny them. He also provided guidance for future constitutional challenges to the travel ban in federal district court.

The decision in *Trump v. Hawaii* was a split decision that fell along ideological lines—liberal and conservative. The "swing" justice and deciding vote in the case was Justice Anthony Kennedy. He joined the majority but wrote a separate concurring opinion, which appeared to be a direct instruction, or perhaps a concerned plea, to Trump and consular officials regarding their use of discretion.

While government officials' words and actions may not all be reviewable by the court, "that does not mean those officials are free to disregard the Constitution and the rights it proclaims and protects," Kennedy wrote. "Indeed, the very fact that an official may have broad discretion, discretion free from judicial scrutiny, makes it all the more imperative for him or her to adhere to the Constitution and to its meaning and its promise."[107] Kennedy insisted, "It is an urgent necessity that officials adhere to these constitutional guarantees [of freedom of belief and expression] and mandates in all their actions, even in the sphere of foreign affairs." He added, "An anxious world must know that our Government remains committed always to the liberties the Constitution seeks to preserve and protect, so that freedom extends outward, and lasts."[108]

A few days later, Kennedy announced his retirement from the Supreme Court, and *Trump v. Hawaii* (2018) would become part of his legacy on the court. Kennedy's decision to defer to Trump and his authority evoked the apprehensions and forewarnings articulated by Democratic-Republican Congressman Albert Gallatin in his response to the Alien Friends Act of 1798 and the tremendous power and discretion it left to President John Adams. "Is that a government of laws which leaves us no security but in the confidence we have in the moderation and patriotism of one man?"[109]

Social Media and Speech Chilling

In April 2017, Jameel Jaffer issued a call for concern regarding Trump's extreme vetting policy and ideological exclusion. As an attorney working at the ACLU, Jaffer had represented Tariq Ramadan and Adam Habib and had challenged their exclusions. Jaffer was now the executive director of the Knight First Amendment Institute at Columbia University, a legal organization that "defends the freedoms of speech and press in the digital age through strategic litigation, research, and public education."[110]

In an article entitled "Censorship at the Border Threatens Free Speech Everywhere," published by *Just Security*, Jaffer warned of potential ideological exclusions under the Trump administration. He described foreign visitors and Americans detained and interrogated about their travels, associations, beliefs, and activities at the border by CBP agents, who also asked for their cellphones or laptops. The Trump administration was considering a requirement that noncitizens disclose their social media handles, in addition to answering questions about their beliefs and associations, as a condition of admission. Jaffer wrote, "The aim is to empower consular and border officials to ensure that would-be visitors to the United States embrace American values, a concept that the Trump administration has not defined."[111]

Jaffer drew on his experience and representation—recalling that in the Habib and Ramadan cases he had learned that under its foreign affairs manual, "the State Department instructed consular officers that the Patriot Act authorized them to exclude foreign nationals who had voiced 'irresponsible expressions of opinion.'" As Trump had mentioned ideological restrictions during the Cold War, Jaffer also looked back at those restrictions. He briefly turned to history and exclusions under the McCarran-Walter Act, mentioning its passage over President Truman's veto and criticisms, as well as the exclusions under it including Dario Fo, Gabriel García Márquez, and Nino Pasti. Such exclusions proved embarrassing to the United States, he said, and were "a testament to official paranoia and closed-mindedness."[112]

What worried Jaffer was not just turning back the clock, but turning back the clock with social media as a tool. He predicted that such a use of social media and revival of ideological exclusion under extreme vetting would be more "pernicious" than during the Cold War. Jaffer noted, everyone carries their expressions, associations, and beliefs on their phones or laptops. Consular officials and CBP agents can inspect texts, as well as tweets, posts, likes, and retweets on social media and interpret their meaning and significance. While such content includes inquiry or browsing and does not necessarily reflect the device owner's views or opinions, now all of it had the potential to be used by officials to exclude individuals at the border or deny visa applications at their discretion.[113]

Jaffer argued that this use of social media would not only lead to capricious and discriminatory exclusions, but also to a chilling effect on expression and association and to self-censorship. Foreign visitors, immigrants, and American citizens inside and outside the United States may be hesitant to follow groups or post, like, or tweet expressions that might be suspicious, fearing that doing so could lead to their exclusion from the United States or from other countries.[114]

A month later, in May 2017, as part of enhanced screening, the State Department required visa applicants to fill out a supplemental form, DS-5535, which asked applicants to list their employment history, contacts and addresses, and social media and email accounts and handles for the past fifteen years.[115] This screening was quite similar to the lists of organizations and affiliations visa applicants had to complete beginning in the 1950s under the McCarran Act.

A year after Jaffer issued his warning, Carrie DeCell, one of his colleagues at the Knight First Amendment Institute, wrote an article in the *Guardian* with an update on Trump's extreme vetting initiative. DeCell described examples of a recent pattern of cases of foreign-born activists who had been denied entry to the United States, as well as an increase of interrogations of American activists and inspections of cell phones and social media at the border.[116] In April 2018, Australian Muslim activist Yassmin Abdel-Magied was scheduled to speak at the PEN World Voices Festival. Upon arrival, CBP agents pulled her aside, inspected her phone, and "following a minute-long review of her case," denied her entry and cancelled her visa. They claimed that Abdel-Magied was traveling on the wrong visa, despite her having obtained that visa for her previous trips to the United States to attend similar events. Shaun King is an American journalist and civil rights activist. Returning from a trip to Cairo with his family, King was detained and questioned about his travels and role in Black Lives Matter. According to King, the CBP agent had "clearly been reading my tweets and knew all about me."[117]

DeCell also included selective deportation as an example of "muzzling" activists and chilling speech under extreme vetting. One case involved New Sanctuary Coalition executive director and immigration activist Ravi Ragbir. An immigrant from Trinidad, Ragbir had been living and working in New York City under an order of deportation after he lost his legal permanent resident status due to a criminal conviction. Ragbir's deportation order was in deferred action, and he was not a priority to be deported. This changed when Ragbir voiced his criticism of Trump's immigration policies, and he was detained during a routine check-in with ICE on January 11, 2018. His lawyers filed a writ of *habeas corpus* to get him released and were successful in their challenge to his selective deportation as a violation of the First Amendment.[118]

It remains unclear for how long the Government will retain records of applicants' social media and other online activities, if it will use social media to continue to monitor applicants and their activities, and how information collected will be interpreted and used to inform immigration decisions. "This is censorship under the guise of immigration enforcement," DeCell wrote. "The public has a right to know how the administration is conducting its new ideological screening test, and at what cost to the broader public discourse." On behalf of the Knight First Amendment Institute, DeCell filed a Freedom of Information Act (FOIA) request and pursued litigation to obtain information about individuals who have been excluded, what information is being collected from visa applicants, and how it is being used.[119]

On June 13, 2018, the Brennan Center for Justice sent a letter to Congress signed by forty-six civil liberties and human rights organizations, including the ACLU and the Knight First Amendment Institute. The letter requested congressional oversight of the Trump administration's extreme vetting policies. It called on Congress to obtain information on the implementation of ideological exclusion and the decisions to grant waivers under the travel ban. Given that the administration provided "no policies, procedures, or guidelines governing the issuance of waivers," the letter demanded that Congress require the State Department and USCIS to provide criteria used for waiver denials and for visa denials.[120]

The letter concluded by asking Congress to "fulfill its constitutional duty to the American people to serve as a check on the Executive."[121] The courts could no longer serve as the only check on the Trump presidency and the travel ban. It was now time for Congress to step in.

The attacks of 9/11 ushered the United States into the War on Terror, with a focus on fear versus freedom. Congress passed new laws including the USA PATRIOT Act and retained and revised material support of terrorist organizations provisions introduced in the 1990s. New agencies in DHS such as USCIS and CBP turned to old methods to suppress dissent and criticism of US foreign and domestic policies, including ideological exclusion. New legal challenges to these exclusions as violating Americans' First Amendment right to receive information and to hear revived old arguments against exclusions as threatening freedom of speech, impeding academic inquiry, undermining democracy, and depicting the United States as a fearful, insecure nation.

In his opinion in *Holder v. Humanitarian Law Project* (2010), Chief Justice Roberts upheld the constitutionality of a statute criminalizing material support to terrorist organizations and deferred to the executive and legislative branches. Roberts issued a similar opinion in *Trump v. Hawaii* (2018), deferring to the executive branch under the plenary power doctrine and the president's authority and ultimate discretion under the presidential proclamation provision in the McCarran-Walter Act. In both cases, judicial deference outweighed First Amendment arguments and protections when restrictions pertained to national security, terrorism, and foreign policy.

David Cole expressed his concern regarding the use of material support statutes as a backdoor to suppression of dissent and guilt by association, which would chill speech and prevent the exercise of First Amendment freedoms. He drew on his litigation from the late 1980s through the 1990s during the transition from the Cold War to the War on Terror, as well as his knowledge of the past and its connection with the present. Jameel Jaffer cited his representation of individuals facing ideological exclusion after 9/11 while working at the ACLU, when he issued his warning about extreme vetting during the Trump administration and DHS officials' use of content on social media to potentially deny visas and bar foreign visitors from entry. Like Cole, Jaffer saw similarities not only with the recent past, but also with the Cold War.

The accounts of the effects of the travel ban included the separation of families and spouses without recourse, long delays, and problems with obtaining waivers.[122] Those within the United States and those barred under the travel ban described its waiver system as discriminatory and its implementation as arbitrary and capricious. Following the Supreme Court's decision in *Trump v. Hawaii*, they brought lawsuits calling its legality into question, as Justice Breyer had done in his dissenting opinion. While the Supreme Court upheld the constitutionality of Trump's travel ban under Section 212(f) of the McCarran-Walter Act, these lawsuits and evaluations of the waiver system by federal courts could curtail or even end its implementation.[123]

On April 10, 2019, Congresswoman Judy Chu (D-CA) and over a dozen of her colleagues in the House of Representatives heeded the call to serve as a check on the executive branch and introduced the "NO BAN Act" (National Origin-Based Antidiscrimination for Nonimmigrants Act). The act was intended to repeal the travel ban and amend the Hart-Celler Act to prohibit discrimination based on religion. It also included congressional oversight and placed limitations on the executive branch's discretion and power to restrict under the presidential proclamation provision. The act required the president, the State Department, and DHS to provide specific evidence to justify a suspension or restriction on entry to the United States and applied strict scrutiny to the president's order, requiring the executive branch to "narrowly tailor the suspension or restriction to meet a compelling government interest."[124]

In late August 2019, Ismail Ajjawi, a seventeen-year-old Palestinian from Lebanon, traveled to the United States to start his freshman year as an undergraduate student at Harvard University. According to Ajjawi, he spent eight hours at Boston Logan International Airport. During this period, CBP agents searched the content on his phone and laptop, questioned him, and then deemed Ajjawi "inadmissible" to enter the United States and revoked his visa. Ajjawi told the *Harvard Crimson* that during the questioning, one of the agents "started screaming at me. She said that she found people posting political points of view that oppose the US on my friend[s] list." He told her, "I have no business with such posts and that I didn't like, [s]hare or comment on them and told her that I shouldn't be held responsible for what others post."[125]

Ajjawi's exclusion received widespread social media and national and international press attention discussing his exclusion. Apparently, he was not the only student who had difficulty entering the United States. A month earlier, Harvard University President Lawrence Bacow wrote to Secretary of State Mike Pompeo and Acting DHS Secretary Kevin McAleenan to complain that international students and instructors were experiencing an increase in visa delays and denials that were "making these scholars' attendance and engagement in the university unpredictable and anxiety-ridden."[126] Harvard University and Ajjawi's scholarship sponsor organization, America-Middle East Educational and Training Service (AMIDEAST), intervened to help Ajjawi gain admission to the United States. Their intervention, in addition to international attention and protests, worked. A week later, Ajjawi was allowed to return to the United States just in time to attend his first day of classes at Harvard on September 3.[127]

Ajjawi's exclusion was precisely what Jaffer and Carrie DeCell had warned could happen if DHS officials used social media to ideologically exclude. The next student, scholar, or visitor might not receive the same attention when he or she is excluded for similar reasons. "The chilling effects of incidents like these ripple through communities far beyond Harvard's incoming freshman class, resulting in widespread self-censorship on social media and threatening intellectual freedom," said DeCell in her response to the Ajjawi case.[128]

When Donald Trump mentioned the Cold War ideological screening test when he introduced extreme vetting, it was a sign that he wanted to go backward. Yet, this process had already begun. The ideological exclusions during the Cold War continued with the shift to the War on Terror. While the McCarran-Walter Act provisions used to ideologically exclude were gone, the use of material support to terrorist organizations had replaced them as a tool of political repression by using guilt by association. The use of social media as a way to suppress dissent through exclusion and deportation was new but the use of associations and expressions to bar or eject individuals from the United States resulting in speech chilling and self-censorship was not. An examination of the War on Terror reveals that perhaps the best description of the history of ideological exclusion and deportation may be Jean-Baptiste Alphonse Karr's epigram, *"plus ça change, plus c'est la même chose"* ("the more that changes, the more it's the same thing").

Conclusion

THE HISTORY OF ideological exclusion and deportation in the United States is not a history about vast numbers of foreign-born visitors or immigrants who were barred or expelled on the basis of belief, expression, or association. For example, between 1900 and 1961, 1,230 "subversive or anarchistic" foreigners were barred from the United States out of 595,435 foreigners who were excluded. Between 1908 and 1961, 1,499 "subversive or anarchistic" foreigners were expelled from the United States out of 492,217 foreigners who were deported.[1]

These numbers may be negligible, but they do not reflect those foreigners who chose to leave or to never apply to visit the United States, those ordered deported but who never left, those detained for months or years, or those who were placed on supervisory parole. These numbers also do not reflect public officials' attempts to suppress the threat of dissent or their perception and depiction of foreigners as the source of subversion. Nor, do these numbers show the exploitation of the vulnerability of foreign-born citizens and noncitizens under the law, or their fear of deportation, exclusion, denaturalization, and detention based on their past or present beliefs, expressions, and associations. These numbers reveal nothing about the chilling effect on expressions of dissent and on freedom of association, and intimidation felt by foreigners inside and outside the United States resulting in self-censorship. Nor can they capture the embarrassment and humiliation caused by the enforcement of ideological restrictions. These numbers will never be able to reflect the damage done to free exchange, literature, scientific discovery, academic inquiry, or to the identity of the United States as a liberal democracy and to its image and reputation abroad.

The history of ideological exclusion and deportation in the United States is not a story of statistics, but rather one of political repression and fear. It is a narrative that can be traced through the passage, use, revision, and repeal of laws, as well as the legal challenges to these laws, which reveal a remarkable consistency and continuity. Discretion and authority, as well as constitutionality and judicial review, have been central to the conflicts that shape this history.

Public officials—including the president, secretary of labor, secretary of state, and the attorney general—have used existing ideological restrictions at their discretion to suppress the threat of dissent or urged members of Congress to pass new ones in the name of national security. Some officials have tried to expel or bar as many foreigners as possible, while others have excluded or deported fewer foreigners, applying their ultimate and interpretive discretion. They struggled to implement restrictions or used prosecutorial discretion to delay or cancel deportations under them. Throughout the twentieth century, use of discretion reflected the personal views of the public officials and the perceptions and politics of the time. It also led to contention over enforcement of these laws—including conflicts among members of presidential administrations, as well as tensions with members of Congress. Public officials who chose to use their authority to prevent deportations or exclusions faced interrogations over their exercise of ultimate, interpretive, and prosecutorial discretion by congressional committees, and officials had to defend themselves against efforts to oust them from their positions.

Tensions also emerged regarding the constitutionality of ideological exclusion and deportation laws. The consolidation of unchecked authority to deport and exclude in the legislative and executive branches of government, which is vulnerable to abuse of power and arguably a violation of the separation of powers, has been a concern since the Alien Friends Act of 1798. Under the plenary power doctrine, the judicial branch defers to the legislative branch, which holds the power to pass, revise, and repeal immigration laws, including ideological exclusion and deportation provisions, and defers to the executive branch, which enforces these laws. This nineteenth century doctrine, based on legal precedent upholding Chinese exclusion, continues to insulate exclusion and deportation cases from substantive judicial review.

First Amendment legal standards and constitutional due process protections for immigrants and noncitizens have also been points of contention that the Supreme Court and Congress have wrestled with throughout the twentieth century and into the twenty-first. The majority of the Supreme Court has acknowledged more rights and protections for citizens and noncitizens within the United States, including under the First Amendment, but it has been reluctant to stray from its application of the plenary power doctrine and deference under it. While the court has expanded judicial safeguards and applied strict scrutiny to restrictions on expression and association to prevent viewpoint discrimination and censorship, it has not extended those safeguards and scrutiny to exclusion cases or these First Amendment protections to foreign noncitizens outside the United States. Congress and the majority of the court have also cast shadows over these constitutional protections by providing a back door to suppression through guilt by association, including the conflation of action and speech within federal statutes that contain provisions that prohibit providing material support to terrorist organizations.

An underlying perpetual fear of subversion, the perception of foreigners as the source of subversion, and the use of ideological exclusion and deportation as a tool of political repression are not relegated to the past. While the persons feared, the beliefs, expressions, and associations deemed subversive, and the methods and technology used have shifted over time, the perceived threat of dissent remains. Congress has passed ideological restrictions, public officials have enforced them, and the Supreme Court has upheld their constitutionality under the plenary power doctrine. This pattern will continue until Congress provides the proper safeguards and oversight to prevent exclusions and deportations on the basis of belief, association, and expression, and the court reevaluates judicial deference under the plenary power doctrine and serves as a stronger check on the legislative and executive branches by applying strict scrutiny and current speech-protective First Amendment standards to ideological exclusions as well as deportations.

ABBREVIATIONS

NOTES

ACKNOWLEDGMENTS

INDEX

Abbreviations

ORGANIZATIONS AND LAWS

ACLU	American Civil Liberties Union
ACPFB	American Committee for Protection of Foreign Born
AEDPA	Antiterrorism and Effective Death Penalty Act of 1996
APA	Administrative Procedure Act
BIA	Board of Immigration Appeals
CBP	US Customs and Border Protection
CCR	Center for Constitutional Rights
DHS	Department of Homeland Security
FBI	Federal Bureau of Investigation
FOIA	Freedom of Information Act
FTO	Foreign Terrorist Organization
HUAC	House Un-American Activities Committee
INS	Immigration and Naturalization Service
IWW	Industrial Workers of the World
NECLC / ECLC	(National) Emergency Civil Liberties Committee
PFLP	Popular Front for the Liberation of Palestine
PLO	Palestine Liberation Organization
SACB	Subversive Activities Control Board
USA PATRIOT Act	Uniting and Strengthening America by Providing Appropriate Tools Required to Intercept and Obstruct Terrorism Act of 2001
USCIS	US Citizenship and Immigration Services

REFERENCES

EGDH vol. 1   Candace Falk, ed., *Emma Goldman: A Documentary History of the American Years, Volume One: Made for America, 1890–1901* (Berkeley: University of California Press, 2003)

EGDH vol. 2   Candace Falk, ed., *Emma Goldman: A Documentary History of the American Years, Volume Two: Making Speech Free, 1902–1909* (Berkeley: University of California Press, 2005)

EGP   Candace Falk, Ronald J. Zboray, and Alice Hall, eds., *The Emma Goldman Papers: A Microfilm Edition* (Alexandria, VA: Chadwyck-Healey, 1990)

FOIA   Freedom of Information Act, US Citizenship and Immigration Services Record Request for "Ernest Esra Mandel"

LABADIE   Joseph A. Labadie Collection, Special Collections Research Center, University of Michigan Library, University of Michigan, Ann Arbor, Michigan

LOC   Manuscript Division, Library of Congress, Washington, DC

MHS   Massachusetts Historical Society

NARA   National Archives and Records Administration, Washington, DC

RBML   Rare Book & Manuscript Library, Columbia University in the City of New York

RNPL   Richard Nixon Presidential Library and Museum, Yorba Linda, California

RRL   Ronald Reagan Library, Digital Library Collection

TAM   Tamiment Library & Robert F. Wagner Labor Archives, Special Collections Center, Elmer Holmes Bobst Library, New York University, New York, New York

Notes

INTRODUCTION

1. Megan Specia, "Palestinian Boycott Activist Denied Entry to United States," *New York Times*, April 12, 2019, A7; Omar Barghouti, "I Co-Founded the BDS Movement. Why Was I Denied Entry to the US?" *Guardian*, April 16, 2019.

2. Nathan Thrall, "BDS: How a Controversial Non-violent Movement Has Transformed the Israeli-Palestinian Debate," *Guardian*, August 14, 2018.

3. Thrall, "BDS."

4. Ruth Eglash, "Israel Imposes Entry Ban on Foreign Boycott Activists," *Washington Post*, March 7, 2017.

5. Thrall, "BDS"; Isaac Stanley-Becker, "University of Michigan Promises to Discipline Faculty in Israel boycott," *Washington Post*, October 11, 2018; "Strengthening America's Security in the Middle East Act of 2019," S.1, 116th Congress (2019–2020), February 5, 2019; Zack Beauchamp, "The Controversy over laws Punishing Israel Boycotts, Explained," *Vox*, January 9, 2019, https://www.vox.com/policy-and-politics/2019/1/9/18172826/bds-law-israel-boycott-states-explained; *NAACP v. Claiborne Hardware Co.*, 458 U.S. 886 (1982).

6. Specia, "Palestinian Boycott Activist Denied Entry to United States."

7. Barghouti, "I Co-Founded the BDS Movement."

8. Hina Shamsi, "ACLU Comment on U.S. Denying Entry to BDS Movement Co-Founder," April 11, 2019, https://www.aclu.org/press-releases/aclu-comment-us-denying-entry-bds-movement-co-founder.

9. Corey Robin, *Fear: The History of a Political Idea* (New York: Oxford University Press, 2004), 2, 16, 180–182, 200, 210.

10. John Higham, *Strangers in the Land: Patterns of American Nativism, 1860–1925* (New Brunswick, NJ: Rutgers University Press, 1955), 4, 8. Higham included ideological exclusion and deportation as part of his examination of a triad of nativism: religious, radical, and racial.

11. Daniel Kanstroom, *Deportation Nation: Outsiders in American History* (Cambridge, MA: Harvard University Press, 2007), 232–240.

12. Aristide R. Zolberg, *A Nation by Design: Immigration Policy in the Fashioning of America* (New York: Russell Sage Foundation, 2006), 15–21.

13. Deirdre Moloney, *National Insecurities: Immigrants and U.S. Deportation Policy since 1882* (Chapel Hill: University of North Carolina Press, 2012), 4; Kanstroom, *Deportation Nation*, 5.

14. William Preston Jr., *Aliens and Dissenters: Federal Suppression of Radicals, 1903–1933* (Cambridge: Harvard University Press, 1963); David Caute, *The Great Fear: The Anti-Communist Purge under Truman and Eisenhower* (New York: Simon & Schuster, 1978); Ellen Schrecker, "Immigration and Internal Security: Political Deportations during the McCarthy Era," *Science & Society* 60, no. 4 (1996–1997): 393–426; Elizabeth Hull, *Taking Liberties: National Barriers to the Free Flow of Ideas* (New York: Praeger, 1990). Legal scholars taking a longer view, include Mitchell C. Tilner, "Ideological Exclusion of Aliens: The Evolution of a Policy," *Georgetown Immigration Law Journal* 2, no. 1 (1987): 1–86, focusing on discussions of law and legal precedent; David Cole, *Enemy Aliens: Double Standards and Constitutional Freedoms in the War on Terrorism* (New York: The New Press, 2003), drawing on history to illuminate his examination of the War on Terror.

15. In addition to Kanstroom, Moloney, and Zolberg, see Edward P. Hutchinson, *Legislative History of American Immigration Policy, 1798–1965* (Philadelphia: University of Pennsylvania Press, 1981); Marion T. Bennett, *American Immigration Policies: A History* (Washington, DC: Public Affairs Press, 1963); Kunal Parker, *Making Foreigners: Immigration and Citizenship Law in America, 1600–2000* (New York: Cambridge University Press, 2015).

16. Geoffrey R. Stone, *Perilous Times: Free Speech in Wartime from the Sedition Act of 1798 to the War on Terrorism* (New York: W. W. Norton, Inc., 2004); Robert Justin Goldstein, *Political Repression in Modern America: From 1870–1976* (Urbana: University of Illinois Press, 2001); Harry Kalven Jr., *A Worthy Tradition: Freedom of Speech in America*, ed. Jamie Kalven (New York: Harper & Row, 1988).

1. SOVEREIGNTY AND SELF-PRESERVATION

1. George Washington's Farewell Address (1796), The Avalon Project: Documents in Law, History, and Diplomacy, Yale Law School, http://avalon.law .yale.edu/18th_century/washing.asp.

2. Stanley Elkins and Eric McKitrick, *The Age of Federalism: The Early American Republic, 1788–1800* (New York: Oxford University Press, 1993), 24–27; Gordon S. Wood, *Empire of Liberty: A History of the Early Republic, 1789–1815* (New York: Oxford University Press, 2009), 53–55, 151–173; Geoffrey R. Stone, *Perilous Times: Free Speech in Wartime from the Sedition Act of 1798 to the War on Terrorism* (New York: W.W. Norton, 2004), 25.

3. Terri Diane Halperin, *The Alien and Sedition Acts of 1798: Testing the Constitution* (Baltimore: Johns Hopkins University Press, 2016), 19–20.

4. Stone, *Perilous Times*, 25–26; Wood, *Empire of Liberty*, 176–178.

5. Wood, *Empire of Liberty*, 197.

6. James Morton Smith, *Freedom's Fetters: The Alien and Sedition Laws and American Civil Liberties* (Ithaca, NY: Cornell University Press, 1956), 5.

7. Wood, *Empire of Liberty*, 198.

8. Smith, *Freedom's Fetters*, 12, 26, 177.

9. Stone, *Perilous Times*, 23.

10. Stone, *Perilous Times*, 22.

11. Smith, *Freedom's Fetters*, 7.

12. Smith, *Freedom's Fetters*, 19.

13. Smith, *Freedom's Fetters*, 23.

14. Halperin, *The Alien and Sedition Acts of 1798*, 35.

15. Halperin, *The Alien and Sedition Acts of 1798*, 34–35; Ashli White, *Encountering Revolution: Haiti and the Making of the Early Republic* (Baltimore: Johns Hopkins University Press, 2010), 125 (describing the fear of Haitian immigrants and "the contagion of rebellion").

16. Halperin, *The Alien and Sedition Acts of 1798*, 22–25.

17. David Wilson, *United Irishmen, United States: Immigrant Radicals in the New Republic* (Ithaca, NY: Cornell University Press, 1998), 43–47.

18. Halperin, *The Alien and Sedition Acts of 1798*, 37.

19. Smith, *Freedom's Fetters*, 9, 14.

20. Jeffrey L. Pasley, *"The Tyranny of the Printers": Newspaper Politics in the Early American Republic* (Charlottesville: University Press of Virginia, 2001), 54–78.

21. Pasley, *"The Tyranny of the Printers,"* 63, 79–80, 91–98.

22. Smith, *Freedom's Fetters*, 9.

23. Smith, *Freedom's Fetters*, 14

24. Smith, *Freedom's Fetters*, 178, 15.

25. "An Act to establish an uniform Rule of Naturalization," 1 Stat. 103 (March 26, 1790).

26. "An act to establish an uniform rule of Naturalization; and to repeal the act heretofore passed on that subject," 1 Stat. 414 (January 29, 1795).

27. "An Act supplementary to and to amend the act, instituted 'An Act to establish an uniform rule of naturalization'; and to repeal the act heretofore passed on that subject," June 18, 1798 (1 Stat. 566).

28. "An Act concerning Aliens," 1 Stat. 570–572 (June 25, 1798).

29. "An Act concerning Aliens."

30. "An Act respecting Alien Enemies," 1 Stat. 577–78 (July 6, 1798).

31. "An act for the punishment of certain crimes against the United States," 1 Stat. 596–97 (July 14, 1798).

32. Stone, *Perilous Times*, 39.

33. Thomas Jefferson to James Madison, June 7, 1798, Founders Online, National Archives, https://founders.archives.gov/documents/Jefferson/01-30-02 -0284.

34. Smith, *Freedom's Fetters*, 63.

35. Annals of Congress, House of Representatives, 5th Congress, 2d Session (June 19, 1798), 1983.

36. Annals of Congress (June 19, 1798), 1980, 1983–1984.

37. Annals of Congress (June 19, 1798), 1978, 1994–1995.

38. Annals of Congress (June 19, 1798), 1986–1987.

39. US Constitution, Amendment X.

40. Annals of Congress (June 19, 1798), 1990.

41. Annals of Congress (June 16, 1798), 1958; (June 19, 1798), 1974–1975, 1980–1981.

42. Annals of Congress (June 19, 1798), 1974–1975.

43. US Constitution, Art. I, Sect., cl. 1.

44. Annals of Congress (June 21, 1798), 2003–2004.

45. Smith, *Freedom's Fetters*, 83; Annals of Congress (June 16, 1798), 1957–1958.

46. Annals of Congress (June 21, 1798), 2008.

47. Jefferson to Madison, May 3, 1798, Founders Online, National Archives, https://founders.archives.gov/documents/Jefferson/01-30-02-0222.

48. *Albany Centinel*, August 7, 1798.

49. Stone, *Perilous Times*, 23, 46.

50. Timothy Pickering to John Adams, October 11, 1798, Founders Online, National Archives, https://founders.archives.gov/?q=Author%3A%22Pickering%2C %20Timothy%22%20Recipient%3A%22Adams%2C%20John%22%20Dates-From %3A1798-10-11&s=1111311111&r=2.

51. John Adams to Timothy Pickering, October 16, 1798, Founders Online, National Archives, https://founders.archives.gov/?q=%20 Author%3A%22Adams%2C%20John%22%20Recipient%3A%22Pickering%2C%20 Timothy%22&s=1111311111&r=50; Smith, *Freedom's Fetters*, 163.

52. Wendell Bird, *Criminal Dissent: Prosecutions Under The Alien And Sedition Acts of 1798* (Cambridge, MA: Harvard University Press, 2020), 327–330.

53. Bird, *Criminal Dissent*, 330–332.

54. Smith, *Freedom's Fetters*, 169–170; Bird, *Criminal Dissent*, 342.

55. John Adams to Timothy Pickering, September 16, 1798, Founders Online, National Archives, https://founders.archives.gov/documents/Adams/99-02-02 -2985.

56. Stone, *Perilous Times*, 48: Bird, *Criminal Dissent*, 350.

57. Wood, *Empire of Liberty*, 261.

58. Timothy Pickering to John Adams, July 24, 1799, Founders Online, National Archives, https://founders.archives.gov/documents/Adams/99-02-02-3803;

Timothy Pickering to John Adams, August 1, 1799, Timothy Pickering Papers, microfilm edition, 69 reels (Boston: MHS), reel 11.

59. Bird, *Criminal Dissent*, 350–352.

60. Smith, *Freedom's Fetters*, 174.

61. Pickering to Adams, August 1, 1799.

62. John Adams to Timothy Pickering, August 13, 1799, Founders Online, National Archives, https://founders.archives.gov/documents/Adams/99-02-02 -3877.

63. Halperin, *The Alien and Sedition Acts of 1798*, 108.

64. Virginia Resolution (1798), The Avalon Project: Documents in Law, History, and Diplomacy, Yale Law School, http://avalon.law.yale.edu/18th_century/virres .asp.

65. Virginia Resolution (1798)

66. Annals of Congress (June 16, 1798), 1956.

67. Congressman Albert Gallatin addressing repeal of the Alien Law, *The Proceedings of the House of Representatives of the United States with Respect to the Petitions Praying for a Repeal of the Alien and Sedition Laws including the Report of a select committee and the speeches of Mr. Gallatin* (Philadelphia: Printed by Joseph Gales, 1799), 20, New-York Historical Society.

68. Gallatin addressing repeal of the Alien Law, 20.

69. Stone, *Perilous Times*, 63, 48–62.

70. John C. Miller, *Crisis in Freedom: The Alien and Sedition Acts* (Boston: Little Brown, 1951), 223.

71. Gerald L. Neuman, *Strangers to the Constitution: Immigrants, Borders, and Fundamental Law* (Princeton: Princeton University Press, 1996), 19.

72. *New York v. Miln*, 36 U.S. 102, 142–143 (1837).

73. Peter Schrag, *Not Fit for Our Society: Immigration and Nativism in America* (Berkeley: University of California Press, 2010), 24–25.

74. Hidetaka Hirota, *Expelling the Poor: Atlantic Seaboard States & the 19th-Century Origins of American Immigration Policy* (New York: Oxford University Press, 2017), 17.

75. Neuman, *Strangers to the Constitution*, 25.

76. Neuman, *Strangers to the Constitution*, 26; Hirota, *Expelling the Poor*, 2.

77. Neuman, *Strangers to the Constitution*, 25–26.

78. Hirota, *Expelling the Poor*, 76–77.

79. Neuman, *Strangers to the Constitution*, 35–36; Daniel Kanstroom, *Deportation Nation: Outsiders in American History* (Cambridge, MA: Harvard University Press, 2007), 98, 100.

80. Aristide R. Zolberg, *A Nation by Design: Immigration Policy in the Fashioning of America* (Cambridge, MA: Harvard University Press, 2006), 177; Roger Daniels, *Asian America: Chinese and Japanese in the United States Since 1850* (Seattle: University of Washington Press, 1988), 33.

81. Kanstroom, *Deportation Nation*, 97–98; Erika Lee, *At America's Gates: Chinese Immigration during the Exclusion Era, 1882–1943* (Chapel Hill: University of North Carolina Press, 2003), 25.

82. Hirota, *Expelling the Poor*, 89.

83. Kanstroom, *Deportation Nation*, 75.

84. Kanstroom, *Deportation Nation*, 85–86.

85. White, *Encountering Revolution*, 125.

86. Neuman, *Strangers to the Constitution*, 35.

87. Kanstroom, *Deportation Nation*, 77. For a description of the Negro Seaman's Acts, see Michael A. Schoeppner, *Moral Contagion: Black Atlantic Sailors, Citizenship, and Diplomacy in Antebellum America* (New York: Cambridge University Press, 2019).

88. US Constitution, Art. VI, cl. 2.

89. *Elkison v. Deliesseline*, 8 F. Cas. 32 (C.C.D. SC, 1823).

90. *Gibbons v. Ogden*, 22 U.S. 1, 196–197 (1824).

91. *Smith v. Turner; Norris v. Boston* consolidated in the "*Passenger Cases*," 48 U.S. 283, 405–408 (1849); Neuman, *Strangers to the Constitution*, 26.

92. James Kettner, *The Development of American Citizenship, 1608–1870* (Chapel Hill: University of North Carolina Press, 1978), 334.

93. Lucy E. Salyer, *Laws Harsh as Tigers: Chinese Immigrants and the Shaping of Modern Immigration Law* (Chapel Hill: University of North Carolina Press, 1995), 9; Charles J. McClain, *In Search of Equality: The Chinese Struggle against Discrimination in Nineteenth-Century America* (Berkeley: University of California Press, 1994), 30.

94. Burlingame Treaty: "Peace, Amity, and Commerce Treaty," 16 Stat. 739 (signed on July 28, 1868) (amending the "Ta-Tsing Treaty" signed on June 18, 1858).

95. "Peace, Amity, and Commerce Treaty," Art. I.

96. "Peace, Amity, and Commerce Treaty," Art. V.

97. Roger Daniels, *Guarding the Golden Door: American Immigration Policy and Immigrants Since 1882* (New York: Hill and Wang, 2004), 13–14; Salyer, *Laws Harsh as Tigers*, 13.

98. "An act to establish an uniform rule of naturalization," 1 Stat. 103, approved March 26, 1790.

99. Salyer, *Laws Harsh as Tigers*, 13. While some Chinese immigrants filed petitions for naturalization in circuit court, arguing that "white" included the Chinese, the court rejected their petitions and held that "white" only applied to members of the "Caucasian race." The Chinese were of the "Mongolian race," and thus, they were not white and could not naturalize.

100. Salyer, *Laws Harsh as Tigers*, 11.

101. Daniels, *Asian America*, 39–43 (describing economic fears that Chinese laborers would be brought to the South and displace freed African Americans working in cotton production or sugar refining); Kanstroom, *Deportation Nation*, 103–104.

102. Page Act, "An act supplementary to the acts in relation to immigration," 18 Stat. 477 (March 3, 1875).

103. "An act supplementary to the acts in relation to immigration," 18 Stat. 477, Sect. 5.

104. "An act supplementary to the acts in relation to immigration," 18 Stat. 477, Sect. 2 & 4.

105. *Henderson et al. v. Mayor of City of New York* and *Commissioners of Immigration* v. *North German Lloyd*, 92 U.S. 259 (1875); *Chy Lung v. Freeman*, 92 U.S. 275 (1875).

106. *Henderson et al. v. Mayor of City of New York*, 259, 270, 280.

107. *Henderson et al. v. Mayor of City of New York*, 273, 275.

108. McClain, *In Search of Equality*, 147; Salyer, *Laws Harsh as Tigers*, 13–14.

109. Angell Treaty of Immigration between the United States and China, 22 Stat. 826, Art. I & II, signed November 17, 1880.

110. Angell Treaty.

111. Salyer, *Laws Harsh as Tigers*, 15.

112. "An act to execute certain treaty stipulations relating to Chinese," 22 Stat. 58, Sect. 1, 14, 15, approved May 6, 1882.

113. "An act to amend 'An act to execute certain treaty stipulations relating to Chinese approved May sixth eighteen hundred and eighty-two,'" 23 Stat. 115, Sect. 4 & 6 (July 5, 1884).

114. Beth Lew-Williams, *The Chinese Must Go: Violence, Exclusion, and the Making of the Alien in America* (Cambridge, MA: Harvard University Press, 2018), 133–136, 171.

115. "A supplement to an act entitled 'An act to execute certain treaty stipulations relating to Chinese,'" 25 Stat. 504, Sect. 1 & 2 (October 1, 1888).

116. *Chae Chan Ping v. United States*, 130 U.S. 581 (1889).

117. *Chae Chan Ping v. United States*, 600–604.

118. *Chae Chan Ping v. United States*, 606.

119. McClain, *In Search of Equality*, 58–63 (describing Field's use of the equal protection clause of the Fourteenth Amendment to strike down California's exclusion of Chinese "lewd" women in *In re Ah Fong*, 1 F. Cas. 213 [C.C.D. Cal. 1874]). Field also used the equal protection clause to invalidate a California hair-clipping ordinance targeting Chinese and "pigtails" in *Ho Ah Kow v. Nunan*, 12 F. Cas. 17 (C.C.D. Cal. 1879).

120. *Chae Chan Ping v. United States*, 595.

121. *Chae Chan Ping v. United States*, 595.

122. *Chae Chan Ping v. United States*, 606.

123. *Chae Chan Ping v. United States*, 604, 606.

124. Matthew Lindsay, "Immigration as Invasion: Sovereignty, Security, and the Origins of the Federal Immigration Power," *Harvard Civil Rights–Civil Liberties Law Review* 45, no. 1 (2010): 31–46 (describing this shift from foreign commerce to self-preservation and national security).

125. *Chae Chan Ping v. United States*, 606.

126. *Chae Chan Ping v. United States*, 606.

127. "An act to regulate Immigration," 22 Stat. 214, Sect. 2 (August 3, 1882).

128. "An act to regulate Immigration," Sect. 1.

129. "An act to regulate Immigration," Sect. 4.

130. "An act in amendment to the various acts relative to immigration and the importation of aliens under contract or agreement to perform labor," 26 Stat.1084, Sect. 1 (March 3, 1891).

131. "An act in amendment to the various acts," Sect. 7 & 8.

132. It was not until the mid-twentieth century that the Supreme Court began to refer to the federal power to exclude or deport foreigners established in these nineteenth-century cases as "plenary." See *Carlson v. Landon*, 342 U.S. 524, 534 (1952).

133. *Nishimura Ekiu v. United States*, 142 U.S. 651, 659 (1892).

134. *Nishimura Ekiu v. United States*, 651, 659.

135. *Nishimura Ekiu v. United States*, 662–663.

136. *Fong Yue Ting v. United States*, 149 U.S. 698, 705–707 (1893). Justice Gray also cited Swiss political philosopher Emmerich de Vattel's *Law of Nations* (1758 in French, 1760 in English) in his decision in *Nishimura Ekiu v. United States* (1892) to support the right to exclude as an inherent power derived from national sovereignty. While the Federalists did not specifically cite Vattel in their debates over passing the Alien Friends Act, his work was very influential in Europe and in the United States during the late eighteenth century, and the Federalists would have been familiar with Vattel's *Law of Nations* and his arguments on sovereignty.

137. *Fong Yue Ting v. United States*, 149 U.S. 698, 746–59 (Field, J. dissenting).

138. *Fong Yue Ting v. United States*, 758.

139. *Fong Yue Ting v. United States*, 759.

140. Kate Holladay Claghorn, *The Immigrant's Day in Court* (New York: Arno Press, 1969), 329–31.

141. *Yamataya v. Fisher*, 189 U.S. 86, 98–101 (1903).

142. While the description "the shot that shocked the world" had been used before to describe President Lincoln's assassination, the phrase appears to have been applied to McKinley's assassination, as well. See, Edward Leigh Pell, James W. Buel, and James P. Boyd, *McKinley and Men of Our Times: Together with the Great Questions with Which They Have Been Identified and Which Are Still Pressing for Solution* (Washington, DC: Historical Society of America, 1901), 189.

2. WAR ON ANARCHY

1. "How the Deed Was Done," *New York Times*, Sept. 7, 1901, 1.

2. "How the Deed Was Done."

3. Murat Halstead, *The Illustrious Life of William McKinley* (Washington, DC: Library of Congress, 1901), 38; "Boston Witness's Story; Says President Prayed that Assassin Might Be Forgiven," *New York Times*, Sept. 8, 1901, 2.

4. Czolgosz, Leon (1873–1901) in "Directory of Individuals," EGDH vol. 1, 525.

5. "Assassin's Trail of Crime from Chicago to the Pacific Coast," *San Francisco Chronicle,* September 8, 1901, repr. in EGDH vol. 1, 461.

6. "Assassin's Trail"; Emma Goldman, *Living My Life* (New York: Dover, 1970 [1931]), 290. "Herr Most and Justus H. Schwab Say Nieman Is Not a Member of the Reds," *New York Times,* September 7, 1901, 5.

7. "Assassin's Trail"; "Assassin Makes Full Confession," *New York Times,* September 8, 1901, A1.

8. Assassin's Trail."

9. "Czolgosz Electrocuted at 7:12 This Morning," *Chicago Tribune,* October 29, 1901, 1.

10. "Wanted to Kill Anarchists," *New York Times,* September 7, 1901, A1.

11. "Wanted to Kill Anarchists."

12. "No Evidence against Emma Goldman," *New York Times,* September 13, 1901, 1.

13. "A Weak Anti-Anarchy Bill," *New York World,* October 28, 1901, 6.

14. "Nation's War on Anarchy Begins," *Chicago Daily Tribune,* September 11, 1901, 2.

15. "The Future of Anarchy in America," *Washington Post,* May 9, 1886, 4.

16. Voltairine de Cleyre, "Anarchism and American Traditions," *Mother Earth* 111, (December 1908–January 1909), repr. in *Anarchy! An Anthology of Emma Goldman's Mother Earth,* ed. Peter Glassgold (New York: Counterpoint, 2000), 29–41.

17. Candace Falk, "Forging Her Place: An Introduction," in EGDH vol. 1, 10.

18. David Rabban, *Free Speech in Its Forgotten Years, 1870–1920* (New York: Cambridge University Press, 1997), 26–27.

19. Paul Avrich, *Anarchist Portraits* (Princeton: Princeton University Press, 1988), 144.

20. Falk, "Forging Her Place," 9.

21. Falk, "Forging Her Place," 14–15.

22. Max Baginski, "The Pioneer of Communist Anarchism in America," *Mother Earth* 7 (March 1911), repr. in *Anarchy! An Anthology of Emma Goldman's Mother Earth,* ed. Peter Glassgold (New York: Counterpoint, 2000), 53–57; Most, Johann (1846–1906) in "Directory of Individuals," EGDH vol. 1, 545.

23. Robert Justin Goldstein, *Political Repression in Modern America: From 1870–1976* (Urbana: University of Illinois Press, 2001), 38.

24. Paul Avrich, *The Haymarket Tragedy* (Princeton, NJ: Princeton University Press, 1986), 215.

25. Avrich, *The Haymarket Tragedy,* 262–263, 268.

26. Goldstein, *Political Repression,* 40.

27. Altgeld's pardon, repr. in "Gov. John P. Altgeld's Pardon of the Anarchists and His Masterly Review of the Haymarket Riot," in Lucy E. Parsons and Albert R. Parsons, *Life of Albert R. Parsons* (Chicago: Lucy E. Parsons, 1915).

28. Falk, "Forging Her Place," 7.

29. Goldman, *Living My Life*, 12–25.

30. Goldman, *Living My Life*, 7–11.

31. Paul Avrich and Karen Avrich, *Sasha and Emma: The Anarchist Odyssey of Alexander Berkman and Emma Goldman* (Cambridge, MA: The Belknap Press of Harvard University Press, 2012), 21–23.

32. Goldman, *Living My Life*, 3–6.

33. Sidney Fine, "Anarchism and the Assassination of McKinley," *Journal of American History* 60 (July 1955): 778.

34. Falk, "Forging Her Place," 14.

35. Fine, "Anarchism and the Assassination of McKinley," 780.

36. Goldman, *Living my Life*, 87; Avrich and Avrich, *Sasha and Emma*, 58.

37. Avrich and Avrich, *Sasha and Emma*, 79.

38. Goldman, *Living my Life*, 105–107.

39. Falk, "Forging Her Place," 14–15; EGDH vol.1, 521. Gaetano Bresci was an Italian anarchist who moved to Paterson, New Jersey, in 1898 and then returned to Italy to assassinate King Umberto I in 1900. His *attentat* was a response to repression in Milan and Sicily. He was considered a martyr within anarchist communities in the United States and Europe.

40. "Anarchist Prisoners in Montjuich," *New York Tribune*, August 15, 1897, 2.

41. "The Anarchists in Germany," *New York Times*, July 30, 1894, 9.

42. "Extradition Order from the French Government," March 16, 1901, repr. in EGDH vol.1, 439.

43. "Anarchist Prisoners in Montjuich," *New York Tribune*, August 15, 1897, 2.

44. "Anarchists Must Go," *Los Angeles Times*, October 9, 1898, 2.

45. Mary S. Barton, "The Global War on Anarchism: The United States and International Anarchist Terrorism, 1898–1904," *Diplomatic History* 39, no. 2 (2015): 309–311.

46. "Anti-Anarchists Confer," *Los Angeles Times*, December 29, 1898, 11.

47. "Assassin Known as Rabid Anarchist," *New York Times*, September 8, 1901, 4.

48. "European Measures against Anarchism," *New York Times*, September 24, 1901, 1.

49. "Propaganda of Death," *Washington Post*, October 6, 1901, 16.

50. "Propaganda of Death."

51. "Physicians Declare that Czolgosz Is Sane," *New York Times*, September 9, 1901, A1.

52. Goldman, *Living My Life*, 290–291, 309; Eric Rauchway, *Murdering McKinley: The Making of Theodore Roosevelt's America* (New York: Hill and Wang, 2003), 101.

53. "Emma Goldman Caught," *New York Sun Times*, September 11, 1901, A1.

54. "Emma Goldman Caught."

55. "No Evidence against Emma Goldman," *New York Times*, September 13, 1901, A1.

56. "No Evidence against Emma Goldman."

57. "New York Likely to Punish Anarchy," *New York Times*, September 13, 1901, A1.

58. Laura Greenwood, "The Anarchist Periodical Press in the United States: An Intertextual Study of *Prison Blossoms, Free Society*, and *The Demonstrator*," unpublished PhD dissertation, Trent University, September 2016.

59. "John Most Is Again Arrested," *New York Times*, September 23, 1901, 1.

60. *People v. Most*, 73 N.Y.S 220, 221 (N.Y. Sp. Sess., 1901).

61. "Most Is Sent to Prison," *Chicago Daily Tribune*, October 15, 1901, 4.

62. *People v. Most*, 73 N.Y.S 220, 221.

63. *People v. Most*, 223.

64. *People v. Most*, 224.

65. Rabban, *Free Speech in Its Forgotten Years*, 132.

66. The First Amendment's prohibition against Congress's infringement on freedom of speech did not apply to state restrictions on speech until the Supreme Court's decision in *Gitlow v. New York*, 268 U.S. 252 (1925).

67. *People v. Most*, 171 NY 423, 432 (NY Court of Appeals, 1902).

68. *People v. Most*, 430.

69. For a description of sex radicals in the late nineteenth century, see Hal D. Sears, *The Sex Radicals: Free Love in High Victorian America* (Lawrence: Regents Press of Kansas, 1977).

70. Notes, *Discontent*, November 13, 1901, 1.

71. Fine, "Anarchism and the Assassination of McKinley," 793. New Jersey and Wisconsin also passed criminal anarchy laws.

72. "Laws for Anarchists," *New York Times*, September 13, 1901, A1.

73. New York Penal Code: "Advocacy of Criminal Anarchy," Art. 14, Sect. 468 (a)–(e), ch. 371 (1902).

74. Candace Falk, "Raising Her Voice: An Introduction," in EGDH vol. 2, 16.

75. Falk, "Raising Her Voice," 16.

76. "The 'Criminal Anarchy' Law," *Mother Earth*, December 10, 1906, 10.

77. James F. Morton, Jr., "The Wise Case," *Discontent*, December 11, 1901, 1; "A Call for Concerted Action," *Lucifer: The Lightbearer*, May 1, 1902, 122–123. Prior to the formation of the Free Speech League, free speech organizations focused specifically on prosecutions under the Comstock Act. In the 1870s, sex radicals formed the National Liberal League and later, the National Defense Association, which sought to "investigate all questionable cases of prosecution under what are now known as the Comstock laws, state and national, and to extend sympathy, moral support, and material aid to those who may be unjustly assailed by the enemies of free speech and press," Rabban, *Free Speech in Its Forgotten Years*, 38–40.

78. Theodore Roosevelt, "First Annual Message," December 3, 1901, Miller Center, University of Virginia, https://millercenter.org/the-presidency/presidential -speeches/december-3-1901-first-annual-message.

79. "A Senate Bill to Keep Out Anarchists," *New York Sun Tribune*, September 11, 1901, A2.

80. "Restricting Immigration," *New York Times*, May 9, 1886.

81. "The Work of Foreign Anarchists," *New York Tribune*, May 6, 1886, 4.

82. "Control of Immigration," *New York Tribune*, May 8, 1886, 1.

83. "The Treatment of Dynamiters," *New York Tribune*, July 28, 1886, 4; "Anarchism and Immigration," *Los Angeles Times*, July 27, 1888, 4.

84. "Report of the Select Committee on Immigration and Naturalization," House of Representatives, 51st Congress, 2d Session, No. 3472, January 15, 1891, 25.

85. "Report of the Select Committee on Immigration and Naturalization," 25–27. "To Restrict Immigration," *New York Times*, January 20, 1889, 16; "To Regulate Immigration," *New York Tribune*, April 17, 1891, 4.

86. "Deportation of Anarchists," *Washington Post*, December 15, 1894, 7.

87. 53 Cong. Rec. H, 8628, daily ed. August 21, 1894, (statement of Rep. Charles Boatner [D-LA]).

88. 53 Cong. Rec. H, 8231, daily ed. August 21, 1894.

89. 53 Cong. Rec. H, 8238, daily ed. August 21, 1894, (statement of Sen. John M. Palmer [D-IL]).

90. 53 Cong. Rec. H, 8241, daily ed. August 6, 1894, (statement of Sen. George F. Hoar [R-MA]).

91. "Mr. Warner's Course on Hill Immigration Bill," *New York Times*, September 23, 1901, A2; 53 Cong. Rec. H, 8628, daily ed. August 21, 1894.

92. 53 Cong. Rec. S, 8240, daily ed. August 6, 1894, (statement of Sen. James H. Kyle [P-SD]).

93. 53 Cong. Rec. S, 8238, daily ed. August 6, 1894 (statement of Sen. John M. Palmer [D-IL]).

94. 53 Cong. Rec. S, 8238, daily ed. August 6, 1894, (statement of Sen. David Hill [R-NY]).

95. Edward P. Hutchinson, *Legislative History of American Immigration Policy, 1798–1965* (Philadelphia: University of Pennsylvania Press, 1981), 112–113.

96. "Plans to Stamp Out Anarchy: Sentiment in Favor of Stringent Prohibitive Laws. At Present There Is No Provision by Which Anarchists Can Be Kept Out of the Country," *New York Times*, September 10, 1901, 2.

97. Senator J. C. Burrows, "The Need for National Legislation against Anarchism," *North American Review* 173 (December 1901): 731.

98. "Alien Immigration Act," March 3, 1903, ch. 1012, Sect. 2 Stat.1213–1222.

99. 57 Cong. Rec.-S, 2805, daily ed. February 28, 1903.

100. "Alien Immigration Act," March 3, 1903, ch. 1012, Sect. 21, 38, 39 Stat.1213–1222.

101. 57 Cong. Rec.-S, 145, daily ed. December 5, 1901. Senator Louis McComas [R-MD] introduced a resolution to the Senate for the exclusion and deportation of anarchists.

102. 57 Cong. Rec.-S, 216, daily ed. December 9, 1901.

103. "The Bill Against Anarchists," *The Nation* 74, no. 1912 (1902): 145–146.

104. Turner, John (1864–1934) in "Directory of Individuals," EGDH vol. 2, 560; "Anarchist Letter-Writing Corp," *Liberty: Not the Daughter but the Mother of Order,* May 16, 1896, 7.

105. "Tour of an Anarchist: A British Socialist Coming to San Francisco," *San Francisco Chronicle,* April 2, 1896, 5; "Anarchists as Labor Organizers," *New York Tribune,* June 17, 1896, 12.

106. "Anarchist John Turner," *Washington Post,* April 24, 1896, 6.

107. "Important for New York," *Free Society,* August 30, 1903, 4.

108. "Emma Goldman to Robert Erskine Ely," October 22, 1903, in Falk, EGDH vol. 2, 111. Goldman does not mention any concern regarding Turner's ability to enter the United States or possible exclusion under the Alien Immigration Act.

109. Commissioner of Immigration on Ellis Island William Williams to Commissioner-General, Bureau of Immigration F. H. Larned, March 29, 1903, in INS, RG 85, Box 50, File 36181, Entry 7, NARA.

110. Commissioner of Immigration on Ellis Island William Williams to Commissioner-General, Bureau of Immigration F. H. Larned, April 2, 1903, RG 85, Box 50, File 36181, Entry 7, NARA.

111. Commissioner-General, Bureau of Immigration F. H. Larned to Commissioner of Immigration on Ellis Island William Williams, March 31, 1903, RG 85, Box 50, File 36181, Entry 7, NARA.

112. Warrant for Deportation: John Turner, No. 41324, Issued by Secretary of Commerce and Labor George B. Cortelyou, October 19, 1903, in *United States ex rel. Turner v. Williams,* 194 U.S. 279 (1904), transcript of record, 4, in *U.S. Supreme Court Records and Briefs, 1832–1978* (Gage, Cengage Learning).

113. "Anarchists Are Raided," *New York Times,* Oct. 24, 1901, 1.

114. "Anarchists Are Raided."

115. Testimony of Inspector John J. McKee, Minutes of Board of Special Inquiry Convened at U.S. Immigration Station, Ellis Island, October 23, 1904, in *United State ex rel. Turner v. Williams,* 194 U.S. 279 (1904), transcript of record, 6.

116. "John Turner to Be Deported," *New York Tribune,* October 25, 1901, 8. Testimony of Inspector Joseph Weldon, Minutes of Board of Special Inquiry Convened at U.S. Immigration Station, Ellis Island, October 23, 1904, in *United States ex rel. Turner v. Williams,* 194 U.S. 279 (1904), transcript of record, 6.

117. Testimony of John Turner, Minutes of Board of Special Inquiry Convened at U.S. Immigration Station, Ellis Island, October 23, 1904, in *United States ex rel. Turner v. Williams,* 194 U.S. 279 (1904), transcript of record, 8.

118. Testimony of John Turner, transcript of record, 9.

119. Petition of John Turner for a writ of *habeas corpus,* filed by Pentecost & Campbell, Attorneys for John Turner, November 11, 1903, in *United States ex rel. Turner v. Williams,* 194 U.S. 279 (1904), transcript of record, 16.

120. Goldman, *Living My Life,* 347–348.

121. "Operation of Our New 'Alien and Sedition Laws,'" *The Public,* November 21, 1903, 526; "Russian Methods in America," *Free Society,* Nov. 29, 1903, 2.

122. "Against Anti-Anarchy Law, Cooper Union Filled," *New York Tribune,* December 4, 1903, 6; "SEEK APPEAL FOR TURNER: Central Union to Ask for Funds to Carry Up Deportation Case," *New York Times,* February 29, 1904, 10.

123. Clarence Darrow, *The Story of My Life* (New York: Charles Scribner's Sons 1932), 41.

124. Darrow, *The Story of My Life,* 53.

125. Darrow, *The Story of My Life,* 97, 100.

126. Masters worked as a lawyer with Darrow from 1903 until 1911. A poet as well as an attorney, Masters later became renowned for his successful collection of poetry in the *Spoon River Anthology* in 1915.

127. Motion of Appellant to Be Admitted to Bail, submitted in *United States ex rel. Turner v. Williams,* 194 U.S. 279 (1904), transcript of record, 1–2.

128. Motion of Appellant, 6–7.

129. Motion of Appellant, 9.

130. Motion of Appellant, 10. Abolished during the French Revolution, *lettres de cachet* were orders signed by the French monarchy authorizing someone's imprisonment or punishment without trial.

131. Motion of Appellant, 10.

132. "John Turner Liberated," *New York Tribune,* March 5, 1904, 4.

133. "Anarchist Turner Tells of His Fight; Was Stared At on Ellis Island as If a Wild Animal," *New York Times,* March 14, 1904, 14.

134. "Anarchist Turner Tells of His Fight."

135. Brief and Argument of Appellant, submitted in *United States ex rel. Turner v. Williams,* 194 U.S. 279 (1904), transcript of record, 40–41, 76.

136. Brief and Argument of Appellant, 107.

137. Brief and Argument of Appellee, submitted in *United States ex rel. Turner v. Williams,* 194 U.S. 279 (1904), transcript of record, 21–24.

138. Brief and Argument of Appellee, 12–16.

139. *United States ex rel. Turner v. Williams,* 194 U.S. 279, 294 (1904).

140. *United States ex rel. Turner v. Williams,* 194 U.S. 292.

141. *United States ex rel. Turner v. Williams,* 194 U.S. 292.

142. *United States ex rel. Turner v. Williams,* 194 U.S. 294.

143. James F. Morton Jr., "Demonstrative," *The Demonstrator,* June 8, 1904, 1.

144. Morton, "Demonstrative."

145. "Too Officious," *The Public,* reprinted in *The Demonstrator,* March 23, 1904, 7.

146. "'REDS' GATHERED IN: BERKMAN AND GOLDMAN Police Break Up Big Meeting of Anarchists—No Resistance," *New York Tribune,* January 7, 1907, 1; "POLICE HAD A 'TIP,': Heard Paterson Anarchists Were Planning 'Demonstration' Here," *New York Tribune,* March 29, 1908, 7.

147. Peter Kropotkin to Emma Goldman, December 16, 1903, in EGDH vol. 2, 127.

148. Ernst Freund, *The Police Power: Public Policy and Constitutional Rights* (Chicago: Callaghan & Company, 1904), 509–513.

149. "Bonaparte Suggests Whip for Anarchists," *New York Times*, August 3, 1906, 1.

150. "Whipping Anarchists," *New York Times*, August 15, 1906, 6.

151. "Article in Mother Earth," December 1906, in EGDH vol. 2, fn.3, 204.

152. Goldman, *Living My Life*, 391.

153. Emma Goldman, "Patriotism: A Menace to Liberty," *Mother Earth*, June 1908.

154. Goldman, *Living My Life*, 428.

155. Transcript of Court-Martial of William Buwalda, First Class Private, Company A, 1st Battalion of Engineers, May 14, 1908, Judge Advocate General Record Group 153, Box 12, File 56990, Entry 17, NARA.

156. "The Week," *The Nation* 86, no. 2240 (1908): 502.

157. William Dudley Foulke, Commissioner, Civil Service Commission, to Charles Joseph Bonaparte, U.S. Attorney General (April 10, 1908), Reel 56, in EGP.

158. Foulke to Bonaparte.

159. Frederick Funston, Commanding General, California, to Fred Ainsworth, Adjutant General, U.S. Department of War (June 30, 1908), Reel 56, in EGP.

160. "To Raise Fund for Buwalda," *San Francisco Chronicle*, January 7, 1909, 13 (quoting Goldman on Buwalda).

161. "Soldier, Released from Alcatraz, to Lecture," *New York Times*, January 13, 1909, 8.

162. Goldman, *Living My Life*, 446.

163. "Five Jurors to Try Anarchists," *San Francisco Chronicle*, January 22, 1909, 16.

164. Goldman, *Living My Life*, 446.

165. Falk, "Raising Her Voice," 66.

166. "Confidential Memo," Immigration Commissioner-General Frank P. Sargent to Immigration Commissioners, September 24, 1907, in EGDH vol. 2, 233. In 1907, Congress revised the Alien Immigration Act of 1903, but left the anarchist provisions intact. The immigration officials cited the 1907 act in their attempts to exclude Goldman.

167. Goldman, *Living My Life*, 411.

168. Goldman, *Living My Life*, 411.

169. Goldman, *Living My Life*, 411.

170. "Confidential Memo," Immigration Commissioner-General Frank P. Sargent to Immigration Commissioners, September 24, 1907, "Federal Warrant for the Arrest of Emma Goldman," November 14, 1907, in Falk, EGDH vol. 2, 233, 254.

171. Goldman, *Living My Life*, 422.

172. Goldman, *Living My Life*, 422.

173. Patrick Weil, *The Sovereign Citizen: Denaturalization and the Origins of the American Republic* (Philadelphia: University of Pennsylvania Press, 2013), 59.

174. At the time of this investigation, Goldman and Kersner had been separated, but they were still legally married.

175. Candice Lewis Bredbenner, *A Nationality of Her Own: Women, Marriage and the Law of Citizenship* (Berkeley: University of California Press, 1998), 15 (quoting act of February 10, 1855, 10 Stat. 604). A vestige of the common law doctrine of coverture, marital derivative citizenship remained federal immigration policy until the Cable Act of 1922.

176. Bredbenner, *A Nationality of Her Own*, 18–19.

177. "An Act to Establish a Bureau of Immigration and Naturalization, and to provide for a uniform rule for the naturalization of aliens throughout the United States," June 29, 1906, 34 Stat. 601, Sect. 15.

178. Weil, *The Sovereign Citizen*, 60.

179. Goldman, *Living My Life*, 449.

180. Weil, *The Sovereign Citizen*, 59.

181. Weil, *The Sovereign Citizen*, 60.

182. Annulment of citizenship of Jacob Kersner, April 8, 1909, in EGDH vol. 2, 416.

183. "Oscar S. Straus to Charles J. Bonaparte," February 11, 1909, in EGDH vol. 2, 410.

184. Weil, *The Sovereign Citizen*, 60.

185. Weil, *The Sovereign Citizen*, 61 (quoting a memorandum from Charles Earl, solicitor of the Department of Commerce and Labor to Oscar Straus, March 21, 1908). Weil notes that a federal court had held that temporary absence did not alter domicile for immigration status purposes.

186. Annual Report of the Commissioner-General of Immigration to the Secretary of Labor, Fiscal Year Ended June 30, 1910 (Washington, DC: Government Printing Office, 1910), 80; Annual Report of the Commissioner-General of Immigration to the Secretary of Labor, Fiscal Year Ended June 30, 1916 (Washington, DC: Government Printing Office, 1916), 84.

187. Richard Bach Jensen, *The Battle against Anarchist Terrorism* (Cambridge: Cambridge University Press, 2014), 290.

188. Barton, "The Global War on Anarchism," 313–317, 325.

189. Barton, "The Global War on Anarchism," 313; Jensen, *The Battle against Anarchist Terrorism*, 250–254.

190. Tim Weiner, *Enemies: A History of the FBI* (New York: Random House, 2012), 10–12; Athan Theoharis, *The FBI & American Democracy: A Brief Critical History* (Lawrence: University of Kansas Press, 2004), 16–17.

191. Emma Goldman, "A Woman Without a Country," *Mother Earth* 4 (May 1909): 81–82.

3. MAKING DEMOCRACY SAFE IN AMERICA

1. David Rabban, *Free Speech in Its Forgotten Years, 1870–1920* (New York: Cambridge University Press, 1997), 77–128.

2. Rabban, *Free Speech in Its Forgotten Years,* 89; Alice Wexler, *Emma Goldman in America* (Boston: Beacon Press, 1984), 178; *Goldman v. Reyburn,* 18 Pa. Dist. R. 883, 884–85 (1909); Bill Lynskey, "'I Shall Speak in Philadelphia': Emma Goldman and the Free Speech League," *Pennsylvania Magazine History & Biography* 133 (April 2009): 167–168.

3. William Preston Jr., *Aliens and Dissenters: Federal Suppression of Radicals, 1903–1933* (Cambridge, MA: Harvard University Press, 1963), 5, 8–10, 42–46.

4. Woodrow Wilson, "Third Annual Message," December 7, 1915, The American Presidency Project, http://www.presidency.ucsb.edu/ws/index.php?pid =29556.

5. Wilson, "Third Annual Message."

6. Geoffrey R. Stone, *Perilous Times: Free Speech in Wartime from the Sedition Act of 1798 to the War on Terrorism* (New York: W.W. Norton, 2004), 153–155. For an analysis of the effects of World War I on American society, citizenship, and culture, see Christopher Capozzola, *Uncle Sam Wants You: World War I and the Making of the Modern American Citizen* (New York: Oxford University Press, 2008).

7. Richard Polenberg, *Fighting Faiths: The Abrams Case, the Supreme Court, and Free Speech* (New York: Viking Penguin, 1987), 36–42.

8. Woodrow Wilson, "Proclamation 1364: Declaring that a State of War Exists between the United States and Germany," April 6, 1917, The American Presidency Project, http://www.presidency.ucsb.edu/ws/?pid=598.

9. Wilson, "Proclamation 1364."

10. Robert Justin Goldstein, *Political Repression in Modern America: From 1870– 1976* (Urbana: University of Illinois Press, 2001), 108–109.

11. "1918 Wartime Measure (An Act to prevent in time of war or departure from or entry into the United States contrary to the public safety)," Pub.L. 65-154, 40 Stat. 559, 65th Congress, enacted May 22, 1918.

12. Jeffrey Kahn, *Mrs. Shipley's Ghost: The Right to Travel and Terrorist Watchlists* (Ann Arbor: University of Michigan Press, 2003), 84 (quoting 65 Proclamation August 8, 1918, 40 Stat. 1829, 1831).

13. Kahn, *Mrs. Shipley's Ghost,* 86.

14. "Selective Draft Law" (An Act to authorize the President to increase temporarily the Military Establishment of the United States), Pub.L. 65-66, 40 Stat. 76, 65th Congress, enacted May 18, 1917.

15. "Espionage Act" (An Act to punish acts of interference with the foreign relations, and the foreign commerce of the United States, to punish espionage, and better to enforce the criminal laws of the United States, and for other purposes), Pub.L. 65-24, 40 Stat. 217, 65th Congress, enacted June 15, 1917.

16. Espionage Act, Sect. 3.

17. "Espionage and Interference with Neutrality," Hearings before the Committee on the Judiciary, H.R. 291 (Washington, DC: Government Printing Office, April 9 and 12, 1917).

18. "Espionage and Interference," 39.

19. "Espionage and Interference," 48–49.

20. Sedition Act, Pub.L. 65-150; 40 Stat. 553, 65th Congress, enacted May 16, 1918.

21. Daniel Kanstroom, *Deportation Nation: Outsiders in American History* (Cambridge, MA: Harvard University Press, 2007), 141–143.

22. Report on the Bisbee Deportations, Made by the President's Mediation Commission to the President of the United States, Bisbee, Arizona, Nov. 6, 1917, repr. in *Official Bulletin* 1, no. 170 (November 27, 1917), 6.

23. Goldstein, *Political Repression*, 116–117; Preston, *Aliens and Dissenters*, 145–151.

24. Stone, *Perilous Times*, 196–197.

25. Rabban, *Free Speech in Its Forgotten Years*, 272. An *amicus curiae* ("friend of the court") brief is submitted by one who is not a party to the case, or solicited by a party, but one who has some information to offer the court pertaining to the case.

26. Rabban, *Free Speech in Its Forgotten Years*, 261.

27. Polenberg, *Fighting Faiths*, 42–48.

28. Paul Avrich and Karen Avrich, *Sasha and Emma: The Anarchist Odyssey of Alexander Berkman and Emma Goldman* (Cambridge, MA: The Belknap Press of Harvard University Press, 2012), 269.

29. "Emma Goldman's Address to Jury," July 9, 1917, The Emma Goldman Papers Project, http://www.lib.berkeley.edu/goldman/pdfs/Speeches -AddresstotheJury.pdf.

30. Rabban, *Free Speech in Its Forgotten Years*, 271 (quoting from Weinberger's appellant brief, 18–21).

31. Avrich and Avrich, *Sasha and Emma*, 276–280.

32. Emma Goldman, *Living My Life* (New York: Dove, 1970 [1931]), 651.

33. "1917 Immigration Act (An act to regulate the immigration of aliens to, and the residence of aliens in, the United States)," Pub.L. 301, 39 Stat. 874, 64th Congress, enacted February 5, 1917.

34. 1917 Immigration Act, Sect. 3.

35. 1917 Immigration Act, Sect. 3.

36. 1917 Immigration Act, Sect. 19.

37. "I.W.W. Deportation Cases," *Hearings before a Subcommittee of the Committee on Immigration and Naturalization*, Statement of W. A. Blackwood, 66th Congress, April 27–30, 1920 (Washington, DC: Government Printing Office, 1920), 76.

38. *United States v. Swelgin*, 254 F. 884 (D.C. Oregon, 1918).

39. *United States v. Swelgin*.

40. "Anarchy and the I.W.W.," *U.S. Immigration Service Bulletin* 1, no. 4 (1918), 1.

41. *Lopez v. Howe,* 259 F. 401, 403–404 (2d Cir. 1919).

42. *Lopez v. Howe,* 404.

43. *Lopez v. Howe,* 404.

44. Secretary of Labor William B. Wilson to Hon. John L. Burnett, Chairman of the Committee on Immigration in the House of Representatives, May 28, 1918, in *U.S. Immigration Service Bulletin* 1, no. 4 (1918), 2.

45. Wilson to Burnett, 2.

46. Wilson to Burnett, 2.

47. Wilson to Burnett, 2.

48. Anarchist Exclusion Act, ch. 186, 40 Stat. 1012, 65th Congress, October 16, 1918, sect. 1, as amended by act of June 5, 1920.

49. Anarchist Exclusion Act, sect. 2.

50. "Bolshevik Propaganda" *Hearings before a Subcommittee of the Committee on the Judiciary,* US Senate, S. Res. 439 and 469, February 11, 1919 to March 10, 1919 (Washington, DC: Government Printing Office, 1919); "Senators Tell What Bolshevism in America Means," *New York Times,* June 15, 1919, 40; Jay Feldman, *Manufacturing Hysteria: A History of Scapegoating, Surveillance, and Secrecy in Modern America* (New York: Anchor Books, 2012), 77.

51. Goldstein, *Political Repression,* 144.

52. Goldstein, *Political Repression,* 144; Stone, *Perilous Times,* 221.

53. "Revolutionary Radicalism: Its History, Purpose and Tactics with an Exposition and Discussion of the Steps Being Taken and Required to Curb It," Report of the Joint Legislative Committee Investigating Seditious Activities, Filed April 24, 1920, in the Senate of the State of New York (Albany, NY: J.B. Lyon Co., 1920); "Raid Rand School, 'Left Wing' and I.W.W. Offices," *New York Times,* June 22, 1919; Marjorie Heins, *Priests of Our Democracy: The Supreme Court, Academic Freedom, and the Anti-Communist Purge* (New York: New York University Press, 2013), 29–30.

54. "Palmer and Family Safe," *New York Times,* June 3, 1919, 1.

55. "Requests $500,000 to Put Down Reds," *Washington Post,* June 13, 1919, 4.

56. "Bureau Expects to Crush Anarchism in America," *Washington Post,* June 4, 1919, 1; Tim Weiner, *Enemies: A History of the FBI* (New York: Random House, 2012),10–12; Athan Theoharis, *The FBI & American Democracy: A Brief Critical History* (Lawrence: University of Kansas Press, 2004), 14–17, 24.

57. "Deport Thirty 'Red' Agitators," *New York Times,* June 29, 1919, 1.

58. "Galleani, Luigi (1861–1931)," in "Directory of Individuals," EGDH vol. 2, 523.

59. Paul Avrich, *Sacco and Vanzetti: The Anarchist Background* (Princeton: Princeton University Press, 1991), 122.

60. Avrich, *Sacco and Vanzetti,* 132–136, 168; "Deport Thirty 'Red' Agitators."

61. Stone, *Perilous Times,* 222–223; Weiner, *Enemies,* 23.

62. Weiner, *Enemies,* 13–14.

63. Weiner, *Enemies*, 13–14.

64. Curt Gentry, *J. Edgar Hoover, the Man and the Secrets* (New York: W.W. Norton, 1991), 69, 74, 75–105.

65. Gentry, *J. Edgar Hoover*, 85–88.

66. Avrich and Avrich, *Sasha and Emma*, 291, 295.

67. Weinberger focused on Goldman's citizenship to prevent her deportation. He argued that Goldman retained her citizenship and Kersner's denaturalization did not affect her status. He also argued that she had derived citizenship through her father, who she claimed became a citizen while she was still a minor. Deirdre Moloney, *National Insecurities: Immigrants and U.S. Deportation Policy Since 1882* (Chapel Hill: University of North Carolina Press, 2012), 175.

68. "Statement by Emma Goldman at Federal Immigration hearing in re deportation," October 27, 1919, The Emma Goldman Papers Project, http://www.lib.berkeley.edu/goldman/pdfs/StatementbyEmmaGoldmanattheFederalHearingREdeportation.pdf.

69. Weiner, *Enemies*, 31.

70. Goldman, *Living My Life*, 717.

71. Goldstein, *Political Repression*, 154–155.

72. Goldstein, *Political Repression*, 156–157; Stone, *Perilous Times*, 223–224; Kanstroom, *Deportation Nation*, 149.

73. Mitchell C. Tilner, "Ideological Exclusion of Aliens: The Evolution of a Policy," *Georgetown Immigration Law Journal* 2, no. 1 (1987): 47; Louis F. Post, *The Deportations Delirium of Nineteen-Twenty: A Personal Narrative of an Historic Official Experience* (Chicago: Charles H. Kerr & Co., 1923), 192.

74. Torrie Hester, *Deportation: The Origins of U.S Policy* (Philadelphia: University of Pennsylvania Press, 2017), 127–128.

75. Goldman, *Living My Life*, 711–712.

76. Post, *The Deportations Delirium*, 148–149.

77. Post, *The Deportations Delirium*, 56–57.

78. Post, *The Deportations Delirium*, 167–187.

79. Post, *The Deportations Delirium*, 202–209.

80. Post, *The Deportations Delirium*, 201.

81. Post, *The Deportations Delirium*, 16–17.

82. Post, *The Deportations Delirium*, 183–187.

83. "Take Steps in House to Impeach Post," *New York Times*, April 16, 1920, 4.

84. "Seeks to Oust Post; Hoch Introduces a Resolution," *Los Angeles Times*, April 16, 1920, 11.

85. "Attorney General A. Mitchell Palmer on Charges Made Against Department of Justice by Louis F. Post and Others: Hearings before the United States House Committee on Rules," House of Representatives, 66th Congress, 2nd session (June 1, 1920); "Palmer Calls Post a Friend to Anarchists," *New York Tribune*, June 2, 1920, 3.

86. Post, *The Deportations Delirium*, 250–274; "Louis Post Defends Rulings on Aliens," *New York Times*, May 9, 1920, 12.

87. Post, *The Deportations Delirium*, 274.

88. National Popular Government League, "To the American People: a Report upon the Illegal Practices of the United States Justice Department," Washington, DC, May 1920.

89. "Lawyers Denounce Raids on Radicals," *New York Times*, May 28, 1920, 6.

90. Hester, *Deportation*, 129. This case is unusual in that Judge Anderson heard it before it reached Post on appeal. He found the Justice Department's conduct so egregious that he agreed to hear it immediately.

91. *Colyer v. Skeffington*, 265 F. 17, 79 (D. Mass. 1920).

92. *Colyer v. Skeffington*, 79.

93. *Colyer v. Skeffington*, 44–47.

94. *Colyer v. Skeffington*, 23–31.

95. "Palmer's Riot Predictions Fail; Nobody Murdered Yet," *New York Tribune*, May 2, 1920, 2.

96. "House Refuses $500,000 Fund Palmer Asked," *New York Tribune*, May 11, 1920, 4.

97. For a detailed account of these negotiations and the difficulties in deporting to Soviet Russia during this period, see Hester, *Deportation*, 118–124, 133–140.

98. Preston, *Aliens and Dissenters*, 262–264.

99. Beverly Gage, *The Day Wall Street Exploded: A Story of America in Its First Age of Terror* (New York: Oxford University Press, 2009), 269.

100. Goldman, *Living My Life*, 725.

101. Goldman, *Living My Life*, 860–888; Emma Goldman, *My Disillusionment in Russia* (London: C.W. Daniel Co., 1925).

102. Avrich and Avrich, *Sasha and Emma*, 331. Goldman had been traveling on a tourist passport, which was due to expire. Colton, an acquaintance, offered his assistance.

103. "Goldman and the Spanish Civil War," The Emma Goldman Papers Project, http://www.lib.berkeley.edu/goldman/MeetEmmaGoldman/emmagoldmanandthe spanishcivilwar.html.

104. Avrich and Avrich, *Sasha and Emma*, 365–371. Goldman is permitted to enter and lecture but only on "nonpolitical" subjects.

105. Avrich and Avrich, *Sasha and Emma*, 372.

106. Avrich and Avrich, *Sasha and Emma*, 381–384.

107. Avrich and Avrich, *Sasha and Emma*, 399.

108. Samuel Walker, *In Defense of American Liberties: A History of the ACLU*, 2nd. ed. (Carbondale: Southern Illinois University Press, 1999), 17.

109. Walker, *In Defense of American Liberties*, 18.

110. Walker, *In Defense of American Liberties*, 18–21.

111. Walker, *In Defense of American Liberties*, 46–47.

112. Walker, *In Defense of American Liberties,* 44.

113. Walker, *In Defense of American Liberties,* 54–60.

114. The Free Speech League had defended not only the IWW in its free speech fights, but also those prosecuted under the Comstock Act for distributing information about contraception, such as Margaret Sanger. Initially, the ACLU took cases concerning the suppression of political or economic speech, but not sexual speech. But by the 1930s, the ACLU began to take these cases and brought constitutional challenges against the Comstock Act and obscenity laws that restricted expression on sex and reproduction. Rabban, *Free Speech in Its Forgotten Years,* 67, 310–312; Laura Weinrib, "The Sex Side of Civil Liberties: United States v. Dennett and the Changing Face of Free Speech," *Law and History Review* 30, no. 2 (2012): 325–386.

115. Rabban, *Free Speech in Its Forgotten Years,* 311.

116. Rabban, *Free Speech in Its Forgotten Years,* 76; Walker, *In Defense of American Liberties,* 53–54, 68.

117. *Masses Publishing Co. v. Patten,* 244 F. 535 (S.D.N.Y. 1917).

118. *Masses Publishing Co. v. Patten,* 540.

119. *Masses Publishing Co. v. Patten,* 246 F. 24 (2d Cir. 1917).

120. *Schenck v. United States,* 249 U.S. 47 (1919).

121. *Schenck v. United States,* 52.

122. *Schenck v. United States,* 52.

123. *Schenck v. United States,* 52.

124. *Schenck v. United States,* 52.

125. *Debs v. United States,* 249 U.S. 211, 216 (1919).

126. *Debs v. United States,* 211, 216.

127. Zechariah Chafee Jr., "Freedom of Speech in War Time," *Harvard Law Review* 32 (June 1919): 932.

128. Chafee, "Freedom of Speech in War Time," 960, 964.

129. Chafee, "Freedom of Speech in War Time," 967–968.

130. Chafee, "Freedom of Speech in War Time," 956.

131. Chafee, "Freedom of Speech in War Time," 958.

132. Chafee, "Freedom of Speech in War Time," 968.

133. Chafee, "Freedom of Speech in War Time," 959.

134. Chafee, "Freedom of Speech in War Time," 960.

135. Stone, *Perilous Times,* 202–203.

136. *Abrams v. United States,* 250 U.S. 616 (1919).

137. *Abrams v. United States,* 624.

138. *Abrams v. United States,* 629 (Holmes, J., dissenting).

139. *Abrams v. United States,* 630.

140. *Gitlow v. New York,* 268 U.S. 652 (1925).

141. *Gitlow v. New York,* 669.

142. *Gitlow v. New York,* 669.

143. *Gitlow v. New York,* 664.

144. *Whitney v. California*, 274 U.S. 357 (1927).

145. *Whitney v. California*, 371.

146. *Whitney v. California*, 379 (Brandeis, J., concurring).

147. *Whitney v. California*, 376.

148. *Whitney v. California*, 377.

149. Zechariah Chafee Jr., *Freedom of Speech* (New York: Harcourt, Brace, and Howe, 1920).

150. Chafee, *Freedom of Speech*, 229–230.

151. Chafee, *Freedom of Speech*, 240.

152. Chafee, *Freedom of Speech*, 281.

153. Chafee, *Freedom of Speech*, 282, 284

154. Chafee, *Freedom of Speech*, 283.

155. Chafee, *Freedom of Speech*, 286

156. Chafee, *Freedom of Speech*, 293.

157. Chafee, *Freedom of Speech*, 292.

158. Chafee, *Freedom of Speech*, 289.

159. Chafee, *Freedom of Speech*, 289.

160. Chafee, *Freedom of Speech*, 291.

161. Chafee, *Freedom of Speech*, 292.

162. Avrich, *Sacco and Vanzetti*, 213, 227.

163. For a discussion of the Wall Street Bombing and of Hoover's career after the bombing, see Gage, *The Day Wall Street Exploded*, 11–37, 125–290, 323–326.

164. For a discussion of the reaction and response to the Sacco and Vanzetti case in the United States and abroad, see Moshik Temkin, *The Sacco-Vanzetti Affair: America on Trial* (New Haven, CT: Yale University Press, 2009).

165. John Higham, *Strangers in the Land: Patterns of American Nativism, 1860–1925* (New Brunswick, NJ: Rutgers University Press, 1955), 11, 312–330.

166. Gary Gerstle, *American Crucible: Race and Nation in the Twentieth Century* (Princeton, NJ: Princeton University Press, 2001), 101–109.

167. Emergency Quota Act, ch. 8, 42 Stat. 5 of May 19, 1921.

168. Immigration Act of 1924, Pub.L. 68–139, 43 Stat. 153, enacted May 26, 1924.

4. DENATURALIZATION, DETENTION, DEPORTATION, AND DISCRETION

1. Aristide R. Zolberg, *A Nation by Design: Immigration Policy in the Fashioning of America* (Cambridge, MA: Harvard University Press, 2006), 268–269.

2. Daniel Kanstroom, *Deportation Nation: Outsiders in American History* (Cambridge, MA: Harvard University Press, 2007), 165.

3. "SAYS 400,000 ALIENS ARE HERE ILLEGALLY; Doak Tells the Senate That 100,000 Are Deportable, and Urges Stricter Law," *New York Times*, January 6, 1931, 5.

4. "Alien Deportations," *Wall Street Journal*, January 7, 1931, 6.

5. Kanstroom, *Deportation Nation*, 214–219. For a discussion of Mexican Removal, see Francisco E. Balderrama and Raymond Rodríguez, *Decade of Betrayal: Mexican Repatriation in the 1930s*, rev. ed. (Albuquerque: University of New Mexico Press, 2006).

6. "Alien Tide Ebb Starts at Length," *Los Angeles Times*, February 11, 1931, 15.

7. "INS Records for 1930s Mexican Repatriations," US Citizenship and Immigration Services, https://www.uscis.gov/history-and-genealogy/our-history /historians-mailbox/ins-records-1930s-mexican-repatriations.

8. "105 Aliens Seized at Seamen's Home," *New York Times*, February 4, 1931, 3.

9. "18 Aliens Seized at Finnish Dance," *New York Times*, February 16, 1931, 17.

10. "18 Aliens Seized at Finnish Dance."

11. "Attacks Raids on Aliens as Illegal," *New York Times*, February 18, 1931, 6.

12. "Fights Ban on Student," *New York Times*, May 15, 1931, 28.

13. "GOVERNMENT TO SEND CHINESE RED TO CHINA; Li Tao Hsuan Loses in Plea to Labor Department That He Be Deported to Russia," *New York Times*, May 23, 1931, 5.

14. "GOVERNMENT TO SEND CHINESE RED TO CHINA"; "Police Clubs Rout Reds at Battery," *New York Times*, May 16, 1931, 2.

15. Emanuel Pollack, "The Case of Li Tao Husan," Labor Research Association records, Folder 26, Box 4, TAM.

16. US National Commission on Law and Observance, "Report on the Enforcement of the Deportation Laws of the United States" (Washington, DC: Government Printing Office, 1931).

17. "Law Body Hits Methods Used in Alien Cases," *Washington Post*, August 8, 1931, 1.

18. US National Commission on Law and Observance, "Report on the Enforcement of the Deportation Laws," 3, 5, 121, 177–179.

19. US National Commission on Law and Observance, "Report on the Enforcement of the Deportation Laws," 178–179.

20. "Doak Denies Blame in Deportations," *New York Times*, August 9, 1931, 5.

21. "Efforts to Stop Deportation of 'Reds' Criticized," *Christian Science Monitor*, July 16, 1931. 4; "Alien Red Backers Are Hit by Doak," *Washington Post*, July 17, 1931, 7.

22. "20,000 to be Deported in 1932, Doak Estimates," *New York Times*, January 7, 1932, 10; "Asks Stiffer Laws on Naturalization; Doak Would Require Aliens to Be Equal of Child 14," *Boston Globe*, December 10, 1931, 5.

23. "Alien Departures Exceeded Immigration in 1932 for First Time in Nation's History," *New York Times*, August 18, 1932, 1.

24. "Doak Hails Benefit in Immigration Cut," *New York Times*, December 10, 1931, 2.

25. Kirstin Downey, *The Woman Behind the New Deal: The Life of Frances Perkins, FDR's Secretary of Labor and His Moral Conscience* (New York: Random House, 2009).

26. "Alien Treatment Investigated Here," *New York Times*, June 27, 1933, 19.

27. "Alien Curb Backed by Miss Perkins," *New York Times*, January 30, 1934, 6.

28. "Senate Gets 'If' Bill to Shield Alien Radicals," *Chicago Daily Tribune*, March 29, 1936, 10.

29. Louise Pettibone Smith, *Torch of Liberty: 25 Years in the Life of the Foreign Born in the U.S.A.* (New York: Dwight-King Publishers, 1959), 44–45; Rachel Ida Buff, *Against the Deportation Terror: Organizing for Immigrant Rights in the Twentieth Century* (Philadelphia: Temple University Press, 2018), 28.

30. Smith, *Torch of Liberty*, 55–60.

31. Smith, *Torch of Liberty*, 61.

32. Smith, *Torch of Liberty*, 61.

33. Smith, *Torch of Liberty*, 62.

34. Louise Pettibone Smith, "In Loving Memory of Abner Green—selfless, unassuming worker on behalf of his fellow men," Box 1, Folder "Administration: Biographical Information—Green, Abner," ACPFB Records, LABADIE.

35. Ann Fagan Ginger, *Carol Weiss King: Human Rights Lawyer, 1895–1952* (Boulder: University Press of Colorado, 1993), xiv–xv, 11–12, 100; Bernard Unti, "Carol Weiss King," *Jewish Women: A Comprehensive Historical Encyclopedia*, February 27, 2009, https://jwa.org/encyclopedia/article/king-carol-weiss.

36. Ginger, *Carol Weiss King*, 12–13, 20–21, Unti, "Carol Weiss King."

37. Ginger, *Carol Weiss King*, 119.

38. "Carol King, Silent Brief Maker," *Christian Science Monitor*, June 9, 1942, 12.

39. Ginger, *Carol Weiss King*, 39.

40. Ginger, *Carol Weiss King*, 40–41.

41. Ginger, *Carol Weiss King*, 41–42.

42. Ginger, *Carol Weiss King*, 40.

43. "Police Clubs Rout Reds at Battery," *New York Times*, May 16, 1931, 2.

44. Smith, *Torch of Liberty*, 63.

45. Smith, *Torch of Liberty*, 63.

46. "Richter, Anti-Nazi, Must Go to Germany," *New York Times*, June 2, 1936, 12.

47. Abner Green, "Deportation of Anti-Nazis," *New York Times*, June 2, 1936, 18; "500 Decry Deportation," *New York Times*, June 14, 1936, 2.

48. Smith, *Torch of Liberty*, 62–63; Buff, *Against the Deportation Terror*, 30.

49. Buff, *Against the Deportation Terror*, 30.

50. Green, "Deportation of Anti-Nazis," 18.

51. Green, "Deportation of Anti-Nazis"; Louis F. Post, *The Deportations Delirium of Nineteen-Twenty: A Personal Narrative of an Historic Official Experience* (Chicago: Charles H. Kerr, 1923), 170–173.

52. Richard Breitman and Alan Kraut, *American Refugee Policy and European Jewry, 1933–1945* (Bloomington: Indiana University Press, 1987), 14–27.

53. "MISS PERKINS HIT OVER ALIEN LAWS; Spanish War Veterans Charge Lax Administration of the Immigration Curbs," *New York Times*, August 24, 1937, 27;

"The Friend of Alien Trouble-Makers," *Chicago Daily Tribune*, September 8, 1934, 12; "Veterans Ask Miss Perkins Be Censured," *Washington Post*, August 13, 1934, 1.

54. Curt Gentry, *J. Edgar Hoover, the Man and the Secrets* (New York: W. W. Norton, 1991), 187–188; "Emma Goldman Wins Permit to Visit Kin," *Washington Post*, January 10, 1934, 1.

55. Paul Avrich and Karen Avrich, *Sasha and Emma: The Anarchist Odyssey of Alexander Berkman and Emma Goldman* (Cambridge, MA: The Belknap Press of Harvard University Press, 2012), 366–369.

56. "Alien Policy Draws Fire," *Los Angeles Times*, March 10, 1935, 2. Many individuals and organizations wrote to Perkins to praise her decision to admit Goldman; see letters and telegrams in Frances Perkins Papers, Folder "Goldman, Emma," Box 73, RBML.

57. George Rosenberger to Frances Perkins, Secretary of Labor, January 15, 1934, Frances Perkins Papers, Folder "Goldman, Emma" Box 73, RBML.

58. Samuel Walker, *In Defense of American Liberties: A History of the ACLU*, 2nd. ed. (Carbondale: Southern Illinois University Press, 1999), 120.

59. "Fish Report Asks Outlawing of Reds as National Menace," *New York Times*, January 18, 1931, 1.

60. Hearings before the Committee on Immigration and Naturalization, "Exclusion and Expulsion of Communists: Suspension, Restriction, and Further Restriction, of Immigration," April 22 and May 5, 1932 (Washington, DC: Government Printing Office, 1932). April 22 & May 5, 1932.

61. Hearings, "Exclusion and Expulsion," 1–14.

62. Hearings, "Exclusion and Expulsion," 16.

63. Hearings, "Exclusion and Expulsion," 15–19.

64. Hearings, "Exclusion and Expulsion," 15–19.

65. Dies Bill, H.R. 8731, 74th Congress, 1st Session, June 29, 1935, Sect. 2–4.

66. Dies Bill, Sect. 6.

67. Dies Bill, Sect. 1.

68. Dies Bill, Sect. 1–15.

69. Kerr-Coolidge Bill, in "Deportation of Aliens," H.R. 6795, 74th Congress, 1st Session, April 9, 10, 11, 1935.

70. Kerr-Coolidge Bill, Sect. 4.

71. Martin Dies, "America for Americans," National Broadcasting Co., May 6, 1935, transcript in "The Alien Menace to America," *Congressional Record*, vol. 79, 74th Congress, 1st Session, 10227–10232 (June 26, 1935).

72. Dies, "America for Americans."

73. Dies, "America for Americans."

74. Robert Justin Goldstein, *Political Repression in Modern America: From 1870–1976* (Urbana: University of Illinois Press, 240.

75. Martin Dies Jr., *The Trojan Horse in America* (New York: Dodd, Mead, 1940).

76. Goldstein, *Political Repression*, 242–243.

77. Kanstroom, *Deportation Nation*, 187–188; Buff, *Against the Deportation Terror*, 59–60.

78. Kanstroom, *Deportation Nation*, 191.

79. Downey, *The Woman Behind the New Deal*, 272–273.

80. "Dies Report Shows Deportation Laws Not Enforced," *Chicago Daily Tribune*, January 4, 1939, 1.

81. Kanstroom, *Deportation Nation*, 191.

82. "Move for Perkins Impeachment on Bridges Case Made in the House," *New York Times*, January 25, 1939, 1.

83. "Move for Perkins Impeachment."

84. "Move for Perkins Impeachment." ; H. Res. 67 *Resolution for the Impeachment of Frances Perkins, Secretary of Labor*, January 24, 1939 (Washington, DC: Government Printing Office, 1939), Frances Perkins Papers, Box 122, RBML.

85. "Miss Perkins Tells Committee Bridges Gets No Favoritism," *New York Times*, February 9, 1939, 1.

86. "Miss Perkins Tells Committee."

87. "Miss Perkins Tells Committee."

88. "Miss Perkins's Defense before House Committee in the Bridges Case," *New York Times*, February 9, 1939, 14.

89. "Miss Perkins's Defense."

90. "House Kills Move for Perkins Trial," *New York Times*, March 25, 1939, 1.

91. Ginger, *Carol Weiss King*, 239.

92. Louis Wood, "Past Communist Membership Held No Ground to Oust Alien," *New York Times*, April 18, 1939, 16.

93. Ginger, *Carol Weiss King*, 238–239.

94. Wood, "Past Communist Membership," 16.

95. Wood, "Past Communist Membership," 16.

96. Ginger, *Carol Weiss King*, 239.

97. *Kessler v. Strecker*, 307 U.S. 22, 29–30 (1939).

98. *Kessler v. Strecker*, 29.

99. *Kessler v. Strecker*, 29.

100. "Miss Perkins Orders Hearing on Bridges," *New York Times*, April 22, 1939, 1.

101. "James M. Landis to Conduct Trial of Harry Bridges," *Washington Post*, May 24, 1939, 24. Concerned about violence at the hearing, Perkins chose the US immigration office on Angel Island as a secure location controlled by the Labor Department, which could limit attendance. See Downey, *The Woman Behind the New Deal*, 283.

102. Ginger, *Carol Weiss King*, 259–260.

103. W. A. MacDonald, "Communist Denied by Bridges as Case against Him Opens," *New York Times*, July 11, 1939, 1.

104. "Bridges Held a Radical, but No Red," *Christian Science Monitor*, December 30, 1939, 1.

105. "Bridges Held a Radical, but No Red."

106. "Landis Absolves Bridges of Charge of Red Affiliation," *New York Times*, December 30, 1939, 4.

107. "Warrant to Oust Bridges Canceled by Miss Perkins," *Washington Post*, January 9, 1940, 1.

108. Gentry, *J. Edgar Hoover*, 245.

109. Ginger, *Carol Weiss King*, 325–330.

110. Gentry, *J. Edgar Hoover*, 244.

111. "Action of Bridges in Congress Likely," *New York Times*, December 31, 1939, 12.

112. Downey, *The Woman Behind the New Deal*, 294–295.

113. Breitman and Kraut, *American Refugee Policy*, 120–123.

114. Gentry, *J. Edgar Hoover*, 245.

115. "Reorganization Plan No. V of 1940," 5 F.R. 2223, 54 Stat. 1238, effective June 15, 1940.

116. 5 Fed. Reg. 3,502 (September 4, 1940).

117. President Roosevelt to Congress, Message regarding "Reorganization Plan No. V," May 22, 1940, https://uscode.house.gov/view.xhtml?req=granuleid:USC -1999-title5a-node78-leaf84&num=0&edition=1999.

118. President Roosevelt to Congress, Message regarding "Reorganization Plan No. V."

119. President Roosevelt to Congress, Message regarding "Reorganization Plan No. V."

120. Alien Registration Act, Pub.L. 76-670, 54 Stat. 670, 76th Congress, June 29, 1940.

121. Kanstroom, *Deportation Nation*, 195.

122. Alien Registration Act, Title I, Sect. 2(a).

123. Alien Registration Act, Title I, Section 3.

124. Alien Registration Act, Title II, Sect. 23.

125. Alien Registration Act, Title III, Sect. 32–33.

126. Alien Registration Act, Title III, Sect. 35–36.

127. "Alien Registration Lauded by Lehman," *New York Times*, August 26, 1940, 17.

128. "Alien Registration Lauded by Lehman."

129. "1940 Nationality Act (An act to revise and codify the nationality laws of the United States in a comprehensive nationality code)," Pub.L. 76-853, 54 Stat. 1137, 76th Congress, October 14, 1940, Chapter III, Sect. 305.

130. 1940 Nationality Act, Chapter III, Sect. 305

131. *Korematsu v. United States*, 323 U.S. 214 (1944).

132. *Korematsu v. United States*, 240–243 (Murphy J., dissenting).

133. Smith, *Torch of Liberty*, 146–163. Smith acknowledges that there is an inherent contradiction between the ACPFB's policies and its lack of legal challenge to Japanese internment. The ACPFB was critical of the internment as unjust. Buff, *Against the Deportation Terror*, 187.

134. Smith, *Torch of Liberty*, 140–144, 152–163.

135. *Schneiderman v. United States*, 320 U.S. 118, 125–126 (1943).

136. *Schneiderman v. United States*, 123–124.

137. Ginger, *Carol Weiss King*, 366.

138. "Carol King, Silent Brief Maker," 12; Ginger, *Carol Weiss King*, x.

139. Ginger, *Carol Weiss King*, 368–369.

140. "Carol King, Silent Brief Maker," 12 (quoting Willkie).

141. "Petitioner's Brief," 27, in *Schneiderman v. United States*, 320 U.S. 118 (1943).

142. "Petitioner's Brief," 28.

143. "Petitioner's Brief," 29.

144. *Schneiderman v. United States*, 154.

145. *Schneiderman v. United States*, 141.

146. *Schneiderman v. United States*, 137.

147. *Schneiderman v. United States*, 141.

148. *Schneiderman v. United States*, 139.

149. *Bridges v. Wixon*, 326 U.S. 135, 139 (1945). Justice Jackson recused himself.

150. *Bridges v. Wixon*, 139.

151. *Bridges v. Wixon*, 139.

152. Ginger, *Carol Weiss King*, 360–361.

153. Ginger, *Carol Weiss King*, 361.

154. Ginger, *Carol Weiss King*, 361.

155. *Bridges v. Wixon*, 139.

156. To file or petition for a writ of *certiorari* is to ask the Supreme Court to review a lower court decision on appeal.

157. *Bridges v. Wixon*, 156–157.

158. *Bridges v. Wixon*, 155.

159. *Bridges v. Wixon*, 156.

160. *Bridges v. Wixon*, 144.

161. *Bridges v. Wixon*, 149.

162. *Bridges v. Wixon*, 143.

163. *Bridges v. Wixon*, 143.

164. *Bridges v. Wixon*, 326 U.S. 135, 174 (Stone, C. J., dissenting).

165. *Bridges v. Wixon*, 166–167.

166. *Bridges v. Wixon*, 167.

167. *Bridges v. Wixon*, 167.

168. *Bridges v. Wixon*, 174.

169. *Bridges v. Wixon*, 326 U.S. 135, 157 (Murphy, J., concurring).

170. *Bridges v. Wixon*, 161.

171. *Bridges v. Wixon*, 162.

172. *Bridges v. Wixon*, 164–165.

173. *Bridges v. Wixon*, 165.

174. *Bridges v. Wixon*, 166.

175. *Bridges v. Wixon,* 166.

176. Lewis Wood, "High Court Blocks Bridges' Expulsion," *New York Times,* June 19, 1945, 9.

177. "Bridges Becomes US Citizen," *New York Times,* September 18, 1945, 12.

178. Ginger, *Carol Weiss King,* 421.

179. Smith, *Torch of Liberty,* 189.

180. Smith, *Torch of Liberty,* 190.

181. Smith, *Torch of Liberty,* 190.

182. Walker, *In Defense of American Liberties,* 127–128.

183. Robert C. Cottrell, *Roger Nash Baldwin and the American Civil Liberties Union* (New York: Columbia University Press, 2000), 262.

184. Cottrell, *Roger Nash Baldwin,* 265; Walker, *In Defense of American Liberties,* 129.

185. Walker, *In Defense of American Liberties,* 129.

186. Walker, *In Defense of American Liberties,* 130–131.

187. Cottrell, *Roger Nash Baldwin,* 270.

188. Walker, *In Defense of American Liberties,* 130–131.

189. Ginger, *Carol Weiss King,* x; Buff, *Against the Deportation Terror,* 11–15. The ACPFB denied it was a Communist-front organization, and Green defended it against such charges.

190. Walker, *In Defense of American Liberties,* 154.

191. Walker, *In Defense of American Liberties,* 122.

192. Edward G. Robinson to Dr. Newson, Dec. 7, 1943, ACPFB Records, Box 1, Folder Administration—Sponsors 1941–1952, LABADIE.

5. AN IRON CURTAIN OF THE WEST

1. For detailed examinations of anti-Communism and McCarthyism in the United States, see David Caute, *The Great Fear: The Anti-Communist Purge under Truman and Eisenhower* (New York: Simon & Schuster, 1978); Ellen Schrecker, *Many Are the Crimes: McCarthyism in America* (Princeton: Princeton University Press, 1998).

2. Herb Block, *"Fire!" Washington Post,* June 17, 1949, 22.

3. Herb Block, "McCarthyism," *Washington Post,* March 29, 1950; Martin Redish, *The Logic of Persecution: Free Expression and the McCarthy Era* (Stanford, CA: Stanford University Press 2005), 23.

4. Redish, *The Logic of Persecution,* 23.

5. Schrecker, *Many Are the Crimes,* xviii.

6. Caute, *The Great Fear,* 28.

7. Alien Registration Act of 1940, 76th United States Congress, 3d session, ch. 439, 54 Stat. 670, 18 U.S.C. Sect. 2385), enacted June 28, 1940, Title II, Sect. 23.

8. Abner Green, *The Deportation Terror: A Weapon to Gag America* (New York: New Century Publishers, 1950), 4.

9. Green, *The Deportation Terror,* 17.

10. Ellen Schrecker, "Immigration and Internal Security: Political Deportations during the McCarthy Era," *Science & Society* 60, no. 4 (1996–1997): 399.

11. Caute, *The Great Fear*, 33.

12. Green, *The Deportation Terror*, 8.

13. Green, *The Deportation Terror*, 8–9.

14. Green, *The Deportation Terror*, 10.

15. Green, *The Deportation Terror*, 5.

16. Green, *The Deportation Terror*, 14.

17. Green, *The Deportation Terror*, 13–14.

18. The Administrative Procedure Act, Pub.L. 79-404, 60 Stat. 237, Sect. 5, 7, and 8 (June 11, 1946).

19. Ann Fagan Ginger, *Carol Weiss King: Human Rights Lawyer, 1895–1952* (Boulder: University Press of Colorado, 1993), 455.

20. Ginger, *Carol Weiss King*, 455.

21. *Wong Yang Sung v. McGrath,* 339 U.S. 33, 53 (1950).

22. Ginger, *Carol Weiss King,* 506.

23. "An act making supplemental appropriations for the fiscal year ending June 30, 1951," 64 Stat. ch. 1052, 1048.

24. Daniel Kanstroom, *Deportation Nation: Outsiders in American History* (Cambridge, MA: Harvard University Press, 2007), 199; Caute, *The Great Fear,* 238.

25. *Bridges v. United States,* 346 U.S. 209 (1953).

26. Kanstroom, *Deportation Nation,* 199.

27. *Dennis v. United States,* 341 U.S. 494, 510 (1951).

28. Ginger, *Carol Weiss King,* 502–503.

29. Referred to as the Mundt-Nixon Bill in 1948 (HR-5852) and reintroduced as the Mundt-Ferguson-Johnston Bill in 1949 (S-2311).

30. It is unclear who coined the term "McCarranism," but it appears in a number of newspaper articles in descriptions of anti-Communism during the early 1950s. See, for example, "Security and Freedom," *Washington Post,* November 9, 1952, B4; "Never Submit, Leader Says," *New York Times,* April 21, 1953, 19.

31. Michael Ybarra, *Washington Gone Crazy: Senator Pat McCarran and the Great American Communist Hunt* (Hanover, NH: Steerforth Press, 2004), 8.

32. Ybarra, *Washington Gone Crazy,* 4.

33. Ybarra, *Washington Gone Crazy,* 464–465.

34. "A Resolution to Make an Investigation of the Immigration System," S. Rep. No. 1515, 81st Cong., 2d Sess. 788 (1950).

35. "A Resolution to Make an Investigation of the Immigration System," 782.

36. "A Resolution to Make an Investigation of the Immigration System," 782.

37. Internal Security Act of 1950, ch. 1024, U.S. Statutes at Large, 81st Cong., II Sess., Ch. 1024, 987–1031 (enacted September 23, 1950).

38. Duane Tananbaum, *Herbert H. Lehman: A Political Biography* (Albany: State University of New York Press, 2016), 335.

39. Internal Security Act of 1950, ch. 1024, Sect. 6(a)(1), incorporating registration requirements from Mundt-Nixon and Mundt-Ferguson.

40. Internal Security Act of 1950, ch. 1024, Sect. 7; "Anti-Red Board Begins Its Duties," *New York Times*, November 2, 1950.

41. Internal Security Act of 1950, ch. 1024, Sect. 12.

42. Internal Security Act of 1950, ch. 1024, Sect. 22 (D).

43. Internal Security Act of 1950, ch. 1024, Sect. 22 (D).

44. Internal Security Act of 1950, ch. 1024, Sect. 22 (1).

45. Internal Security Act of 1950, ch. 1024, Sect. 22 (5).

46. Jay Walz, "Law to Bar Subversives Cause of Much Confusion," *New York Times*, October 15, 1950, E7.

47. Laurence Burd, "All Alien Visas Held Up Under Anti-Red Law," *Chicago Daily Tribune*, October 13, 1950, 20.

48. Mitchell C. Tilner, "Ideological Exclusion of Aliens: The Evolution of a Policy," *Georgetown Immigration Law Journal* 2, no. 1 (1987): 62.

49. Walter H. Wagonner, "US Cancels Visas for Entering Here," *New York Times*, October 13, 1950, 1.

50. Sam Falk, "Maestro of La Scala Is Detained With 30 Others under Alien Act," *New York Times*, October 13, 1950, 14.

51. "Italian Singer for 'Met' Opera among 90 Held under Alien Law," *Washington Post*, October 11, 1950, 6.

52. "Szigeti Released at Ellis Island; Admitted to U.S.," *New York Times*, November 21, 1950, 7.

53. Howard Taubman, "Opera Hit Hard by New Alien Ban," *New York Times*, October 11, 1950, 41.

54. "Interned Pianist Temporarily Free; Stay in Country till Saturday," *New York Times*, October 10, 1950, 17.

55. "95 Passengers Held Under Security Act," *New York Times*, October 11, 1950, 1.

56. Richard Mowrer, "Austrian Communists Mold McCarran Act to Own Use," *Christian Science Monitor*, December 6, 1950, 5.

57. Mowrer, "Austrian Communists," 5.

58. Mowrer, "Austrian Communists," 5.

59. "Graham Greene Visa Held Up for Inquiry," *New York Times*, February 3, 1952, 1.

60. "State of Fear in America: Mr. Graham Greene's Concern," *Manchester Guardian*, February 20, 1952, 7.

61. "State of Fear in America," 7.

62. "At America's Gateways," *New York Times*, February 6, 1952, 28.

63. Immigration and Nationality Act of 1952, Pub.L. 82-414, 66 Stat. 163, (enacted June 27, 1952).

64. Immigration and Nationality Act of 1952, ch. 4, Sect. 212(28)(I)(ii)(a).

65. Immigration and Nationality Act of 1952, ch. 4, Sect. 212(28)(I)(i). An "innocent joiner" is defined as a voluntary member who is under sixteen, a forced member under the law, or "for purposes of obtaining employment, food rations, or other essentials of living or where necessary for such purposes."

66. "President's Message to Congress Vetoing the Immigration and Nationality Act," Pub. Papers 445, June 25, 1952, repr. in "Whom We Shall Welcome," Report of President's Commission on Immigration and Naturalization (Washington, DC: Government Printing Office, January 1, 1953), 280. Truman later formed a Special Commission on Immigration and Naturalization to analyze, critique, and reform the implementation and enforcement of immigration restrictions by consular officials and INS officers. It produced a report in 1953 called "Whom Shall We Welcome."

67. Immigration and Nationality Act of 1952, ch. 4, Sect. 104(a); Tilner, "Ideological Exclusion of Aliens," 272.

68. "President's Message to Congress Vetoing the Immigration and Nationality Act," 446.

69. Immigration and Nationality Act of 1952, ch. 4, Sect. 212(a)(28)(I).

70. Immigration and Nationality Act of 1952, ch. 3, Sect. 223 (b)(3).

71. "Chaplin Gives Up Re-Entry Permit," New York Times, April 16, 1953, 1.

72. "Senator Assails Chaplin," New York Times, May 14, 1949, 19; Statement of Hon. Harry P. Cain, "Communist Activities Among Aliens and National Groups," Hearings before the Subcommittee on Immigration and Naturalization, Senate Judiciary Committee, 81st Congress, 1st sess., S. 1832 (May 13, 1949), 101–105.

73. John Sbardellati and Tony Shaw, "Booting a Tramp: Charlie Chaplin, the FBI, and the Construction of the Subversive Image in Red Scare America," Pacific Historical Review 72, no. 4 (2003), 514–520.

74. Sbardellati and Shaw, "Booting a Tramp," 519 (describing the desire to use a morality charge against Chaplin to offset any bad publicity from ideological grounds, and concern over the inability to use that charge and barring reentry to Chaplin because the McCarran-Walter Act did not go into effect until December 24, 1952).

75. "M'Granery Lashes Comedian Chaplin," Los Angeles Times, October 3, 1952, 25; "Chaplin Must Prove Case," New York Times, October 29, 1952, 32; Kenneth S. Lynn, Charlie Chaplin and His Times (New York: Simon & Schuster, 1997), 484–489. According to Lynn, McGranery's devout Catholicism led to his hatred of Chaplin. McGranery's anti-Communism was coupled, if not overshadowed, with his disgust for Chaplin's treatment of women and rumors that he paid for two illegal abortions. It was Chaplin's morals that drove McGranery's desire to exclude and question him, rather than the actor's politics. The newspapers focused on Chaplin's politics as the reason behind McGranery's denial of re-entry. See Sbardellati and Shaw, "Booting a Tramp," 508–509 (describing the FBI's and McGranery's focus on Chaplin's relationship with Joan Barry, including charges under the Mann Act for

paying for her transport across state lines and her paternity suit against him, as potential grounds for exclusion).

76. "Chaplin Gives Up Re-Entry Permit," 1.

77. "Chaplin Says 'Lies' Led Him to Quit U.S.," *Washington Post*, April 18, 1953, 15; Charlie Chaplin, *My Autobiography* (New York: Simon & Schuster, 1964), 468.

78. Graham Greene, "Dear Mr. Chaplin," *New Republic*, October 13, 1952, 5.

79. "American Visa Policy and Foreign Scientists," *Bulletin of the Atomic Scientists* 8, no. 7 (1952): 210–259.

80. "Eminent Scientists Give Their Views on American Visa Policy," *Bulletin of the Atomic Scientists* 8, no. 7 (1952): 217.

81. "Eminent Scientists Give Their Views on American Visa Policy," 218.

82. Victor Weisskopf, "Report on the Visa Situation," *Bulletin of the Atomic Scientists* 8, no. 7 (1952): 221.

83. Weisskopf, "Report on the Visa Situation," 221.

84. Edward Shils, "America's Paper Curtain," *Bulletin of the Atomic Scientists* 8, no. 7 (1952): 214–215.

85. Shils, "America's Paper Curtain," 210–211, 215.

86. M. Louis LePrince Ringuet, "French Physicists and the U.S. Visas," *Bulletin of the Atomic Scientists* 8, no. 7 (1952): 247.

87. "Whom We Shall Welcome," Report of President's Commission on Immigration and Naturalization (Washington, DC: Government Printing Office, January 1, 1953), 161–163.

88. *Shaughnessy v. Pedreiro*, 349 U.S. 48 (1955).

89. Abner Green, "New York Conference to Repeal the Walter-McCarran Law and Defend Its Victims." February 27, 1954, Folder 2, 1951–54, Box 1, ACPFB Papers, TAM.

90. Green, "New York Conference."

91. "Annual Report of the Immigration and Naturalization Service for the Fiscal Year Ended June 30, 1956" (Washington, DC: Justice Department), 67, 95–96, 119.

92. Jerilyn Fisher, "Rose Chernin 1901–1995," *Jewish Women's Archive*, February 27, 2009, http://jwa.org/encyclopedia/article/chernin-rose.

93. Green, "New York Conference."

94. Rachel Ida Buff, *Against the Deportation Terror: Organizing for Immigrant Rights in the Twentieth Century* (Philadelphia: Temple University Press, 2018), 220.

95. Immigration and Nationality Act of 1952, ch. 4, Sect. 340 (a).

96. Caute, *The Great Fear*, 240.

97. "Warrant for Arrest of Alien," May 14, 1953, Folder C.B.'s Arrest for Deportation, Box 22, Cedric Belfrage Papers, TAM.

98. Cedric Belfrage, *The Frightened Giant: My Unfinished Affair with America* (New York: Weekly Guardian Associates, 1957), 228.

99. Abner Green, "Report, for National Conference to Defend the Rights of Foreign Born. New York December 11, 12 1954," Folder 2, 1951–54, Box 1, ACPFB Papers, TAM.

100. Green, "New York Conference."

101. Richard M. Fried, *Nightmare in Red: The McCarthy Era in Perspective* (New York: Oxford University Press, 1990), 189 (quoting Saltzman).

102. *Siminoff, et al. v. P.A. Esperdy*, 267 F.2d 705 (2d Cir. 1959).

103. Caute, *The Great Fear*, 238–239. It is unclear how Heikkinen would have made such applications when Finland and Canada refused to accept him, and presumably neither country would have issued him a passport.

104. *Heikkinen v. United States*, 355 U.S. 273 (1958).

105. Caute, *The Great Fear*, 239.

106. Immigration and Nationality Act of 1952, ch. 4, Sect. 244 (c).

107. "Fact Sheet on Walter-McCarran Law Supervisory Parole Provisions," 1956, Folder 4 1956–59, Box 1, ACPFB Papers, TAM. Immigration and Nationality Act of 1952, ch. 4, Sect. 244(d).

108. Ginger, *Carol Weiss King*, 521.

109. *Butterfield v. Zydok*, 342 U.S. 524, 525 (1952).

110. *Butterfield v. Zydok*, 526.

111. Ginger, *Carol Weiss King*, 532.

112. ACLU Records, Box 828, Subject Files Freedom of Belief, Expression and Association, Freedom of Movement 1947–1976, Seeley G. Mudd Manuscript Library, Princeton University (containing correspondence regarding visa denials and recommendations to contact politicians and bureaucrats on foreign visitors' behalf as the only recourse. Constitutional challenges in exclusion cases were not recommended).

113. ACLU Records, Box 828, Folder 23, Tuteur, Charles, A., 1952–53, Subject Files Freedom of Belief, Expression and Association, Freedom of Movement 1947–1976, Seeley G. Mudd Manuscript Library, Princeton University (correspondence between Louis Joughin and Edward Meyerding).

114. Samuel Walker, *In Defense of American Liberties: A History of the ACLU*, 2nd ed. (Carbondale: Southern Illinois University Press, 1990), 210–211 (some members resigned and others were not reelected to the Board).

115. Caute, *The Great Fear*, 245.

116. Caute, *The Great Fear*, 249.

117. Green, *The Deportation Terror*, 3–22.

118. Correspondence, Papers of ACPFB, Box 1, Folder Administration—Sponsors 1941–1952, LABADIE.

119. Edward G. Robinson to ACPFB, November 20, 1950, ACPFB Records, Box 1, Folder Administration—Sponsors 1941–1952, LABADIE.

120. Abner Green to Marion Hathway, May 22, 1950, ACPFB Records, Box 1, Folder Administration—Sponsors 1941–1952, LABADIE.

121. Abner Green to Harriet Ida Pickens, March 9, 1951, ACPFB Records, Box 1, Folder Administration—Sponsors 1941–1952, LABADIE.

122. Louise Pettibone Smith, *Torch of Liberty: 25 Years in the Life of the Foreign Born in the U.S.A.* (New York: Dwight-King Publishers, 1959), 281.

123. Green, "New York Conference."

124. Abner Green to All Defense Committees, April 25, 1955, Folder 3, 1955, Box 1, ACPFB Papers, TAM.

125. "Subpoena from NY Attorney General," August 10, 1955, Folder 3, 1955, Box 1, ACPFB Papers, TAM.

126. Abner Green, "Statement," June 13, 1957, Folder 4, 1956–59, Box 1, ACPFB Papers, TAM.

127. Louise Pettibone Smith to ACPFB members, 1958, Folder 4, 1956–59, Box 1, ACPFB Papers, TAM.

128. *American Committee for Protection of Foreign Born v. SACB*, 380 U.S. 503 (1965) (remanding the case to SACB for fact-finding and reconsideration). In 1974, the New York Supreme Court dismissed the New York attorney general's injunction against the ACPFB and its designation as a charitable organization.

129. Finding Aid, ACPFB Records, LABADIE, https://quod.lib.umich.edu/s /sclead/umich-scl-acpfb?view=text.

130. ACPFB Records, Box 1, Folder Council Meetings Minutes 1973–76, LABADIE.

131. ACPFB Records, Box 1, Folder Administration Dissolution of ACPFB (1982), LABADIE.

132. *United States ex rel. Knauff v. Shaughnessy*, 338 U.S. 537, 539 (1950).

133. *United States ex rel. Knauff v. Shaughnessy*, 542.

134. *United States ex rel. Knauff v. Shaughnessy*, 543.

135. *United States ex rel. Knauff v. Shaughnessy*, 542–543.

136. *United States ex rel. Knauff v. Shaughnessy*, 544.

137. *United States ex. rel. Knauff v. Shaughnessy*, 338 U.S. 537, 551 (Jackson, J., dissenting).

138. *United States ex rel. Knauff v. Shaughnessy*, 550.

139. Kanstroom, *Deportation Nation*, 205.

140. *Harisiades v. Shaughnessy*, 342 U.S. 580, 590 (1952).

141. *Harisiades v. Shaughnessy*, 586–587.

142. *Harisiades v. Shaughnessy*, 588.

143. *Harisiades v. Shaughnessy*, 590.

144. *Harisiades v. Shaughnessy*, 590.

145. *Harisiades v. Shaughnessy*, 590, 592.

146. *Carlson v. Landon; Butterfield v. Zydok*, 342 U.S. 524 (1952). King argued the companion case *Butterfield v. Zydok*.

147. *Carlson v. Landon*, 534.

148. *Carlson v. Landon*, 538.

149. *Carlson v. Landon*, 538.

150. *Carlson v. Landon*, 541.

151. *Carlson v. Landon*, 542.

152. *Shaughnessy v. Mezei*, 345 U.S. 206 (1953).

153. *Shaughnessy v. Mezei*, 208.

154. *Shaughnessy v. Mezei*, 216.

155. *Shaughnessy v. Mezei*, 345 U.S. 206, 228 (Jackson, J. dissenting).

156. *Shaughnessy v. Mezei*, 219.

157. *Shaughnessy v. Mezei*, 225.

158. *Shaughnessy v. Mezei*, 227.

159. *United States v. Witkovich*, 353 U.S. 194, 198 (1957).

160. *United States v. Witkovich*, 200.

161. *United States v. Witkovich*, 201–202.

162. *Rowoldt v. Perfetto*, 355 U.S. 115, 116–118 (1957).

163. *Rowoldt v. Perfetto*, 117.

164. *Rowoldt v. Perfetto*, 118.

165. *Galvan v. Press*, 347 U.S. 522, 528 (1954).

166. *Rowoldt v. Perfetto*, 120.

167. *Gastelum-Quinones v. Kennedy*, 374 U.S. 469, 480 (1963).

168. *Gastelum-Quinones v. Kennedy*, 477.

169. *Gastelum-Quinones v. Kennedy*, 478.

170. Marion T. Bennett, *American Immigration Policies: A History* (Washington, DC: Public Affairs Press, 1963), 341.

171. *Yates v. United States*, 354 U.S. 298, 320 (1957).

172. *Kent v. Dulles*, 357 U.S. 116 (1958).

173. *Baggett v. Bullitt*, 377 U.S. 360 (1964).

174. *Albertson v. Subversive Activities Control Board*, 382 U.S. 70 (1965); *United States v. Robel*, 389 U.S. 258 (1967) (overturning expulsion of defense facility employee for being a Communist upon his registration with the attorney general under the McCarran Act and invalidated Truman's loyalty-security program).

175. *Lamont v. Postmaster General*, 381 U.S. 301 (1965).

176. *Red Lion Broadcasting Co. v. F.C.C.*, 395 U.S. 367 (1969).

177. *Tinker v. Des Moines Community School District*, 393 U.S. 503 (1969).

178. For a discussion of academic freedom during McCarthyism, see Ellen Schrecker, *No Ivory Tower: McCarthyism & the Universities* (New York: Oxford University Press, 1986).

179. *Shelton v. Tucker*, 364 U.S. 479, 487 (1960).

180. *Keyishian v. Board of Regents*, 385 U.S. 589, 603 (1967).

181. *Brandenburg v. Ohio*, 395 U.S. 444, 447 (1969).

182. Arthur M Schlesinger, Jr., *Robert Kennedy and His Times* (New York: First Mariner Books, 1978), 435; Abba Schwartz, *The Open Society* (New York: William Morrow, 1968), 25.

183. John F. Kennedy, *Nation of Immigrants* (New York: Harper & Row, 1964). Originally an essay written by Kennedy in 1958, this was updated and published as a book in 1964.

184. Schlesinger, *Robert Kennedy and His Times*, 434–436;

185. For a discussion of refugee policy legislation during the Cold War, see Carl Bon Tempo, *Americans at the Gate: The United States and Refugees during the Cold War* (Princeton, NJ: Princeton University Press, 2009).

186. Schwartz, *The Open Society*, 138–138, 171–172.

187. Schwartz, *The Open Society*, 142. Migration and Refugee Assistance Act of 1962, Pub. L. 87-510, June 28, 1962, 76 Stat. 121 (22 U.S.C. 2601 et seq.).

188. Schwartz, *The Open Society*, 4.

189. Schwartz, *The Open Society*, 26.

190. Schwartz, *The Open Society*, 22. Director of the Passport Office, Ruth Shipley, and her successor, Frances Knight, were staunch anti-Communists and supporters of McCarthyism. Caute, *The Great Fear*, 246.

191. Schwartz, *The Open Society*, 200.

192. Schwartz, *The Open Society*, 22, 37.

193. Schwartz, *The Open Society*, 37.

194. Schwartz, *The Open Society*, 33–37, 46; Caute, *The Great Fear*, 246 (describing similar fear in the passport office).

195. Immigration and Nationality Act of 1952, 66 Stat. 182, 8 U.S.C. Sect. 1182(d)(3)(A).

196. US-Soviet Cultural Exchange Agreement, "Lacy-Zaroubin Agreement," January 27, 1958, Special to the *New York Times*, "Text of the Joint Communique of U.S. and Soviet Union on Cultural Exchanges," *New York Times*, January 28, 1958, 8.

197. Tad Szulc, "Visa Denial Bars Leftist's Debate," *New York Times*, April 7, 1962, 2.

198. Schwartz, *The Open Society*, 47.

199. Schwartz, *The Open Society*, 46–47.

200. [Letter to the Editor] Frank Tennenbaum, "Visa Policy Assailed," *New York Times*, May 1, 1962, 36.

201. Schwartz, *The Open Society*, 47.

202. Schwartz, *The Open Society*, 48–49.

203. Schwartz, *The Open Society*, 49.

204. Schwartz, *The Open Society*, 18.

205. Schwartz, *The Open Society*, 19.

206. Schwartz, *The Open Society*, 5–7.

207. Schwartz, *The Open Society*, 15, 121–125; Edward P. Hutchinson, *Legislative History of American Immigration Policy, 1798–1965* (Philadelphia: University of Pennsylvania Press, 1981), 364–377; "Ex-Rep. Michael A. Feighan, 87; Architect of '65 Immigration Law," *New York Times*, March 20, 1992.

208. Schwartz, *The Open Society*, 21.

209. Henry Raymont, "Leftist Novelist Is Barred by U.S.," *New York Times,* February 28, 1969, 35.

210. "The Fuentes Incident," *New York Times,* March 5, 1969, 46.

211. Henry Raymont, "Fuentes Incident Revives Dispute," *New York Times,* March 3, 1969, 7.

6. THE RETURN OF MCCARRANISM

1. Jan Willem Stutje, *Ernest Mandel: A Rebel's Dream Deferred* (London: Verso Books, 2009), 40.

2. Tariq Ali, "Capitalism's Optimistic Critic," *Guardian,* July 22, 1995, 3.

3. Stutje, *Ernest Mandel,* 94; Geoffrey Hodgson, "Ernest Mandel, 1923–1995," *Economic Journal* 107, no. 440 (1997): 160.

4. Patrick Seale and Maureen McConville, *Red Flag / Black Flag: French Revolution 1968* (New York: Ballantine Books, 1968), 82; Stutje, *Ernest Mandel,* 185. According to Stutje, Mandel was barred from France until 1981.

5. FOIA—"Mandel, Ernest," signed waiver for Ernest Mandel—1968 and report on granting waiver in 1962.

6. John Kifner, "Student Revolutionaries Seek Bigger Causes," *New York Times,* September 25, 1968, 31.

7. Immigration and Nationality Act of 1952, 66 Stat. 182, 8 U.S.C. Sect. 1182(a)(28)(D) and (G)(v).

8. Immigration and Nationality Act of 1952, Sect. 1182(d)(3)(A).

9. Richard Nixon, "Address Accepting the Presidential Nomination at the Republican National Convention in Miami Beach, Florida," August 8, 1968, C-SPAN, https://www.c-span.org/video/?c4612766/law-order-richard-nixon-1968 -presidential-acceptance-speech.

10. Richard Nixon, "Address to the Nation on the War in Vietnam," November 3, 1969, Miller Center, University of Virginia, https://millercenter.org/the -presidency/presidential-speeches/november-3-1969-address-nation-war-vietnam.

11. Milton Viorst, "Attorney General Mitchell's Philosophy Is 'The Justice Department Is an Institution for Law Enforcement, Not Social Improvement': The Mitchell Philosophy," *New York Times,* August 10, 1969, SM10.

12. James Rosen, *The Strong Man: John Mitchell and the Secrets of Watergate* (New York: Doubleday, 2008), 77–79.

13. "Wiretaps by US Triple to 382,061 since 1968," *Boston Globe,* August 16, 1971, 11.

14. Rosen, *The Strong Man,* 80.

15. Rosen, *The Strong Man,* 80.

16. "The Pragmatist," *Newsweek,* December 8, 1969, 45.

17. "The Pragmatist," 45.

18. FOIA—March 14, 1962—granting waiver of ineligibility.

19. FOIA—August 5, 1968—granting waiver of ineligibility.

20. NECLC Press Release, June 13, 1970, in "Mandel Case Press," NECLC Collection, Box 130, Case Files Series IV "Mamis to Mandel," in RBML; Ernest Mandel to Alta Fowler (in French), October 23, 1969, in "Mandel," NECLC Collection, Box 130, Case Files Series IV "Mamis to Mandel" in RBML.

21. Ernest Mandel to Alta Fowler (in French), October 30, 1969, in "Mandel," NECLC Collection, Box 130 in RBML.

22. NECLC Press Release, June 13, 1970.

23. Ernest Mandel to Alta Fowler (in French), October 30, 1969.

24. Ernest Mandel to Alta Fowler (in French), October 23, 1969.

25. Barbara Watson to Leonard Boudin, November 6, 1969, in "Mandel v. Mitchell Correspondence," NECLC Collection, Box 130 in RBML.

26. FOIA—Vera Glaser and Malvina Stephenson, "Mitchell's Comments Televised," *Washington Evening Star*, December 2, 1969.

27. "Rogers May Act to Let Marxist in U.S," *Los Angeles Times*, November 28, 1969, 13.

28. "Mitchell Bars Belgian Marxist from U.S. Visit," *New York Times*, November 27, 1969, 1.

29. "Mitchell Bars Belgian Marxist from U.S. Visit," 1.

30. "Mitchell Bars Belgian Marxist from U.S. Visit," 1.

31. "Mitchell Bars Belgian Marxist from U.S. Visit," 1.

32. "Mitchell Bars Belgian Marxist from U.S. Visit," 1.

33. "The Pragmatist," 45.

34. FOIA—Vera Glaser and Malvina Stephenson, "Mitchell's Comments Televised."

35. FOIA—James F. Greene to Leonard Boudin, February 13, 1970.

36. FOIA—Greene to Arno Mayer [undated] responding to Telegram—Arno Mayer to AG Mitchell, December 1, 1969.

37. FOIA—Greene to Arno Mayer [undated].

38. "Students Hear a Red by Tape and Phone," *New York Times*, October 19, 1969, 68.

39. "Students Hear a Red by Tape and Phone," 68.

40. George Novack, *The Speech Nixon and Mitchell Tried to Ban: Ernest Mandel's Revolutionary Strategy in the Imperialist Countries* (New York: Pathfinder Press, Inc., 1970), 3 (quoting Galbraith), in "Mandel v. Mitchell Correspondence," NECLC Collection, Box 130 in RBML.

41. Novack, *The Speech Nixon and Mitchell Tried to Ban*, 3 (quoting Galbraith).

42. Letter to the Editor, "Ban on Ernest Mandel," *New York Times*, October 25, 1969, 32.

43. FOIA—Robert F. Goheen to John Mitchell, December 6, 1969.

44. FOIA—Robert F. Goheen to John Mitchell.

45. FOIA—Robert F. Goheen to John Mitchell.

46. FOIA—Alan Simpson to Attorney General Mitchell, December 9, 1969.

47. FOIA—MIT, Boston U. & Harvard U. Petition to Attorney General Mitchell, November 18, 1969.

48. FOIA—MIT, Boston U. & Harvard U. Petition.

49. FOIA—Kingman Brewster Jr. to John Mitchell, December 28, 1969.

50. FOIA—Norman Birnbaum to John Mitchell, December 1, 1969.

51. "... and Abroad," *New York Times,* October 28, 1969, 46.

52. "McCarranism Revisited," *New York Times,* November 27, 1969, 28.

53. "Mitchell's Fearful Policy," *Chicago Daily News,* December 30, 1969, 8.

54. "Mitchell's Fearful Policy," 8.

55. "Can Col. Collins Explain This?" *Chicago Daily Tribune,* December 22, 1969, 24.

56. FOIA—William Faris to Congressman Howard Robison, November 27, 1969.

57. FOIA—William Faris to Congressman Howard Robison.

58. "Marxist Attributes Denial of U.S. Visa to Rules He Broke," *New York Times,* November 29, 1969, 11.

59. Novack, *The Speech Nixon and Mitchell Tried to Ban,* 6.

60. Novack, *The Speech Nixon and Mitchell Tried to Ban,* 6.

61. Novack, *The Speech Nixon and Mitchell Tried to Ban,* 6.

62. The ECLC changed its name to the NECLC in 1968. The ECLC is introduced in Chapter 5.

63. Leonard Boudin to George Novack and Ralph Schoenman, December 23, 1969, in "Mandel v. Mitchell Correspondence," NECLC Collection in RBML.

64. Nick Ravo, "Leonard Boudin, Civil Liberties Lawyer, Dies at 77," *New York Times,* November 26, 1989, 45.

65. *Kent v. Dulles,* 357 U.S. 116 (1958).

66. *Lamont v. Postmaster General,* 381 U.S. 301 (1965).

67. *Zemel v. Rusk,* 381 U.S. 1, 16–17 (1965).

68. "Justice Dept. Bars Visa to Belgian Marxist," *Washington Post,* November 27, 1969, A40.

69. "Justice Dept. Bars Visa to Belgian Marxist," A40.

70. Author interview with Professor David Rosenberg, May 1, 2018; Reminiscences of Leonard Boudin (1987), page 530, Oral History Archives at RBML. See *Red Lion Broadcasting Co. v. FCC,* 395 U.S. 367, 390 (1969) establishing the right to hear or "listen"; *Keyishian v. Board of Regents,* 385 U.S. 589, 603 (1967) describing academic freedom as a "special concern of the First Amendment." Rosenberg also mentioned *Sweezy v. New Hampshire,* 354 U.S. 234 (1957) as influencing his strategy and due process arguments and the importance of free expression within universities.

71. Author interview with Professor David Rosenberg.

72. Leonard Boudin to George Novack and Ralph Schoenman, December 23, 1969, in "Mandel v. Mitchell Correspondence," NECLC Collection, Box 130 in RBML.

73. Leonard Boudin to George Novack and Ralph Schoenman, December 23, 1969; Memo: George Novack to Leonard Boudin, "Re: Ernest Mandel Case Legal Fund," July 6, 1970, in "Mandel v. Mitchell Correspondence," NECLC Collection, Box 130 in RBML.

74. Complaint, *Mandel v. Mitchell*, dated March 18, 1970, par. 6, in "Mandel," NECLC Collection, Box 130 in RBML.

75. Amended Complaint, *Mandel v. Mitchell*, dated May 11, 1970.

76. Amended Complaint, par. 18.

77. Amended Complaint, par. 18.

78. Amended Complaint, par. 22.

79. "Designation of Judges," *Mandel v. Mitchell*, signed by US Court of Appeals for Second Circuit Chief Judge J. Edward Lumbard, dated June 16, 1970, in "Mandel," NECLC Collection, Box 130 in RBML.

80. NECLC Press Release, June 19, 1970, in "Mandel Case Press," NECLC Collection in RBML.

81. "U.S. Visa Is Denied to Widow of Dubois," *New York Times*, May 5, 1970, 35.

82. "U.S. Visa Is Denied to Widow of Dubois," 35.

83. "U.S. Visa Is Denied to Widow of Dubois," 35.

84. *Communist Party v. Subversive Activities Control Board*, 367 U.S. 1 (1961).

85. Graham Du Bois disputed accounts that they had renounced their American citizenship after becoming citizens of Ghana. She wrote that her husband had ignored a request from the US government to come to the embassy in Ghana and renounce his citizenship. Shirley Graham Du Bois to Richard P. Stevens, April 29, 1970, "Papers of Du Bois, Shirley Graham, 1896–1977," Arthur and Elizabeth Schlesinger Library on the History of Women in America, Harvard University.

86. "Biography," in finding aid for "Papers of Du Bois, Shirley Graham, 1896–1977."

87. Gerald Horne, *Race Woman: The Lives of Shirley Graham Du Bois* (New York: New York University Press, 2000), 242–243; "U.S. Visa Is Denied to Widow of Dubois," 35.

88. "Visa Schizophrenia," *Afro-American*, May 23, 1970, 4.

89. "Ask Visa for Mrs. Dubois," *New York Amsterdam News*, May 9, 1970, 42.

90. Horne, *Race Woman*, 245.

91. "Ask Visa for Mrs. Dubois," 42.

92. Shirley Graham Du Bois to Richard P. Stevens, April 13, 1970, "Papers of Du Bois, Shirley Graham, 1896–1977."

93. Kenneth R. Cole Jr. to Bud Krogh, May 27, 1970 (describing Moynihan memo and Nixon's reaction to it), White House Central Files, Subject Files, EX IM/D—Immigration and Naturalization [1969–1970], BOX 1 in RNPL.

94. Raymond Farrell to Bud Krogh, June 12, 1970, White House Central Files, Subject Files, EX IM/D—Immigration and Naturalization [1969–1970], BOX 1 in RNPL.

95. Raymond Farrell to Bud Krogh.

96. Bud Krogh to Kenneth R. Cole Jr., June 15, 1970, White House Central Files, Subject Files, EX IM / D—Immigration and Naturalization [1969–1970], BOX 1 in RNPL.

97. Bud Krogh to Kenneth R. Cole Jr.

98. John Ehrlichman to Richard Nixon, June 24, 1970, White House Central Files, Subject Files, EX IM / D—Immigration and Naturalization [1969–1970], BOX 1 in RNPL. Ehrlichman made this recommendation to Nixon, but he did not mention Krogh's comments.

99. Raymond Farrell to Bud Krogh, August 11, 1970, White House Central Files, Subject Files, EX IM / D—Immigration and Naturalization [1969–1970], BOX 1 in RNPL.

100. Author interview with Tariq Ali, June 1, 2018. Ali did not pursue litigation and chose not to challenge his exclusion.

101. "Pakistani Student Is Denied Visa for Speech in U.S," *New York Times,* December 3, 1969, 9.

102. Abdeen M. Jabara to Shirley Graham Du Bois, April 3, 1970, "Papers of Du Bois, Shirley Graham, 1896–1977."

103. *Mandel v. Mitchell,* 325 F. Supp. 620, 634 (E.D.N.Y. 1971).

104. *Mandel v. Mitchell,* 634.

105. *Mandel v. Mitchell,* 633.

106. *Mandel v. Mitchell,* 632.

107. *Mandel v. Mitchell,* 629.

108. *Mandel v. Mitchell,* 629.

109. *Mandel v. Mitchell,* 325 F. Supp. 620, 640 (Bartels, J., dissenting).

110. *Mandel v. Mitchell,* 648.

111. *Mandel v. Mitchell,* 642.

112. Norman Birnbaum to Ernest Mandel, April 9, 1971, in "Mandel Case File," NECLC Collection, Box 130 in RBML.

113. Appellant Brief for United States, *Mitchell v. Mandel,* submitted to the Supreme Court on March 2, 1972, 20–22, under *Kleindienst v. Mandel,* 408 U.S. 753 (1972) in *U.S. Supreme Court Records and Briefs, 1832–1978* (Gage, Cengage Learning).

114. Appellant Brief for United States, *Mitchell v. Mandel,* 33–34.

115. Appellant Brief for United States, *Mitchell v. Mandel,* 35, 39.

116. Appellees Brief for Ernest Mandel, David Mermelstein, Wassily Leontief, Norman Birnbaum, Robert L. Heilbroner, Robert Paul Wolff, Louis Menashe, Noam Chomsky, and Richard A. Falk, *Mitchell v. Mandel,* submitted to the Supreme Court on April 5, 1972, 34, under *Kleindienst v. Mandel,* 408 U.S. 753 (1972) in *U.S. Supreme Court Records and Briefs, 1832–1978* (Gage, Cengage Learning).

117. Appellees Brief for Ernest Mandel et al., *Mitchell v. Mandel,* 12, 15–17, 31–33.

118. Oral Arguments, "Kleindienst v. Mandel," April 18, 1972, Oyez, https://www.oyez.org/cases/1971/71-16.

119. Oral Arguments.

120. Oral Arguments.

121. A.C.L.U. *Amicus Curiae* brief, *Mitchell v. Mandel,* submitted to the Supreme Court on April 4, 1972, 19–22, under *Kleindienst v. Mandel,* 408 U.S. 753 (1972) in *U.S. Supreme Court Records and Briefs, 1832–1978* (Gage, Cengage Learning).

122. A.C.L.U. *Amicus Curiae* brief, 21.

123. A.C.L.U. *Amicus Curiae* brief, 22.

124. Notes for Conference, [undated], LOC, Papers of Harry A. Blackmun, Box 145, Folder 1 Opinions, Case No: 71-16 "K v. Mandel" 1971 Supreme Court Term.

125. Justice Thurgood Marshall to Chief Justice Warren E. Burger, May 3, 1972, LOC, Thurgood Marshall Papers, Supreme Court Case Files - OT 1971, Opinions Appellate - 71-16 Kleindienst v. Mandel, Box 87, Folder 9.

126. Log Sheet, LOC, Papers of Harry A. Blackmun, Box 133, Folder 9, Case No: 71-16 "K v. Mandel" 1971 Supreme Court Term.

127. Oral Argument and Conference Notes, [undated], LOC, Papers of Harry A. Blackmun, Box 145, Folder 1 Opinions, Case No: 71-16 "K v. Mandel" 1971 Supreme Court Term.

128. *Kleindienst v. Mandel,* 408 U.S. 753 (1972). Mitchell appealed the US District Court's decision, and later resigned to manage President Nixon's reelection campaign. Richard Kleindienst replaced him as attorney general on June 12, 1972.

129. *Kleindienst v. Mandel,* 759–761.

130. *Kleindienst v. Mandel,* 759–762.

131. *Kleindienst v. Mandel,* 764.

132. *Kleindienst v. Mandel,* 764.

133. *Kleindienst v. Mandel,* 765.

134. *Kleindienst v. Mandel,* 760

135. *Kleindienst v. Mandel,* 768–769.

136. *Kleindienst v. Mandel,* 769.

137. *Kleindienst v. Mandel,* 769–770.

138. *Kleindienst v. Mandel,* 770.

139. *Kleindienst v. Mandel,* 770.

140. *Kleindienst v. Mandel,* 770.

141. *Kleindienst v. Mandel,*767.

142. *Kleindienst v. Mandel,* 766.

143. *Kleindienst v. Mandel,* 408 U.S. 753, 772 (Douglas, J., dissenting).

144. *Kleindienst v. Mandel,* 774.

145. *Kleindienst v. Mandel,* 774.

146. *Kleindienst v. Mandel,* 408 U.S. 753, 775 (Marshall, J., dissenting).

147. *Kleindienst v. Mandel,* 782.

148. *Kleindienst v. Mandel,* 782–783.

149. *Kleindienst v. Mandel,* 777.

150. *Kleindienst v. Mandel*, 778.

151. *Kleindienst v. Mandel*, 778.

152. *Kleindienst v. Mandel*, 785.

153. Mandel to NECLC, September 9, 1972, "Mandel," NECLC Collection, Box 130 in RBML.

154. Mandel to NECLC.

155. *United States v. United States District Court*, 407 U.S. 297, 321 (1972).

156. "Atty. Gen. Mitchell Waives Lennon Visa," *Los Angeles Times*, August 29, 1970, A6.

157. Jon Wiener, *Come Together: John Lennon in His Time* (Chicago: University of Illinois Press, 1991), 96–99.

158. "Lennon, Yoko Ono Liable to Deportation," *Washington Post*, March 16, 1972, K8.

159. David Bird, "Lindsay Deplores Action to Deport Lennon as a 'Grave Injustice,'" *New York Times*, April 29, 1972, 33.

160. Wiener, *Come Together*, 233.

161. "American Hospitality," *Newsday*, May 2, 1972, 38.

162. "Love It and Leave It," *New York Times*, May 2, 1972, 42.

163. Kenneth S. Lynn, *Charlie Chaplin and His Times* (New York: Simon & Schuster, 1997), 525 (noting that Chaplin had made a "conciliatory political statement" to obtain a visa, but "no one in the Nixon administration had shown the slightest inclination to oppose his return").

164. Leon Wildes, *John Lennon vs. the USA: The Inside Story of the Most Bitterly Contested and Influential Deportation Case in United States History* (Chicago: ABA Publishing, 2016), 140–143.

165. Wildes, *John Lennon vs. the USA*, 7–8. Thurmond also sent a copy of the same letter he sent to Mitchell to William Timmons, assistant to the president for legislative affairs; see Strom Thurmond to William Timmons, February 4, 1972, White House Central Files, Subject Files, EX A–Z—Immigration and Naturalization [1971–1972], BOX 2 in RNPL.

166. *Lennon v. INS*, 527 F.2d 187 (2d Cir. 1975).

167. Arnold H. Lubasch, "Deportation of Lennon Barred by Court of Appeals," *New York Times*, October 8, 1975, 42.

168. *Lennon v. INS*, 195.

169. Peter Schrag, *Test of Loyalty: Daniel Ellsberg and the Rituals of Secret Government* (New York: Simon and Schuster, 1974), 329–330, 355–356; "A Background Paper on Leonard Boudin Prepared for White House by Hunt," *New York Times*, July 19, 1974, 16.

170. Gene Blake, "Judge Dismisses Ellsberg Charges: Actions by U.S. Offend Justice, Byrne Declares," *Los Angeles Times*, May 12, 1973, A1.

171. Stutje, *Ernest Mandel*, 249.

7. ONE DOOR CLOSES, ANOTHER OPENS

1. The Final Act of the Conference on Security and Cooperation in Europe, August 1, 1975, 14 I.L.M. 1292 (Helsinki Declaration), http://www1.umn.edu /humanrts/osce/basics/finact75.htm.

2. The Final Act of the Conference on Security and Cooperation in Europe.

3. Act of August 17, 1977, Pub.L. No. 95–105, Title I, Sect. 112, 91 Stat. 844. "For the purposes of achieving greater United States compliance with the provisions of the [Helsinki accords] and for purposes of encouraging other signatory countries to comply with those provisions."

4. "Foreign Relations Authorization Act, 1980 and 1981," *Congressional Record Proceedings and Debate*—Senate, 96th Congress, 1st Sess., (May 10, 1979), 10564-10565.

5. Foreign Relations Authorization Act, Fiscal Year 1978, Pub. L. No. 95–105, Title I Sect. 112, 91 Stat. 844, 848 (1979).

6. Immigration and Nationality Act of 1952, 66 Stat. 182, 8 U.S.C. Sect. 1182(a)(29).

7. Immigration and Nationality Act of 1952, Sect. 1182(a)(27).

8. Abba Schwartz, *The Open Society* (New York: William Morrow, 1968), 38–39.

9. Ronald Reagan, Address before a Joint Session of Congress on the State of the Union, February 6, 1985, https://www.reaganlibrary.gov/research/speeches/20685e.

10. Bernard Weintraub, "President Accuses 5 'Outlaw States' of World Terror," *New York Times*, July 9, 1985, A1. Reagan included Guatemala, Libya, North Korea, and Iran on the list.

11. David C. Wills, *The First War on Terrorism: Counter-Terrorism Policy during the Reagan Administration* (New York: Rowman & Littlefield, 2003), 6.

12. *Allende v. Shultz*, 845 F.2d 1111, 1113 (1st Cir. 1988).

13. Patrick E. Tyler, "U.S. Denies Allende Widow Visa for Speech," *Washington Post*, March 4, 1983, 2.

14. Tyler, "U.S. Denies Allende Widow Visa for Speech," 2.

15. Tyler, "U.S. Denies Allende Widow Visa for Speech," 2; "Salvador Allende's Widow Denied Entry Visa by US," *Boston Globe*, March 4, 1983, 4.

16. *Allende v. Shultz*, 845 F.2d 1111, 1113 (1st Cir. 1988).

17. *City of New York v. Baker*, 878 F.2d 507, 510 (D.C. Cir. 1989).

18. Burt Neuborne and Steven R. Shapiro, "The Nylon Curtain: America's National Border and the Free Flow of Ideas," *William and Mary Law Review* 26, no. 5 (1985): 725.

19. Steven R. Shapiro, "Ideological Exclusions: Closing the Border to Political Dissidents," *Harvard Law Review* 100, No. 4 (1987): 930, 935.

20. Neuborne and Shapiro, "The Nylon Curtain," 725; Stuart Taylor Jr., "The Unwelcome Mat Is Out for Ideological Undesirables," *New York Times*, July 15, 1984, E5.

21. Michael Koncewicz, *They Said No to Nixon: Republicans Who Stood Up to the President's Abuses of Power* (Oakland: University of California Press, 2018), 52–63.

22. Rick Atkinson, "Congressmen, Others Denounce Denial of Visas to Critics of U.S.," *Washington Post,* December 3, 1983, A12.

23. Atkinson, "Congressmen, Others Denounce Denial of Visas to Critics of U.S.," A12.

24. Taylor, "The Unwelcome Mat"; Kevin O'Neill, "A Vestige of McCarthyism," *Newsday,* August 14, 1985, 65.

25. "Why Fear Foreigners' Free Speech?" *New York Times,* November 13, 1986, A30.

26. "Why Fear Foreigners' Free Speech?" A30; "Prejudicial to US Interests," *Boston Globe,* March 5, 1983, 14; "Nervous Nellies at the Gates," *New York Times,* March 14, 1984, A14.

27. "A World Safe from Democracy," *Boston Globe,* December 3, 1983, 1.

28. Barney Frank, *Frank: A Life in Politics from the Great Society to Same-Sex Marriage* (New York: Farrar, Straus and Giroux, 2015), 6–7.

29. Frank, *Frank,* 115–116, 124–126.

30. Duane Tananbaum, *Herbert H. Lehman: A Political Biography* (Albany: State University of New York Press, 2016), 334.

31. Tananbaum, *Herbert H. Lehman,* 355–356

32. Mitchell C. Tilner, "Ideological Exclusion of Aliens: The Evolution of a Policy," *Georgetown Immigration Law Journal* 2, no. 1 (1987): 63.

33. Tananbaum, *Hebert H. Lehman,* 337–338, 349; David Caute, *The Great Fear: The Anti-Communist Purge under Truman and Eisenhower* (New York: Simon & Schuster, 1978), 39–40.

34. "The Fuentes Incident," *New York Times,* March 5, 1969, 46.

35. Deborah Cohn, "Carlos Fuentes: Fostering Latin American–U.S. Relations during the Boom," *Inti: Revista de literatura hispánica* no. 75, article 3 (April 2012): 12.

36. Linda Greenhouse, "Redefining the Boundaries: Who May Come In; Pro & Con: What Price An Anarchist?," *New York Times,* April 10, 1988, E5.

37. Greenhouse, "Redefining the Boundaries," E5.

38. "Exclusion and Deportation Amendments of 1983," Hearing before the Subcommittee on Immigration, House Judiciary Committee, 98th Congress, 2d sess., H.R. 4509 and H.R. 5227 (June 28, 1984).

39. "Exclusion and Deportation Amendments of 1983," 5. Text of H.R. 4509 "To amend the Immigration and Nationality Act with respect to the grounds for exclusion and deportation of aliens."

40. "Exclusion and Deportation Amendments of 1983," 40–41.

41. "Exclusion and Deportation Amendments of 1983," 86.

42. "Exclusion and Deportation Amendments of 1983," 93.

43. "Exclusion and Deportation Amendments of 1983," 93.

44. "Exclusion and Deportation Amendments of 1983," 88.

45. Tom Bernstein, "Ideas Not Welcome!" *New York Times,* July 15, 1980, 19.

46. "Exclusion and Deportation Amendments of 1983," 89.

47. "Exclusion and Deportation Amendments of 1983," 91–92.

48. "Exclusion and Deportation Amendments of 1983," 140–141, 174.

49. "Exclusion and Deportation Amendments of 1983," 140–148, 174.

50. Jeri Laber, "Why Some Writers Are Not Welcome Here," *New York Times,* April 29, 1984, 28.

51. "Exclusion and Deportation Amendments of 1983," 160–161, 166.

52. "Exclusion and Deportation Amendments of 1983," 162.

53. "Exclusion and Deportation Amendments of 1983," 163–167.

54. "Exclusion and Deportation Amendments of 1983," 163.

55. "Exclusion and Deportation Amendments of 1983," 170.

56. "Exclusion and Deportation Amendments of 1983," 168.

57. *Fiallo v. Bell,* 430 U.S. 787, 794–799 (1977).

58. "Exclusion and Deportation Amendments of 1983," 169.

59. Frank, *Frank,* 116.

60. "Exclusion and Deportation Amendments of 1983," 138.

61. "Exclusion and Deportation Amendments of 1983," 130.

62. "Exclusion and Deportation Amendments of 1983," 130–136, 174.

63. "Exclusion and Deportation Amendments of 1983," 132–133.

64. Kristin Helmore, "Would William Shakespeare Get a Visa?" *Christian Science Monitor,* May 30, 1984.

65. Helmore, "Would William Shakespeare Get a Visa?"

66. Curt Suplee, "Conferees See Threat to Civil Liberties," *Washington Post,* September 19, 1984.

67. Suplee, "Conferees See Threat to Civil Liberties."

68. Suplee, "Conferees See Threat to Civil Liberties."

69. Elizabeth Mehren, "The PEN Mightier in Imagination than the State?: George Shultz Speech Enlivens 28th Worldwide Writers' Congress in N.Y.," *Los Angeles Times,* January 15, 1986.

70. George P. Shultz, "The Writer and Freedom," Secretary of State address before PEN International Conference, January 12, 1986, New York City, published in US Department of State, Bureau of Public Affairs, *DC Current Policy,* No. 782, 1, in Roberts, John G., Files, Immigration and Naturalization, Box 37 (2 of 3), RRPL.

71. Shultz, "The Writer and Freedom," 2.

72. Shultz, "The Writer and Freedom," 2–3.

73. Shultz, "The Writer and Freedom," 3.

74. Shultz, "The Writer and Freedom."

75. "If Mr. Shultz Is Serious about Visas," *New York Times,* Jan. 18, 1986, 26.

76. Shultz, "The Writer and Freedom."

77. "ABA Resolution," February 1, 1986, folder "Immigration and Naturalization" (2 of 3), Box 37, John G. Roberts Jr. Files, RRL.

78. 8 U.S.C. Sect. 1182(f). Later in 1986, Reagan would issue Proclamation 5517, suspending entry to Cuban nationals as immigrants, except for those with immediate relatives in the United States.

79. Proclamation 4865—High seas interdiction of illegal aliens, September 29, 1981, NARA, https://www.archives.gov/federal-register/codification/proclamations/04865.html.

80. Proclamation 5377—Suspension of entry as nonimmigrants by officers or employees of the Government of Cuba or the Communist Party of Cuba, October 4, 1985, NARA, https://www.archives.gov/federal-register/codification/proclamations/05377.html.

81. [Memorandum] John G. Roberts Jr. to Fred F. Fielding and Richard A. Hauser, February 4, 1986, folder "Immigration and Naturalization" (2 of 3), Box 37, John G. Roberts Jr. Files, RRL.

82. [Memorandum] John G. Roberts Jr. to Fred F. Fielding.

83. [Memorandum] Fred F. Fielding to Abraham D. Sofaer, February 4, 1986, folder "Immigration and Naturalization" (2 of 3), Box 37, John G. Roberts Jr. Files, RRL.

84. [Memorandum] John G. Roberts Jr. to Richard A. Hauser, February 20, 1986, folder "Immigration and Naturalization" (2 of 3), Box 37, John G. Roberts Jr. Files, RRL.

85. "Exclusion and Deportation of Aliens," Hearing before the Subcommittee on Immigration, House Judiciary Committee, 100th Congress, 1st sess., H.R. 1119 (June 23, 1987), 6, 17.

86. "Exclusion and Deportation of Aliens," 11.

87. "Exclusion and Deportation of Aliens," 29–30.

88. "Exclusion and Deportation of Aliens," 183.

89. "Exclusion and Deportation of Aliens," 190–191.

90. Foreign Relations Authorization Act, Fiscal Years 1988 and 1989, Pub. L. No. 100–204, Title IX Sect. 901, 101 Stat. 1331, 1399–1400 (1987).

91. S. Rep. No. 100–75, 100th Congress, 1st Sess. (1987), 11.

92. "Foreign Relations Authorization Act," Sect. 901(b)(2) (1988), as amended by 102 Stat. 2268-36.

93. *Abourezk v. Reagan*, 592 F.Supp. 880, 884–886 (D.D.C. 1984).

94. *Abourezk v. Reagan*, 887–888.

95. *Allende v. Shultz*, 605 F. Supp. 1220, 1223 (D.Mass 1985).

96. *Allende v. Shultz*, 1225–1227.

97. *Abourezk v. Reagan*, 785 F. 2d 1043, 1047 (DC Cir. 1986).

98. *Abourezk v. Reagan*, 1057.

99. *Abourezk v. Reagan*, 1056–1058.

100. *Abourezk v. Reagan*, 1061.

101. *Abourezk v. Reagan*, No. 83-3739, 1988 WL 59640 (D.D.C. June 7, 1988).

102. *City of New York v. Baker*, 878 F.2d 507, 509–511 (D.C. Cir. 1989).

103. *Allende v. Shultz*, 845 F.2d 1111, 1116–1121 (1st Cir. 1988).

104. Nick Ravo, "Leonard Boudin, Civil Liberties Lawyer, Dies at 77," *New York Times*, November 26, 1989, 45.

105. David Cole, *Enemy Aliens: Double Standards and Constitutional Freedoms in the War on Terrorism* (New York: The New Press, 2003), 158–161.

106. Stephen Engelberg, "Greater Access to Terrorism Data Is Sought for Immigration Agency," *New York Times*, February 6, 1987, A15.

107. David Cole and James X. Dempsey, *Terrorism and the Constitution: Sacrificing Civil Liberties in the Name of National Security* (New York: The New Press, 2006), 45.

108. *Rafeedie v. INS*, 688 F.Supp. 729, 731–733 (D.D.C. 1988).

109. *Rafeedie v. INS*, 752–754.

110. *Rafeedie v. INS*, 754–755.

111. Cole and Dempsey, *Terrorism and the Constitution*, 40–42.

112. *ADC v. Meese*, 714 F. Supp. 1060, 1063–1064 (D. Cal. 1989).

113. *ADC v. Meese*, 1084.

114. *ADC v. Meese*, 1082.

115. *ADC v. Meese*, 1084.

116. Immigration Act, Pub. L. No. 101–649, Stat. 4978 (1990).

117. Immigration Act, Sect. 601(a)(3)(A).

118. Immigration Act, Sect. 601(a)(3)(C)(ii).

119. Immigration Act, Sect. 601(a)(3)(B)(ii).

120. Immigration Act, Sect. 601(a)(3)(C)(iii).

121. Immigration Act, Sect. 601(a)(3)(B)(i)(II).

122. Cole and Dempsey, *Terrorism and the Constitution*, 131–132.

123. Cole and Dempsey, *Terrorism and the Constitution*, 137–146.

124. Cole and Dempsey, *Terrorism and the Constitution*, 49–51.

125. *Reno v. ADC*, 525 U.S. 471, 487–488 (1999).

126. *Reno v. ADC*, 491–492.

8. WAR ON TERROR

1. Jennifer Loven, "South Asians, Arabs, Muslims Implore Nation Not to Avenge Terrorist Attacks on Those Who Merely Look like the Hijacker," *Atlanta Daily World*, September 23, 2001, 6.

2. David Cole, *Enemy Aliens: Double Standards and Constitutional Freedoms in the War on Terrorism* (New York: The New Press, 2003), 26–46.

3. "Americans States of Mind: Anxiety and Resolve," *New York Times*, October 10, 2001, A18.

4. George W. Bush, "Address to the Joint Session of the 107th Congress," September 20, 2001, http://georgewbush-whitehouse.archives.gov/infocus /bushrecord/documents/Selected_Speeches_George_W_Bush.pdf.

5. Bush, "Address to the Joint Session of the 107th Congress."

6. Cole, *Enemy Aliens*, 57.

7. "Uniting and Strengthening America by Providing Appropriate Tools Required to Intercept and Obstruct Terrorism (USA PATRIOT Act) Act of 2001," Pub. L. No. 107–56, 115 Stat. 272 (2001).

8. USA PATRIOT Act.

9. Russ Feingold, "On Opposing the U.S.A. Patriot Act," October 12, 2001, http://www.archipelago.org/vol6-2/feingold.htm.

10. John Ashcroft, Testimony Senate Judiciary Committee, December 6, 2001. https://www.justice.gov/archive/ag/testimony/2001/1206transcriptsenatejudiciary committee.htm.

11. ACLU, "Safe and Free," October 16, 2002, https://www.aclu.org/news/aclu -mobilizes-members-and-supporters-nationwide-keep-america-safe-and-free.

12. Mark Hertsgaard, "How the Pentagon punished NSA whistleblowers," *Guardian*, May 22, 2016; Hugh Handeyside and Esha Bhandari, "Warrantless Border Searches of Smartphones Are Skyrocketing. We're Suing to Stop Them." ACLU, September 13, 2017, https://www.aclu.org/blog/privacy-technology/privacy -borders-and-checkpoints/warrantless-border-searches-smartphones-are; "Federal Court Rules Suspicionless Searches of Travelers' Phones and Laptops Unconstitutional," Electronic Frontier Foundation, November 12, 2019, https://www.eff.org /press/releases/federal-court-rules-suspicionless-searches-travelers-phones-and -laptops.

13. For a discussion of the history of watchlists, see Jeffrey Kahn, *Mrs. Shipley's Ghost: The Right to Travel and Terrorist Watchlists* (Ann Arbor: University of Michigan Press, 2013).

14. For a discussion of the conflation of Muslim and Middle Eastern immigrants and Arab Americans and terrorism, see Khaled A. Beydoun, *American Islamophobia: Understanding the Roots and Rise of Fear* (Berkeley: University of California Press, 2018).

15. "Why Countering Violent Extremism Programs Are Bad Policy," Brennan Center for Justice, September 9, 2019, https://www.brennancenter.org/our-work /research-reports/why-countering-violent-extremism-programs-are-bad-policy; Chris Rickerd, "Homeland Security Suspends Ineffective, Discriminatory Immigration Program," ACLU, May 6, 2011, https://www.aclu.org/blog/speakeasy/homeland -security-suspends-ineffective-discriminatory-immigration-program.

16. Cole, *Enemy Aliens*, 47–74.

17. ACLU, "The Excluded: Ideological Exclusion and the War on Ideas," April 20, 2007, https://www.aclu.org/other/excluded-ideological-exclusion-and -war-ideas.

18. ACLU, "The Excluded," 5–6.

19. ACLU, "The Excluded," 6–8.

20. ACLU, "The Excluded," 16–17.

21. ACLU, "The Excluded," 13–15.

22. ACLU, "The Excluded," 15.

23. Jay Tolson, Anna Mulrine, and Elizabeth Bryant, "Should This Man Come to the U.S.?" *U.S. News & World Report* 137, no. 20 (2004): 76–79.

24. Tolson, Mulrine, and Bryant, "Should This Man Come to the U.S.?"; Elaine Sciolino, "A Muslim Scholar Raises Hackles in France," *New York Times*, November 16, 2003, A3; Tariq Ramadan, "Too Scary for the Classroom?" *New York Times*, September 1, 2004, A19.

25. Stephen Kinzer, "THREATS AND RESPONSES: THE TEACHER; Muslim Scholar Loses U.S. Visa as Query Is Raised," *New York Times*, August 26, 2004, A14.

26. Peter Slevin, "Lacking Visa, Islamic Scholar Resigns Post at Notre Dame," *Washington Post*, December 15, 2004, A6.

27. USA PATRIOT Act, Section 411(a)(1)(A)(iii)(VI).

28. "Muslim Scheduled to Teach at Notre Dame Has Visa Revoked," *Los Angeles Times*, August 25, 2004, A23.

29. Tariq Ramadan, "Why I'm Banned in the USA," *Washington Post*, October 1, 2006, B1.

30. Kinzer, "THREATS AND RESPONSES: THE TEACHER," A14.

31. "A Foreign Scholar Kept Out," *New York Times*, September 6, 2004, A16.

32. *American Academy of Religion, American Association of University Professors, et al. v. Michael Chertoff; Condoleezza Rice*, Complaint for Declaratory and Injunctive Relief, filed with the US District Court, Southern District of New York, January 25, 2006, https://www.aclu.org/sites/default/files/pdfs/complaint012506.pdf.

33. *American Academy of Religion, American Association of University Professors, et al. v. Napolitano*, 573 F.3d 115, 118–121 (2d. Cir., 2009).

34. *American Academy of Religion, American Association of University Professors, et al. v. Napolitano*, 121–122, 127.

35. US Department of Treasury, "U.S. Designates Five Charities Funding Hamas and Six Senior Hamas Leaders as Terrorist Entities," August 22, 2003, https://www.treasury.gov/press-center/press-releases/Pages/js672.aspx.

36. *American Academy of Religion, et al. v. Napolitano*, 221–222.

37. Ramadan, "Why I'm Banned in the USA."

38. Ramadan, "Why I'm Banned in the USA."

39. Ramadan, "Why I'm Banned in the USA."

40. *American Academy of Religion, American Association of University Professors, et al. v. Michael Chertoff*, No. 06 Civ. 588, 2007 U.S. Dist. (S.D.N.Y. Dec. 20, 2007), 32

41. *American Academy of Religion, American Association of University Professors, et al. v. Michael Chertoff*, 26–32.

42. *American Academy of Religion, et al. v. Napolitano*, 117–120.

43. *American Academy of Religion, et al. v. Napolitano*, 117–118.

44. *American Academy of Religion, et al. v. Napolitano*, 119–121, 134, 138.

45. Benjamin Weiser, "Scholar May Receive New Chance to Get Visa," *New York Times*, July 18, 2009, A14.

46. ACLU, "Federal Appeals Court Rules in Favor of U.S. Organizations that Challenged Exclusion of Prominent Muslim Scholar," July 17, 2009, https://www.aclu.org/news/federal-appeals-court-rules-favor-us-organizations-challenged-exclusion-prominent-muslim.

47. ACLU, "Federal Appeals Court Rules in Favor of U.S. Organizations that Challenged Exclusion of Prominent Muslim Scholar."

48. Sarah Lyall, "In Shift, U.S. Lifts Visa Curbs on Professor," *New York Times*, January 21, 2010, A6.

49. Kirk Semple, "At Last Muslim Scholar Visits," *New York Times*, April 8, 2010, A29.

50. Semple, "At Last Muslim Scholar Visits."

51. Neil MacFarquhar, "U.S. Stymied 21 Years, Drops Bid to Deport 2 Palestinians," *New York Times*, November 1, 2007, A18; "A Shameful Prosecution," *New York Times*, February 14, 2007, A26.

52. Cole, *Enemy Aliens*, 17–72, 85–183.

53. David Cole and James X. Dempsey, *Terrorism and the Constitution: Sacrificing Civil Liberties in the Name of National Security* (New York: New Press, 2006), 1–21.

54. Cole and Dempsey, *Terrorism and the Constitution*, 163–164.

55. Cole and Dempsey, *Terrorism and the Constitution*, 164–165.

56. *Holder v. Humanitarian Law Project*, 130 S.Ct. 2705 (2010), 2712.

57. *Holder v. Humanitarian Law Project*, 2710.

58. *Holder v. Humanitarian Law Project*, 2728, 2736.

59. *Holder v. Humanitarian Law Project*, 2729.

60. *Holder v. Humanitarian Law Project*, 2729 (quoting AEDPA Section 301 (a)(7) "Findings and Purpose").

61. *Holder v. Humanitarian Law Project*, 130 S.Ct. 2705, 2731 (Breyer, J., dissenting).

62. *Holder v. Humanitarian Law Project*, 2734.

63. *Holder v. Humanitarian Law Project*, 2736.

64. *Holder v. Humanitarian Law Project*, 2740.

65. David Cole, "The Roberts Court's Free Speech Problem," *New York Review of Books*, June 28, 2010, https://www.nybooks.com/daily/2010/06/28/roberts-courts-free-speech-problem/.

66. Cole, "The Roberts Court's Free Speech Problem."

67. Cole, "The Roberts Court's Free Speech Problem."

68. Marc Lynch, "Attempts to Designate Muslim Brotherhood as a Terrorist Organization Have Failed Before. Why Is It Returning Now?" *Washington Post*, May 1, 2019; Andrew March, "Designating the Muslim Brotherhood a "terrorist organization" puts academic researchers at risk," *Washington Post*, January 25, 2017.

69. For a discussion of the implications of material support for social media, see Nina I. Brown, "Fight Terror, Not Twitter: Insulating Social Media from Material Support Claims," *Loyola LA Entertainment Law Review* 37, no. 1 (2017).

70. George Washington's Farewell Address (1796), The Avalon Project: Documents in Law, History, and Diplomacy, Yale Law School, http://avalon.law .yale.edu/18th_century/washing.asp.

71. Donald Trump, Presidential Campaign Announcement, June 16, 2015, http://time.com/3923128/donald-trump-announcement-speech/.

72. Ron Nixon and Linda Qui, "Trump's Evolving Words on the Wall," *New York Times,* January 18, 2018, https://www.nytimes.com/2018/01/18/us/politics/trump -border-wall-immigration.html.

73. Jenna Johnson and Abigail Hauslohner, "'I Think Islam Hates Us': A Timeline of Trump's Comments about Islam and Muslims," *Washington Post,* May 20, 2017, https://www.washingtonpost.com/news/post-politics/wp/2017/05/20/i-think -islam-hates-us-a-timeline-of-trumps-comments-about-islam-and-muslims/.

74. Tessa Berenson, "Donald Trump Proposes 'Extreme Vetting' for Immigrants," *Time,* August 15, 2016, http://time.com/4452970/donald-trump -immigration-isis-terrorism/.

75. Anthony Romero to Donald Trump, *New York Times,* November 11, 2016, https://www.aclu.org/letter/aclu-letter-president-elect-trump-published-new-york -times.

76. Rebecca Kheel, "ACLU to Trump: 'See You in Court,'" *The Hill,* November 11, 2016, https://thehill.com/policy/defense/305216-aclu-pledges-to-use-full -firepower-if-trump-pursues-deportations-muslim-ban.

77. Jason DeParle, "How Stephen Miller Seized the Moment to Battle Immigration," *New York Times,* August 18, 2019, A1; Nick Miroff and Josh Dawsey, "The Adviser Who Scripts Trump's Immigration Policy," *Washington Post,* August 17, 2019.

78. Donald Trump, Executive Order 13769: "Protecting the Nation from Foreign Terrorist Entry into the United States," January 27, 2017, https://www .whitehouse.gov/presidential-actions/executive-order-protecting-nation-foreign -terrorist-entry-united-states/ (citing Section 212(f) of the Immigration and Nationality Act, codified as 8 U.S.C. 1182(f) as the statutory basis to support his Executive Order and suspension of entry).

79. Trump, Executive Order, 13769, Section 1.

80. Trump, Executive Order 13769, Sections 3–5; Michael D. Shear and Helene Cooper, "Trump Bars Refugees and Citizens of 7 Muslim Countries," *New York Times,* January 28, 2017, A1.

81. Ron Nixon, "Homeland Security Officials Caught Off Guard by First Entry Ban, Report Concludes," *New York Times,* January 20, 2018, A16.

82. Jonah Engel Bromwich, "Lawyers Mobilize at Nation's Airports after Trump Ban," *New York Times,* January 29, 2017, https://www.nytimes.com/2017/01/29/us /lawyers-trump-muslim-ban-immigration.html.

83. Andy Newman, "Highlights: Reaction to Trump's Travel Ban," *New York Times,* January 29, 2017, https://www.nytimes.com/2017/01/29/nyregion/trump -travel-ban-protests-briefing.html.

84. Leslie Stahl, "The ACLU's Surprising New Political Strategy, Modeled in Part after the NRA," *60 Minutes*, March 10, 2019, https://www.cbsnews.com/news/the-aclu-surprising-new-political-strategy-modeled-in-part-after-the-national-rifle-association-60-minutes/.

85. Michael D. Shear, Nicholas Kulish and Alan Feuer, "Judge Blocks Trump Order on Refugees amid Chaos and Outcry Worldwide," *New York Times*, January 29, A1.

86. Hillel Smith and Ben Harrington, "Overview of Travel Ban Litigation and Recent Developments," Congressional Research Service, April 23, 2018, https://fas.org/sgp/crs/homesec/LSB10017.pdf.

87. Smith and Harrington, "Overview of Travel Ban Litigation and Recent Developments."

88. *Trump v. International Refugee Assistance Project*, 582 US ___ (2017), https://www.supremecourt.gov/opinions/16pdf/16-1436_l6hc.pdf.

89. Smith and Harrington, "Overview of Travel Ban Litigation and Recent Developments."

90. *Trump v. Hawaii*, Brief of Respondents State of Hawaii et al. in opposition, filed January 12, 2018, https://www.supremecourt.gov/DocketPDF/17/17-965/27771/20180112172848825_Trump%20v.%20Hawaii%20Brief%20in%20Opposition.pdf.

91. *Trump v. Hawaii*, Brief in of Respondents.

92. Amy B. Wang, "Trump Asked for a Muslim Ban, Giuliani Says—Ordered a Commission to Do It 'Legally,'" *Washington Post*, January 29, 2017.

93. *Trump v. Hawaii*, Reply of Petitioner Donald J. Trump, President of the United States, et al., filed January 16, 2018, https://www.supremecourt.gov/DocketPDF/17/17-965/27843/20180116122242163_17-965%20Trump%20v.%20Hawaii.pdf.

94. *Korematsu v. United States*, 323 U.S. 214 (1944).

95. Justice Department, "Confession of Error: The Solicitor General's Mistakes during Japanese-American Internment cases," May 20, 2011, https://www.justice.gov/archives/opa/blog/confession-error-solicitor-generals-mistakes-during-japanese-american-internment-cases.

96. "COURT OVERTURNS A WAR CONVICTION: Ruling for Japanese-American Praised by Those Wanting U.S. to Admit Injustice," *New York Times*, November 11, 1983, B7; Julie Johnson, "President Signs Law to Redress Wartime Wrong," *New York Times*, August 11, 1988, A16.

97. *Korematsu v. United States*, 323 U.S. 214, 246 (Jackson, J. dissenting).

98. *Trump v. Hawaii*, 138 S. Ct. 2392, 2400–2402 (2018).

99. *Trump v. Hawaii*, 2046–2411.

100. *Trump v. Hawaii*, 2420–2421.

101. *Trump v. Hawaii*, 2423.

102. *Trump v. Hawaii*, 138 S. Ct. 2392, 2433 (Sotomayor, J., dissenting).

103. *Trump v. Hawaii*, 2441.

104. *Trump v. Hawaii*, 2447–2448.

105. *Trump v. Hawaii*, 138 S. Ct. 2392, 2429-2431 (Breyer, J. dissenting).

106. *Trump v. Hawaii*, 2431–2433.

107. *Trump v. Hawaii*, 138 S. Ct. 2392, 2424 (Kennedy, J. concurring).

108. *Trump v. Hawaii*, 2424.

109. Congressman Albert Gallatin addressing repeal of the Alien Law, *The Proceedings of the House of Representatives of the United States with Respect to the Petitions Praying for a Repeal of the Alien and Sedition Laws Including the Report of a Select Committee and the Speeches of Mr. Gallatin* (Philadelphia: Printed by Joseph Gales, 1799), 20, New-York Historical Society.

110. Knight First Amendment Institute at Columbia University, "About the Knight Institute," https://knightcolumbia.org/page/about-the-knight-institute.

111. Jameel Jaffer, "Censorship at the Border Threatens Free Speech Everywhere," *Just Security*, April 14, 2017, https://www.justsecurity.org/39986/censorship-border -extreme-vetting-free-speech./.

112. Jaffer, "Censorship at the Border."

113. Jaffer, "Censorship at the Border."

114. Jaffer, "Censorship at the Border."

115. Moshe Shulman, Who Needs a Border Wall When You Have DS-5535?" *New York Times*, October 24, 2018; US Department of State, Supplemental Questions for Visa Applicants, https://www.nafsa.org/_/File/_/amresource/DS5535.pdf.

116. Carrie DeCell, "Trump's 'Extreme Vetting' Is Muzzling Activists and Shutting Them Out," *Guardian*, April 20, 2018.

117. DeCell, "Trump's 'Extreme Vetting.'"

118. Derek Hawkins, "Ravi Ragbir Case: Federal Judge Blasts ICE for 'Cruel' Tactics, Frees Immigrant Rights Activist Ravi Ragbir," *Washington Post*, January 20, 2018; "ICE Tried to Deport an Immigration Activist. That May Have Been Unconstitutional," *New York Times*, April 28, 2019, SR8.

119. Hawkins, "Ravi Ragbir Case"; "Knight Institute v. DHS, FOIA Suit for Records on Ideological Exclusion and Social Media Monitoring," https://knightcolumbia.org /content/knight-institute-v-dhs-foia-suit-records-ideological-exclusion-and-social -media-monitoring.

120. "Brennan Center and 46 Organizations Demand Congressional Oversight of Trump's Muslim Ban and Extreme Vetting," June 13, 2018, https://www .brennancenter.org/analysis/brennan-center-and-46-organizations-demand -congressional-oversight-trumps-muslim-ban-and

121. "Brennan Center and 46 Organizations Demand Congressional Oversight."

122. Shoba Sivaprasad Wadhia, *Banned: Immigration Enforcement in the Time of Trump* (New York: New York University Press, 2019), 22–26; Faiza Patel, Harsha Panduranga, and Tom McBrien, "The Muslim Ban: A Family Separation Policy," Brennan Center for Justice, June 26, 2019, https://www.brennancenter.org/blog /muslim-ban-family-separation-policy.

123. Robert Tsai, "Trump's Travel Ban Faces Fresh Legal Jeopardy," *Politico Magazine,* March 27, 2019, https://www.politico.com/magazine/story/2019/03/27/trump-travel-ban-lawsuit-supreme-court-unconstitutional-226103.

124. Text H.R. 2214–116th Congress, April 11, 2019, "To Transfer and Limit Executive Branch Authority to Suspend or Restrict the Entry of a Class of Aliens."

125. Shera S. Avi-Yonah and Delano R. Franklin, "Incoming Harvard Freshman Deported after Visa Revoked," *Harvard Crimson,* August 27, 2019, https://www.thecrimson.com/article/2019/8/27/incoming-freshman-deported/.

126. Karen Zraick and Mihir Zaveri, "Harvard Student Says He Was Barred From U.S. over His Friends' Social Media Posts," *New York Times,* August 28, 2019, A14.

127. Shera S. Avi-Yonah and Delano R. Franklin, "Harvard Student Previously Denied Entry to the United States Arrives at Harvard," *Harvard Crimson,* September 3, 2019, https://www.thecrimson.com/article/2019/9/3/harvard-student-turned-away-arrives/.

128. Zraick and Zaveri, "Harvard Student Says He Was Barred From U.S. Over His Friends' Social Media Posts," A14.

CONCLUSION

1. Marion T. Bennett, *American Immigration Policies: A History* (Washington, DC: Public Affairs Press, 1963), 339, 341.

Acknowledgments

Threat of Dissent is the culmination of my exploration of the interplay between the past and present and the intersection of immigration, radicalism, and civil liberties in American history. My interest in this interplay and intersection began when I was an undergraduate student at Columbia University and continued over the course of two decades. I am indebted to many historians, educators, scholars, lawyers, librarians, archivists, colleagues, friends, and family members for their encouragement and assistance during this long intellectual journey.

While at Columbia, I was fortunate to study with some brilliant professors, including Eric Foner, who supervised my senior honors thesis and served on my doctoral dissertation committee. One of the greatest historians of his generation, Eric continues to inform his readers and to inspire his former students through his pathbreaking scholarship and his teaching a "usable past." I am so grateful to Eric for his support and guidance along the way.

I began writing about law and history in one of my undergraduate courses taught by the late Alan Brinkley, whose excellent lectures and scholarship were only exceeded by his kindness and generosity. Two outstanding historians and teachers, Kim Phillips-Fein and Elizabeth Blackmar, urged me to continue to pursue my interest in legal history and to expand my research on radicalism and freedom of speech. The late Paul Avrich, the preeminent scholar of anarchism in the United States, guided and supported my research. I fondly remember our conversations over lunch or coffee, when we discussed the anarchist movement and his writing on Alexander Berkman. It was a pleasure to know him and an honor to cite his work in my own.

I first met Maeva Marcus twenty years ago when she hired me to conduct research for her invaluable *Documentary History of the Supreme Court of the United States, 1789–1800*. I am grateful to Maeva not only for sparking my interest in constitutional history, but also for her friendship and her dedication to finding ways to advance legal history education.

ACKNOWLEDGMENTS

I received my law degree from American University Washington College of Law, and I thank all of my superb professors—in particular, Congressman Jamie Raskin (D-MD), my First Amendment law professor, and Muneer Ahmad, my immigration law professor, who encouraged me to read and write about ideological exclusion during the early years of the War on Terror. I am also grateful to James May for his instructive and enlightening legal history classes, as well as for taking the time to read early drafts of my work and supporting my decision to obtain a PhD in history, which set me on the path to writing this book.

While I was pursuing my doctorate at New York University, Linda Gordon, Brigitte Bedos-Rezak, Martha Hodes, Molly Nolan, Andrew Needham, and William Nelson provided helpful observations and suggestions as I explored my interest in ideological exclusion and deportation in the United States. Andrew also gave me some excellent advice and recommendations as I began to learn more about this history and to develop this narrative.

My doctoral advisor, Thomas Bender, guided me through graduate school with his patience, professionalism, and breadth of knowledge. A leading intellectual, urban, and cultural historian, Tom provided astute and insightful comments on my research and writing, which led me to focus on the dynamics behind restrictions on immigration and on freedom of speech.

I am so grateful to the late Marilyn Young for her generosity and encouragement during and after my time in graduate school. Marilyn was a remarkable teacher and influential scholar who specialized in US foreign policy and wrote about America's wars. She was incredibly supportive of my desire to write this book and enthusiastic about its contribution to Cold War scholarship. She also took the time to introduce me to the Society for Historians of American Foreign Relations, as well as to the Center for the United States and the Cold War and its seminar held at the Tamiment Library. The publication of *Threat of Dissent* remains bittersweet because I will never be able to thank Marilyn and present her with a signed copy.

The late Michael Nash, a labor historian and director of the Tamiment Library and Robert F. Wagner Labor Archives, encouraged me to conduct research in the library's archival collection and arranged for me to present my research at the Cold War Center's seminar. Thank you to all of the seminar presenters who shared their work with me over the years and the seminar attendees who offered their suggestions when I presented mine.

Ellen Schrecker, the foremost expert on McCarthyism and academic freedom in the United States, was the commentator on the first paper I presented at the Cold War seminar. She provided not only illuminating critiques but also suggestions on where to find additional sources. This book could not have been written without her encouragement and guidance. At the Cold War seminar I also met Marjorie Heins, a former staff attorney for the American Civil Liberties Union who writes about censorship, academic freedom, and the Cold War. I am grateful to Marge for her important work and for her helpful advice and support.

I thank my many friends and colleagues for their guidance and camaraderie as I began to examine cases of ideological exclusion and deportation in the United States, including Anelise Shrout, Jeannette Estruth, David Weinfeld, Lilly Tuttle, Dylan Yeats, Natalie Blum-Ross, Peter Wirzbicki, David Rainbow, Thomas Fleischman, Bekah Friedman, Alexander Manevitz, Atiba Pertilla, Tracy Neumann, Paul Kershaw, and especially my friend Ashley Minihan for her assistance translating archival documents.

After law school, I worked for American University's General Counsel, Mary Kennard, and for attorneys Hisham Khalid, Bethany Bridgham, Justin Perillo, and Thi Nguyen-Southern. I thank them for creating a warm and collaborative work environment and for being so supportive as I started writing this book. I later worked as a historical walking tour guide for Big Onion Walking Tours in New York City. I am grateful to Seth Kamil, the president of Big Onion, for the opportunity to draw on my research and talk about immigration law and history with students of all ages, local New Yorkers, and visitors from across the country and around the world.

In 2016, I became the inaugural Judith S. Kaye Fellow for the Historical Society of the New York Courts. It has been an honor to contribute to the society's educational programs to bring law and history to students, lawyers, and the public. I thank Marilyn Marcus, John Siffert, Helaine Barnett, Troy McKenzie, John Q. Barrett, and Allison Morey for their support, encouragement, and interest in my book, as well as William Hinrichs at Bard High School Early College and the students in my "Civil Rights, Civil Liberties, and the Empire State" course.

A special thank you goes to Candace Falk, editor and director of the Emma Goldman Papers Project, who urged me to examine Goldman's ideological deportation as part of my interest in radicalism and freedom of speech. Her edited volumes, *Emma Goldman: A Documentary History of the American Years,* have been an indispensable resource for writing this book. I also thank associate editor Barry Pateman for his research guidance in locating anarchist newspapers and archival sources.

New York University and the Society for Historians of American Foreign Relations generously provided grants, which enabled me to conduct research at the Tamiment Library, the Rare Book and Manuscript Library at Columbia University, the Library of Congress and National Archives in Washington, DC, the Richard Nixon Presidential Library and Museum, and the Special Collections Research Center at the University of Michigan in Ann Arbor. I am grateful to all the librarians and archivists who assisted me, and especially Julie Herrada, Curator of the Joseph A. Labadie Collection, who helped me to navigate the American Committee for Protection of Foreign Born records, and Marian Smith, the former Senior Historian for the US Citizenship and Immigration Services History Office, who shared her extensive knowledge of immigration records and assisted me in filing a Freedom of Information Act request, which was essential in order to write this book.

Thank you to Deirdre Moloney for her hospitality while I was conducting research at Princeton University and to the late Norman Birnbaum for discussing his remembrances of his role in the Ernest Mandel case. I also thank writer and activist Tariq

Ali for taking the time to speak with me about Ernest Mandel, as well as former American Civil Liberties Union legal director Melvin Wulf and Harvard Law Professor David Rosenberg for discussing their civil liberties litigation and the legal challenge to Mandel's exclusion from the United States.

I was fortunate to receive two fellowships, which enabled me to conduct research for this book and offered opportunities to talk about my work. I thank the Massachusetts Historical Society for the Marc Friedlaender Fellowship and all the staff and librarians for their assistance, including Conrad E. Wright, Katheryn Viens, Anna Clutterbuck-Cook, and Sabina Beauchard, as well as Peter Drummey for his guidance and for locating a copy of President Adams's signed blank warrant, which appears in Chapter 1. The Andrew W. Mellon Foundation and the New-York Historical Society provided a year-long fellowship to conduct research. I thank Michael Ryan, Louise Mirrer, Jennifer Schantz, Marci Reaven, Valerie Paley, Nina Nazionale, Lindsay King, Schuyler Schuler, Rebecca Grabie, Crystal Toscano, Ted O'Reilly, and Mariam Touba for their assistance and support, as well as research fellows Sarah Gronningsater, Joseph Murphy, Frank Cirillo, and Michael Hattem for their helpful suggestions.

The Organization of American Historians, the Society for Historians of American Foreign Relations, and the Law and Society Association provided opportunities to present my research at their annual conferences. I thank all attendees, panelists, and colleagues for their comments and questions, including Roger Daniels, Linda Kerber, Matthew Frye Jacobson, Paul Kramer, Moshik Temkin, Sam Lebovic, Rachel Ida Buff, Yael Schacher, Hidetaka Hirota, Lucy Salyer, María Cristina García, Jane Hong, Anil Kalhan, Matthew Guariglia, Carly Goodman, Torrie Hester, Ryan Archibald, Sarah Snyder, Ruth Wasem, Melvin Urofsky, David Rabban, and Adam Goodman.

I am grateful to Indiana University Maurer School of Law and the *Indiana Journal of Global Legal Studies* for inviting me to discuss my work at their symposium conference in 2011 and for publishing my article, "Global Anti-Anarchism: the Origins of Ideological Deportation and the Suppression of Expression" in vol. 19, no. 1 (2012), portions of which are reprinted in Chapter 2.

Immigration historians Kevin Kenny and Katherine Benton-Cohen read the entire manuscript and recommended its publication. I thank them for their support and insightful analysis, thorough review, and sage advice. Both also generously took the time to meet with me to discuss their comments and to address any questions. I am grateful to Harvard University Press for publishing this book and to everyone on the production team who assisted in its publication. I also thank my first editor, Thomas LeBien, for his encouragement, support, and belief in this book's contribution. When Thomas decided to pursue another career opportunity, I was very fortunate that Heather Hughes was chosen as my new editor. Heather provided excellent edits to help improve my manuscript and guidance to assist me in clearing the hurdles and steps toward publication. I am so grateful to Heather for bringing her expertise, as well as her patience and care, to this process.

ACKNOWLEDGMENTS

I could never have written this book without the support and encouragement of dear friends and family members, including Scott Parker, Patrick Inniss, Lawrence Newman, Susan Rossman, Patricia Guerrin, Maddalena Marinari, Bryan Messerly, Einav Rabinovitch-Fox, Robyn Schwartz, Tiffany Williams, Maria Ter-Mikaelian, Howard Gillette, Margaret Marsh, Jon Wakelyn, Joyce Walker, Dale Smith, and Christine Worobec. Several who are no longer with us were also historians and educators, and I hope that in some way my scholarship honors their memory: Jean and Louis Joughin, David E. Kyvig, James W. Mooney, Janet Oppenheim, and Malcolm Rossman.

Threat of Dissent is dedicated to my parents. My mother, Deborah A. Kraut, is one of the toughest, smartest, and most resilient women I have ever known. She has always used her experiences and wisdom to help others, and I appreciate that she has done the same for me. My father, Alan M. Kraut, is an exceptional historian and teacher, as well as a thoughtful mentor and a *mensch*. Some of my favorite childhood memories are of our long walks and talks together, when he shared his love of history and enthusiasm for learning about the past. I am eternally grateful to my mother and father for being such wonderful parents, and for their unconditional love and unwavering support while I wrote this book and began to forge my path as an advocate, scholar, and educator.

Index

House Committee on Immigration and
Naturalization, 99–100
House Judiciary Committee, 103–104, 191
House Rules Committee, 76
House Subcommittee on Immigration,
Refugees, and International Law, 151,
191, 203
House Un-American Activities Committee
(HUAC), 101–102, 117, 118, 122, 125, 130,
134–135, 139, 150–151
Hsuan, Li Tao, 92, 97
Humanitarian Law Project (HLP), 229–231
Humphrey, Hubert, 190
Hungary: immigrants from, 144–145

Iberian Anarchist Federation, 79
Ideological exclusion: Alien Friends Act
(1798) on, 3, 9, 13, 15–25, 27, 34, 53, 241;
Barghouti's, 1–2; citizenship restrictions
and, 4, 29, 30, 110 (see also Denaturalization; Naturalization); Cold War-era, 10,
118, 120–154, 186–189, 191 (see also
McCarranism); democracy safeguarding
via, 64–89; denaturalization as, 4 (see also
Denaturalization); explicit, 4–5 (see also
Immigration laws); First Amendment and
(see First Amendment rights); Great
Depression-era, 90–110, 116, 146; implicit,
4–5 (see also Discretion); national identity
and, 8, 197 (see also National identity);
overview of history of, 1–10, 248–250;
political repression via, 3, 7–8, 249 (see also
Political repression); retaliatory, 4–5, 155,
180, 184, 215; Sedition Act (1798) and,
16–17, 19, 21–24, 34, 82, 172; selective,
4–5, 13, 216–217, 243 (see also Discretion);
terrorism as justification for, 10, 184–189,
191, 192, 201, 203–205, 210–215, 216–217,
218–247; see War on Anarchy
Illegal Immigration Reform and Immigrant
Responsibility Act (IIRIRA, 1996), 216–217
Immigrants: anarchism blamed on, 37, 39,
40–42, 47, 76–77; British, 14, 134–135;
Chinese, 26, 28–32, 92, 260n99, 260n101,
261n119; denaturalization of (see Denaturalization); fear of political repression of,

7, 18–19, 134; Finnish, 92, 135; French, 14,
16, 19–20; German, 65, 68, 95, 97–98, 107,
110, 127, 145–146; Great Depression-era
statistics on, 93; Greek, 123, 142; Haitian,
14, 27, 141, 202; Hungarian, 144–145;
ideological exclusion and deportations of
(see Deportations; Ideological exclusion);
indentured servitude of, 26; inferior and
degenerate labels for, 88; internment of,
65, 110, 122, 237–238, 239–240, 282n133;
Irish, 14, 21–22, 25–26; Italian, 110,
127–128, 135; Japanese, 32, 35, 110, 122,
237–238, 239–240, 282n133; Korean,
135–136; labor agitation blamed on,
63–64; laws on (see Immigration laws);
Mexican, 91–92, 141, 232; Muslim, 222,
223–227, 232–233, 234–241; registration
requirement for, 15, 65, 109–110; Russian,
73, 135, 136–137; terrorism and
scapegoating of, 218, 222, 232; Ukrainian,
135. See also Foreigners; Refugees
Immigration Act (1882), 32, 91
Immigration Act (1891), 32, 47
Immigration Act (1917), 67–69, 71, 100, 105
Immigration Act (1990), 213–214, 216, 222
Immigration and Customs Enforcement, US
(ICE), 220, 243
Immigration and Nationality Act (1952). See
McCarran-Walter Act (1952)
Immigration and Naturalization Service
(INS): Communist deportations by, 100,
102, 130; deportation hearings lacking
impartiality in, 133; formation of, 90; on
invalidity of deportation hearings, 124;
Mandel's file at, 159, 161; prosecutorial
discretion of, 180; raids by, 92; reorganization of in War on Terror, 220; terrorism
response of, 210–212, 216–217; transfer
to Justice Department, 107–108
Immigration laws: commerce regulation
and, 18, 27–29; consular control system
and, 89; enforcement of, 32–33, 35; explicit
restrictions in, 4–5; First Amendment
intersection with, 5–6, 8–9, 37, 53,
156; likely to become a public charge
exclusions in, 25–26, 32–33, 91, 98, 233;